D0405456

Also by Drew Gilpin Faust

Mothers of Invention: Women of the Slaveholding
South in the American Civil War

Southern Stories: Slaveholders in Peace and War

The Creation of Confederate Nationalism: Ideology
and Identity in the Civil War South

James Henry Hammond and the Old South:
A Design for Mastery

A Sacred Circle: The Dilemma of the Intellectual
in the Old South, 1840–1860

THIS REPUBLIC OF SUFFERING

THIS REPUBLIC
OF SUFFERING

Death and the
American Civil War

DREW GILPIN FAUST

Alfred A. Knopf　　New York　　2008

THIS IS A BORZOI BOOK
PUBLISHED BY ALFRED A. KNOPF

Portions of this book originally appeared in Civil War Times
and Harvard Magazine.

Library of Congress Cataloging-in-Publication Data
Faust, Drew Gilpin.
This republic of suffering: death and the American
Civil War / Drew Gilpin Faust.—1st ed.
p. cm.
Includes bibliographical references and index.
ISBN-13: 978-0-375-40404-7
1. United—States—History—Civil War, 1861–1865—Social
aspects. 2. United States—History—Civil War,
1861–1865—Psychological aspects. 3. United States—History—
Civil War, 1861–1865—Influence. 4. Death—Social
aspects—United States—History—19th century.
5. Death—United States—Psychological aspects—History—19th century.
6. Burial—Social aspects—United States—History—19th century.
7. Burial—United States—Psychological aspects—History—
19th century. I. Title.
E468.9.F385 2008
973.7'1—dc22 2007014658

Manufactured in the United States of America
Published January 10, 2008
Reprinted Three Times
Fifth Printing, February 2008

IN MEMORY

OF

MCGHEE TYSON GILPIN

1919–2000

Captain, U.S. Army
Commanding Officer
Military Intelligence Interpreter Team #436
6th Armored Division

Wounded, August 6, 1944
Plouviens, France

Silver Star
Purple Heart
Croix de Guerre

Contents

Illustrations

Preface

Mortality defines the human condition. "We all have our dead—we all have our Graves," a Confederate Episcopal bishop observed in an 1862 sermon. Every era, he explained, must confront "like miseries"; every age must search for "like consolation." Yet death has its discontinuities as well. Men and women approach death in ways shaped by history, by culture, by conditions that vary over time and across space. Even though "we all have our dead," and even though we all die, we do so differently from generation to generation and from place to place.[1]

In the middle of the nineteenth century, the United States embarked on a new relationship with death, entering into a civil war that proved bloodier than any other conflict in American history, a war that would presage the slaughter of World War I's Western Front and the global carnage of the twentieth century. The number of soldiers who died between 1861 and 1865, an estimated 620,000, is approximately equal to the total American fatalities in the Revolution, the War of 1812, the Mexican War, the Spanish-American War, World War I, World War II, and the Korean War combined. The Civil War's rate of death, its incidence in comparison with the size of the American population, was six times that of World War II. A similar rate, about 2 percent, in the United States today would mean six million fatalities. As the new southern nation struggled for survival against a wealthier and more populous enemy, its death toll reflected the disproportionate strains on its human capital. Confederate men died at a rate three times that of their Yankee counterparts; one in five white southern men of military age did not survive the Civil War.[2]

But these military statistics tell only a part of the story. The war killed civilians as well, as battles raged across farm and field, as

encampments of troops spread epidemic disease, as guerrillas en-
snared women and even children in violence and reprisals, as draft
rioters targeted innocent citizens, as shortages of food in parts of the
South brought starvation. No one sought to document these deaths
systematically, and no one has devised a method of undertaking a
retrospective count. The distinguished Civil War historian James
McPherson has estimated that there were fifty thousand civilian
deaths during the war, and he has concluded that the overall mortality rate for the South exceeded that of any country in World War I
and that of all but the region between the Rhine and the Volga in
World War II. The American Civil War produced carnage that has
often been thought reserved for the combination of technological
proficiency and inhumanity characteristic of a later time.[3]

The impact and meaning of the war's death toll went beyond the
sheer numbers who died. Death's significance for the Civil War generation arose as well from its violation of prevailing assumptions
about life's proper end—about who should die, when and where, and
under what circumstances. Death was hardly unfamiliar to mid-
nineteenth-century Americans. By the beginning of the 1860s the
rate of death in the United States had begun to decline, although
dramatic improvements in longevity would not appear until late in
the century. Americans of the immediate prewar era continued to be
more closely acquainted with death than are their twenty-first-
century counterparts. But the patterns to which they were accustomed were in significant ways different from those the war would
introduce. The Civil War represented a dramatic shift in both incidence and experience. Mid-nineteenth-century Americans endured a
high rate of infant mortality but expected that most individuals who
reached young adulthood would survive at least into middle age.
The war took young, healthy men and rapidly, often instantly,
destroyed them with disease or injury. This marked a sharp and
alarming departure from existing preconceptions about who should
die. As Francis W. Palfrey wrote in an 1864 memorial for Union soldier Henry L. Abbott, "the blow seems heaviest when it strikes down
those who are in the morning of life." A soldier was five times more

likely to die than he would have been if he had not entered the army. As a chaplain explained to his Connecticut regiment in the middle of the war, "neither he nor they had ever lived and faced death in such a time, with its peculiar conditions and necessities." Civil War soldiers and civilians alike distinguished what many referred to as "ordinary death," as it had occurred in prewar years, from the manner and frequency of death in Civil War battlefields, hospitals, and camps, and from the war's interruptions of civilian lives.[4]

In the Civil War the United States, North and South, reaped what many participants described as a "harvest of death." By the midpoint of the conflict, it seemed that in the South, "nearly every household mourns some loved one lost." Loss became commonplace; death was no longer encountered individually; death's threat, its proximity, and its actuality became the most widely shared of the war's experiences. As a Confederate soldier observed, death "reigned with universal sway," ruling homes and lives, demanding attention and response. The Civil War matters to us today because it ended slavery and helped to define the meanings of freedom, citizenship, and equality. It established a newly centralized nation-state and launched it on a trajectory of economic expansion and world influence. But for those Americans who lived in and through the Civil War, the texture of the experience, its warp and woof, was the presence of death. At war's end this shared suffering would override persisting differences about the meanings of race, citizenship, and nationhood to establish sacrifice and its memorialization as the ground on which North and South would ultimately reunite. Even in our own time this fundamentally elegiac understanding of the Civil War retains a powerful hold.[5]

Death transformed the American nation as well as the hundreds of thousands of individuals directly affected by loss. The war created a veritable "republic of suffering," in the words that Frederick Law Olmsted chose to describe the wounded and dying arriving at Union hospital ships on the Virginia Peninsula. Sacrifice and the state became inextricably intertwined. Citizen soldiers snatched from the midst of life generated obligations for a nation defining its purposes and polity through military struggle. A war about union, citizenship, freedom, and human dignity required that the government attend to the needs of those who had died in its service. Execution of these newly recognized responsibilities would prove an important vehicle for the expansion of federal power that characterized the transformed postwar nation. The establishment of national cemeteries and the emergence of the Civil War pension system to care for both the dead and their survivors yielded programs of a scale and reach unimaginable before the war. Death created the modern American union—not just by ensuring national survival, but by shaping enduring national structures and commitments.[6]

Civil War Americans often wrote about what they called "the work of death," meaning the duties of soldiers to fight, kill, and die, but at the same time invoking battle's consequences: its slaughter, suffering, and devastation. "Work" in this usage incorporated both effort and impact—and the important connection between the two. Death in war does not simply happen; it requires action and agents. It must, first of all, be inflicted; and several million soldiers of the 1860s dedicated themselves to that purpose. But death also usually requires participation and response; it must be experienced and handled. It is work to die, to know how to approach and endure life's last moments. Of all living things, only humans consciously anticipate death; the consequent need to choose how to behave in its face—to worry about how to die—distinguishes us from other animals. The need to manage death is the particular lot of humanity.[7]

It is work to deal with the dead as well, to remove them in the literal sense of disposing of their bodies, and it is also work to remove them in a more figurative sense. The bereaved struggle to separate themselves from the dead through ritual and mourning. Families and communities must repair the rent in the domestic and social fabric, and societies, nations, and cultures must work to understand and explain unfathomable loss.

This is a book about the work of death in the American Civil War. It seeks to describe how between 1861 and 1865—and into the

"The True Defenders of the Constitution." Engraving from a drawing by James Walker. Harper's Weekly, *November 11, 1865.*

decades that followed—Americans undertook a kind of work that history has not adequately understood or recognized. Human beings are rarely simply passive victims of death. They are actors even if they are the diers; they prepare for death, imagine it, risk it, endure it, seek to understand it. And if they are survivors, they must assume new identities established by their persistence in face of others' annihilation. The presence and fear of death touched Civil War Americans' most fundamental sense of who they were, for in its threat of termination and transformation, death inevitably inspired self-scrutiny and self-definition. Beginning with individuals' confrontation with dying and killing, the book explores how those experiences transformed society, culture, and politics in what became a broader republic of shared suffering. Some of the changes death brought were social, as wives turned into widows, children into orphans; some were political, as African American soldiers hoped to win citizenship and equality through their willingness both to die and to kill; some were philosophical and spiritual, as the carnage compelled Americans to seek meaning and explanation for war's destruction.

Every death involved "the great change" captured in the language and discourse of nineteenth-century Christianity, the shift from this life to whatever might come next. A subject of age-old concern for believers and nonbelievers alike, the existence and nature of an after-life took on new urgency both for soldiers anxious about their own deaths and for bereaved kin speculating on the fate of the departed. And even if spirits and souls proved indeed immortal, there still remained the vexing question of bodies. The traditional notion that corporeal resurrection and restoration would accompany the Day of Judgment seemed increasingly implausible to many Americans who had seen the maiming and disfigurement inflicted by this war. Witnesses at field hospitals almost invariably commented with horror on the piles of limbs lying near the surgeon's table, dissociated from the bodies to which they had belonged, transformed into objects of revulsion instead of essential parts of people. These arms and legs seemed as unidentifiable—and unrestorable—as the tens of thousands of missing men who had been separated from their names. The integral relationship between the body and the human self it housed was as shattered as the wounded men.[8]

Bodies were in important ways the measure of the war—of its achievements and its impact; and indeed, bodies became highly visible in Civil War America. Commanders compared their own and enemy casualties as evidence of military success or failure. Soldiers struggled for the words to describe mangled corpses strewn across battlefields; families contemplated the significance of newspaper lists of wounds: "slightly, in the shoulder," "severely, in the groin," "mortally, in the breast." They nursed the dying and buried their remains. Letters and reports from the front rendered the physicality of injuries and death all but unavoidable. For the first time civilians directly confronted the reality of battlefield death rendered by the new art of photography. They found themselves transfixed by the paradoxically lifelike renderings of the slain of Antietam that

"Confederate Dead at Antietam, September 1862."
Photograph by Alexander Gardner. Library of Congress.

Mathew Brady exhibited in his studio on Broadway. If Brady "has not brought bodies and laid them in our dooryards and along the streets, he has done something very like it," wrote the *New York Times*.[9]

This new prominence of bodies overwhelmingly depicted their destruction and deformation, inevitably raising the question of how they related to the persons who had once inhabited them. In the aftermath of battle survivors often shoveled corpses into pits as they would dispose of animals—"in bunches, just like dead chickens," one observer noted—dehumanizing both the living and the dead through their disregard. In Civil War death the distinction between men and animals threatened to disappear, just as it was simultaneously eroding in the doctrines of nineteenth-century science.[10]

The Civil War confronted Americans with an enormous task, one quite different from saving or dividing the nation, ending or maintaining slavery, or winning the military conflict—the demands we customarily understand to have been made of the Civil War generation. Americans North and South would be compelled to confront—and resist—the war's assault on their conceptions of how life should end, an assault that challenged their most fundamental assumptions about life's value and meaning. As they faced horrors that forced them to question their ability to cope, their commitment to the war, even their faith in a righteous God, soldiers and civilians alike struggled to retain their most cherished beliefs, to make them work in the dramatically altered world that war had introduced. Americans had to identify—find, invent, create—the means and mechanisms to manage more than half a million dead: their deaths, their bodies, their loss. How they accomplished this task reshaped their individual lives—and deaths—at the same time that it redefined their nation and their culture. The work of death was Civil War America's most fundamental and most demanding undertaking.

THIS REPUBLIC OF SUFFERING

CHAPTER I

DYING

"To Lay Down My Life"

"Dying—annuls the power to kill."
EMILY DICKINSON, 1862

No one expected what the Civil War was to become. Southern secessionists believed northerners would never mobilize to halt national division or that they would mount nothing more than brief and ineffective resistance. South Carolina senator James Chesnut boldly promised to drink all the blood that might be shed as a result of the Confederate declaration of independence.[1] When military confrontation began to seem inevitable, northerners and southerners alike expected it to be of brief duration. The North entered the First Battle of Bull Run in the summer of 1861 anticipating a decisive victory that would quash the rebellion; Confederates thought the Union would quickly give up after initial reverses. Neither side could have imagined the magnitude and length of the conflict that unfolded, nor the death tolls that proved its terrible cost.

A number of factors contributed to these unanticipated and unprecedented losses. The first was simply the scale of the conflict itself. As a South Carolinian observed in 1863, "The world never saw such a war." Approximately 2.1 million northerners and 880,000 southerners took up arms between 1861 and 1865. In the South, three out of four white men of military age became soldiers. During the American Revolution the army never numbered more than 30,000 men.[2]

Changing military technology equipped these mass armies with new, longer-range weapons—muzzle-loading rifles—and provided some units, by the latter stages of the war, with dramatically increased firepower in the form of breech-loading and even repeating rifles. Railroads and emerging industrial capacity in both North and South made resupply and redeployment of armies easier, extending the duration of the war and the killing.

Yet for all the horrors of combat, soldiers dreaded dying of disease even more. Death from illness, one Iowa soldier observed, offered "all of the evils of the battlefield with none of its honors." Twice as many Civil War soldiers died of disease as of battle wounds. The war, Union surgeon general William A. Hammond later observed, was fought at the "end of the medical middle ages." Neither the germ theory nor the nature and necessity of antisepsis was yet understood. A wave of epidemic disease—measles, mumps, and smallpox—swept through the armies of volunteers in the early months of war, then yielded precedence to the intractable camp illnesses: diarrhea and dysentery, typhoid and malaria. Nearly three-quarters of Union soldiers suffered from serious bowel complaints in every year of the war; by 1865 the sick rate for diarrhea and dysentery was 995 per thousand. Contamination of water supply from camp latrines was a key cause of these illnesses, as it was of typhoid. "The camp sink," one 1862 description of an all-too-typical Union bivouac reported, "is located between the tents and the river. It is covered with fresh earth twice a week . . . The men, however, generally make use of the ground in the vicinity." Ether and chloroform had made military surgery a more plausible and widespread response to wounds, but lacking an understanding of antisepsis, physicians routinely spread infection with unclean instruments and dressings. After the Battle of Perryville in 1862, water was so scarce that Union surgeons performing amputations almost around the clock did not wash their hands for two days. Gangrene was so commonplace that most military hospitals had special wards or tents for its victims.[3]

Civil War soldiers had many opportunities to die and a variety of ways in which to do so. A war that was expected to be short-lived

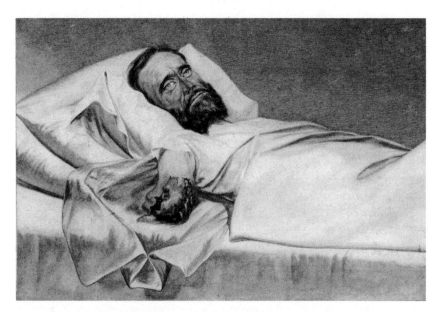

Milton Wallen, Company C, First Kentucky Cavalry, in a prison hospital. "Dying of Gangrene." Watercolor by Edward Stauch. National Museum of Health and Medicine, Armed Forces Institute of Pathology.

instead extended for four years and touched the life of nearly every American. A military adventure undertaken as an occasion for heroics and glory turned into a costly struggle of suffering and loss. As men became soldiers and contemplated battle, they confronted the very real possibility of death. They needed to be both willing and ready to die, and as they departed for war, they turned to the resources of their culture, codes of masculinity, patriotism, and religion to prepare themselves for what lay ahead. This was the initial work of death.

"Soldier," a Confederate chaplain reminded his troops in 1863, "your business is to die."[4] Men in Civil War America went to war talking of glory and conquest, of saving or creating a nation, and of routing the enemy. But at the heart of the soldier's understanding of his duty rested the notion of sacrifice. E. G. Abbott was far from alone when he explained his motivation for entering the Union army. "I came into this war," he wrote, "to lay down my life."[5] As a Confederate soldier prayed, "my first desire should be not that I might escape death but that my death should help the cause of the right to triumph."[6] The rhetoric of service—to nation, to God, to comrades—rationalized the violence of this devastating war by casting it as the instrument of both nationalist and Christian imperatives: soldiers would die for God and Country. "I did not go to war to murder. No! and . . . Our dear Lord knows it and he will stand by me," wrote John Weissert of Michigan, describing how "my hair stood on ends" as he surveyed the gruesome aftermath of battle.[7] Focusing on dying rather than on killing enabled soldiers to mitigate their terrible responsibility for the slaughter of others. As men saw themselves mirrored in the faces of those expiring around them, they struggled to come to terms with the possibility and the significance of their own annihilation. Dying assumed clear preeminence over killing in the soldier's construction of his emotional and moral universe.

Civil War soldiers were, in fact, better prepared to die than to kill, for they lived in a culture that offered many lessons in how life should end. But these lessons had to be adapted to the dramatically changed circumstances of the Civil War. The concept of the Good Death was central to mid-nineteenth-century America, as it had long been at the core of Christian practice. Dying was an art, and the tradition of *ars moriendi* had provided rules of conduct for the moribund and their attendants since at least the fifteenth century: how to give up one's soul "gladlye and wilfully"; how to meet the devil's temptations of unbelief, despair, impatience, and worldly attachment; how to pattern one's dying on that of Christ; how to pray. Texts on the art of dying proliferated with the spread of vernacular printing, culminating in 1651 in London with Jeremy Taylor's *The Rule and Exercise of Holy Dying*. His revision of the originally Catholic *ars moriendi* proved not just a literary achievement but an intellectual triumph that firmly established the genre within Protestantism.[8]

By the nineteenth century Taylor's books had become classics, and the tradition of the *ars moriendi* was spread both through reprints of earlier texts and through more contemporary considerations of the Good Death. Often these more modern renditions appeared in new contexts and genres: in sermons that focused on one or two aspects of the larger subject; in American Sunday School Union tracts distributed to youth across the nation; in popular health books that combined the expanding insights of medical science with older religious conventions about dying well; and in popular literature, with the exemplary deaths of Dickens's Little Nell, Thackeray's Colonel Newcome, or Harriet Beecher Stowe's Eva. So diverse and numerous were these representations of the Good Death that they reached a wide spectrum of the American population at midcentury, and they would become a central theme within the songs, stories, and poetry of the Civil War itself. By the 1860s many elements of the Good Death had been to a considerable degree separated from their explicitly theological roots and had become as much a part of respectable middle-class behavior and expectation in North and South as they were the product or emblem of any particular religious affiliation. Assumptions about the way to die remained central within both Catholic and Protestant faiths, but they had spread beyond formal religion to become a part of more general systems of belief held across the nation about life's meaning and life's appropriate end.[9]

The Good Death proved to be a concern shared by almost all Americans of every religious background. An overwhelming majority of Civil War soldiers, like Americans generally in the 1860s, was Protestant, and Protestant assumptions dominated discussions about death. But the need for wartime unity and solidarity produced an unprecedented level of religious interaction and cooperation that not only brought Protestant denominations together but to a considerable degree incorporated Catholics and Jews as well. The war encouraged a Protestant ecumenism that yielded interdenominational publication societies, common evangelical gatherings, and shared charitable efforts, like the Christian Commission, through which thousands of volunteers ministered to both spiritual and bodily needs of Union soldiers. But Civil War ecumenism extended beyond Protestantism. Catholic chaplains in both Union and Confederate armies remarked on the effective cooperation among pastors and soldiers of differing religious affiliations. In one incident that became legend, Father William Corby offered a ceremony of general absolution to a brigade of Union troops before their engagement at Gettysburg. "Catholic and non-Catholic," Corby wrote, "showed a profound respect, wishing at this fatal crisis to receive every benefit of divine grace that could be imparted." The chaplain added generously that "general absolution was intended for all ... not only for our brigade, but for all, North or South, who were susceptible of it and who were about to appear before their Judge."[10]

Even Jewish soldiers, who constituted less than three-tenths of a percent of Civil War armies, joined this common religiosity. Michael Allen, Jewish chaplain of a Pennsylvania regiment, held nondenominational Sunday services for his men, preaching on a variety of topics, including proper preparation for death. Although we today tend to assume sharp differences between Jewish and Christian views of death, and particularly the afterlife, these contrasts appeared far less dramatic to mid-nineteenth-century Americans. Drawing on traditions stretching back at least to Maimonides, Jews of the Civil War era shared Christians' anticipation of what one condolence letter called "a better life" to come. Rebecca Gratz of Philadelphia could comfort her sister-in-law that her son, killed at the Battle of Wilson's Creek, and his distraught father "shall be united in another world." Civil War death thus narrowed theological and denominational differences. The shared crisis of battle yielded a common effort to make the notion of a Good Death available to all.[11]

Americans North and South agreed upon death's transcendent importance. A tract distributed to Confederate soldiers by the Presbyterian Church warned that "death is not to be regarded as a mere event in our history. It is not like a birth, or a marriage, or a painful accident, or a lingering sickness." It has an "importance that cannot be estimated by men." Death's significance arose from its absolute and unique permanence. "Death fixes our state. Here [on Earth] everything is changing and unsettled. Beyond the grave our condition is unchangeable." The moment of death could thus offer a glimpse of this future. "What you are when you die, the same will you reappear in the great day of eternity. The features of character with which you leave the world will be seen in you when you rise from the dead." How one died thus epitomized a life already led and predicted the quality of life everlasting. The *hors mori,* the hour of death, had therefore to be witnessed, scrutinized, interpreted, narrated—not to mention carefully prepared for by any sinner who sought to be worthy of salvation. The sudden and all but unnoticed end of the soldier slain in the disorder of battle, the unattended deaths of unidentified diseased and wounded men denied these consolations. Civil War battlefields and hospitals could have provided the material for an exemplary text on how not to die.[12]

Soldiers and their families struggled in a variety of ways to mitigate such cruel realities, to construct a Good Death even amid chaos, to substitute for missing elements or compensate for unsatisfied expectations. Their successes and failures influenced not only the last moments of thousands of dying soldiers but also the attitudes and outlook of survivors who contended with the impact of these experiences for the rest of their lives.

Perhaps the most distressing aspect of death for many Civil War Americans was that thousands of young men were dying away from home. As one group of Confederate prisoners of war observed in a resolution commemorating a comrade's death in 1865, "we... deplore that he should die... in an enemys land far from home and friends." Most soldiers would have shared the wishes of the Georgia man whose brother sadly wrote after his death in Virginia, "he always did desire... to die at home." Death customs of the Victorian era centered on domestic scenes and spaces; hospitals housed the indigent, not respectable citizens. As late as the first decade of the twentieth century, fewer than 15 percent of Americans died away from home. But the four years of civil war overturned these conventions and expectations, as soldiers died by the thousands in the company of strangers, even enemies. As a South Carolina woman remarked in 1863, it was "much more painful" to give up a "loved one [who] is a stranger in a strange land."[13]

Civil War soldiers experienced an isolation from relatives uncommon among the free white population. The army, moreover, segregated men from women, who in the nineteenth century bore such significant responsibility for the care of both the living and the dead. As a hospital volunteer remarked of the Army of the Potomac, "of this hundred thousand men, I suppose not ten thousand were ever entirely without a mother's, a sister's, or a wife's domestic care before."[14]

Family was central to the *ars moriendi* tradition, for kin performed its essential rituals. Victorian ideals of domesticity further reinforced these assumptions about death's appropriate familial setting. One should die among family assembled around the deathbed. Relatives would of course be most likely to show concern about the comfort and needs of their dying loved one, but this was ultimately a secondary consideration. Far more important, family members needed to witness a death in order to assess the state of the dying person's soul, for these critical last moments of life would epitomize his or her spiritual condition. The dying were not losing their essential selves, but rather defining them for eternity. Kin would use their observations of the deathbed to evaluate the family's chances for a reunion in heaven. A life was a narrative that could only be incomplete without this final chapter, without the life-defining last words.[15]

Last words had always held a place of prominence in the *ars moriendi* tradition. By the eighteenth century "dying declarations" had assumed—as they still retain—explicit secular importance: a special evidentiary status excepting them from legal rules excluding hearsay. People believed final words to be the truth, both because they thought that a dying person could no longer have any earthly motivation to lie, and because those about to meet their maker would not want to expire bearing false witness. As sermonizers North and South reminded their congregations: "A death-bed's a detector of the heart."[16]

Last words also imposed meaning on the life narrative they concluded and communicated invaluable lessons to those gathered around the deathbed. This didactic function provided a critical means through which the deceased could continue to exist in the lives of survivors. The teachings that last words imparted served as a lingering exhortation and a persisting tie between the living and the dead. To be deprived of these lessons, and thus this connection, seemed unbearable to many nineteenth-century Americans left at home while their sons, fathers, husbands, and brothers died with their words unrecorded or even unheard.

Americans thus sought to manage battlefield deaths in a way that mitigated separation from kin and offered a substitute for the traditional stylized deathbed performance. Soldiers, chaplains, military nurses, and doctors conspired to provide the dying man and his family with as many of the elements of the conventional Good Death as possible, struggling even in the chaos of war to make it possible for men—and their loved ones—to believe they had died well. Spiritual wounds demanded attention as powerfully as did those of the flesh. Battle deaths belonged to those at home as well as those in the field. The traditions of *ars moriendi* defined civilians as participants in war's losses and connected soldiers to those behind the lines. Both parties worked to ensure that soldiers would not die alone.[17]

Soldiers endeavored to provide themselves with surrogates: proxies for those who might have surrounded their deathbeds at home. Descriptions of battle's aftermath often remark on the photographs found alongside soldiers' corpses. Just as this new technology was capable of bringing scenes from battlefield to home front, as in Brady's exhibition of Antietam dead in New York, more often the reverse occurred. A dead Yankee soldier at Gettysburg was found with an ambrotype of three children "tightly clasped in his hands." The ultimately successful effort to identify him created a sensation, with magazine and newspaper articles, poems, and songs celebrating the devoted father, who perished with his eyes and heart focused on eight-year-old Franklin, six-year-old Alice, and four-year-old Frederick. But Amos Humiston was far from the only man to die clutching a photograph. Denied the presence of actual kin, many dying men removed pictures from pockets or knapsacks and spent their last moments communicating with these representations of absent loved ones. "I have often thought," William Stilwell wrote to his wife, Molly,

Amos Humiston dies holding an ambrotype of his three children.
"An Incident at Gettysburg." Frank Leslie's Illustrated Newspaper,
January 2, 1864.

in Georgia, "if I have to die on the battlefield, if some kind friend would just lay my Bible under my head and your likeness on my breast with the golden curls of hair in it, that it would be enough."[18]

In military hospitals, nurses frequently cooperated in the search for substitute kin, permitting delirious soldiers to think their mothers, wives, or sisters stood nearby. In a famous lecture she delivered across the country in the years after the war, Clara Barton described her crisis of conscience when a young man on the verge of death mistook her for his sister Mary. Unable to bring herself actually to address him as "brother," she nevertheless kissed his forehead so that, as she explained, "the act had done the falsehood the lips refused to speak."[19]

Perhaps Clara Barton was familiar with some of the popular Civil War–era songs that portrayed her situation almost exactly: the plea of the expiring soldier requesting his nurse to "Be My Mother Till I Die," or even the lines of the nurse herself:

> *Let me kiss him for his mother,*
> *Or perchance a sister dear;*
>
> . . . .
>
> *Farewell, dear stranger brother,*
> *Our requiem, our tears.*

This song was so widely sung it prompted a reply, which was published as an "ANSWER TO: Let Me Kiss Him for His Mother." Written in the voice of those who remained at home, the ballad expressed gratitude to the women caring for the wounded at the same time that it sought to reassure wives and mothers that their loved ones were not dying alone.

> *Bless the lips that kissed our darling,*
> *As he lay on his death-bed,*
> *Far from home and 'mid cold strangers*
> *Blessings rest upon your head.*
>
> . . . .
>
> *O my darling! O our dead one!*
> *Though you died far, far away,*
> *You had two kind lips to kiss you,*
> *As upon your bier you lay*
>
> . . . .
>
> *You had one to smooth your pillow,*
> *You had one to close your eyes.*[20]

The original song and its "answer" represented an interchange, a nationwide conversation between soldiers and civilians, between men and women, as they worked together to reconstruct the Good Death amid the disruptions of war, to maintain the traditional connections between the dying and their kin that defined the *ars moriendi*. The inability to witness the last moments of a brother, husband, or child shattered expectations about an appropriate earthly conclusion to these important human connections. A father who arrived to find his son just hours after he died of wounds received at Fredericksburg wrote feelingly of his disappointment—and described his vision of how his son's life should have ended. "If I could have got to our child, and spoken loving and encouraging words to him, and held his dear hand in mine, and received his last breath: but it was not so to be." Yet denied his deathbed role, the parent had at least achieved one of his purposes: he had acquired definite knowledge of his son's fate.[21]

Because no effective or formal system of reporting casualties operated on either side during the war, it became customary for the slain soldier's closest companions at the time of his death to write a letter to his next of kin, not just offering sympathy and discussing the disposition of clothes and back pay but providing the kind of information a relative would have looked for in a conventional peacetime deathbed scene. These were condolence letters intended to offer the comfort implicit in the narratives of the *ars moriendi* that most of them contained. News of a Good Death constituted the ultimate solace—the consoling promise of life everlasting.[22]

Some soldiers tried to establish formal arrangements to ensure the transmission of such information, to make sure that not just the fact but a description of their death would be communicated to their families. In 1862 Williamson D. Ward of the 39th Indiana made a pact with several members of his company to provide this assurance for one another. "We promised each other" that if any were wounded or killed, "we would see that they were assisted off the field if wounded and if dead to inform the family of the circumstances of death." In the Union prison at Fort Delaware, captured Confederate officers formed a Christian Association with a similar purpose. The group's minute book recorded their resolution, passed on January 6, 1865, "making it the duty" of the organization "to ascertain the name of every Confederate off[icer] dying in this prison and the attendant circumstances, and to transmit the same to their nearest friends or relatives."[23]

But even without the formality of such resolutions, soldiers performed this obligation. After Gettysburg W. J. O'Daniel informed Sarah Torrence of the death of her husband, Leonidas, explaining that the two of them "went into battle side by side," promising each other "if one go[t] hurt to do all we could for him." The letter represented the final fulfillment of that obligation. William Fields wrote to Amanda Fitzpatrick about how her husband had passed his last hours in a Richmond hospital at the very end of the war: "As you in all probability have not heard of the death of your husband and as I was a witness to his death I consider it my duty to write to you although I am a stranger to you." Duty similarly motivated I. G. Patten of Alabama to respond with "Aufaul knuse" to a letter that arrived in camp from I. B. Cadenhead's wife almost two weeks after his battlefield death. Another Confederate castigated himself for not stopping in the aftermath of an 1863 battle to record an enemy soldier's last words and transmit them to his family. In retrospect, this seemed to the young rebel a far more egregious failure than not providing water to the thirsty man.[24]

Remarkably similar North and South, condolence letters constitute a genre that emerged from the combination of the assumptions of *ars moriendi* with the "peculiar conditions and necessities" of the Civil War. These letters sought to make absent loved ones virtual witnesses to the dying moments they had been denied, to link home and battlefront, and to mend the fissures war had introduced into the fabric of the Good Death. In camp hospitals nurses and doctors often assumed this responsibility, sending the bereaved detailed descriptions not just of illnesses and wounds but of last moments and last words. Some hospital personnel even played the role of instructors in the art of dying, eliciting final statements and cueing their patients through the enactment of the Good Death. When Jerry Luther lay wounded in 1862, a physician urged him to send a last message to his mother. Another soldier, asked by a doctor for his last words to send home, responded by requesting the doctor to provide them. "I do not know what to say. You ought to know what I want to say. Well, tell them only just such a message as you would like to send if you were dying." The expiring soldier clearly regarded the doctor as an expert in *ars moriendi* as well as in medicine. This was a ritual the physician must understand far better than he. The war encouraged not just the performance of the traditions of *ars moriendi* but their dissemination. Chaplains North and South saw this instruction as perhaps their most important obligation to the soldiers in their spiritual charge, a duty Catholic father William Corby described as "the sad consolation of helping them . . . to die well."[25]

Sometimes soldiers would attempt to eliminate intermediaries and narrate their deaths directly. Many carried letters to be forwarded to loved ones if they were killed. Sergeant John Brock of the 43rd U.S. Colored Infantry described men bidding each other farewell as they awaited battle near Petersburg. "One corporal from the state of Maine," he reported, "handed me a letter, together with his money and watch. 'Write my wife,' said he, 'in case that anything should happen to me.' "[26]

Some men managed to write home themselves as they lay dying, speaking through pens instead of from the domestic deathbeds war had denied them. These letters are particularly wrenching, in part because last words of more than a century ago appear seemingly unmediated on the page, speaking across the years, serving as a startling representation of immortality to a twenty-first-century reader. Jeremiah Gage of Mississippi wrote his mother after Gettysburg, "This is the last you may ever hear from me. I have time to tell you I died like a man."[27]

Bloodstains cover James Robert Montgomery's 1864 letter from Spotsylvania to his father in Camden, Mississippi. A private in the Confederate signal corps, twenty-six-year-old Montgomery reported that a piece of shell had "horribly mangled" his right shoulder. "Death," he wrote, "is inevitable." But if the stained paper makes his wounds seem almost tangible, his assumptions about death emphasize the years that distance him from our own time. "This is my last letter to you," he explains. "I write to you because I know you would be delighted to read a word from your dying son." His choice of the word "delight" here—a term that seems strikingly inappropriate

within our modern understanding—underlines the importance accorded the words of the dying. Even as his father faced the terrible
news of his son's death, Montgomery expected him to have the
capacity to be delighted by the delivery of his son's last thoughts.
And even in extremis Montgomery followed the generic form of the
Civil War death letter. By the middle of the 1864 Wilderness campaign, Montgomery may well have had a good deal of practice at
writing such letters to other families. Now he could use this proficiency in composing his own.[28]

Montgomery died four days later. His close comrade Ethelbert
Fairfax wrote to confirm his death and to describe James's last
moments to his family. "I have never witnessed such an exhibition
of fortitude and Christian resignation as he showed. In this sad
bereavement you will have the greatest of all comforts in knowing
that he had made his peace with god and was resigned to his
fate . . . He retained consciousness to the last . . . His grave is marked."
Marked but never found. Montgomery's family never realized their
hope to bring his body home to Mississippi.[29]

Letters describing soldiers' last moments on Earth are so similar,
it is as if their authors had a checklist in mind. In fact, letter writers
understood the elements of the Good Death so explicitly that they
could anticipate the information the bereaved would have sought
had they been present at the hour of death: the deceased had been
conscious of his fate, had demonstrated willingness to accept it, had
shown signs of belief in God and in his own salvation, and had left
messages and instructive exhortations for those who should have
been at his side. Each of these details was a kind of shorthand, con-
veying to the reader at home a broader set of implications about the
dying man's spiritual state and embodying the assumptions most
Americans shared about life and death.[30]

Condolence letters invariably addressed the deceased's awareness
of his fate. It was, of course, desirable for the dying man to be conscious and able to confront his impending demise. Only if he was
facing death's inevitablity would he clearly reveal the state of his soul
in his last utterances. One of the Civil War's greatest horrors was that

it denied so many soldiers this opportunity by killing them suddenly, obliterating them on the battlefield and depriving them of the chance for the life-defining deathbed experience. Letter writers were honest in reporting such unsatisfactory deaths, explaining to loved ones at home that they were not alone in being deprived of the last words of the departed.

Sudden death represented a profound threat to fundamental assumptions about the correct way to die, and its frequency on the battlefield comprised one of the most important ways that Civil War death departed from the "ordinary death" of the prewar period. When two soldiers calmly eating dinner in a tent in South Carolina were instantly and unexpectedly killed by a shell lobbed from nearby Sullivan's Island, Samuel A. Valentine of the legendary Massachusetts 54th wrote that although he had seen many comrades die, this incident was especially upsetting, and he declared that he had "never had anything to rest on me so much in my life." The suddenness, the lack of preparation, made these deaths a particularly "awful sight."[31]

Readiness was so important in determining the goodness of a death that soldiers often tried to convince themselves and others that even what appeared to be sudden had in fact been well prepared. The soldier unable to speak after being wounded on the field had, letter writers frequently reassured kin, expressed his faith and demonstrated his anticipations of salvation in the days or weeks before his fatal encounter. When John L. Mason was killed just outside Richmond in October 1864, a comrade wrote to his mother to explain he "died almost instantly without speaking or uttering a word after being struck." But the letter went on to assure her that there still remained "much for consolation" in his death, for even though Mason had been unable to say so, there was evidence that he was "willing and ready to meet his saviour." The preceding summer he had told his comrades that he "felt his sins were forgiven & that he was ready and resigned to the Lord's will & while talking he was so much overjoyed that he could hardly suppress his feelings of delight."[32]

A sermon delivered in honor of a deceased New York soldier gave this paradox of prepared unpreparedness theological foundation. Reverend Alexander Twombly reminded the assembled congregation that no such thing as sudden death exists in God's eyes, that the length of a human life is exactly what God intends it to be. "God's time in taking every Christian home, is the full harvest time in that soul's earthly course." Such words served as both consolation and exhortation: if God is ready, we had better be too. As an 1863 obituary discourse for a Michigan soldier admonished, "Sinner, Procrastinate not. Let his sudden death be to thee a warning."[33]

An anticipated death could never be sudden, and thus soldiers' premonitions came to play an important role in their work of preparation. Many letters announcing the deaths of comrades commented on the deceased's forebodings that a particular encounter would indeed prove fatal. These men provided themselves with time for the all-important spiritual preparation one could use effectively only when face-to-face with unavoidable death. Sure knowledge—even of death—seemed preferable to persisting uncertainty, for it restored both a sense of control and the possibility for the readiness so central to the *ars moriendi*. On the night before his last battle in Virginia in 1862, Willie Bacon had told his comrades of his conviction he would die. "Strange and mysterious," remarked the preacher who delivered his funeral sermon, "is the fact that God so often permits the shadow of death to be thrown upon us, that we may prepare ourselves for his coming." L. L. Jones anticipated that he would be killed in the fighting in Missouri in the summer of 1861 and so provided his wife with his dying sentiments before he went into combat. "I wish you to have my last words and thoughts," he wrote. "Remember me as one who always showed his worst side and who was perhaps better than he seemed. I shall hope to survive and meet you again ... but it may not be so, and so I have expressed myself in the possible view of a fatal result." He was killed in his first battle. Early in the war W. D. Rutherford of South Carolina remarked to his fiancée upon "how we find ourselves involuntarily longing for the worst," so as simply not to be caught unaware. Rutherford confronted three more years of such uncertainty and "longing" before he was killed in Virginia in October 1864.[34]

Wounded or sick soldiers who knew they had not long to live were explicit about being prepared, articulating their acceptance of their fate. J. C. Cartwright wrote with sadness to inform Mr. and Mrs. L. B. Lovelace of Georgia that their son had died in April 1862 in Tennessee. But, he reassured them, "he was conscious all the time and expressed a willingness to die." T. Fitzhugh wrote Mrs. Diggs to report the death of her beloved husband in June 1863. He lived "but a short while" after being shot by the Yankees, but "he was in his right mind at the time of his death" and "was perfectly resigned." A nurse in a Virginia military hospital informed the mother of a deceased patient that he had been "conscious of his death and . . . not afraid but willing to die," which she reassuringly interpreted as "reason to believe that he is better off" now than in this world of woe.[35]

Witnesses eagerly reported soldiers' own professions of faith and Christian conviction, for these were perhaps the most persuasive evidences that could be provided of future salvation. As T. J. Hodnett exclaimed to his family at home after his brother John's 1863 death from smallpox, "Oh how could I of Stud it if it had not bin for the bright evidence that he left that he was going to a better world." Hodnett was deeply grateful that John's "Sole seme to be . . . happy" as he passed his last moments singing of a heaven with "no more triels and trubble nor pane nor death." Captain A. K. Simonton of North Carolina and Isaac Tucker of New Jersey fought on different sides of the conflict, but both died with the words "My God! My God!" on their lips. Tucker was not a "professed and decided follower of Jesus," but his regular attendance at church, his calm in the face of death, and his invocation of the divinity at the end suggested grounds for fervent hope about his eternal future. Simonton's presentiment of his end, his attention in the weeks before his death to "arranging his business for both worlds," indicated that he too was ready to greet his maker, as he indeed did with his last words.[36]

When soldiers expired unwitnessed and unattended, those report-

"The Letter Home." Charcoal and graphite drawing by Eastman
Johnson, 1867. Minneapolis Institute of Arts.

ing their deaths often tried to read their bodies for signs that would reveal the nature of their last moments—to make their silence somehow speak. Their physical appearance would communicate what they had not had the opportunity to put into words. Many observers believed, as one war correspondent put it, that the "last life-expression of the countenance" was somehow "stereotyped by the death blow" and preserved for later scrutiny and analysis. A witness to the death of Maxcy Gregg wrote to the general's sisters that "the calm repose of his countenance indicated the departure of one, at peace with God." In words meant to offer similar assurance to grieving relatives, a Confederate soldier reported the death of a cousin in 1863: "His brow was perfectly calm. No scowl disfigured his happy face, which signifies he died an easy death, no sins of this world to harrow his soul as it gently passed away to distant and far happier realms." Clearly such a face could not be on its way to hell. A Michigan soldier, however, found just such evidence in the appearance of some "rebels" already many hours dead. "Even in death," he wrote, "their traits show how desperate they are and in what situation their conscience was. Our dead look much more peaceful." Witnesses eagerly reported any evidence of painless death, not just to relieve the minds of loved ones about the suffering a soldier might have had to endure but, more importantly, because an easy death suggested the calmness, resignation, and quick passage to heaven that the bereaved so eagerly hoped for as they contemplated the fate of their lost kin.[37]

Peaceful acceptance of God's will, even when it brought death, was an important sign of one's spiritual condition. But if resignation was necessary for salvation, it was not sufficient. Condolence letters detailed evidence of sanctified behavior that absent relatives had not been able to witness. When Henry Bobo, a Mississippi private, died of wounds received near Richmond in the summer of 1862, his cousin wrote from the field to assure Henry's parents that their son had a better chance of getting to heaven than they might think. There had been, he reported, a "great change" in Henry's "way of living" in the months just before his death. Although he had never actually become a professed Christian, Henry had quit swearing and had begun to lead a Christian life. I. B. Cadenhead's sergeant tried similarly to reassure the soldier's widow after her husband's death outside Atlanta in the summer of 1864. "I have had several conversations with him upon the subject of death he sayed to me their was one thing that he was sorry for & that [was] he had not united himself with the church before he left home." When Asahel Nash was killed in the fall of 1862, his parents wrote their nephews, who had served in the First Ohio with their son, to secure information about his life as well as his death. "We want you to write all you can about Asahel . . . How were his morals?" The army, they feared, was "a poor place to improve good habits."[38]

Perhaps Walter Perry had succumbed to the temptations of camp life, for his brother Frank reported that the soldier expressed great anxiety about his past behavior as he lay dying after Antietam. Frank wrote his family in Georgia that Walter at first "said that he hoped he was prepared to meet his God in a better world than this," but he knew "he had been a bad, bad, very bad boy." Frank hastened to assure the dying man that Christ had come to save such sinners. And when Walter failed to mention any of the family by name in his last hours, Frank emphasized that he had nonetheless addressed them implicitly by repeating "Good by, *Good by to you all.*" Striving to fit his brother's life and words into the model of the Good Death, Frank Perry consoled his family with a report of Walter's expressed hope to "meet *us all in Heaven.*" But hope in this case seemed to fall considerably short of certainty.[39]

In a letter to his wife informing her of her brother George's death in 1864, Frank Batchelor worked hard to transform the deceased into a plausible candidate for salvation. Batchelor admitted that George "did not belong to the visible body of Christ's Church," but cited his "charity," "his strong belief in the Bible," and his rejection of the sins of "envy hatred and malice" to offer his wife hope for her brother's fate. Batchelor confirmed himself "satisfied" that George was "a man of prayer" and had no doubt at last "found the Savior precious to his sole" before he died. "This being so," Batchelor happily concluded, his wife could comfort herself with the knowledge she would meet her brother again "in the green fields of Eden."[40]

Just as the bereaved looked for persuasive evidence of salvation, so too were they eager for last messages from dying kin. Reports of parting communications to loved ones appeared in almost every condolence letter. Sanford Branch wrote his mother in Georgia after the First Battle of Bull Run to say his brother John's last words were "about you." After Private Alfred G. Gardner of Rhode Island was shot at Gettysburg, he charged his sergeant to tell his wife he died happy. T. J. Spurr of Massachusetts expired uttering the word "Mother"; Wiley Dorman "asked for his Mother the last word he spoke." Fathers often exhorted children to complete their education, help their mothers, and say their prayers. With these words dying soldiers brought the names and spirits of absent loved ones to their deathbeds and left their survivors with wishes and instructions that outlived their source. For those at home, news of these final messages reinforced the sense of connectedness to lost kin. Neither family nor soldier was left entirely alone, for these deathbed invocations of absent loved ones worked in some measure to overcome separations. Home and battlefront collaborated in the work of managing the unprecedented realities of Civil War death.[41]

Soldiers' efforts to provide consolation for their survivors altered the traditions of the *ars moriendi*. New kinds of death required changed forms and meanings for consolation. When Civil War condolence letters enumerated evidence of the deceased's Christian achievements, designed to show his eligibility for salvation, the writer often included details of the soldier's military performance, his patriotism, and his manliness. "Tell my mother," one soldier said, "I have stood before the enemy fighting in a great and glorious cause." In a letter to the widow of a comrade who had died the preceding day, T. Fitzhugh reported all the customary information: her husband had been resigned to death, was conscious of his fate, and sent his love to his wife and children. But he also added that the soldier had "died a glorious death in defense of his Country."[42]

The image of the Christian soldier encompassed patriotic duty within the realm of religious obligation. But in some instances patriotism and courage seemed to serve as a replacement for evidence of deep religious faith. After Ball's Bluff, Oliver Wendell Holmes Jr. lay severely wounded, wondering if his religious skepticism was going to put him "en route for Hell." A "deathbed recantation," he believed, would be "but a cowardly giving way to fear." With willful profanity, he declared, "I'll be G-d'd if I know where I'm going." But he urged his physician to write home in case of his death to say that he had done his duty. "I was very anxious they should know that."[43]

Holmes's worried acknowledgment of his failure to conform to expected belief and behavior ironically affirms the cultural power of the prevailing Christian narrative. Some nonbelievers hoped that patriotism would substitute for religious conviction in ensuring eternal life. A dying Confederate asked a friend, "Johnnie if a boy dies for his country the glory is his forever isn't it?" He would have found the views of David Cornwell of the Eighth Illinois reassuring. "I couldn't imagine," he mused, "the soul of a soldier who had died in the defense of his country being consigned to an orthodox hell, whatever his opinion might be of the plan of salvation."[44]

Cornwell's views, widely held in both armies, seemed to many Protestant clergy an unwarranted theological departure generated by earthly needs rather than transcendent truths. As the *Army and Navy Messenger,* published in Virginia by the interdenominational Evangelical Tract Society, warned in 1864, patriotism was not piety. "It is not the blood of man, but *'the blood of Jesus Christ that cleanseth from all sin.' "*[45]

Despite clerical efforts, the boundary between duty to God and duty to country blurred, and dying bravely and manfully became an important part of dying well. For some soldiers it almost served to take the place of the more sacred obligations of holy living that had traditionally prepared the way for the Good Death. Letters comforting Wade Hampton after his son Preston was killed in the fall of 1864 emphasized this juxtaposition of military and Christian duty and sacrifice. William Preston Johnston urged Hampton to remember that his son's "heroism has culminated in martyrdom," which should serve as a "consolation for the years he might have lived." James Connor's letter to Hampton structured the imperatives of Christianity, military courage, and masculinity into a hierarchy of solace. "Your best consolation will I know my dear Genl," he wrote, "be drawn from higher than earthly sources[;] still some alleviation of the sorrow is to be drawn from the reflection that Preston died as he had lived, in the path of duty and honor. Young as he was he had played a man's part in the war."[46]

Although Christian principles remained paramount, considerations of courage and honor could also offer "some alleviation of the sorrow" and thus came to play a significant role in Civil War conceptions of holy living and holy dying. A letter written from North Carolina in 1863 to inform William K. Rash that "your son R. A. Rash is no more" is striking in its deviation from the conventional model. It includes no mention of God or religion, simply reporting the ravages of "the Grim monster Death." All the more significant, then, is its invocation of the only comfort available in the absence of appeal to the sacred: "But one consolation he died in full discharge of his duty in the defence of his home & Country." Patriotism and piety converged in what was at once a newly religious conception of the nation and a newly worldly understanding of faith.[47]

For some, even the reassurance of manly duty bravely accomplished remained unavailable. Commanding officers, chaplains, nurses, and friends did all within their power to cast each death as good, to offer grounds for hope to the bereaved. As one postwar chronicler explained, the Catholic Sisters of Mercy who nursed eighteen-year-old David Brant "wrote to his father the least painful account possible of the poor son's death." Indeed, attendants of the dying may not have simply waited to report a Good Death but worked instead to compel it by demanding courage and calmness

A Bad Death. "The Execution of the Deserter William Johnson."
Harper's Weekly, *December 28, 1861.*

from the moribund or even, as Catholic nurses and chaplains frequently reported, winning consent for last-minute baptisms. These observers were struggling to manage and mitigate some of the horror of the slaughter they encountered daily.[48]

But sometimes what one Confederate chaplain called "fond and comforting hope" was all but impossible. Hugh McLees, a missionary to South Carolina regiments, noted that "the deathbed of an impenitent and unpardoned sinner is a very awful place yet it is the one where I have been often called to stand." To stand—but not to describe, for there was little motivation to communicate such distressing information to survivors. But depictions of Bad Deaths could serve as "edifying" examples. Reports of painful, terrifying deaths offered powerful warnings. Father Louis-Hippolyte Gache, a Confederate chaplain, found Freemasons especially likely to die badly, obstinate in rejecting faith to the end. Gache described a man who cursed both him and the church in his "last agony" and thus left his family with a "twofold bereavement: they mourned his physical, and with much more grief, his spiritual death."[49]

Perhaps the most widespread version of the Bad Death appeared in the narratives of soldiers' executions that can be found not only in newspapers and religious publications but in almost every surviving soldier's diary and every substantial collection of soldiers' letters. Punishment for desertion or for crimes like murder or rape, executions were more frequent in the Civil War than in any American conflict before or since. They were rituals customarily staged before assemblies of troops and were designed to make a powerful impression and serve a distinct disciplinary purpose. The *Charleston Mercury* described soldiers seized by "uncontrollable emotion" as their division formed three sides of a square to witness the execution of ten deserters. Soldiers who sat on their coffins as they awaited the firing squad or stumbled up the steps to the gallows served as an unforgettable warning to those who would die well rather than in shame and ignominy. An execution compelled its witnesses literally to confront death and to consider the proper path toward life's final hour. In the case of execution of deserters, the ceremony offered a particularly pointed contrast between the Good Death in combat and the disgraceful end meted out to those seeking to escape battle's terrors.[50]

Executions provided more than just negative examples. The condemned served in many cases as exemplars of hope, for chaplains worked to save these unfortunates from "the second death" and to use them to transmit a compelling educational message. Calm resignation, last-minute expressions of repentance, the enactment of elements of the Good Death even at the foot of the gallows, sometimes even an address from the prisoner urging his fellow soldiers to "beware of his untimely fate"—all provided indelible messages about both good living and good dying, ones that witnesses took very much to heart. These deaths, remarked Catholic chaplain William Corby, "were harder on the nervous system than the scenes witnessed in the middle of a battle, where there is rattle, dash, and excitement to nerve one up for the occasion." As a Confederate private remarked in a letter to his wife, seeing a man die this way was "awful"—at once horrible and inspiring of awe. Almost any soldier could have written the words penned by one witness to an execution in 1863: "I don't think I shall ever forget the scene."[51]

Military executions made a forceful statement about the need to be prepared to die. As the condemned prisoner scrambled to change his eternal fate with a last-minute conversion or repentance, he reinforced the centrality of readiness to the Good Death. Spiritual preparedness was of course the essence of dying well, but men often demonstrated readiness in more temporal ways. Many popular renditions of the *ars moriendi* emphasized the importance of settling one's worldly affairs. A man who arranged for a burial plot on a furlough home was clearly contemplating his mortality, disposing of earthly preoccupations so that his death might bring a satisfactory conclusion to life's narrative.

Many soldiers recognized their precarious situation by composing wills. "Knowing the uncertainty of life & the uncertainty of death," Private Edward Bates of Virginia proceeded to arrange for the disposition of his twenty-five dollars of personal property. David Coe of Clarke County, Virginia, composed a will at the very occasion of his enlistment at the Berryville Post Office in June 1861. Calling for pen, ink, and paper, he conscripted postal patrons to serve as witnesses. "As I am about to leave home in these war of the Sothren Confedersey, I leave all I am worth...to my wife." Thomas Montfort of Georgia found it "sad and melancholy" to see men before battle "preparing for the worst by disposing of their property by will" at the same time the surgeon sharpened his instruments, soldiers readied lint for bandages, and men scattered sand around artillery emplacements, "not for health or cleanliness, but to drink up human blood." As his unit awaited a Union attack on Savannah's Fort Pulaski, Montfort passed his time "witnessing wills" for comrades.[52]

Although the affluent were more likely to prepare wills, many soldiers of lesser means also sought to specify the distribution of their assets, perhaps to try to exert some control over a future in which they would play no part. Attendants in military hospitals often solicited oral declarations from dying soldiers in order to know what to do with their effects. John Edwards's dying wishes, recorded as his "Noncuptative Will," by Mr. Hill at the hospital of the 53rd Virginia in April 1862, requested that the forty dollars in his possession be sent to his sister because he knew he was "bound to die."[53]

Soldiers' personal possessions often took on the character of *memento mori*, relics that retained and represented something of the spirit of the departed. Burns Newman of the Seventh Wisconsin Volunteers undertook the "painful duty" of informing Michael Shortell's father of his son's death near Petersburg the preceding evening. "Enclosed," he continued, "send you some trinkets taken from his person by my hand. Think you will prize them as keepsakes." A Bible, a watch, a diary, a lock of hair, even the bullet with which a son or a brother had been killed could help to fill the void left by the loved one's departure, and could help make tangible a loss known only through the abstractions of language.[54]

In a more figurative sense, condolence letters reporting the details of soldiers' deaths served as *memento mori* for kin working to understand wartime loss. Survivors rewrote these narratives of Good Deaths using the condolence letter as a rough draft for a range of printed genres designed to impose meaning and purpose on war's chaos and destruction. Obituaries often replicated the structure and content of condolence letters, frequently even quoting them directly, describing last moments and last words and assessing the likelihood of a deceased soldier's salvation. William James Dixon of the Sixth Regiment of South Carolina Volunteers, his obituary reported, had not entered the army as a believer, though he had always "maintained a strictly moral character." Several battles, however, impressed him with "the mercy of God in his preservation," so that before his death at Chancellorsville he had "resolved to lead a new life." His loved ones could, the *Daily South Carolinian* assured them, safely "mourn not as those who have no hope" and could be certain "that their loss is his eternal gain."[55]

Civil War Americans worked to construct Good Deaths for themselves and their comrades amid the conditions that made dying—and living—so terrible. As war continued inexorably onward and as death tolls mounted ever higher, soldiers on both sides reported how difficult it became to believe that the slaughter was purposeful and that their sacrifices had meaning. Yet the narratives of the *ars moriendi* continued to exert their power, as soldiers wrote home about comrades' deaths in letters that resisted and reframed war's carnage.

Men did so not simply to mislead the bereaved in order to ease their pain—a ruse that historian Jay Winter attributes to the self-consciously deceptive letters from the Western Front in World War I. As Roland Bowen of the 15th Massachusetts responded to a friend's request for "all the particulars" about a comrade's death at Antietam, "I fear they will do you no good and that you will be more mortified [devastated] after the facts are told than you are now. Still you ask it and wither it be for the better or worse not a word shall be [kept] from you."[56]

Although the authors of Civil War condolence letters did try their utmost to cast the deaths they described in the best possible light, their efforts are striking in their apparent commitment to honesty, their scrupulousness in reporting when a deceased soldier's faith had been suffused with doubt, when his behavior had been less than saintly. Civil War soldiers seem themselves desperately to have wanted to believe in the narratives they told and in the religious assumptions that lay behind them. The letters may have served in part as a way of reaching across the chasm of experience and horror that separated battle and home front, as an almost ritualized affirmation of those very domestic understandings of death that had been so profoundly challenged by circumstances of war, as a way of moving symbolically out of the meaningless slaughter back into the reassuring mid-nineteenth-century assumptions about life's meaning and purpose. Narratives of dying well may have served as a kind of lifeline between the new world of battle and the old world at home.[57]

In the eyes of a modern reader, men often seem to have been trying too hard as they sought to present evidence of a dead comrade's ease at dying or readiness for salvation. But their apparent struggle provides perhaps the most eloquent testimony of how important it was for them to try to maintain the comforting assumptions about death and its meaning with which they had begun the war. In face of the profound upheaval and chaos that civil war brought to their society and to their own individual lives, Americans North and South held tenaciously to deeply rooted beliefs that would enable them to make sense out of a slaughter that was almost unbearable. Their Victorian and Christian culture offered them the resources with which to salve these deep spiritual wounds. Ideas and beliefs worked to assuage, even to overcome the physical devastation of battle. And yet death ultimately remained, as it must, unintelligible, a "riddle," as Herman Melville wrote, "of which the slain / Sole solvers are."[58] Narratives of the Good Death could not annul the killing that war required. Nor could they erase the unforgettable scenes of battlefield carnage that made soldiers question both the humanity of those slaughtered like animals and the humanity of those who had wreaked such devastation.

CHAPTER 2

KILLING

"The Harder Courage"

"I am aposed to one man killing another [but] . . . I shall fight."
THEOPHILUS PERRY

Tolstoy once wrote that what fascinated him about war was "its reality"—not the strategies of generals or the maneuvers of troops but "the actual killing." He was "more interested," he explained, "to know in what way and under the influence of what feelings one soldier kills another than to know how the armies were arranged at Austerlitz and Borodino."[1] Killing is battle's fundamental instrument and purpose. And in the Civil War it was killing, not dying, as Orestes Brownson observed in 1862, that demanded "the harder courage," for it required the more significant departure from soldiers' understandings of themselves as human beings and, in mid-nineteenth-century America, as Christians.

Most Civil War combatants were very like one another—metaphorically, if not literally, brothers, in the oft-repeated trope of the war. When racial difference eroded this common identity, killing became easier, as in the many reported instances of atrocities against black soldiers, such as the infamous 1864 massacre at Fort Pillow. But in most circumstances and for most individuals during the war, killing posed a problem to be overcome. In this respect Civil War soldiers were hardly different from their fellow combatants in other wars. Studies of warriors in ancient times, in Napoleonic armies, in World Wars I and II, and in the Falklands confirm the judgment of

Lieutenant Colonel Dave Grossman, U.S. Army Retired, specialist in military psychology and former West Point faculty member, that "man is not by nature a killer." Indeed, he often resists even firing his weapon.[2]

But just as human beings die differently in different times and places, they come to kill differently too. Human reluctance to murder expresses itself within a particular historical and cultural moment. Civil War killing, like death more generally, required work—intellectual and psychological effort to address religious and emotional constraints, as well as adaptation to the ways this particular war's technologies, tactics, and logistics shaped the experience of combat.

The first challenge for Civil War soldiers to surmount was the Sixth Commandment. Dying exemplified Christian devotion, as Jesus had demonstrated on the cross, but killing violated fundamental biblical law. As one Texas recruit explained his fears, fighting in battle seemed "the most . . . blasphemous thing perhaps on earth." Sermons and religious publications North and South invoked and explored the traditional "just war" doctrine, emphasizing that killing was not merely tolerated but required in God's service. There is "nothing in the demands of a just and defensive warfare at variance with the spirit and duties of Christianity," an oft-reprinted tract for soldiers emphasized. Citing a variety of Old Testament texts, the *Confederate Baptist* insisted that men were exempt from the commandment not to kill "when lawful war calls for the slaying of our country's foes." While southerners most often appealed to self-defense against invasion as the source of the war's justness, they invoked as well the notion of divine sanction for a holy war in which they served as Confederate crusaders. Northerners just as avidly claimed God for their side as they fought to save a nation that represented "the last best hope of earth." "I am aposed to one man killing another," a Union soldier wrote to "Friends at Home," but, he continued, "when we are atacked and our lives are in danger by a gang of men aposed to the best government on earth I shall fight." As emancipation emerged as an explicit war aim after 1862, northerners increasingly cited the sin of slavery as a religious justification for the use of violence. In 1864 the *Christian Recorder,* published by the African Methodist Episcopal Church, editorialized on "The War and Its Design," inquiring when war and killing are acceptable and concluding that the goal of over-turning the wrong of slavery made the conflict a righteous one and its carnage justifiable.[3]

Such arguments offered permission to kill, or at least softened deeply held prohibitions against it. But soldiers and even comman-ders still struggled with taking other men's lives. Union general in chief Winfield Scott observed before First Bull Run how thin a line separated war from murder. "No Christian nation," he insisted, "can be justified in waging war in such a way as shall destroy five hundred and one lives, when the object of the war can be attained at a cost of five hundred. Every man killed beyond the number absolutely required is murdered." From his perspective in 1861, Scott would have regarded the ultimate slaughter of hundreds of thousands and the profligate squandering of lives that was to come at places like Malvern Hill, Marye's Heights, Cold Harbor, and Gettysburg as unforgivable. Scott's successor as Union commander, George B. McClellan, shared this aversion to killing. "When he had to lose lives he was almost undone," observed historian T. Harry Williams. Gen-eral George Gordon Meade believed that in order to ensure minimal losses on both sides, the North should prosecute the war "like the afflicted parent who is compelled to chastise his erring child, and who performs the duty with a sad heart." It was in this context that Meade's bloody victory at Gettysburg would seem appalling, and that Grant's casualties in the spring campaigns of 1864 would be attacked as "butchery."[4]

As they took up arms and, in the phrase they commonly used to describe initiation into battle, went "to see the elephant," individual soldiers worried about their direct personal responsibility for killing. A Massachusetts man wrote of his first experience under fire in Bal-timore in April 1861, when a mob of irate southern sympathizers attacked Union troops heading through the city to Washington. Edwin Spofford pulled the trigger almost without thinking after a

*"The Sixth Regiment of the Massachusetts Volunteers
Firing into the People, Baltimore, April, 1861."*
Frank Leslie's Illustrated Newspaper, *April 30, 1861.*

soldier standing next to him was killed. "The man who shot him fell dead by my rifle," he wrote. "I felt bad at first when I saw what I had done, but it soon passed off, and as I had done my duty and was not the aggressor, I was soon able to fire again and again." Duty and self-defense released him from an initial sense of guilt and helped him to do the work of a soldier. Implicit yet present here too was the motive of revenge. Spofford came to kill almost as a reflex, as a response to what he saw as the murder of the comrade beside him.[5]

As the intensity of this war and the size of its death tolls mounted in the months and years that followed, vengeance came to play an ever more important role, joining principles of duty and self-defense in legitimating violence. The desire for retribution could be almost elemental in its passion, overcoming reason and releasing the restraints of fear and moral inhibition for soldiers who had witnessed the slaughter of their comrades. Hugh McLees of South Carolina wrote of the struggle not to abandon his principles in his treatment of a group of Union prisoners. "I saw some nasty blue Yankees in the cars at Atlanta," he wrote in 1864,

> and as I looked at our poor Boys there with their grisly wounds and some of them cold in death I could much more easily have taken a dagger and said to them see there what a carnival of blood you have made and as you love it take still more that of your own hearts take that with what you have already drunk I could more easily have done that than I could act toward them in the part that I know a truly brave magnanimous man must ever act toward a foe in his power and unarmed. May God give me grace to live a Christian.

As it reiterated "take...that...take that," McLees's letter home enacted in language the violence he had abjured; the pen freed him to express a brutality he had resisted with dagger or sword. Yankee Oliver Norton proved less controlled after his messmates fell victim to Confederate fire, for he abandoned all thoughts of magnanimity or Christianity. The feeling "uppermost in my mind," he explained, "was a desire to kill as many rebels as I could."[6]

Once the constraints of conscience and custom loosened, some soldiers, especially in the heat of combat, could seem almost possessed by the urge to kill. A soldier in action became "quite another being," one of "almost maniac wildness," with eyes darting, nostrils flared, and mouth gasping, a correspondent for a southern newspaper observed. A *New York Tribune* reporter at Shiloh described this frightening transformation. "Men lost their semblance of humanity," he wrote, "and the spirit of the demon shone in their faces. There was but one desire, and that was to destroy." It was difficult for him to think of these men as Christian soldiers, or even as beings who were fully human.[7]

Soldiers, too, found themselves surprised by the power of some comrades' exhilaration. Byrd Willis of the Army of Northern Virginia wrote in his journal about seeing a member of his unit "jumping about as if in great agony" during an 1864 skirmish. "I immediately ran up to him to ascertain when he was hurt & if I could do any thing of him—but upon reaching him I found that he was not hurt but was executing a species of Indian War Dance around a Poor Yankee (who lay on his back in the last agonies of death) exclaiming I killed him! I killed him! Evidently carried away with excitement & delight, I left James to continue his dance." Numbers of Civil War letters and diaries describe similar instances of soldiers playing at being Indians—imitating war whoops, painting their faces with mud or soot from cartridges in what they saw as Indian style—when going into battle. By replacing their own identities with those of men they regarded as savages, they redefined their relationship both to violence and to their prewar selves.[8]

The emerging delight in killing was not restricted to the heat of battle. Confederate artillery officer Osmun Latrobe described his pleasure contemplating a job well done after Antietam: "I rode over the battlefield, and enjoed the sight of hundred[s] of dead Yankees. Saw much of the work I had done in the way of several limbs, decapitated bodies, and mutilated remains of all kinds. Doing my soul good. Would that the whole Union army were as such, and I had had my hand in it." For Latrobe, this "work" represented a successful execution of his duties as a soldier. Vengeance was simply a form of justice, the mutilated bodies equivalent to the biblical eye and tooth of retribution. Half a year later Latrobe would be celebrating "glorious heaps of Yankee dead" after Chancellorsville. Sergeant William Henry Redman was in pursuit of Confederates retreating after Gettysburg when he wrote his mother of his near obsession with destroying the rebels who had dared invade the North. "I am only satisfied nowadays when I am fighting the enemy. The proper time to fight him is while he is on our northern soil. I shall kill every one of them that I can."[9]

Although Union and Confederate soldiers often struggled, at least initially, with killing, men throughout history have reported loving combat, and the Civil War was no exception. Union officer John W. De Forest explained that "to fire at a person who is firing at you is somehow wonderfully consolatory and sustaining; more than that, it is exciting and produces in you the so-called joy of battle." Although De Forest described the comfort of shooting in self-defense, he also revealed how he escaped an oppressive sense of victimhood through action against his enemy; he was at once justified and empowered by battle's intensity. Frank Coker of Georgia tried to explain to his wife how despite battle's horrors, "there is an excitement, a charm, an inspiration in it that makes one wish to be where it is going on." For some men from rural areas, battle took on the character of the hunt, with its sense of sport and pleasure. A Texas officer exulted as the enemy fell before him, "Oh this is fun to lie here and shoot them down." To a Union soldier near Harrison's Landing, Virginia, in 1862, battle "seemed like play for we would be laughing and talking to each other yelling and firing away. One fellow would say 'Watch me pop that fellow.' Another fellow said, 'I dropped a six foot secesh.' "[10]

Far from finding reluctance about killing among his comrades, H. C. Matrau of the Union's Iron Brigade explained to his parents how military training seemed only to enhance an innate brutality. A month of drilling in bayonet attacks led him to conclude, "It is strange what a predilection we have for injuring our brother man, but we learn the art of killing far easier than we do a hard problem in arithmetic." Surprised at this discovery, Matrau began to revise his understanding of human nature and its capacities. Many soldiers found that society's powerful inhibitions against murder were all too easily overcome.[11]

Yet the particular social and technological circumstances of the Civil War posed significant challenges to the art of killing as it had been practiced in earlier conflicts. Armies of the mid-nineteenth century were accustomed to fighting in ordered ranks to control soldiers and compel their firing and killing. The mechanism of drill and the almost automatic movements imposed by military discipline worked together with the organization of troops in close ranks to lessen soldiers' self-doubt and inhibitions about killing—as well as any desire or chance they might have to flee. Men acted as part of a whole, which both removed an element of agency from the individual and encompassed him within the pressures and solidarity of the group.

As a Confederate soldier waiting to enter combat cried to a rabbit he saw loping across the battlefield amid heavy fire, " 'Run, cotton-tail . . . If I hadn't got a reputation to sustain, I'd travel too!' "[12]

But the Civil War departed in significant ways from what had come before. It was fought with new weapons, significantly more technologically advanced even than those generally available in the Mexican War a decade and a half earlier. Instead of the smoothbore musket, which could accurately reach targets up to about one hundred yards away, almost all Civil War infantry North and South were, by the middle of the war, equipped with rifles with an effective range of a three hundred yards. By the end of the war the introduction of breechloaders, chiefly among some units of the Union army, further enhanced lethality by permitting soldiers to reload rapidly, rather than at the pace of two to three shots a minute common with muzzle-loading rifles. Civil War armies marked a significant departure from previous conflicts as well, for this war generated a mass mobilization of common citizens and forces of unprecedented size. The approximately three million Americans North and South who ultimately served in the course of the conflict were not trained professionals, schooled in drill and maneuver, but overwhelmingly volunteers with little military knowledge or experience.[13]

Combined with the enhanced firepower and range of Civil War weapons, the minimal training of volunteer forces and the sheer size of the armies brought increased disorder to battle and less direct control by officers over troops. In addition, most Civil War battlefields were not open terrain but were covered with woods and scrub that undermined the orderly command of long battle lines. Although costly frontal assaults remained common till nearly the end of the war, by the latter stages of the conflict troops began to be employed in looser order and even in trench warfare, as the construction of earthworks and field fortifications became routine. As a result, soldiers became far less likely to fight in close-order battle formation where they fired on command; they had more independence in deciding when and whether to discharge their weapons.

Dave Grossman suggests that this independence may have

prompted many Civil War soldiers to express their aversion to killing by failing to discharge their weapons. He cites as evidence the discovery of 24,000 loaded rifles on the field after Gettysburg; half these weapons held more than one load. Given how long it took to load and fire a rifle—using powder, ball, ramrod, percussion cap—he calculates that 95 percent of these soldiers should have been shot with an empty weapon if they had indeed been actively engaged in trying to kill the enemy. Grossman believes that "most of these discarded weapons on the battlefield at Gettysburg represent soldiers who had been unable or unwilling to fire their weapons in the midst of combat and then had been killed, wounded, or routed."[14]

There is little surviving evidence with which to assess the accuracy of Grossman's assertion about high rates of nonfiring by Civil War soldiers; his claim is based chiefly on extrapolations from studies of other wars, studies that are themselves contested. The intriguing puzzle of multiply loaded guns may have other explanations: for example, a soldier's pure panic, or his failure amid the din of battle to realize a weapon had not discharged. But some anecdotal evidence of resistance to firing does exist. One Confederate soldier at Chickamauga made a dramatic show of his refusal to kill. Instead of aiming at the enemy, he shot straight up into the air while "praying as lustily as ever one of Cromwell's Roundhead's prayed." When his captain threatened to shoot him, a comrade reported his reply: "You can kill me if you want to, but I am not going to appear before my God with the blood of my fellow man on my soul." Willing to remain "exposed to every volley of the enemy's fire," the soldier was ready to give his life rather than take that of another.[15]

Subsequent wars introduced forms of combat with levels of impersonality and anonymity that reduced the burden of individual responsibility endured by Civil War infantry. Many of the bombs and missiles used in twentieth-century warfare, for example, almost entirely separated the killer from his victims. The crew of the *Enola Gay* or the specialists targeting precision weapons in the First Gulf War had a very different relationship to killing than the Civil War soldier—or the twenty-first-century enlisted man on the ground in

Afghanistan or Iraq. Physical distance between enemies facilitates emotional distance from destructive acts. But fewer than 10 percent of Civil War troops were artillerymen, who lobbed shot, shell, or canister toward a distant enemy, and even these targets were usually close enough to be clearly identifiable as men. Most Civil War wounds were inflicted by minié balls shot from rifles: 94 percent of Union injuries were caused by bullets; 5.5 percent by artillery; and less than 0.4 percent by saber or bayonet. Although Civil War weapons did have significantly increased range, infantry engagements, even as they grew to involve tens of thousands of men, remained essentially intimate; soldiers were often able to see each other's faces and to know whom they had killed. Historian Earl Hess asserts that despite the capabilities of the new rifles, most combat occurred at a distance of about one hundred yards, even though, as one Yankee soldier explained, "when men can kill one another at six hundred yards they generally would prefer to do it at that distance." S. H. M. Byers of Iowa remembered one terrible battle where "lines of blue and gray" stood "close together and fire[d] into each other's faces for an hour and a half," and after Gettysburg, Union soldier Henry Abbott wrote his father of opposing "rows of dead . . . within 15 and 20 feet apart, as near hand to hand fighting as I ever care to see."[16]

The growth in size of battlefields between the Civil War and the two World Wars of the next century influenced the kinds of interactions that took place upon them. In Civil War engagements, *The Penguin Encyclopedia of Modern Warfare* calculates, the ratio of soldiers to space on the field averaged one man per 260 square meters; by the end of World War II, the ratio rose to one per 28,000 square meters. With its large volunteer armies, its longer-range weapons, and its looser military formations, the Civil War thus placed more inexperienced soldiers, with more firepower and with more individual responsibility for the decision to kill, into more intimate, face-to-face battle settings than perhaps any other war in history. Absent the reassurance provided by distance or controlling discipline or combat experience, many Civil War soldiers were likely to have struggled as they decided when and even whether to fire at men who were visibly very like themselves.[17]

For many soldiers, the horror of killing was exemplified by sharp-shooters, whose work appeared simply to be "cold blooded murder." Sniping was a fundamental reality of Civil War military life, and rifles made marksmen accurate up to a distance of almost half a mile. Other technological innovations, the telescopic sight and the breech-loading rifle, further enhanced the sharpshooter's lethality. Confederate sharpshooters' units required men to be able to hit a target at six hundred yards with open sights. A Vermont recruiting poster for "The Sharp Shooters of Windham County" announced, "No person will be enlisted who cannot when firing at the distance of 200 yards, at a rest, put ten consecutive shots in a target, the aver-age distance not to exceed five inches from the centre of the bull's eye to the centre of the ball."[18]

Soldiers often described bullets whizzing by even as they sat com-posing their letters home. "Dear Brother, Wife and All," Isaac Had-den wrote to his family in New York from Virginia in June 1864, "There was a man this moment shot in the belly 20 feet from me which is nothing unusual in this country. It is worth a man's life to go to sh-t here." To shoot a man as he defecated, or slept, or sat cooking or eating, or even as he was "sitting under a tree reading Dickens," could not easily be rationalized as an act of self-defense. Soldiers in camp wanted to think themselves off duty as targets as well as killers, and they found the intentionality and personalism involved in picking out and picking off a single man highly disturbing. Union sharpshooting units customarily wore green uniforms to serve as camouflage, and Confederates came to refer to these marksmen as "snakes in the grass."[19]

The cool calculation, the purposefulness, and the asymmetry of risk involved in sharpshooting rendered it even more threatening to basic principles of humanity than the frenzied excesses of heated battle. When twelve soldiers from a regiment of Union sharpshoot-ers were taken prisoner in Virginia in 1864, a local Petersburg news-paper argued for their execution: "in our estimation they are nothing

"The Army of the Potomac—A Sharp-Shooter on Picket Duty."
Engraving from an oil painting by Winslow Homer.
Harper's Weekly, *November 15, 1862.*

but murderers creeping up & shooting men in cold blood & should receive the fate of murderers." After enduring twenty-four days of steady and debilitating sniper fire between Union and Confederate troops near Port Hudson, Louisiana, John De Forest confessed, "I could never bring myself to what seemed like taking human life in pure gayety." Men who had displayed great courage in battle had broken down "under the monotonous worry" generated by sniper fire. De Forest judged it a "sickening, murderous, unnatural, uncivilized way of being." Men who could kill others in this way were not men as De Forest had before the war understood them to be; they violated his assumptions about both human nature and human civilization; he believed they undermined what defined their human selves.[20]

Dehumanizing the enemy is a common means of breaking down restraints against killing. Military training and propaganda often explicitly encourage such behavior, and soldiers themselves are inventive at differentiating and demeaning those whom they are assigned to destroy—be they Krauts or Nips or Slopes, to cite three twentieth-century examples. In the mid-nineteenth century, racism served to place African American soldiers in particular peril. Even in the Union army the 180,000 black soldiers who enlisted beginning in 1862 faced degrading inequalities in pay and opportunity. Constituting nearly 10 percent of federal forces, they served under white officers and were overwhelmingly assigned to labor details and fatigue duty rather than entrusted with the responsibilities of combat.

For Confederates, black troops represented an intolerable provocation. To permit blacks to serve as soldiers, Howell Cobb of Georgia declared, suggested "our whole theory of slavery is wrong." These inferior beings, he believed, were incapable of the courage required for battle. But for white southerners, the issue was not primarily one of racial theories. The terrifying actuality of a force of armed black men seemed equivalent to a slave uprising launched by the federal government against the South. White southerners feared and detested African American troops. Mary Lee, who had endured three years on the front lines in embattled Winchester, Virginia, felt "more unnerved" by the appearance of black Union soldiers in 1864 "than by any sight I have seen since the war [began]."[21]

Confederate soldiers regarded black troops as "so many devils," whose very presence in the South justified their deaths. As the *Arkansas Gazette* proclaimed, "Arming negroes, as soldiers or otherwise, or doing any thing to incite them to insurrection is a worse crime than the murder of any one individual: Therefore, all officers and soldiers . . . guilty of such practices . . . should be punished as murderers." Southern soldiers did victimize black Yankees, with atrocities that ranged from slaughter of prisoners to mutilation of the dead. W. D. Rutherford of South Carolina boldly declared his intentions in a letter he sent to his wife before an 1864 engagement with a regiment of U.S. Colored Troops: "The determination in our army is to kill them all and spare not." The Fort Pillow massacre of April 1864, when Nathan Bedford Forrest's men killed nearly two-thirds of the approximately three hundred black soldiers present, most after they had surrendered, was only the most notorious of such incidents. Others were perhaps even more grisly. At a battle at Poison Springs, Arkansas, which occurred in the same month as Fort Pillow, the First Kansas Colored Volunteer Infantry lost 117 dead and only about half as many wounded. This was a suspicious ratio in itself, as numbers of wounded almost always far exceed numbers of slain. A Confederate officer described bodies "scalped & . . . nearly all stripped . . . No black prisoners were taken." A Union soldier confirmed "that the inhuman and blood thirsty enemy . . . was engaged in killing the wounded wherever found." But a local newspaper defended the Confederate actions as entirely consistent with the larger purposes of the war, "We cannot treat negroes . . . as prisoners of war without a destruction of the social system for which we contend . . . We must claim the full control of all negroes who may fall into our hands, to punish with death, or any other penalty." Slavery required subordination and control, and arming men elevated and empowered them.[22]

It was not just African American soldiers who were at risk of southern retribution. A Texas officer described with some amazement his unit's engagement with a black regiment near Monroe, Louisiana: "I never saw so many dead negroes in my life. We took no prisoners, except the white officers, fourteen in number; these were lined up and shot after the negroes were finished. Next day they were thrown into a wagon, hauled to the Ouchita river and thrown in. Some were hardly dead—that made no difference—in they went."[23]

Even black teamsters or servants working for the federals were at risk, and male slaves suspected of fleeing to join the Union army were more than fair game for Confederate rage. A Confederate major described an incident in which black civilians accompanying Union troops were slaughtered. "The battle-field was sickening . . . no orders, threats or commands could restrain the men from vengeance on the negroes, and they were piled in great heaps about the wagons, in the tangled brushwood, and upon the muddy and

"The War in Tennessee—Rebel Massacre of the Union
Troops After the Surrender at Fort Pillow, April 12."
Frank Leslie's Illustrated Newspaper, *May 7, 1864.*

trampled road." All too often, however, orders and commanders encouraged rather than restrained such atrocities. Private Harry Bird reported that Confederates after the Battle of the Crater in 1864 quieted wounded black soldiers begging for water "by a bayonet thrust." Bird welcomed the subsequent order "to kill them all"; it was a command "well and willingly . . . obeyed." General Robert E. Lee, only a few hundred yards away, did nothing to intervene.[24]

Jefferson Davis himself had approved the execution of four captured black soldiers in the fall of 1862, and Secretary of War James Seddon declared in April 1863 that "the Department has determined that negroes captured will not be regarded as prisoners of war." General Kirby Smith, commander of the Trans Mississippi Department, even admonished an officer who had shown himself too merciful to black combatants. "I have been unofficially informed," he wrote, "that some of your troops have captured negroes in arms. I hope this may not be so, and that your subordinates who may have been in command of capturing parties may have recognized the propriety of giving no quarter to armed negroes and their officers."[25]

In the case of black soldiers and the officers who surrendered the privileges of whiteness by consenting to lead them, "propriety" seemed all too often to dictate murder. Killing was not simply justified but almost required, even when such action demanded suspension of fundamental rules of war and humanity. In practice, it would prove impossible for Confederates to maintain a policy of killing all black prisoners, at least in part because of threatened Union reprisals. Some African Americans were treated as prisoners of war, as were, for example, the approximately one hundred men incarcerated at Andersonville. But violence against black soldiers and their white officers was extensive and widely discussed among northern soldiers and civilians alike.[26]

Well before white atrocities stoked an intensified desire for vengeance, black soldiers approached war's violence differently from white Americans. Their understanding of why the war was righteous and why their fighting was justified grew out of their knowledge of centuries of suffering under slavery, as well as from their own personal experiences of cruelty and oppression. As T. Strother explained in a letter to the *Christian Recorder,* the newspaper of the African Methodist Episcopal Church,

To suppose that slavery, the accursed thing, could be abolished peacefully and laid aside innocently, after having plundered cradles, separated husbands and wives, parents and children; and after having starved to death, worked to death, whipped to death, run to death, burned to death, lied to death, kicked and. cuffed to death, and grieved to death; and, worst of all, after having made prostitutes of a majority of the best women of a whole nation of people . . . would be the greatest ignorance under the sun.

Slavery manufactured death, Strother charged; it was itself a kind of warfare perpetrated against blacks; to take arms against it was by definition an act of self-defense, an assertion of manhood and a claim for personal liberation. "Those who would be free must strike the blow," a young soldier explained in 1863. Blacks fought to define and claim their humanity, which seemed to many inseparable from avenging the wrongs of a slave system that had rendered them property rather than men.[27]

It would come to seem ironic to many observers, both during the war and later, that manhood should be defined and achieved by killing. Writing the history of the black experience in war and Reconstruction in 1935, W. E. B. DuBois found it "extraordinary ... that in the minds of most people ... only murder makes men. The slave ... was humble; he protected the women of the South, and the world ignored him. The slave killed white men; and behold, he was a man!" In fact, like other Civil War soldiers, African Americans wrote often of dying and of Christian sacrifice as fundamental purposes of their military service. "Wounded Colored Soldiers in Hospital" after the 1863 assault on Fort Wagner cast themselves as "soldiers for Jesus" and assured the readers of the northern black press that "if all our people get their freedom, we can afford to die." Black soldiers did die in dramatic numbers; one-fifth of the approximately 180,000 who served did not survive the war, although disease proved a far more deadly killer than combat. (Overall, twice as many soldiers died of disease as from battle wounds; ten times as many black soldiers did.) But these deaths promised political as well as spiritual redemption. Black soldiers sought to win a place in the polity, as citizens and as men, through their willingness to give up their lives. "When you hear of a white family that has lost father, husband or brother," wrote a corporal from the Third U.S. Colored Troops reporting the loss of ten comrades in South Carolina, "you can say of the colored man, we too have borne our share of the burden." Black and white northerners could honor heroic black deaths, even if, as historian Alice Fahs points out, the racist assumptions of many whites made them "only

"Unidentified Sergeant, U.S. Colored Troops."
Rare Book, Manuscript, and Special Collections
Library, Duke University.

too willing to celebrate the manhood of black soldiers who no longer had any manhood to exercise."[28]

Perhaps the most dramatic such celebration, one that became for many African Americans emblematic of the meaning of black service and sacrifice, was the New Orleans funeral of Captain André Cailloux in August 1863. The *Christian Recorder* judged the event "one of the most extraordinary exhibitions brought forth by this rebellion." And exhibition it was: of black courage, accomplishment, and solidarity, as well as the strength of a black claim to citizenship in a restored American nation.

Cailloux was one of approximately 11,000 free people of color in antebellum New Orleans. A literate artisan and a property owner, he served as secretary of one of the city's many Afro-Creole mutual benefit societies. After the fall of New Orleans to federal forces in the spring of 1862, Cailloux helped recruit a company for the Union army. Founded upon a long tradition of military service by New Orleans's free people of color, including a critical role in aiding Andrew Jackson against the British in 1815, the Louisiana Native Guards claimed distinctions denied other units of nonwhite soldiers, such as the right to serve under company officers from their own community. Killed as he led his men in a charge at Port Hudson on May 27, 1863, Cailloux was the first of only a few black officers to die in the war. For all his courage and respectability, André Cailloux was in the eyes of the Confederates simply a man who deserved not just death but dishonor for his presumption in taking up arms against a superior race. Despite a truce called to permit the removal of the dead and wounded, rebel sharpshooters prevented Union troops from retrieving the bodies of black soldiers. Cailloux lay on the field until July 8, when Port Hudson surrendered. After forty-one days exposed to the elements, his body could be identified only because of a ring he still wore.[29]

Cailloux's funeral in New Orleans later in the month was intended to compensate for this humiliation. One wonders too if it was in some sense understood—at least by the northern press—as a counterpoint to the elaborate ceremonies that had surrounded the burial of Confederate hero Stonewall Jackson, who had died just days before Cailloux was killed. In New Orleans "immense crowds of colored people" made the streets "almost impassable," the newspapers reported. Benevolent societies lined Esplanade Street for more than a mile. A parade of fellow soldiers and civic society members accompanied the coffin, draped in an American flag and borne by a hearse pulled by a team of fine horses, to St. Louis Cemetery. A Catholic priest, who had been censured and suspended by the Louisiana archbishop because of his antislavery sympathies, performed the service and "called upon all to offer themselves, like Cailloux had done, martyrs to the cause of justice, freedom and good government. It was a death the proudest might envy." The *Union,* newspaper of the free black community, concluded that Captain Cailloux's death had "vin-

"Funeral of the Late Captain Cailloux."
Harper's Weekly, *August 29, 1863.*

dicated his race from the opprobrium with which it was charged."
Certainly, his death became a symbol for the northern antislavery
cause and particularly for black abolitionists. The flag Cailloux had
carried at Port Hudson was prominently displayed at the National
Negro Convention presided over by Frederick Douglass in October
1864. Cailloux's death—configured as heroic sacrifice—made a powerful case for blacks' right to citizenship in the nation they had given
so much to save.[30]

But in the eyes of many African Americans, the focus on death
and Christian sacrifice only seemed to combine with widespread
military atrocities to perpetuate a disturbing tradition of black victimhood. From the front in Virginia, reporter George Stephens hastened to assure his readers at the New York *Weekly Anglo-African* that
"we do not wish to make . . . [them] think that we are anxious to
meet death on the battlefield . . . or to use the language of a contemporary, 'go out gaily to meet death as to our bride.' " The suffering of
bondage sufficed; now justice required that others be the objects of

violence. Part of establishing equality would be evening this score. Vengeance and retribution played a prominent place in blacks' understanding of the rationale for war's destructiveness, as well as for the violent acts of individual men.[31]

A popular poem that appeared in several versions in the black press illustrated this conception of achieving equity through equivalent suffering. A "brave Confederate chief" is killed in battle and is carried home to his mother, who greets the death of her only son with "frantic sorrow." Her "aged slave" comes to offer not consolation but justice. "Missus," she declares, "we is even, now." The white mother had sold all ten of her slave's children, so now neither woman has any remaining offspring; the two mothers are alone together in their common loss. The mistress must now, in the words of her slave, "to the just Avenger bow." The war is God's instrument for balancing the accounts of righteousness:

> *Yea! although it tarry long,*
> Payment shall be made for wrong![32]

This notion of fitting retribution also lay at the heart of Frederick Douglass's view of the war and of black soldiers' role within it. The most prominent voice of the northern black community, Douglass understood the centrality of violence to slavery from his own experience in bondage. He had been beaten, he had fought back, and he had fled; he retained few illusions about the likelihood of white southerners giving up their peculiar institution without a desperate struggle. Douglass believed he had reclaimed his own "manly independence" by fighting and overcoming the brutal white overseer Covey. In Douglass's view, slaves had the absolute right to rise up and kill their masters, and his sympathy for John Brown had arisen from this premise. Douglass embraced a redemptive as well as an instrumental view of bloodshed; violence was not simply effective but instructive and liberating. The war's brutality, he wrote, served as a "blazing illustration" of the fundamental truth that "there is no more exemption for nations than for individuals from the just retribution due to flagrant and persistent transgression." But the Civil War's "tears and blood," he believed, "may at last bring us to our senses."[33]

Black soldiers entered battle not just deeply invested in the war's outcome but strongly motivated to kill in service of their cause. Already victims of generations of cruelty in slavery, they saw themselves to be simply balancing accounts as they struggled for the freedom that would equalize their condition. They were fighting, they repeated again and again, for "God, race and country"—for righteousness, equality, and citizenship. But as the war continued and black troops experienced rising numbers of atrocities at the hands of Confederate troops who singled them out for special cruelty and humiliation, many African American soldiers felt even more entitled to vengeance and even more eager to kill. They knew, too, that they would be given no quarter if captured by southerners, who were likely either to shoot them or to send them into slavery—regardless of whether they had been slaves or had even lived below the Mason-Dixon line before the war.[34]

Cordelia Harvey, sent south by the governor of Wisconsin to provide aid to the state's wounded, wrote from Mississippi late in April 1864 to describe the anger and determination of black soldiers. "Since the Fort Pillow tragedy," she explained, "our colored troops & their officers are awaiting in breathless anxiety the action of Government... Our officers of negro regiments declare they will take no more prisoners—& there is death to the rebel in every black mans eyes. They are still but terrible. *They will fight*... The negroes know what they are doing." A black regiment, she reported, had already hanged a Chicago cotton merchant who had dared to say that he believed the rebels "did right" in killing the blacks on a nearby plantation during a recent raid.[35]

News of Fort Pillow prompted cries for vengeance from northern blacks. Soldiers should not cease fighting "until they shall have made a rebel to bite the dust for every hair of those... of our brethren massacred at Fort Pillow... give no quarter; take no prisoners... then, they will respect your manhood," wrote one correspondent to the

Christian Recorder. But Henry M. Turner, the black chaplain of the First U.S. Colored Infantry, worried about the position "highly endorsed by an immense number of both white and colored people, which I am sternly opposed to, and that is, the killing of all the rebel prisoners taken by our soldiers." Even if the rebels had "set the example," such actions represented an "outrage upon civilization and ... Christianity." Turner urged black soldiers to disappoint those who expected them to behave brutally; they should instead claim a moral superiority to their enemies. Vengeance, as another black chaplain emphasized, belonged to the Lord.[36]

In March 1865 the ringing cadences of Lincoln's Second Inaugural would echo the widespread black understanding of the war's carnage as divine punishment for the sin of slavery. Advocating "malice toward none," urging that Americans "judge not that we be not judged," Lincoln nevertheless suggested the possibility that in the Civil War God himself had judged—not in designating a victor but in exacting the lives of so many Americans. The deaths brought about by the Civil War were less a Christian sacrifice than an atonement. "If God wills that it continue," Lincoln proclaimed just a little more than a month before the end of the war, "until every drop of blood drawn with the lash, shall be paid by another drawn with the sword, as was said three thousand years ago, so still it must be said, 'the judgments of the Lord are true and righteous altogether.' "[37]

Lincoln's eloquence was perhaps matched by the passion of an elderly woman slave who saw in the work of death and killing the conflict's fundamental purpose. Mary Livermore, Union nurse, described a wartime encounter with an African American woman she had known years before during Livermore's service as a governess on a southern plantation. Aunt Aggy had waited through decades of cruelty to see "white folks' blood . . . a-runnin' on the ground like a riber." But she had always had faith "it was a-comin. I allers 'spected to see white folks heaped up dead. An' de Lor', He's keept His promise, an' 'venged His people, jes' as I knowed He would. I seed 'em dead on de field, Massa Linkum's sojers an' de Virginny sojers, all heaped togedder . . . Oh, de Lor' He do jes' right, if you only gib Him time enough to turn Hisself."[38]

Slavery gave the war's killing and dying a special meaning for black Americans; the conflict was a moment for both divine and human retribution, as well as an opportunity to become the agent rather than the victim of violence. Killing was for black soldiers—as well as for black civilians like Aunt Aggy—the instrument of liberation; it was an act of personal empowerment and the vehicle of racial emancipation. To kill and to be, as soldiers, permitted to kill was ironically to claim a human right.

In the aftermath of battle, when the intensity and the frenzy dissipated, when the killing at least temporarily ceased, when reason returned, soldiers confronted the devastation they had created and survived—"the unmistakable evidence," as one soldier put it after Spotsylvania, "that death is doing its most frightful work." William Dean Howells later wrote of the lasting impact of the Civil War on James Garfield, a Union general and later U.S. president: "at the sight of these dead men whom other men had killed, something went out of him, the habit of a lifetime, that never came back again: the sense of the sacredness of life and the impossibility of destroying it." Dead men whom other men had killed: there was the crux of the matter. Battle was, as a North Carolina soldier ruefully put it, "majestic murder." The carnage was not a natural disaster but a man-made one, the product of human choice and human agency. Neither North nor South had expected the death tolls that Civil War battles produced, and the steadily escalating level of destruction continued to amaze and horrify. The Mexican War had claimed approximately 13,000 U.S. lives, of which fewer than 2,000 had been battle deaths; the First Battle of Bull Run in August 1861 had shocked the nation with its totals of 900 killed and 2,700 wounded. By the following spring at Shiloh, Americans recognized that they had embarked on a new kind of war, as the battle yielded close to 24,000 casualties, including approximately 1,700 dead on each side. Shiloh's number of killed and wounded exceeded the combined totals of all the major engagements of the war that had preceded it. The summer's fighting on the Virginia Peninsula would escalate the carnage yet again. "We used to think that the battle of Manassas was a great affair," Confederate Charles Kerrison wrote home to South Carolina in July 1862, "but it was mere child's play compared with those in which we have lately been engaged." By the time of Gettysburg a year later, the Union army alone reported 23,000 casualties, including 3,000 killed; Confederate losses are estimated between 24,000 and 28,000; in some regiments, numbers of killed and wounded approached 90 percent. And by the spring of 1864 Grant's losses in slightly more than a month approached 50,000.[39]

Faced with the Civil War's unprecedented slaughter, soldiers tried to make sense of what they had wrought. As they surveyed the scene at battle's end, they became different men. For a moment they were relieved of the demand to kill; other imperatives—of Christianity, of humanity, of survival rather than courage or duty—could come again to the fore. And now they had time to look at what was around them. Union colonel Luther Bradley described this transformation:

> Of all the horrors the horrors of the battlefield are the worst and yet when you are in the midst of them they don't appal one as it would seem they ought. You are engrossed with the struggle and see one and another go down and say, "there goes poor so-and-so. Will it be my turn next." Your losses and dangers don't oppress you 'till afterwards when you sit down quietly to look over the result or go out with details to bury the dead.

Dealing with the "afterwards" required work lest, as a Confederate soldier worried after Shiloh, the spectacle "dethrone reason or pervert the judgment." Henry C. Taylor wrote to his parents in Wisconsin after a grim night collecting the dead and wounded from an 1863 battle in Kentucky, "I did not realize anything about the fight when we were in action, but the battlefield at midnight will bring one to a realizing sense of war. I never want to see such a sight again. I cannot give such a description of the fight as I wish I could. My head is so full that it is all jumbled up together and I can't get it into any kind of shape." But he could draw one clear and revealing conclusion: "Tell Mrs Diggins not to let her boy enlist."[40]

Soldiers struggled to communicate to those eager to know their fate at the same time that they themselves struggled to understand what they saw. Why indeed were they still alive? As one Indiana soldier wrote in his diary in 1864, his "best men" had fallen around him, yet "I am not better than they." William Stilwell of Georgia confessed to his wife the day after Antietam, "I am in good health this morning as far as my body is concerned, but in my mind I am perplexed." Unable to explain, soldiers tried to describe, invoking the raw physicality of carnage and suffering. Even as survivors they could not escape the literal touch of death, which assaulted the senses. First there was the smell. "The dead and dying actually stink upon the hills," W. D. Rutherford wrote his wife after the Seven Days Battles around Richmond. For a radius of miles, the "mephitic effluvia" caused by rotting bodies ensured that even if the dead were out of sight, they could not be out of mind. And then there were the thousands of bodies. Men had become putrefied meat, not so much killed as slaughtered, with "nothing to distinguish them from so many animals." Stepping accidentally on a dead man's leg felt to James Wood Davidson's "boot-touch like a piece of pickled pork—hard and yet fleshy," and he leaped back with alarm. Soldiers looked with horror upon bodies that seemed to change color as they rotted, commenting frequently upon a transformation that must have borne considerable significance in a society and a war in which race and skin color were of definitive importance. "The faces of the dead," one northern Gettysburg veteran described, "as a general rule, had turned black—not a purplish discoloration, such as I had imagined in reading of the 'blackened corpses' so often mentioned in descriptions of battlegrounds, but a deep bluish *black*, giving to a corpse with black hair the appearance of a negro."[41]

Witnesses to battle's butchery often wrote of the impossibility of crossing the field without walking from one end to the other atop the dead. "They paved the earth," a soldier wrote after the Battle of Williamsburg in 1862. Grant found the same after Shiloh: "I saw an open field . . . so covered with dead that it would have been possible to walk across the clearing, in any direction, stepping only on dead bodies without a foot touching the ground." With grim precision Eugene Blackford described a two-acre area at Fredericksburg containing 1,350 dead Yankees; others estimated stretches of a mile or more at Antietam or Shiloh where every step had to be planted on a dead body. Men were revolted both by the dishonor to the slain beneath their feet and by the pollution represented by such distasteful contact with the dead. Like a modern snapshot, this oft-repeated representation of battle's horror graphically portrayed in the freeze-frame of a picture what soldiers could not narrate in a sequence of words. With vividness and detail, for the senses rather than for the reason or intellect, this recurrent image communicated the unspeakable.[42]

Men wept. Even as he acknowledged that "it does not look well for a soldier to cry," John Casler of the Stonewall Brigade knew "I could not help it." Benjamin Thompson of the 111th New York affirmed that after Gettysburg "no words can depict the ghastly picture." He "could not long endure the gory, ghastly spectacle. I found my head reeling, the tears flowing and my stomach sick at the sight." Colonel Francis Pierce confessed that "such scenes completely unman me." Battle changed the living to the dead, humans into animals, and strong men into "boys . . . crying like children"—or perhaps even into women with their supposed inability to control their flowing tears. As Walter Lee wrote his mother from the front in June 1862, "I don't believe I am the same being I was two weeks ago, at least I don't think as I used to and things don't seem as they did."[43]

One way soldiers became different men was by resisting and repressing the unbearable horror. "The feelings of a soldier walking over his first battle-field and over his second, are widely different," a southern newspaper observed. Men wrote of "hardening," numbing, or becoming "calloused" or even indifferent to others' deaths as well as to the prospect of their own. A Union surgeon, surrounded in Virginia by "a horrible spectacle of human misery," saw this transformation in attitude as a blessing, regarding it as a "wise provision of divine providence that man can accommodate himself to any & every circumstance, at first no matter how revolting." A seasoned soldier could sleep or eat amid the bodies of the dead; "all signs of emotion . . . or ordinary feelings of tenderness and sympathy" disappeared. With a gesture that reflected either a jocular insensitivity or an ironic anger that may well have shocked and surprised his wife, Isaac Hadden of New York invited her to join him at dinner "in the enemy's rifle pits where the dead lay around crawling away with dear little worms called maggots . . . I was kind of hungry and got used to the pretty sights." Union colonel Charles Wainwright reported that when another soldier fell against him proclaiming himself a dead man, "I had no more feeling for him, than if he had tripped over a stump and fallen; nor do I think it would have been different had he been my brother." Private Wilbur Fisk of Vermont resorted to irony in his attempt to depict soldiers' changing attitudes: "The more we get used to being killed, the better we like it."[44]

Soldiers acted with as little concern as if it were not men but "hogs dying around them." Human life diminished sharply in value, and the living risked becoming as dehumanized as the dead. Soldiers perhaps found it a relief to think of themselves not as men but as machines—without moral compass or responsibility, simply the instruments of others' direction and will. As a common soldier, Angus Waddle believed he was "but a machine by which fame and glory is manufacted for some great Gen.' " Texan Elijah Petty explained to his wife that "we have no right to think. Others have been appointed to think for us and we like the automation must kick (or work) when the wire is pulled." Civilians caring for the fallen in battle's immediate aftermath adopted a similar strategy. Katherine Wormeley, who served on a hospital ship during the Peninsula Campaign, believed that to permit herself to "feel acutely at such times is merely selfish." It was imperative "to put away all feeling. Do all you can, and be a machine—that's the way to act; the only way."[45]

While many soldiers welcomed this numbing as a means of escaping the horrors around them, others worried about the implications of such detachment. "The fact that many men get so accustomed to the thing, that they can step about among the heaps of dead bodies, many of them their friends and acquaintances[,] without any particular emotion, is the worst of all," a Federal officer observed. Indifference to suffering and death was "demoralizing," a failure to care about what should matter most in human life. A religious tract widely distributed in the Confederate army issued a stern "WARNING TO SOLDIERS." "Guard against unfeeling recklessness," it cautioned. "By familiarity with scenes of violence and death, soldiers often become apparently indifferent to suffering and anguish, and appear to be destitute of the ordinary sensibilities of our humanity." Hardening represented in the eyes of the church an abandonment of the compassion that lay at the core of human and Christian identity. Loss of feeling was at base a loss of self—a kind of living death that could make even survivors casualties of war.[46]

Killing was the essence of war. But it also challenged men's most fundamental assumptions about the sanctity of their own and other human lives. Killing produced transformations that were not readily reversible: the living into the dead, most obviously, but the survivors into different men as well, men required to deny, to numb basic human feeling at costs they may have paid for decades after the war ended, as we know twentieth- and twenty-first-century soldiers from Vietnam to Iraq continue to do; men who, like James Garfield, were never quite the same again after seeing fields of slaughtered bodies destroyed by men just like themselves.

CHAPTER 3

BURYING

"New Lessons Caring for the Dead"

"This is not how we bury folks at home."
ROLAND E. BOWEN, 15TH MASSACHUSETTS,
SEPTEMBER 28, 1862

However stunned, exhausted, and overwhelmed, soldiers at the end of battle had more work to do. The carnage created by the Civil War's major engagements, and even the casualties of smaller skirmishes, presented an immediate challenge to those still reeling from the fighting's physical and emotional impact. Soldiers had to disregard their own misery and attend to the wounded and dead. The sheer number of bodies requiring disposal after a Shiloh, an Antietam, or a Gettysburg defied both administrative imagination and logistical capacity, for each death posed a pressing and grimly pragmatic problem: What should be done with the body?

Nineteenth-century Americans confronted this crisis of the Civil War slain within a broader context of assumptions about appropriate treatment of the dead. Humanity, not just particular humans, was at stake. As the trustees of the Antietam National Cemetery would explain in 1869, "One of the striking indications of civilization and refinement among a people is the tenderness and care manifested by them towards their dead."[1]

Why do living humans pay attention to corpses? There is, of course, the compelling need for disposal. But that is simply the most tangible and immediate problem dead bodies pose. In 1854, well before the intrusions of war, *Harper's New Monthly Magazine* offered an extended consideration of the subject. Its editor, Henry Raymond, founder of the *New York Times* and one of Lincoln's strongest wartime supporters, speculated whether the "sacredness of the human body" was a notion too outdated for a modern era of science and progress. Invoking history, philosophy, religion, and reason, he insisted otherwise. "There ever has been, in all places, in all ages, among all classes and conditions of mankind, a deep-feeling in respect to the remains of our earthly mortality." The body, the essay continued, is not simply a possession, "like a picture, a book, a garment, or any thing else that once *belonged* to the deceased." In the corpse, rather, there remains "something of the former selfhood." And, in the terms of prevailing Protestant doctrine, something of the future and immortal selfhood as well. The human body is "not like any other portion of matter," for it "will be raised again—yea, the same body."[2]

Redemption and resurrection of the body were understood as physical, not just metaphysical, realities, and therefore the body, even in death and dissolution, preserved "a surviving identity." Thus the body required "sacred reverence and care"; the absence of such solicitude would indicate "a demoralized and rapidly demoralizing community." The body was the repository of human identity in two senses: it represented the intrinsic selfhood and individuality of a particular human, and at the same time it incarnated the very humanness of that identity—the promise of eternal life that differentiates human remains from the carcasses of animals, who possess neither consciousness of death nor promise of either physical or spiritual immortality. Such understandings of the body and its place in the universe mandated attention even when life had fled; it required what always seemed to be called "decent" burial, as well as rituals fitting for the dead.[3]

Civil War soldiers worried deeply about their own remains, especially as they began to encounter circumstances that made customary reverence all but impossible. A South Carolinian wrote from the Virginia front that "some how I have a horor of being thrown out in a neglected place or bee trampled on as I have seen a number of graves here." His hope was to be transported home. Jeremiah Gage of the 11th Mississippi felt differently. As he lay dying at Gettysburg, he wrote to urge his mother not to regret that she would be unable to retrieve his body. With his last words, he asked "to be buried like my comrades. But deep, boys deep, so the beasts won't get me." Confederate Thomas J. Key shared the same gruesome concern: "It is dreadful to contemplate being killed on the field of battle without a kind hand to hide one's remains from the eye of the world or the gnawing of animals and buzzards." Another northern soldier expressed a different worry with his last breath: "don't let the rebels get me." To be returned to the bosom of family or, failing that, at least to be honorably buried with one's comrades and preserved from the desecrations of enemies, human and otherwise: these concerns were shared by soldiers North and South.[4]

When the war began, military officials on both sides sought to establish regularized burial procedures, in no small part because decaying bodies and the "effluvia" that emanated from them were believed to pose serious threats to public health. Many of the deaths in the initial months of the conflict arose from epidemics of diseases like measles and mumps that broke out as men, often from isolated rural areas, crowded together in army camps and exposed one another to new illnesses. Both North and South ordered military hospitals to establish burial grounds. Each hospital of the Union army was charged to provide a "dead house," for storage of corpses prior to burial and for post-mortem examinations. When circumstances permitted, hospital personnel kept careful records of those interred, provided them with respectful burials, and, if the army remained stationary for a period of time, maintained graves. In Virginia in 1861, for example, accounts of the Confederate hospital at Culpeper showed regular sums expended to local laborers for digging graves and making coffins for interments in its well-tended cemetery.[5]

But as war escalated and troops began to clash on the battlefield, these cemeteries became entirely inadequate for those who were dying at the scene of the fighting, on scattered grounds, or in hastily

"Soldiers' Graves near General Hospital, City Point, Virginia."
Library of Congress.

established field hospitals. At the end of the war, a former Union hospital steward remembered ruefully the failure to maintain careful records of the dead. Field hospitals, he explained, were organized on an emergency basis. "Everything . . . was therefore hurriedly arranged. You will therefore understand the seeming want of order in the burial of the dead . . . It was with the greatest difficulty and with terrible exertion on the part of my associates and myself that we were able to care for the sick and wounded—hence the little apparent care for those who were beyond help." As a Union chaplain put it, "We learned new lessons as to caring for the soldier dead, or as to the necessity of failing to care for them in the exigencies of more active warfare."[6]

The First Battle of Bull Run late in July 1861 yielded casualties that galvanized military officials to reconsider their lack of preparation for so many fallen. In September the Union army issued General Orders no. 75, making commanding officers responsible for burial of soldiers who died within their jurisdiction and for submission of a form recording their deaths to the office of the adjutant general. A little more than six months later, General Orders no. 33 detailed more elaborate instructions:

> In order to secure, as far as possible, the decent interment of those who have fallen, or may fall, in battle, it is made the duty of Commanding Generals to lay off plots of ground in some suitable spot near every battlefield, so soon as it may be in their power, and to cause the remains of those killed to be interred, with headboards to the graves bearing numbers, and, when practicable, the names of the persons buried in them. A register of each burialground will be preserved, in which will be noted the marks corresponding to the headboards.[7]

"As far as possible . . . when practicable": the very language reveals how utopian a measure this would prove. The structures and resources that would have been necessary to implement such policies were hardly even imagined, much less provided: the Union army had no regular burial details, no graves registration units, and until 1864 no comprehensive ambulance service. As late as Second Bull Run, in August 1862, a Union division took the field without a single ambulance available for removal of casualties. The Confederate army passed analogous regulations specifying the commanders' duty to bury the dead, dispose of their effects—and even pay their laundry bills. But they gave no more systematic attention to how these exhortations might actually be heeded than did their northern counterparts. Burying the dead after a Civil War battle seemed always to be an act of improvisation, one that called upon the particular resources of the moment and circumstance: available troops to be detailed, prisoners of war to be deployed, civilians to be enlisted.[8]

This lack of capacity and preparation was evident in the length of time it took to attend to the dead. Battlefield exigencies often delayed care for the wounded, much less the slain. If a military advantage seemed threatened, commanders might well reject flags of truce proposed for removal of casualties from the field. During the Peninsula Campaign of 1862, for example, Union colonel Henry Weeks reported to his commanding officer from Hanover Court House, Virginia, "the refusal of the enemy to admit our burial party." Soldiers often lay on the field dead or dying for hours or even days until an engagement was decided. Josiah Murphey of Nantucket reported on June 6, 1864, that casualties from the Battle of Cold Harbor remained where they had fallen for three days. At last a twenty-four-hour flag of truce interrupted the unrelieved fighting and enabled soldiers to bury their dead. A northern paper explained Grant's rejection of a forty-eight-hour "cessation of hostilities" to bury the dead during this spring 1864 campaign: "Lee was on his knees begging for time to bury his dead. But in this cruel war the business of generals is with the living." Civilians and soldiers alike began to understand the meaning and urgency of the phrase they so often intoned: "Let the dead bury the dead."[9]

More often delay resulted from the failure to mobilize necessary manpower and resources for the task. The Battle of Antietam, September 17, 1862, the bloodiest single day of combat in American history, left both Union and Confederate armies staggering. Lee slowly limped southward, leaving the field—and the dead of both sides—to the Union army. McClellan appeared to be paralyzed by the magnitude of the engagement and failed to take strategic advantage of his victory by pursuing the Confederate army. A similar paralysis seemed to grip his troops as they confronted the devastation before them. Twenty-three thousand men and untold numbers of horses and mules lay killed or wounded. A Union surgeon reported that a week after the battle "the dead were almost wholly unburied, and the stench arising from it was such as to breed a pestilence." He described "stretched along, in one straight line, ready for interment, at least a thousand blackened bloated corpses with blood and gas protruding from every orifice, and maggots holding high carnival over their

"A Burial Party After the Battle of Antietam."
Photograph by Alexander Gardner. Library of Congress.

heads." A nurse arriving more than ten days later found men still scattered on the field.[10]

Some commanders at Antietam had detailed squads to inter the dead soon after the fighting ceased. New Yorker Ephraim Brown, who had proudly captured a rebel flag during the battle on September 17, found himself ordered two days later to bury Confederates along the line of his earlier triumph. His detail counted 264 bodies along a stretch of about fifty-five yards. Brown may have resented having his valor rewarded with this grisly obligation, as units were sometimes assigned to burial duty in response to some military infraction or shortcoming. S. M. Whistler of the 130th Pennsylvania ruefully reported that three days after the Battle of Antietam his regiment, "by reason of having incurred the displeasure of its brigade commander, was honored in the appointment as undertaker-in-

"Antietam. Bodies of Confederate Dead Gathered for Burial."
Photograph by Alexander Gardner. Library of Congress.

chief" for a "particular part of the field." In a gesture that was at once practical and punitive, officers often ordered prisoners of war to bury their own dead. A Confederate officer, for example, after an engagement later in the war, seemed to take satisfaction from the discomfort of Union prisoners "assigned to bury their neglected dead. The sight of their unburied comrades rotting in the woods & fields revolted them."[11]

Origen Bingham of the 137th Pennsylvania was comparatively rested after the Battle of Antietam because his regiment had been held in reserve. But then he and his men found themselves confronting "the most disagreeable duty that could have been assigned to us; tongue cannot describe the horible sight." The soldiers had been killed on Wednesday, September 17; the 137th arrived on the field on Sunday. Although Union corpses had already been interred, probably by their own units and comrades, hundreds of Confederates remained. Bingham secured permission from the provost marshal's office to buy liquor for his men because he believed they would be able to carry out their orders only if they were drunk. These were hardly conditions that encouraged respectful treatment of the deceased, and indeed ribald jokes and inebriated revelry abounded. Another burial party, overwhelmed by the number of bodies, tried a different means of making its task manageable. A squad of exhausted Union soldiers threw fifty-eight Confederates down the well of a local farmer who had unwisely abandoned his premises.[12]

The Battle of Gettysburg the following summer presented an even greater challenge, for the fighting stretched over three days, delaying attention to the dead as military demands on the living continued unabated. By July 4, an estimated six million pounds of human and animal carcasses lay strewn across the field in the summer heat, and a town of 2,400 grappled with 22,000 wounded who remained alive but in desperate condition. One Union medical officer, who was assuming responsibility for burying those he could not save, reported that he lacked even basic tools: "I had not a shovel or a pick . . . I was compelled to send a foraging party to the farmhouses, who, after a day's labor, procured two shovels and an ax." So many bodies lay unburied that a surgeon described the atmosphere as almost intolerable. Residents of the surrounding area complained of a "stench" that persisted from the time of the battle in July until the coming of frost in October. A young boy remembered that everyone "went about with a bottle of pennyroyal or peppermint oil" to counteract the smell.[13]

Responsibility for the dead usually fell to the victor, for it was his army that held the field. Early in the war soldiers expressed outrage when the defeated abandoned their comrades without providing for their burial. "No set of heathens in the world was ever guilty of such acts," a Georgia soldier proclaimed after First Bull Run in July 1861. "They never did come back to bury the first one of their dead." This was a scruple abandoned as rapidly as the bodies themselves. "I can-

Black soldiers serving as burial detail. "Burying the
Dead Under a Flag of Truce, Petersburg, 1864."
Frank Leslie's Illustrated Newspaper, *September 3, 1864.*

not delay to pick up the debris of the battlefield," Union major general Meade baldly declared after his army's costly success at Gettysburg in July 1863. When two of his comrades were shot down trying to retrieve the body of their colonel near Winchester in 1862, Confederate Theodore Fogel explained to his parents, "I knew it was not right to expose myself in that way. Colonel Holmes was dead, and it was not right for us to risk our lives simply to get his body off the field." The needs of the living increasingly trumped the dignity of the departed.[14]

Practical realities dictated that retreating armies did not have time to attend to the dead but had to depend on the humanity of their opponents, who predictably gave precedence to their own casualties. This discrimination arose largely from ties of feeling with departed comrades, but there may have been an element of tactical calculation as well. Confederate surgeon John Wyeth described how by the end of the long night after the Confederate victory at Chickamauga, "most of the Confederate dead had been gathered in long trenches and buried; but the Union dead were still lying where they fell. For its effect on the survivors it was the policy of the victor to hide his own losses and let those of the other side be seen." Sometimes, especially if armies found themselves on the move, enemy dead were not buried at all but were left to rot in places where troops found their bones as they circled back over ground where earlier engagements had been fought. Frank Oakley of Wisconsin encountered skeletons from the First Battle of Bull Run as he fought the Second thirteen months later; soldiers at Spotsylvania and the Wilderness in 1864 continually stumbled upon human debris from the Chancellorsville battle that had taken place almost exactly a year before.[15]

Armies developed burial techniques intended to make the daunting task of disposal of bodies manageable, but these procedures seemed horrifying even to many of those who executed them. Burial parties customarily collected the dead in a single location on the field by tying each soldier's legs together, passing the rope around his torso, and then dragging him to a row of assembled bodies. A bayonet, heated and bent into a hook, could keep a soldier from having to touch what was often a putrescent corpse. The burial detail might then dig a grave, place a body in the hole, cover it with dirt from the next grave, and continue until the line of corpses was covered. But such individuation was usually reserved for one's comrades and for circumstances where sufficient time and resources were available. Enemy dead were more likely to be buried in large pits. G. R. Lee described the procedure in his unit: "long trenches were dug about six feet wide and three to four deep. The dead were rolled on blankets and carried to the trench and laid heads and feet alternating so as to save space. Old blankets were thrown over the pile of bodies and the earth thrown on top." One soldier worried that the process as he witnessed it after Shiloh reduced men to the status of animals or perhaps even vegetables. "They dig holes," he wrote, "and pile them in like dead cattle and have teams to draw them together like picking up pumpkins."[16]

Confederates at Gettysburg were buried in trenches containing

"Dead Confederate Soldiers Collected for Burial.
Spotsylvania, May 1864." Library of Congress.

150 or more men, often hurled rather than laid to rest. Sometimes the rotting bodies ruptured, compelling burial parties to work elsewhere until the stench had dissipated. Soldiers stomped "on top of the *dead* straightening out their legs and arms and *tramping* them down so as to make the hole contain as many as possible." The press of circumstance could, on occasion, require mass burial even of one's own men. A Connecticut chaplain remembered a desperate encounter that killed twenty-three of his company during the very last days of the war: "The best that we could do in the brief interval of our stay was to bury our dead hurriedly in a common grave . . . in a long trench by the wayside, the officers by themselves, and the enlisted men near them." Mass graves obviously obliterated the names of their occupants, although the living often tried to ensure that per-

sonal items remained with the bodies, preserving at least the possibility of later disinterment and identification. Trenches might also be marked, like one at Antietam, with a simple wooden sign indicating "80 rebels buried here." Customarily, northern and southern soldiers were interred separately; a Union colonel expressed outrage when he discovered an instance of military hospitals burying the dead indiscriminately, with no "distinction between the graves of our Brave men who have died for our cause, and the grave of the worthless invaders of our soil. This," he proclaimed, "is all wrong." He could only think this had been the fault of the "*Undertaker* who cares only to get his money for covering their heads with earth." Separate sections of the hospital cemetery should be selected "and the bodies kept separate," he insisted.[17]

Weary soldiers took advantage of natural trenches and existing declivities. After Second Bull Run eighty-five dead were laid beside a ridge created by a railroad excavation and then "covered by the levelling of the embankment over them as the most expeditious manner of burial." James Eldred Phillips of Virginia described burying the dead in the spring 1863 campaign by placing men "down in deep gulleys on either side of the road and the dirt was dug from the side to cover them over." But spring storms followed, and Phillips learned, "after getting some distance down the road," that "heavy rainfall had washed up all of the men that were buried in the gulley . . . and carried them down toward Fredericksburg."[18]

Haste and carelessness frequently yielded graves so shallow that bodies and skeletons reappeared, as rain and wind eroded the soil sheltering the dead and hogs rooted around battlefields in search of human remains. For men buried on the field, coffins were out of the question; a blanket was the most a man could hope for as a shroud. As a northern relief worker reported about burials in Virginia in 1864, "None have been buried in coffins since the campaign commenced." At war's outset, many Americans would have designated the coffin as the basic marker of the "decency" that distinguished human from animal interment, and they would have agreed with

*"A Burial Trench at Gettysburg." Photograph by
Timothy H. O'Sullivan. Library of Congress.*

John J. Hardin, an Indiana volunteer, who found it "dreadful . . . to see the poor soldier just thrown in a ditch an covered over without any box."[19]

Burials like these dehumanized the dead and appalled many of the living. A Union chaplain observed that in pit burials bodies were "covered over much the same as farmers cover potatoes and roots to preserve them from the frost of winter; with this exception, however: the vegetables really get more tender care . . . Circumstances prevent such tenderness from being extended to the fallen hero." Frequently corpses were quite literally naked—or clad only in underwear, which still permitted a distinction between Yankee and Confederate corpses, for northerners customarily wore wool and southerners cotton. Soldiers desperate for clothing robbed the dead with little feeling of propriety or remorse, and thieves and scavengers appeared on battlefields immediately after the end of hostilities. At the end of the Battle of Franklin in 1864 needy Confederate soldiers even stripped

"Rebel Soldiers After Battle 'Peeling' (i.e. Stripping) the Fallen Union Soldiers." Frank Leslie's Illustrated Newspaper, *February 13, 1864.*

the bodies of their own generals, six of whom lay dead on the field. Captured at Spotsylvania, Union surgeon Daniel Holt recognized a friend among the two hundred dead Yankees "stretched out before a trench half full of water into which they were to be thrown at the convenience of their captor. Entirely naked."[20]

Soldiers worried that the piles of dead might include those still living, unable to speak or let their presence be known or "extricate themselves from their former comrades." William Gore of New York related the frightening experience of a fellow soldier in Virginia who described a "narrow escape from the grave" already dug, when a nurse happened to intervene and indicate she would arrange to have his body sent home to friends. While he lay awaiting shipment, he returned to consciousness—and soon to duty. Since at least the late eighteenth century Americans had displayed deep anxiety about premature burial, devising coffins with bells and special protocols for resuscitation to prevent interment of the living. These concerns represented a fundamental uncertainty about the boundary between life and death, a doubt that included the metaphysical quandaries of immortality, as well as the physiological definition of vitality. Coming to terms with the Civil War's death toll began for many Americans with the difficulty of simply identifying and recognizing the end of life.[21]

When bodies remained in the control of their comrades and when troops were not hurried off to new encounters, dead soldiers fared better. Companies and regiments regularly preempted officially designated burial details by assuming responsibility for their own dead. Frequently closest comrades had sworn to provide one another with "a decent burial," and men searched the field in the nights and days after great battles to locate missing friends and relatives. Soldiers did the best they could to make such interments respectful. A comrade of Private Albert Frost of the Third Maine described his efforts when he discovered Frost missing after the third day at Gettysburg. He and a companion received permission to return to where they had last seen Frost alive.

> We found him face down and with many others the flesh eaten (in that hot climate) by maggots, but not so bad but that we could recognize him. When we went to bury him, all we could find to dig a grave was an old hoe in a small building. The bottom of the grave was covered with empty knapsacks, then we laid in our beloved brother and covered him with another knapsack, and over all put as much earth as we could find. The grave was dug at the foot of a large tree. We then found a piece of a hard wood box cover and cut his name on it with a jacknife and nailed it to the tree at the head of his grave.[22]

Albert Frost's burial illustrates many of the central components of what we might call friendly burial on the field. His comrades expended considerable effort and ingenuity to provide him the dignity of an individual and identifiable grave. They tried to compensate for the general unavailability of coffins in the immediate aftermath of battle by using abandoned knapsacks to shield him from direct contact with the earth, thus providing the covering critical to the notion of a "decent burial"—of a human rather than an animal.

In the earliest years of the war, when coffinless burials had not yet become commonplace, Yankees and Confederates alike expressed their distress and struggled to find acceptable substitutes. One inventive Union soldier, unwilling to permit his uncle to be buried without some barrier between his body and the bare earth, discovered a hollow log to serve as a coffin. By the time of Gettysburg, Albert Frost's companions had abandoned all hope of even a substitute coffin and simply covered the body. The soldiers chose a spot near a tree—no doubt as much to serve as a landmark as an aesthetic feature of the gravesite—and they tried as well to mark the place of burial. Wooden panels from boxes of hardtack (the "cast-iron" crackers that served as an army staple), pieces of board from ammunition boxes, and crossed fence rails all routinely became makeshift grave markers.

Some soldiers enacted other rituals of respect for the dead: brief prayers either with or without the participation of a chaplain. Confederate Thomas Key described the burial of two soldiers in 1864 accompanied by Bible readings, prayers, and a hymn "in the midst of a heavy cannonading and singing of minié balls." James Houghton of Michigan, "wishing to know that my tent mate was deasently buried," returned to the field after Gettysburg and found that others had already performed the task in the course of interring dozens of his fellow soldiers. Houghton was satisfied that "all the painess possible was taken in their burial...in some cases their Blody garments were removed and washed and dried on limbs of treas then Replased." Nurses in field hospitals performed services over the dead when time and circumstances permitted, but as the conflict wore on, these opportunities seemed to diminish. For months after assuming her duties, Confederate Fannie Beers explained, "I insisted upon attending every dead soldier to the grave and reading over him a part of the burial service. But it had now [by the fall of 1862] become impossible. The dead were past help; the living *always* needed succor."[23]

In their efforts to find and honor comrades amid the bodies of thousands, soldiers demonstrated their resistance to the war's casual

Coffined and coffinless dead side by side. The former were likely officers. "Burial of Federal Dead. Fredericksburg, 1864." Photograph by Timothy H. O'Sullivan. Library of Congress.

erasure of the meaning of individual human life. As a Connecticut chaplain revealingly explained,

> To say that two thousand or twenty thousand men are killed in a great battle, or that a thousand of the dead are buried in one great trench, produces only a vague impression on the mind at the fullest. There is too much in this to be truly personal to you. But to know one man who is shot down by your side, and to aid in burying him, while his comrades stand with you above his open grave,

is a more real matter to you than the larger piece of astounding information.[24]

Soldiers paid homage to their dead comrades out of respect for the slain men, endeavoring to reclaim the individual and what *Harper's* had called "its . . . selfhood" from the impersonal and overwhelming carnage. But they also did it for themselves: to reassert their own commitment to the sanctity of human life and the integrity of the human self. They were reaffirming the larger purposes of their own existence and survival and hoping that if they were killed others would similarly honor them.

But some individuals inevitably seemed to matter more than others. Officers received privileged treatment on the field—at the hands of the enemy, who customarily returned their bodies, as well as from their own men. In 1864 J. W. McClure of South Carolina described to his wife a practice common throughout the war: a flag of truce used for the exchange of "bodies of prominent officers" who had been killed and left in enemy hands. By contrast, when Robert Gould Shaw died leading his black troops in an assault on Fort Wagner in 1863, Confederates explicitly dishonored him and his abolitionist commitments by refusing to surrender his body and interring it in a trench with his black soldiers.[25]

Both Union and Confederates provided their own dead officers with privileged treatment. In Richmond's Hollywood Cemetery, where men were brought from surrounding battlefields throughout the war, the informal practice of burying officers together and apart from their men soon led to the establishment of an officially separate Officers' Section. After the Battle of Cedar Mountain in 1862 most of the Federal dead lay unburied for days, although the bodies of their officers were packed in charcoal and sent to Washington, where they were to be placed in metallic coffins and shipped to their homes across the North. Confederate Charles Kerrison described a similar differentiation in treatment according to rank when he attempted to retrieve the body of his brother Edwin, a private killed in the spring of 1864. When one of four officers for whom metallic coffins had been provided proved lost, Kerrison hoped he might appropriate the surplus casket for Edwin. But he seemingly never questioned that a higher-ranking soldier should have been provided a coffin while his brother had none. A Texas soldier was less accepting. "The officers get the honor," he wrote, "you get nothing. They get a monument, you get a hole in the ground and no coffin." Oliver Wendell Holmes, searching for his son in the bloody aftermath of Antietam, took these contrasts for granted: "The slain of higher condition, 'embalmed' and iron cased, were sliding off the railways to their far homes; the dead of the rank and file were being gathered up and committed hastily to the earth."[26]

A Commission of Inquiry investigating the conditions of Union prisoners of war in 1864 reported that these distinctions persisted and perhaps even intensified in captivity. Dead Yankee enlisted men at one prison camp were thrown into a cellar where they might be devoured by rats and dogs before being carted off for burial, while officers, "secured by contributions, made up among themselves, metallic coffins and a decent, temporary deposit in a vault... until they could be removed to the North." This systematic privileging of rank marked the fact that an officer was in a quite literal sense some body. When captured Yankee surgeon Daniel Holt watched Confederate burial squads deny that identity to a group of his dead comrades, he forcefully articulated his conviction that their status in life ought to have carried over into death. "It is a sad, sad sight," he wrote to his wife, "to see men who at home occupied position and place, possessing wealth... deposited as they are here, in the ground, with nothing but a blanket and mother earth over them." Coffins, embalming, shipment home, a marked and honored grave: these were the privileges that Civil War Americans were most eager to provide their dead comrades and kin.[27]

It was not just soldiers who had to deal with the dead in the days after fighting ceased. Combat respected no boundaries, spreading across farms, fields, and orchards, into gardens and streets, presenting civilians with bodies in their front yards, in their wells, covering their corn or cotton fields. The capacities of existing cemeteries in

*"A Contrast: Federal Buried, Confederate Unburied, Where
They Fell on the Battlefield of Antietam." Caption and
photograph by Alexander Gardner. Library of Congress.*

towns like Richmond and Atlanta were taxed, then exceeded, as
communities struggled to provide graves for the escalating numbers
of the fallen.

After three days of battle Gettysburg confronted the problem of
7,000 slain men and 3,000 dead horses, far too many for Union
troops—who held the field as Lee rapidly retreated southwards—to
inter with adequate dispatch. Civilians joined in the burial of the
dead out of both sympathy and necessity. Fifty Confederates lay on
George Rose's fields; seventy-nine North Carolinians had fallen in a
perfect line on John Forney's farm; the widow Leister confronted fifteen dead horses in her front yard; Joseph Sherfy's barn, which had
been used as a field hospital, was left a burnt ruin, with "crisped and
blackened limbs, heads and other portions of bodies" clearly visible
in the rubble.[28]

*One of the estimated 1.5 million horses and mules killed
in the war. Sketch by Alfred R. Waud. Library of Congress.*

No single Virginia battle matched Gettysburg's toll of killed and
wounded, but the fighting in the corridor between Washington and
Richmond extended over years rather than days, incorporating local
residents into what seemed to be a permanent landscape of war. The
Peninsula Campaign of 1862 compelled Richmond's Hollywood
Cemetery to acquire additional acreage in order to provide for the
soldiers dying in nearby battles as well as in the city's numerous
military hospitals. Sometimes the pressure of burials at Hollywood
became so great that as many as two hundred bodies would be awaiting interment. Chaplain Joseph Walker explained how he worked to
be at once respectful and efficient in his treatment of the dead. "It was
our habit to have one service for several bodies that were uncovered in
adjacent graves varying the service to suit the numbers, or have a general service over the coffins while still above ground." Strangers visiting the cemetery often joined these observances, providing mourners
for those who had died far from home and claiming their lives and sacrifice for the broader community of Virginia and the South.[29]

The emergence of this impersonal connection with the dead, one
independent of any direct ties of kin or friendship, was a critical evolution in the understanding of war's carnage. The soldiers being

interred did not belong just to their friends and relatives; their loss was more than just a diminution of their own families; these men were more than simply individual selves. In rituals like those at Hollywood, the fallen were being transformed into an imagined community for the Confederacy, becoming a collective in which a name or identity was no longer necessary. These men were now part of the Confederate Dead, a shadow nation of sacrificed lives to be honored and invoked less for themselves than for the purposes of the nation and the society struggling to survive them. These soldiers could no longer contribute to the South's military effort, but they would serve other important political and cultural purposes in providing meaning for the war and its costs.[30]

One instance of a southern soldier buried by strangers became quite literally iconic, first within the Civil War South and then in the maintenance of Confederate memory after the war. *The Burial of Latané*, painted by Virginian William D. Washington in 1864, portrays the interment of a young lieutenant, killed during J. E. B. Stuart's legendary ride around McClellan's army during the Peninsula Campaign of 1862. William Latané, the only Confederate casualty of the expedition, was left behind enemy lines, amid civilians surrounded by Union forces. Slaves built his coffin and dug his grave, and a white Virginia matron read the burial service over his remains. The women in attendance were all socially prominent, and the story became well known in nearby Richmond. Poet John Thompson, a former editor of the *Southern Literary Messenger*, commemorated the event in broadside verse extolling those

> *Strangers, yet sisters, who with Mary's love*
> *Sat by the open tomb and weeping looked above.*
>
> . . . .
>
> *Gently they laid him underneath the sod*
> *And left him with his fame, his country, and his God.*[31]

Artist Washington decided in 1864 to portray the incident in paint and assembled a number of Richmond ladies to pose for his effort.

The Burial of Latané, *1864. Painting by William D. Washington.*
The Johnson Collection.

The completed canvas was first hung in his small Richmond studio, where it attracted "throngs of visitors" eager to see this depiction of Christian and Confederate sacrifice. Soon the press of crowds forced its relocation to the halls of the Confederate capitol. There a bucket was placed beneath the painting for contributions to the Confederate cause. After the war Washington arranged for engravings of the painting. These were widely distributed in a promotional effort undertaken by the *Southern Magazine,* a publication founded in 1871 to honor Confederate memory. The prints enjoyed what historian Frank Vandiver has called "fantastic popularity" and became a standard decorative item in late-nineteenth-century white southern homes.[32]

Created in the midst of war, the painting undertook important cultural work, linking southern war death to Christian tradition and iconography through the representation of a Confederate *pietà.* The black slaves and white women whom Washington depicted burying the Confederate hero represented the artist's effort to impart broader meaning to Latané's demise by connecting it to a community that extended well beyond the white men who had fought alongside him. By 1864 both the Confederacy and the institution of slavery were disintegrating, rendering Washington's depiction of home front solidarity and military glory at once illusory and telling. The painting seeks to define and celebrate Confederate nationalism, identifying the soldier's corpse as at once the source of and the meaning for the body politic.

The women who buried Latané found themselves conscripted into the work of death by a war that invaded their homes and communities. Other civilians volunteered, traveling from afar by the hundreds, determined that their loved ones not suffer and die among strangers. Many families of moderate means flocked to battlefields in order to reclaim bodies, encase them in coffins, and escort them home. A focus of wonder and horror, battle sites in fact became crowded with civilians immediately after the cessation of hostilities: besides relatives in search of kin, there were scavengers seeking to rob the dead, entrepreneurial coffin makers and embalmers, and swarms of tourists attracted by the hope of experiencing the "sublimity of a battle scene" or simply, as one disgusted soldier put it, "gratifying their morbid curiosity." A Massachusetts soldier who lay suffering in an Antietam field hospital after the amputation of his leg clearly resented these gawkers. "People come from all parts of the country. Stare at us but do not find time to do anything," he complained.[33]

But most civilians appeared out of earnest desperation to locate and care for loved ones. The death of relatives far away from families and kin was, as we have seen, particularly disruptive to fundamental nineteenth-century understandings of the Good Death, assumptions closely tied to the Victorian emphasis on the importance of home and domesticity. Moreover, inadequacies in the means of reporting casualties in both North and South reinforced civilians' desire to repossess the bodies of loved ones in order to be certain they were truly dead and had not just been misidentified. As a South Carolina

*"Maryland and Pennsylvania Farmers Visiting the Battlefield
of Antietam While the National Troops Were Burying the Dead
and Carrying Off the Wounded." From a sketch by F. H. Schell.*
Frank Leslie's Illustrated Newspaper, *October 18, 1862.*

woman wrote in anguish to her sister, "O Mag you don't know how
sorry I am about Kits dying I cant think of nothing else . . . did they
open the coffin it looks like you all ought to have seen for certain
whether it was him or not and how he was put away."[34]

At the beginning of the war, when losses were still expected to be
small in number, several states in the North announced their determination to bring every slain soldier home. As late as 1863 Governor
Andrew Gregg Curtin of Pennsylvania declared that, at the family's
request, the state would pay the cost of removing a body from Gettysburg for reburial within the state, and several other northern
states sent official agents to assist citizens in the removal of their lost
kin. In response to early deaths the members of some army units
joined in informal arrangements for returning bodies to loved
ones. In November 1861 a Union regiment "voted . . . to raise money

enough to send home the body of everyone who dies," and in 1862 a Pennsylvania soldier wrote his parents that he and his comrades had contributed $140 to embalm and ship the bodies of two soldiers killed in his company.[35]

Mounting death tolls soon made such sweeping intentions unrealizable. A number of both state-aided and voluntary organizations, such as the Pennsylvania State Agency, the Louisiana Soldiers Relief Association, the Central Association of South Carolina, and the New England Soldiers Relief Association, nevertheless continued to help individual citizens bring their loved ones home. Late in 1863, for example, the record books of the Pennsylvania State Agency noted funds advanced to Alice Watts to transport her and her "husband Thomas Watts late a private" in the 24th Pennsylvania Volunteers. Cities and towns sometimes offered desperate residents assistance as well.[36]

In the North, as casualties mounted and war grew more intense, the Sanitary Commission played an increasingly significant role in burials and in handling the dead. This enormous philanthropic organization and its network of thousands of volunteers and hundreds of paid agents worked to provide needed supplies and assistance to soldiers. Sometimes agents in the field assumed care of hospital graveyards and registries of death; others worked to arrange for burials in the aftermath of battle; still others assisted families in locating lost loved ones and providing for their shipment home.[37]

After the bloody battles in the West during the last year and a half of the war, Sanitary Commission agents in Chattanooga, for example, worked with a network of their counterparts in northern cities to return Union soldiers' remains. M. C. Read arranged for disinterment of bodies, embalmers' services, metallic cases, and shipping costs, telegraphing families when their loved ones were at last en route home. "BODY OF MAJ. R. ROBBINS GOES NORTH TODAY," he wired on June 16, 1864. Often families deposited funds with a commission agent in the North to cover anticipated expenditures associated with locating and returning kin and to avoid the difficulties of transferring money to the front.[38]

During a six-month period in 1864 the Chattanooga office handled thirty-four requests for disinterments, chiefly though not exclusively the bodies of officers. In October Mary Brayton, a Sanitary Commission worker in Cleveland, wrote in search of Henry Diebolt of Company A, 27th Ohio, who had been killed May 28 in Dallas, Georgia. "The grave is about 1½ miles from Dallas near the cemetery & has a headboard properly marked," she explained. "Metallic case preferred. Forward soon as possible." The family of George Moore of Illinois had more specific and personal requests. "Have the undertaker secure a lock of his hair as a memento," the commission agent wrote. "Let his face be uncovered, and inform us when the body is shipped."[39]

When armies moved operations, commission agents often made records of camp graveyards so that soldiers' bodies might at some future point be reclaimed. Orange Judd gathered details of burials when the Union army undertook a "change of base" from Belle Plain, Virginia, in May 1864, and he assembled them into an elaborate map. The graves had been marked with headboards made of cracker boxes and inscribed with penciled names, but Judd feared these might easily be "obliterated by storm or by the enemy" if the ground changed hands. His effort, he hoped, would "enable friends to find the bodies indicated." He outlined twenty-six graves, mostly with names and regiments attached. Six bodies remained unknown, but he offered descriptions that he thought might prove useful. "About 23; Black hair, Intelligent Countenance, Buried May 15." In nearby Port Royal commission records of another cemetery mapped twenty-three graves, including three plots occupied by soldiers who had arrived in ambulances "with their pockets cut off and all records gone." They had been robbed of both their possessions and their identities while they lay on the field. With the departure of Union troops from the vicinity imminent, the commission agent reported, "the graves were put under the guard of george Smith A colored man who lives just south of the ground & who will do all he is allowed to do to keep them in order."[40]

The resources of the Sanitary Commission stretched only so far, however. For the most part the bereaved were forced to rely upon themselves and upon the emerging network of embalmers, undertakers, and private "agents," who followed the armies, finding work and profit for themselves in assisting grieving families who had little idea of how to find or retrieve their lost husbands, brothers, and sons. Undertaker W. R. Cornelius, who worked regularly with the Sanitary Commission in Tennessee, also offered his services to families directly. He reported that he "shipped colonels, majors, captains and privates by the carload some days," sending them both to the Union and to the Confederacy. Sometimes families procured friends to locate missing loved ones and arrange for the return of bodies; sometimes they set off themselves, often arriving at the battlefield unsure whether they had come to nurse a wounded man or to transport his body home.[41]

In March 1863 Henry Bowditch left Boston by train as soon as he received a telegram reporting that his son Nathaniel had been wounded. "DANGEROUS. COME AT ONCE," a cousin and fellow soldier had wired. "It was like a dagger in my heart when I first heard the horrible news," the father wrote. But in the course of the trip Bowditch grew hopeful and "bought books and papers calculated to amuse a wounded man." When he descended onto the platform in Washington, however, a friend who met him brought the news that Nathaniel was dead. Bowditch, a prominent physician who had himself volunteered his medical services in Virginia the preceding fall, was taken by train and wagon to the camp of the First Massachusetts Cavalry, where he was reunited with his dead son. There he was able to gain some comfort by hearing from Nat's fellow officers "beautiful things" about his courage and his profession of faith and hope as he died. Yet he still found himself almost incapacitated by the shock of Nat's death. "I scarcely know what to think or do," he wrote his wife. "I seem almost stunned by the news." Eventually Nathaniel Bowditch's embalmed body was shipped home and buried beneath a stone likeness of his saber in Cambridge's Mount Auburn Cemetery.[42]

Even those of privilege and position faced challenges as they sought to retrieve and honor their dead. Henry Bowditch, already distressed by the lack of ambulances and more general provision for the wounded in the Union army, now saw the direct results of this lack of system in the death of his son, who had lain unattended on the field. His son's death, he recognized, gave him "greater moral influence" to pursue his cause. The state, he insisted in a pamphlet published in the fall of 1863, had an obligation to its soldiers. "If any government under Heaven ought to be *paternal,* the United States authority, deriving, as it does, all its powers from the people, should surely be such, and should dispense that power, in full streams of benignant mercy upon its soldiers." Bowditch's arguments not only contributed to the establishment of a comprehensive ambulance system by the following year but articulated a logic of obligation that applied not just to the wounded but also to the dead.[43]

Stanley Abbott's brother left home under circumstances very like Bowditch's, after being notified by a telegram that Stanley had been wounded in the chest at Gettysburg. Although the message insisted, "Doctor says not mortal," Abbott died the next day. His brother arrived promptly enough to find his grave easily. Procuring a coffin was more difficult, however, for thousands of other parents, wives, and siblings were searching for them as well. After five days he at last succeeded and shipped his brother home, one of an estimated fifteen hundred Yankee bodies privately expressed to relatives after Gettysburg, even though the commanding Union officer ultimately felt compelled to prohibit disinterments in the heat of August and September in deference to the "health of the . . . community."[44]

Confederate officers were often retrieved and escorted home by slaves who had accompanied them into service. More than six thousand blacks traveled with Lee's army into Pennsylvania in 1863, and Colonel Edward Porter Alexander, who had himself brought two slaves with him from the South, described the scene at the end of the battle: "Negro servants hunting for their masters were a feature of the landscape that night." Elijah, property of Colonel Isaac Avery, was determined to bring his body back to North Carolina, but in the chaos of Lee's retreat he managed to get the corpse only as far as Maryland, where it was buried. Peter, who belonged to General James Johnston Pettigrew, and Joe, owned by General William Dorsey Pender, were more successful; both accompanied their masters' remains home to the South after their deaths in the Gettysburg campaign.[45]

The Adams Express Company and its Confederate counterpart, the Southern Express, did a booming business during the war, establishing careful and elaborate regulations for the safe and sanitary transport of bodies. At the beginning of the conflict many bodies were shipped in wooden coffins, but weather and delays created situations that led Adams to require metal caskets. Joseph Jeffries was one of dozens of entrepreneurs who flocked to Gettysburg after the battle to sell their services in retrieving and shipping bodies. He advertised "METALLIC COFFINS . . . Warranted Air-Tight" that would not only meet shipping requirements but could "be placed in the Parlor without fear of any odor escaping therefrom." A "zinc-lined box covered with cloth plated mounting" for expressing Captain R. G. Goodwin of Massachusetts cost fifty dollars in 1862, no small sum even for a person of some means. No wonder one shipping agent, at least, continued to be presented with wooden coffins. He responded by creating a small cemetery to hold the bodies he could not send and, in one particularly demanding week, buried more than forty men. At the end of the war these bodies were at last disinterred and returned to their families.[46]

Bowen Moon of New York refused to be daunted by shipping regulations when he went in search of his brother-in-law William Salisbury after Antietam. A soldier from Salisbury's regiment described his dead comrade's gravesite, and Moon managed to purchase a serviceable, if not elegant, wooden coffin from one of several local carpenters now devoting themselves to filling the sudden and almost overwhelming demand. Moon hired a local farmer to help him exhume the body. Even though Salisbury shared his grave with two other men and even though two weeks had passed since the battle, Moon was able to identify him with little difficulty. But he faced an unexpected setback when the railroad refused to accept the consignment, insisting it "did not carry dead bodies that had begun to decompose." Moon caulked the coffin, bribed the baggage manager, and succeeded in bringing Salisbury's remains home.[47]

Some Americans had attempted before the war to preserve bodies by using coffins that rested corpses on ice, and such inventions grew ever more elaborate as families sought to retrieve growing numbers of war dead for burial at home. The Staunton Transportation Company, for example, distributed handbills to civilians thronging Gettysburg in July and August 1863, promising that its new "Transportation Case preserves the body in a natural state and [as] perfect condition as when placed in it for any distance or length of time in any weather." The case was "so arranged as to readily expose the face of the dead for inspection," and the broadside promised that it would seem "as though the subject had died on the day of arrival at home." It worked because "ITS CONSTRUCTION makes it a portable refrigerator." J. B. Staunton offered a variety of other services to the bereaved: regular coffins, "exhumers and guides who had surveyed the whole Battle-field," as well as "Deodorizers and Army Disinfectionists."[48]

But even the elaborate refrigeration mechanism of the Staunton Transportation Case could not rival the advances in bodily preservation achieved by the spread of embalming. Significant technological advances had been made in the process in the years just prior to the war, as Americans adopted and patented chemical embalming procedures that had been known in Europe since the first decades of the century. In the 1850s embalming had been chiefly used not to prepare bodies for funerals but to contribute to the study of anatomy and pathology by providing cadavers preserved for dissection. It was during the war that embalming first became more widely practiced, not just generating a transformation in physical treatment of the dead but establishing a procedure that would serve as a foundation for the emergence of the funeral industry and the professionalization of the undertaker.

But more was operating here than purely practical concerns about how to arrest decomposition of bodies in order to ship them home. Americans did not want to endure the unprecedented separation

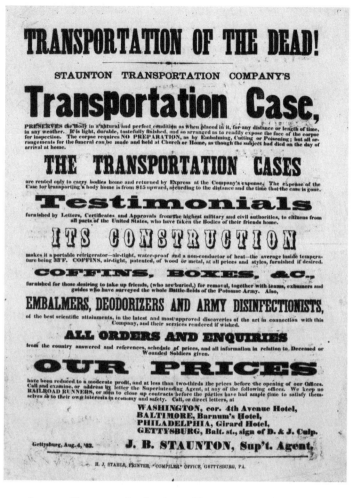

Staunton Transportation Company. "Transportation of the Dead!"
The Library of Company of Philadelphia.

from deceased kin that war had introduced. Families sought to see their lost loved ones in as lifelike a state as possible, not just to be certain of their identity but also to bid them farewell. Embalming offered families a way to combat at least some of the threats the war posed to the principles of the Good Death. To contemplate one's husband, father, or son in a state of seemingly sleeplike repose was a means of resisting death's terror—and even, to a degree, its reality; it offered a way of blurring the boundary between life and death.

Corpses, at least those that had not been dismembered in combat, could be made to look lifelike, could be made to appear as if they were on the verge of awakening in a new life to come.[49]

Embalming attracted attention early in the war when the body of Union colonel Elmer Ellsworth, killed in Alexandria, Virginia, on May 24, 1861, by a Confederate sympathizer, was preserved. Ellsworth had been a law clerk in Lincoln's Springfield office, and the press, in this moment before casualties became commonplace, detailed every aspect of his death, from his heroic sacrifice of life, to the honoring of his body in state in the White House, to his lifelike corpse. His embalmer, Thomas Holmes, became the best-known practitioner of the war, setting up an establishment in Washington, D.C., where he embalmed more than four thousand soldiers at a price of one hundred dollars each. The war made him a wealthy man.[50]

Neither the Union nor the Confederate government routinely provided for embalming deceased soldiers. Surgeons would sometimes offer this service to prominent individuals who died in army hospitals, and the undertakers contracted by the federal government to assist with disposal of the dead might do embalming for a fee charged to grieving families or comrades. In a spirit of benevolent paternalism, Union officers sometimes arranged for special care of the bodies of their men. For example, a captain left directions with a nurse at a hospital of the Army of the Potomac, "TO THE EMBALMER AT FALMOUTH STATION: You will please embalm the body of Elijah Clifford, a private of my company. Do it properly and well, and as soon as it is done send me word, and I will pay your bill at once. I do not want this body expensively embalmed, but well done, as I shall send it to Philadelphia." For a private, "well done" was seemingly good enough.[51]

Embalming remained much rarer in the Confederacy than in the North, no doubt because the invaded South was compelled to focus more directly on survival than on elaborate treatments of the dead. But embalmers advertised throughout the war in the Richmond press, announcing their readiness to perform "disinfections" and directing potential customers to newly opened field offices on the sites of recent battles. Dr. William MacClure promised "persons at a

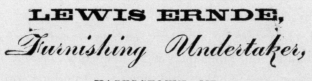

Business card for undertaker Lewis Ernde, Hagerstown, Maryland.
The Library Company of Philadelphia.

distance" that "BODIES OF THE DEAD" would be "Disinterred, Disinfected, and SENT HOME" from "any place within the Confederacy." While the southern funeral industry remained far less developed and embalming far less common than in the North well into the twentieth century, the oldest funeral home in the South, G. A. Diuguid and Sons in Lynchburg, Virginia, handled 1,251 soldiers in 1862, including both Union and Confederates embalmed and sent home for burial.[52]

The Virginia battlefields provided a booming business for undertakers of both North and South, and Washington, D.C., included three embalmers in its 1863 City Directory. Dr. F. A. Hutton of 451 Pennsylvania Avenue took a full page to advertise his services. "Bodies Embalmed by us NEVER TURN BLACK! But retain their natural color and appearance . . . so as to admit of contemplation of the person Embalmed, with the countenance of one asleep." Embalming promised to transform death into slumber. Like MacClure, Hutton pledged "particular attention paid to obtaining bodies of those who have fallen on the Battle Field." Embalmers advertised both themselves and the process by exhibiting preserved bodies—often unknown dead simply collected from the field and embalmed—as Thomas Holmes did on undertakers' premises in downtown Washington, in Georgetown, and in Alexandria. Happily, no record survives of an unsuspecting mother or wife coming upon her lost loved one displayed in a store window.[53]

For all its increase in popularity, embalming provoked ambivalence and suspicion. Embalmers were frequently accused of extortionate and dubious practices, and they were disturbing, too, in their intimacy with the dead. A Yankee reporter revealingly described his encounter with an embalmer who was following Union troops toward Richmond during the Peninsula Campaign of 1862. "He was a sedate, grave person, and when I saw him, standing over the nude ... corpse, he reminded me of the implacable vulture ... His battery and tube were pulsing like ones heart and lungs, and the subject was being drained at the neck ... 'If you could only make him breathe, Professor,' said an officer standing by. The dry skin of the embalmer broke into chalky dimples, and he grinned very much as a corpse might do: 'Ah!' he said, '*then* there would be money made.' " Public discomfort with embalmers appeared most often in regard to this issue of money and the unsettling commodification of the dead that their business represented. In an expression of dismay at the war's emerging market of death, a Yankee newspaperman reported— and, one suspects, at least partly invented—a conversation with an especially ambitious and frank embalmer: " 'I would be glad to prepare private soldiers. They were wuth a five dollar bill apiece. But, Lord bless you, a colonel pays a hundred, and a brigadier-general two hundred. There's lots of them now, and I have cut the acquaintance of everything below a major. I might,' he added, 'as a great favor, do a captain, but he must pay a major's price. I insist upon that! Such windfalls don't come every day. There won't be another such killing for a century.' " Making a killing seemed to be in every sense the work at hand.[54]

The U.S. Army was deluged with anguished protests from families of dead soldiers who believed they had been cheated by embalmers operating near the battlefront. An officer at City Point, Virginia, protested to Inspector James A. Hardie in 1864 that "scarcely a week passes that I do not receive complaints against one or another of these embalmers ... [They] are regarded by the medical department

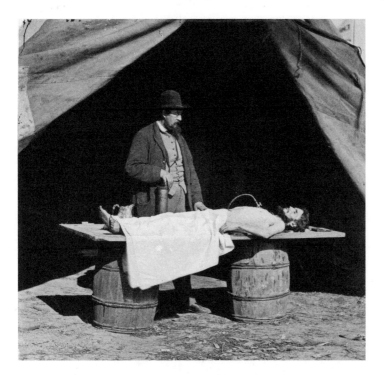

"Embalming Surgeon at Work on Soldier's Body."
Library of Congress.

of the army generally as an unmitigated nuisance ... the whole system as practised here is one of pretension, swindling, and extortion." In 1863 a case was lodged against Hutton & Williams, "EMBALMERS OF THE DEAD" in Washington. Hutton was imprisoned and the company's records were seized. The suit alleged that the pair regularly recovered and embalmed soldiers without permission and then demanded payment from grieving families, threatening to disinter or refuse to return the bodies if their conditions were not met.

In the fall of 1864 Timothy Dwight of New York pursued a grievance with Secretary of War Stanton against Dr. Richard Burr, a prominent Washington embalmer, claiming that Burr was guilty of extortion for preying upon him in his distress after "the loss of a most excellent Boy." Burr defended his fee of one hundred dollars to the provost marshal, saying his employees had risked their lives recover-

"Dr. Bunnell's Embalming Establishment in the Field
(Army of the James)." Library of Congress.

ing the body from near the picket line and then carrying it several hundred yards under fire. He had then disinfected the body "by means of my embalming fluid and charcoal" and enclosed it in a zinc coffin, sealed it, and shipped it—clearly warranting, he insisted, his charges. On January 9, 1865, General Ulysses Grant responded to the chorus of grievances by withdrawing all embalmers' permits and ordering them beyond the lines. The distances separating the dead and their loved ones nevertheless continued to encourage embalming, in spite of great uneasiness about the practice and widespread hostility toward its practitioners.[55]

Embalming was expensive. So were refrigerated cases; so too were trips to battlefields to recover kin. Richer Americans had resources to invest in managing and resisting death that their poorer countrymen and -women lacked. All but taken for granted through much of the war, this differential treatment began to be challenged as the federal government assumed new responsibility for the war dead. In 1862, in response to logistical problems presented by the growing number of bodies, the U.S. Congress passed a measure giving the president power to purchase grounds "and cause them to be securely enclosed, to be used as a national cemetery for the soldiers who shall die in the service of the country." Without any appropriation or formal policy with which to implement this legislative action, the War Department established cemeteries as emergency circumstance demanded—chiefly near concentrations of military hospitals where many dead required burial. But under the terms of this measure, five cemeteries of a rather different character were created in the course of the war. These were burial grounds for the dead of a particular battle, usually established when a lull in active operations made such an undertaking possible. Three of these cemeteries, Chattanooga, Stones River, and Knoxville, were created by Union generals, and two, Antietam and Gettysburg, by joint actions of northern states whose citizens had participated in the battles. In each case the purpose of the effort extended well beyond simply meeting the need for disposing of the dead. These cemeteries were intended to memorialize the slain and celebrate the nation's fallen heroes. Gettysburg represented a particularly important turning point. The large numbers of casualties in that bloody battle were obviously an important factor in generating action, but it is not insignificant that the carnage had occurred in the North, in a town that had not had the opportunity to grow accustomed to the horrors of the constant warfare that had battered Virginia for two long years. Gettysburg made the dead—and the problem they represented—starkly visible to northern citizens, so many of whom flocked to the small Pennsylvania town in the aftermath of battle. Perhaps even more critical was the fact that the North had resources with which to respond, resources not available to the hard-pressed Confederacy.[56]

The impetus for the Gettysburg cemetery arose from a meeting of state agents in the weeks after the battle. With financial assistance from Union states that had lost men in the engagement, David Wills, a Gettysburg lawyer, arranged to purchase seventeen acres adjoining an existing graveyard. In October contracts were let for the reburial of Union soldiers in the new ground at a rate of $1.59 for each body. In November Lincoln journeyed to help dedicate the new Soldiers' National Cemetery. This ceremony and the address that historian Garry Wills has argued "remade America" signaled the beginning of a new significance for the dead in public life. Perhaps the very configuration of the cemetery can explain the force behind this transformation. The cemetery at Gettysburg was arranged so that every grave was of equal importance; William Saunders's design, like Lincoln's speech, affirmed that every dead soldier mattered equally regardless of rank or station. This was a dramatic departure from the privileging of rank and station that prevailed in the treatment of the war dead and different even from the policies of the Chattanooga cemetery that would be created later in the year.[57]

The establishment of the Gettysburg cemetery marked the beginning of significant shifts in attitude and policy produced by the nation's confrontation with Civil War slaughter. Chaplain H. Clay Trumbull wrote of "new lessons" imposed by the necessities of war, as Americans North and South endured and even practiced ways of handling the dead that would previously have seemed unthinkable. Not only did these actions dishonor the slain by treating them more like animals than humans; they diminished the living, who found themselves abandoning commitments and principles that had helped to define their essential selves. Out of the horror of Civil War burials, there grew, even in the midst of the conflict itself, a variety of efforts to resist these unwanted transformations, to establish different sorts of "lessons" as the product of the nation's experience of war. Civil War Americans worked to change death in ways that ranged from transforming the actual bodies of the dead through embalming to altering the circumstances and conditions of interment by establishing what would become the national cemetery system and a massive postwar reburial program—the latter federally sponsored in the North but also executed on a far smaller scale by private voluntary actions in the South.[58]

The engagement of the Union government in these matters, first made highly visible in the Gettysburg dedication ceremonies, acknowledged a new public importance for the dead. No longer simply the responsibility of their families, they, and their loss, now belonged to the nation. These men had given their lives that the nation might live; their bodies, repositories of their "selfhood" and "surviving identity," as *Harper's* had put it, deserved the nation's recognition and care. The dead, as well as the living, had claims upon a government "deriving," as Henry Bowditch proclaimed in his plea for ambulances, "all its powers from the people."[59]

Yet these soldiers' selfhood and their identity were also inseparable from their names. The project of decently burying the Civil War dead required more than simply interment. The work of locating the missing and naming the tens of thousands of men designated as "unknown" would prove one of the war's most difficult tasks.

NAMING

"The Significant Word UNKNOWN"

Men thrown by the hundreds into burial trenches; soldiers stripped of every identifying object before being abandoned on the field; bloated corpses hurried into hastily dug graves; nameless victims of dysentery or typhoid interred beside military hospitals; men blown to pieces by artillery shells; bodies hidden by woods or ravines, left to the depredations of hogs or wolves or time: the disposition of the Civil War dead made an accurate accounting of the fallen impossible. In the absence of arrangements for interring and recording overwhelming numbers, hundreds of thousands of men—more than 40 percent of deceased Yankees and a far greater proportion of Confederates—perished without names, identified only, as Walt Whitman put it, "by the significant word UNKNOWN."[1]

To a twenty-first-century American, this seems unimaginable. The United States expends more than $100 million each year in the effort to find and identify the approximately 88,000 individuals still missing from World War II, Korea, and Vietnam. The obligation of the state to account for and return—either dead or alive—every soldier in its service is unquestioned. But these assumptions are of quite recent origin. There have been many revolutions in warfare in the last century and a half. Although perhaps less dramatic than transformations of military technology and organization, changing attitudes toward the dead and missing have profoundly altered the practices and experience of war—for soldiers and civilians alike. Only with the Korean War did the United States establish a policy of identifying and repatriating the remains of every dead soldier. Only with World War I did soldiers begin to wear official badges of identity—what came to be known as dog tags. Only with the Civil War did the United States create its system of national cemeteries and officially involve itself with honoring the military dead. It was the Civil War, as Walt Whitman observed, that made the designation "UNKNOWN" become "significant."[2]

The dead of the Mexican War received no official attention until 1850, two years after the conflict ended, when the federal government found and reinterred 750 soldiers in an American cemetery in Mexico City. These bodies represented only about 6 percent of the soldiers who had died, and not one body was identified. But with the Civil War, private and public belief and behavior gradually shifted. This was a war of mass citizens' armies, not of professional, regular forces; it was a war in which the obligation of the citizen to the nation was expressed as a willingness to risk life itself. In its assault upon chattel slavery, the conflict fundamentally redefined the relationship between the individual and the nation. This affirmation of the right to selfhood and identity reflected beliefs about human worth that bore other implications, for the dead as well as the living.[3]

Central to the changes that have occurred since the 1860s is the acknowledgment of the importance of information: of knowing whether a soldier is dead or alive, of being able to furnish news or provide the bereaved with the consoling certainty represented by an actual body. But in 1861, neither the Union nor the Confederate government recognized this as a responsibility. With the outbreak of war both North and South established measures for maintaining records of deceased soldiers, requiring forms to be filled out at army hospitals and sent in multiple copies to Washington or Richmond. Significantly, however, not one of these copies, nor any other sort of official communication, was designated for the family of the dead. And the obstacles to fulfilling even this plan seemed daunting. Samuel P.

Moore, surgeon general of the Confederate army, felt compelled in 1862 to issue a circular deploring the "indifference" of his medical officers to record keeping. But his exhortations apparently had little effect. When a January 1864 article in the *Charleston Mercury* summarized the preceding year's casualties, the newspaper concluded, "These returns show a great deal of negligence by Captains and Surgeons in reporting the deaths of soldiers." In the North field commanders interpreted reporting requirements to apply only to rear areas, so in April 1862 the War Department issued General Orders no. 33 to include the combat zone in its efforts to provide for the identification of the dead. But as we have seen, this measure employed language—"as far as possible . . . when practicable"—that made it more an aspiration than an order, and commanders treated it as such. General Orders no. 33 made no provision for implementing its goals and designated no special troops for graves registration duties. And like earlier measures, it assumed no responsibility for reporting deaths to those who waited at home.[4]

In both North and South those on the home front struggled to fill the void of official intelligence. In the days after a major engagement Union and Confederate newspapers covered their pages with eagerly awaited reports. Sarah Palmer of South Carolina reflected the agonies of northerners and southerners alike when she wrote after Second Bull Run, "I do feel too anxious to see the papers and get the list of casualties from Co. K and yet I dread to see it." Although civilians crowded news offices and railroad junctions waiting for information, the lists were notoriously inaccurate and incomplete.[5]

The sources of intelligence for these published lists varied. Sometimes the newspaper report of a regiment's dead and wounded was preceded by a statement from a chaplain indicating he had collected the information. Indeed, in some commands, this was officially the chaplain's duty, although that did not necessarily mean he carried it out. One infuriated nurse at a Nashville hospital complained that instead of performing this obligation, the chaplain there spent his time "pitching quoits." Many regiments—more than half in the Con-

Searching the casualty lists. Detail from "News of the War."
Drawn by Winslow Homer. Harper's Weekly, *June 14, 1862.*

federate and two-fifths in the Union army—did not have chaplains at all.[6]

Often an officer introduced the list. In some instances civilians representing charitable organizations assembled the data, recognizing that military officials were too occupied with the concerns of the living to make this a priority. W. P. Price, who represented a South Carolina relief agency, tried to establish a formal system and reported from Atlanta in June 1864 that he had made arrangements for colonels of Carolina regiments to furnish him with regular reports, "by which means I hope to be enabled to furnish correct lists." But, he continued, his plan seemed imperiled because "I regret to state that several important letters [with information] sent from the field . . . have miscarried."[7]

Lists frequently included statements acknowledging the inadequacy of their information. As a Confederate newspaper stated in 1863, "Of Company I, 38 men were lost in action. 31 of these are accounted for as prisoners. The remaining seven," the article conjectured, "must have been killed." Sons or brothers listed as "slightly wounded" often turned out to be dead, and husbands reported as "killed in action" later appeared unharmed. "I have known so many instances where families have been held in agonised suspense for days by the report of relatives being dangerously wounded when they were not," one Confederate wrote to an anxious mother in South Carolina. Mathew Jack Davis of the 19th Mississippi kept his family in suspense for four years. "I had been reported killed on the day I was captured," he related. "I read my own obituary." Joseph Willett of New York hastened to reassure his sister after the Battle of the Wilderness, "You may have heard before you read this that I was killed or wounded but allow me to contradict the report." Journalist Henry Raymond, founder of the *New York Times,* rushed to Virginia in 1863 in response to news of his brother's death. He engaged an embalmer but could not locate the body, so he went to army headquarters to inquire. Instead of answering his query, an aide produced his brother, quite alive and well. Yankee private Henry Struble was not only listed as a casualty after Antietam but assigned a grave after his canteen was found in the hands of a dead man he had stopped to help. After the war ended, Struble sent flowers every Memorial Day to decorate his own grave, to honor the unknown soldier it sheltered and perhaps to acknowledge that there but for God's grace he might lie. Recipients of bad news repeated and cherished such narratives, hoping that a different story with a happier ending might emerge, and denying as long as possible the reality and finality of death.[8]

More reliable and certainly more consoling than casualty lists were the personal letters that custom required a dead soldier's closest friends and immediate military superiors to write to his relatives. But months often passed before soldiers in the field found time, circumstance, or strength to write. These communications were, moreover, dependent upon the vicissitudes of the postal service, which, in the Confederacy, grew increasingly unreliable. Southerners complained that by 1864 so many of the postal clerks in Richmond had been conscripted into the army that the mail between the Virginia theater and the home front had entirely broken down.[9]

Voluntary organizations worked to fill the void left by the failure of military and governmental officials to provide information to families. In the North both the Christian Commission and the Sanitary Commission, the two most significant Union-wide charitable efforts to grow out of the war, came to regard communication with families as central to their efforts. The Christian Commission proclaimed its commitment in words printed at the top of each page of the stationery it distributed to soldiers at the front: "The U.S. Christian Commission send this sheet as a messenger between the soldier and his home. Let it hasten to those who wait for tidings." In just three months during the spring of 1864 the commission reported that it had supplied 24,000 quires of paper and envelopes to the Army of the Potomac, and in the days after large battles it transported hundreds of letters from military hospitals and camps to nearby post offices. After Sherman's army reached Savannah in December 1864, the commission delegates who had been following his troops rented rooms and installed fifty writing desks, where soldiers produced three hundred letters a day.[10]

In cases of soldiers' grave illness or death, commission delegates—the unpaid volunteers upon whom the work of the organization rested—wrote in their behalf, composing letters "for soldiers still lingering" or "to carry 'last words.'" It was one of the fundamental responsibilities of its five thousand delegates, as the commission described it, "to spare no pains to give immediate and accurate information of the wounded and dead to those who waited" at home, and the commission estimated they had written more than 92,000 letters for soldiers by the end of the war. General field agents, regional supervisors of the commission, reported the active effort that delegates undertook to identify the dead in order to be able to send news to loved ones. After the Battle of Chattanooga, one agent related with satisfaction, "We were able to fill out many home letters, by the memoranda gathered during the night from the lips of the dying and

*"The United States Christian Commission Office at 8th and H Streets,
Washington, D.C., 1865." Library of Congress.*

from the letters and diaries found on the dead. Ordinarily, unless the
body had been robbed, in the inside breast pocket of the blouse there
would be a letter from friends, a photograph, a Christian Commission Testament, or a hymn-book, with the name and regiment and
home address."[11]

In 1864 the commission organized the Individual Relief Department, designed to respond to inquiries about the fate of individual
soldiers. "To answer these letters often involved a long and difficult
search, first at the regiment, then at the field hospital, then in the
post hospital or camp," Reverend Lemuel Moss, home secretary of
the commission, remembered in 1868. But often the information
could indeed be found. Anna H., "a little girl," wrote the commission
seeking her father because her mother was "almost crazy" with the

anxiety of having heard nothing for four weeks. "This is the third letter we have sent off," she reported, as she begged "for any one to send us back an answer whether my dear father is dead or alive ... If we cannot pay you, the Lord will. Do please be so kind, and answer this letter." The commission sadly informed her that her father was already buried.[12]

As part of its effort to collect information more systematically, the commission distributed printed notebooks to enable delegates in the field to keep records of the soldiers whom they assisted, information that could easily be passed along to the central Relief Department. A Christian Commission Death Register from Virginia in 1864 provided columns for names, units, dates of death, and "particulars" and "remarks" that usually included an assessment of the deceased's religious state, as well as details about the disposition of his body. Part of the impetus for the commission's desire to communicate with families was to provide, where possible, the reassurance that many of these soldiers had indeed died Good Deaths, with the commission delegate often having served as evangelist as well as surrogate kin and record keeper. S. B. Smith appeared in the register as "a chris[tian] and ready to die," but Samuel Green's religious condition was "unknown"; and George Ewing was decidedly "not a Christian." One soldier's family would not be notified because "address of relatives not discoverable"; the dying man could only "shake or nod in negative or affirmative response to a question." Joseph Kramer's "friends [were] unknown," so in his case as well there was "no letter written." George Besse "seemed like a good boy, spoke tenderly of his friends, expressed some religious feeling and seemed to welcome the offer to pray with him and in several instances he joined with apparent fervor ... He had by his pillow the likeness of mother and sister." The commission delegate recorded with evident gratification this example of dying well. Marcus Flambury affirmed "In God I trust" after a half hour conversing with a commission delegate, who surely reported this encouraging indication of salvation to Flambury's family. But another soldier, troubled and deeply troubling, was past all help—in this world and the next: he appeared in the register as "Self suicide" after he shot himself. Early entries in the register listed gravesites in a hospital cemetery by row and number; later entries became more schematic, as they began to report battlefield rather than hospital deaths and to describe interments with far less specificity.[13]

In the closing year of the war Christian Commission representatives became increasingly involved not just in providing information to families but in working to ensure the preservation of the identities of the dead. The night after the Battle of Nashville in December 1864, the general field agent for the Army of the Cumberland described commission delegates searching the field to "gather up the dead, identify them through their comrades, if possible, and mark them by a card." The delegates had assumed the role of a volunteer graves registration service. After Appomattox the following spring, Christian Commission representatives would search battlefields and burying grounds around Petersburg and Richmond, locating, recording, and protecting soldiers' graves. Ultimately the commission published this list of interments together with the records of the dead in several Confederate prisons, a total of eight thousand names, "for gratuitous distribution among the friends of the lost." In the course of the war the Christian Commission had come to recognize that its pastoral duties, its concerns for "spiritual consolation," and its commitment to Christian souls also involved a commitment to Christian bodies and to the individual identity of the immortal self. This was a service they performed both to comfort the survivors and to demonstrate appropriate respect for the dead, each one of whom was a candidate for divine salvation.[14]

The Sanitary Commission approached the work of naming the dead rather differently, in keeping with the more general contrasts that distinguished the two agencies. While the Christian Commission was motivated by humanitarian sympathy and religious benevolence, the Sanitarians regarded such an approach as unduly sentimental, lacking the hard-headed realism and the order and discipline necessary to a modern age and a modern war. Working through a system of paid agents, the Sanitary Commission derided the amateurishness inherent in the volunteer efforts of the Christian Commission. The United States Sanitary Commission sought to bring dispassionate principles of science and efficiency to bear on the national crisis; relief efforts, while necessary, seemed less important than the establishment of rules of military organization that would maximize prevention of disease and effective management of wounds. Its Bureau of Vital Statistics, its inspections of camps and of soldiers, represented important manifestations of the effort to use the war as a kind of natural scientific experiment. "The vast proportions of our national Armies," wrote Charles Stillé in his official report of commission activities during the war, "... afforded facilities not likely to occur again ... and it would have been most unfortunate had the opportunities thus afforded for the study of large numbers of men in their hygienic and physiological relations, been suffered to pass unimproved." Led by well-connected members of a wealthy elite, the Sanitary Commission attained a size and financial strength, as well as a public influence and reach, that far exceeded that of the Christian Commission.[15]

But just as the Christian Commission was compelled by the demands of war to redirect its focus to this world from the next, so the Sanitarians—especially agents amid the misery of the battlefields—found themselves inevitably caught up in the pressing human needs of the moment. In the problem of handling the unidentified dead and wounded, issues of order and humanitarianism converged. Recognizing that before the desired revolution of science and prevention could be effected, "a vast amount of suffering would ensue" requiring "methodical and large measures of relief," the commission had established early in the war a Special Relief Service, which undertook such activities as distributing extra clothing, procuring special foods for the sick, helping discharged soldiers to find their way home, distributing reading matter, and answering inquiries about missing soldiers. Like the Christian Commission, the Sanitary Commission came to regard itself as a "great medium of intercommunication between the people and the Army," and it was soon overwhelmed with requests for information.[16]

Dedicated to order and system, the Sanitarians created a bureaucracy to meet the growing demand. Late in 1862 the commission established a Hospital Directory through which it hoped to "supply a greatly needed want" by centralizing information on the name and condition of every soldier admitted to a Union military hospital. On the third floor of the commission's office in downtown Washington, D.C., three full-time clerks copied data from the daily reports of dozens of hospitals into large ledgers. The directory began to advertise in order to announce its new services to the public. "Having seen your notice in the paper of your establishment of information of missing sogers," John Herrick of Michigan declared, "I now write to find out what has become of my brother which I hav not heard from since august last." Herrick thought he might have been "wounded at the battle of bullrun or antietam," and he urged the directory to investigate.[17]

By March 1863 three additional bureaus had been established in Philadelphia, New York, and Louisville to divide responsibility for all 233 army general hospitals. Commission officers did not simply wait for patients to arrive in hospitals; "as soon as the roar of the battle had ceased," Sanitary agents accompanied relief workers onto the field in order to make lists of the dead and wounded. "While bodily suffering was relieved by one class of agents, every effort was made by the other to cheer and encourage the sufferer by an assurance that his friends at home should know, at once, his exact condition."[18]

During the directory's first year, some 13,000 specific inquiries were submitted and 9,203 answered. By early 1865 more than a million names had been recorded in office ledgers. Gathering information about all these men was no small feat. On July 4, 1863, for example, John Bowne of the Washington directory office left for Gettysburg to procure names of casualties from what he already knew had been a momentous battle. But five days later he complained that "the returns are coming provokingly and sadly slow." Survivors were more concerned with caring for the wounded and burying the dead than with reporting on their fate. Bowne had found "by experience it is only when in a state of rest that the officers notice my communications." Nearly two weeks after the battle Bowne had eight thousand names of Gettysburg's fallen entered into his ledgers, but he observed that the directory's records had never been "so confused... and so unsatisfactory from their want of fullness." Reports from field hospitals were riddled with errors and omissions, often lacked dates, and were frequently illegible, "written with the faintest lead pencil." Directory officials hired extra help and even "encroached on the Lord's Day" to accomplish their task, for it seemed a permissible "work of mercy." But the scale of death at Gettysburg challenged the fledgling directory's capacity, and six weeks after the battle, the register of dead and wounded remained woefully incomplete.[19]

Many requests for information went unanswered, with the two words "not found" marked on the letter of inquiry. But sometimes the directory was able to transmit wonderfully comforting news. Richard Deering responded himself when his regiment was asked to provide information about him, and he jovially reported that he was "alive and kicking." Often, however, directory officials relieved "harrowing suspense" with replies that were devastating in their "painful certainty." The superintendent of the Washington office described the daily scene of applicants arriving in person for news: "A mother has not heard anything of her son since the last battle; she hopes he is safe, but would like to be assured—there is no escape—she must be told that he has fallen upon the 'federal altar'; an agony of tears bursts forth which seem as if it would never cease... A father... with pale face and tremulous voice, anxious to know, yet dreading to hear, is told that his boy is in the hospital a short distance off;... while tears run down his cheeks, and without uttering another word [he] leaves the room."[20]

After the bloody battles in Virginia in the spring of 1864, when Grant's army suffered 65,000 casualties in about seven weeks, the Washington directory office was almost overwhelmed with families and friends in search of news. "Never before," a June 1864 report declared, "has the throng of inquirers been so urgent and anxious... Frequently as early as 6 o clk in the morning have the visitors

"Nurses and Officers of the United States Sanitary Commission at
Fredericksburg, Virginia, During the Wilderness Campaign, 1864."
Library of Congress.

besieged our rooms and not until eleven at night was it safe to close
the doors to obtain the much needed rest before again entering upon
the daily routine of relief and consolation." Three days of slaughter at
Gettysburg the year before paled in comparison with the relentless
pressure of the Wilderness, Spotsylvania, Cold Harbor: battles that
followed one another without respite as Grant strove to inflict a
mortal blow on his outnumbered enemy.[21]

Most inquiries to directory offices came not through personal visits but in the mail, in letters that survive to provide a window into the heartrending specificity of war's cost. In March 1863 Peter Williams inquired from Michigan: "It is with the greates Ancitey that I pen a few lines to you to know the ware abouts ... of my brother Arthur Williams ... I have not heard from him for five month ... he may have died sconce pleas answer as soon as you get this." Susannah Hampton from New York wrote to the Philadelphia directory two months after Gettysburg in search of her son:

> will you please to inform me at your earliest convenience whether my son Joseph H. Hampton a member of company A 72 regiment N.Y. State vols Excelsior is alive or dead if alive and wounded please be so kind as to state what his wounds are and where he lies and if cared for and if Dead Oh pray let me know it and relieve my anxiety ... I have heard all kinds of rumors about him and his miseries until they have left me in a state bordering on phrensy.[22]

Amid all these compelling stories, John Bowne found himself especially engaged by the tribulations of a young woman who feared she had been deserted rather than bereaved but had no intention of quietly enduring the injustice she believed she had suffered. "Mrs Biddy Higgins alias Hayes," a domestic working for a respectable Philadelphia family, wrote in search of her husband, Peter Hayes, alias Higgins—"the latter being his real name"—a member of a New York Artillery regiment:

> I was married to him by the name of Higgins by the Priest of the Cathedral, 18th and Logan Square Philadelphia about nine months ago. He was 15 months in the U.S. General Hospital West Philadelphia and was sent away to his Regiment last July, I think, but *I never heard from him afterwards at all He never wrote to me,* although he knows *perfectly well* my address, having been here scores of times. This makes me a little suspicious that he might *possibly perhaps* have been married *previously* to somebody else, as he

acted lovingly towards me and we *never* had a difference or *even angry word* at any time, so it is *too bad* of him to desert me. Now as you are organization to help the poor, I hope you will be kind enough to find out for me 1st *Where Peter Hayes comes from* and who are his family and friends where he formerly lived before entering the Army, so I may write to them to enquire about him. Perhaps you could ask him this 1st before you ask him 2nd what reason he has for *never* writing to me or even letting me know where he was, or ever sending me any money at all, although I have been very ill and I do not think he could have been a very steady young man in his morals, and I have always been modest and of *excellent* character beyond any doubt, never running after the men, but he came *for a year* before I was married to him to the family where I had been a servant for many years and who will give me the best of characters.

Please reply soon as I am so much worried in my mind "Mrs Biddy Higgins alias Hayes"[23]

Bowne determined he would "try to do what I can for Mrs Biddy Higgins as I think she has been hard dealt by." But within a week of her letter, she appeared in person at the directory office to report that she had received a letter from her husband with money and a daguerreotype and that she expected him home on furlough in a few days. "So Biddy is all right," a directory official scribbled on her file. She was among the lucky ones.[24]

Ultimately the commission estimated it successfully answered 70 percent of requests for information. Although its war-end report acknowledged that this service had differed "essentially" from anything the commission had originally expected to do, it "was the work, perhaps of all others, the . . . most gratifying of any undertaken by the Commission." Even as they amassed their dispassionate statistics and implemented comforting bureaucratic order and discipline in their efforts to name the dead, the Sanitarians became humanitarians and sentimentalists in spite of themselves.[25]

The Confederacy, lagging behind the North in both men and

matériel, also faced greater shortages of information. The South had not experienced the same explosion of voluntary associations that had characterized the North in the prewar years and never developed centralized wartime charitable organizations like the Sanitary and Christian commissions. But Confederates also sought means to systematize the collection of information about casualties and ways to make that intelligence available to kin. The Louisiana Soldiers' Relief Association, for example, promised to provide information to "friends at home" about any Louisiana recruit serving in Virginia, and the Central Association and the South Carolina Relief Depot endeavored to gather information for South Carolinians. Southern religious newspapers often printed "Soldiers' Guides," gathered from hospital censuses, listing news and location of the killed and wounded.[26]

Less philanthropically inclined individuals also sought to meet the demand for information. Across Virginia a number of southerners worked the battlegrounds offering themselves as paid agents to Confederate families in search of information. In the spring of 1864 the eighteen-year-old son of South Carolina's prominent Middleton family disappeared in Virginia. His father, Oliver, procured the services of a representative who scoured camps and hospitals in search of information about the missing soldier. Oliver Jr. had fallen at Cold Harbor, but a survey of all field hospitals, an inquiry to the Confederate commissioner of prisons, a query to the Union prison at Camp Lookout, and interviews with men from his company all proved fruitless. "I will still endeavor to learn the exact fate of your son," P. Hunter promised. At last, through a friend, the father learned of his son's death in a farmhouse close to the field and secured details about the location of his grave under a nearby apple tree. The boy's consoling last words were "tell my father I died like a Middleton." Oliver Sr. immediately began to make arrangements to bring the body home.[27]

In northern cities entrepreneurs also established themselves as agents who would seek missing soldiers for a fee. An enterprise on Bleecker Street in New York City, for example, called itself the "U.S.

Army Agency" and advertised in *Harper's Weekly* in 1864 for "legal heirs seeking information as to whereabouts of Soldiers killed or wounded in Battle." In return for their efforts in locating men, they would claim a share of the deceased's back pay or the widow's pension—thus the appeal to "legal heirs."[28]

Missing information about soldiers' deaths often had practical as well as emotional significance. In the South claims for back pay, as well as for the Confederate funeral allowance—$45 for an officer and $10 for an enlisted man—had to be accompanied by proof of death. Military record keeping was so imperfect that, as the superintendent of claims for Alabama put it, "frequently the fact and date of death cannot be ascertained" because "repeated orders of the Adjutant and Inspector General have not been fully appreciated and complied with." Most often a "final statement" procured from the company commander of the deceased soldier had to substitute for absent documentation. In the North, passage of an 1862 act providing pensions for widows as well as dependent sisters and mothers of dead soldiers made similar evidence necessary for those wishing to claim these benefits. Securing required documentation was no easy task, and families with the means often turned to agents who proffered themselves as experts in negotiating the Union or Confederate army bureaucracies.[29]

Even when information was accurate and available—through newspaper casualty lists or the offices of a charitable organization or from a paid agent—it was often not delivered until long after the event. Weeks or months of waiting were common. In South Carolina, for example, the first casualty lists from the Wilderness appeared in the newspapers ten days after the battle. No wonder a Confederate officer took advantage of rank and privilege—and the fortuitous residence of his family near a telegraph line—to send a telegram home after every engagement reporting simply, "I am well."[30]

His decision to take the matter of providing information into his own hands typified the behavior of many Civil War participants,

*"I am well." Telegram from William Drayton Rutherford to Sallie
Fair Rutherford, July 6, 1862. South Caroliniana Library.*

who devised a variety of means to ensure that their fate would be
reported. Although no official identification badges were issued by
either army, soldiers, aided in some cases by enterprising civilians,
devised their own precursors to the dog tag. A Union burial party
working late on the night of July 4, 1863, to inter the Gettysburg
dead came across the body of a boy of about nineteen. In his pocket
they found "a small silver shield with his name, company, and regiment engraved upon it." They copied the information onto a wooden
headboard for his grave and forwarded the shield to his father. Soldiers in the Union army could purchase badges from sutlers in the
field or from a variety of establishments on the home front that
advertised regularly in the press. The badges seem to have been far
less commercially available in the South, but Confederate soldiers
invented their own substitutes. A pocket Bible inscribed with name
and address and even instructions about notification of kin served
quite effectively. Many Union soldiers adopted such informal meth-

Advertisement for soldiers' identification badges. Frank Leslie's
Illustrated Newspaper, *September 10, 1864.*

ods as well. Josiah Murphey of Nantucket made sure always to have
a used envelope addressed to him "somewhere about me so that if
killed in battle my friends might know what became of me."[31]

Stories have become legendary of soldiers scribbling their names
on bits of paper and pinning them to their uniforms before engagements they expected to be especially bloody—such as Meade's
planned attack on Lee's field fortifications at Mine Run in 1863 or
Grant's suicidal assault at Cold Harbor the next year. After Oliver

"I am Capt O W Holmes, 20th Mass V, Son of
Oliver Wendell Holmes, MD, Boston."
"I wrote the above when I was lying in a little house on the field
of Antietam which was for a while within the enemy's lines,
as I thought I might faint & so be unable to tell who I was."
Note written by Oliver Wendell Holmes Jr.
Harvard Law School Library.

Wendell Holmes Jr. was shot at Antietam and taken to a field hospital in a nearby house, he was afraid he would faint or die and be left nameless, so he wrote on a slip of paper, "I am Capt. O. W. Holmes 20th Mass. V Son of Oliver Wendell Holmes, M.D. Boston." Holmes recovered and kept the paper for the rest of his life. These soldiers' terror that their identities would be obliterated expressed itself with a grim and almost dispassionate practicality. They confronted the enormity of death with ingenious attempts to control at least one of its particulars. If a soldier could not save his life, he hoped at least to preserve his name.[32]

Soldiers had many allies among the civilian population in their effort to maintain their identities and to provide for notification of kin. Katherine Wormeley, serving on a Union hospital ship during the Peninsula Campaign, used the same method as the fatalistic soldiers. "So many nameless men come down to us, speechless and dying," she wrote, "that now we write the names and regiments of the bad cases and fasten them to their clothing, so that if they are speechless when they reach other hands, they may not die like dogs." To die without an identity seemed to Wormeley equivalent to surrendering one's humanity, becoming no more than an animal. Nursing pioneer Clara Barton kept a series of small—one imagines pocket—notebooks into which she entered information about the families of dying soldiers so that when time permitted she could write to the survivors. The diary of T. J. Weatherly, a South Carolina physician who attended Confederate troops in Virginia, served a

Receiving what one soldier called "Aufaul knuse." Detail
from "News of the War." Drawn by Winslow Homer.
Harper's Weekly, *June 14, 1862.*

similar purpose. "Columbus Stephenson, Bethany Church, Iredell County, NoCa," he noted on a torn and undated page, "to be written to about the death &c of Lt. Thomas W. Stephens[on]."

It is not hard to envision Dr. Weatherly asking Thomas Stephenson for his father's name and address as he consoled him in his last moments. "AA Hewlett, Summerville Ala for Capt Hewlett; Mrs. S Watkins Wadesboro NC for S J Watkins 14th NC," Weatherly's list continued.[33]

Walt Whitman may have been the most famous of those who wrote from hospitals to notify kin of soldiers' deaths. In 1862 the poet traveled to Virginia in search of his brother George, reported wounded after the Battle of Fredericksburg. George's injuries proved superficial, but Whitman was deeply affected by his glimpse of war. Like many other Americans first encountering the aftermath of battle, Whitman was struck most forcefully by the sight in front of a Union field hospital of a "heap" of amputated "feet, legs, arms, hands, &c.," pieces of humans who like the nation itself had been dismembered as a result of reasoned and would-be benevolent human intent. War's ironies and man's destructiveness both lay represented in that bloody pile. Whitman felt that any "cares and difficulties" he might have known seemed "trifling" in the face of such horrors: "Nothing we call trouble seems worth talking about." The war and its suffering soldiers became his preoccupation. "Who are you . . . Who are you . . . ?" he asked the dead, and concluded these soldiers represented "the majesty and reality of the American common people." In these men lay the true meaning of the war. Whitman served, as literary critic M. Wynn Thomas has written, as "a surrogate mourner of the dead—one who took it on himself to do what the relatives could not do: to remember the dead man in the very presence of the corpse."[34]

Whitman became a tireless hospital visitor, spending seven or eight hours each day ministering to patients, chiefly in Washington, D.C., where almost fifty thousand men lay sick and wounded. His efforts were less medical than consolatory; he provided rice puddings, small amounts of spending money, stamped envelopes and stationery, peaches, apples, oranges, horseradish, undershirts, socks, soap, towels, oysters, jellies, horehound candy—and love, comfort, and "cheer." And he himself wrote hundreds of letters—often, he reported, more than a dozen a day—for soldiers unable to do this for themselves. After suffering with his family the torments of uncertainty about George's fate, Whitman understood well the importance of communication between battle and home front. "I do a good deal of this," he wrote to the *New York Times,* "writing all kinds, including love letters . . . I always encourage the men to write, and promptly write for them." He often wrote, too, to inform relatives of soldiers' deaths. A revolutionary poet—*Leaves of Grass* has been said to represent "an absolute discontinuity with the traditions of English verse"—Whitman introduced no innovations to the genre of the condolence letter. Instead he provided families with the information they expected and needed:

> Your son, Corporal Frank H. Irwin, was wounded near Fort Fisher, Virginia, March the 25, 1865 . . . He died the first of May . . . Frank . . . had everything requisite in surgical treatment, nursing &c . . . He was so good and well-behaved . . . At . . . times he would fancy himself talking . . . to children or such like, his relatives I suppose, and giving them good advice . . . He was perfectly willing to die . . . and was perfectly resign'd . . . I do not know his past life, but I feel as if it must have been good.

Irwin's behavior in dying, Whitman concluded, "could not be surpass'd. And now like many other noble and good men, after serving his country as a soldier, he has yielded up his young life . . . in her service." This was, Whitman assured the grieving mother, a prepared death, a willing death, a patriotic death—certainly a Good Death. And even though Whitman was himself not in any sense an orthodox Christian believer, he closed his letter by offering Frank Irwin's family a carefully worded consolation of faith: "there is a text, 'God doeth all things well'—the meaning of which, after due time, appears to the soul."[35]

"Ward K at Armory Square Hospital in Washington, D.C.," one of the hospitals Walt Whitman visited regularly. Library of Congress.

In his poem "Come Up from the Fields Father," Whitman imagined the family that received a letter like those he wrote. In Ohio's "vital and beautiful" fall, "all prospers well." Apples and grapes ripen; the wheat is ready for cutting. But amid this harvest of life, news arrives of war's harvest of death. A letter comes to the farm's family, written not by their son Pete but in another's hand. It reports his gunshot wound but does not yet communicate the more terrible truth that "he is dead already" by the time the letter arrives. It is a letter that will destroy the mother, as a rifle has already destroyed the son.[36]

John O'Neal, a Gettysburg physician, did not send letters to bereaved families, but he kept a record of the names and locations of Confederate graves he encountered as he traveled about the county visiting patients. These were men already dead, well past O'Neal's medical ministrations, but he felt nevertheless a sense of obligation that led him to document their often hasty interments in hope of someday transmitting the information to family or friends. Into his journal, scribbled in a little bound volume entitled "The Physician's Handbook of Practice," he entered, alongside patients' names and ailments, lists of dead Confederates, their companies, regiments, and gravesites: "2nd Corps Ground, Back of Schwartz Barn No 1 Crew J. Co. K 8 Fla No 2 Farmer N, Co G. 7 N.C. Died July 26."[37]

Individuals did not just wait for letters or published casualty lists to obtain news about the dead and wounded; they also made use of the press to request information or to share information they had been able to acquire. In both North and South civilians took out personal advertisements to announce the condition of prisoners and the fate of the missing. These notices were used to communicate across the divide of Civil War—to provide southerners with news from the North and vice versa. In 1864, for example, a Richmond paper published a notice placed by Union general Benjamin Butler. Directed to the attention of a Confederate naval surgeon, Butler's advertisement reported that his son and a friend were alive and had been taken prisoner at the end of June. "They are both well and at [the Union prisoner of war camp at] Point Lookout. I have taken leave to write this note to relieve your anxiety." He had spoken to the young prisoner, he continued, "in a personal interview." Butler and the Confederate surgeon had almost certainly been acquainted before the war, and ties of friendship and humanitarianism combined in this instance to yield information about two of the war's missing. A personal advertisement in a Richmond paper announced to "Hon. R.W.B. of South Carolina—your son Nat is a prisoner at Point Lookout, unwounded, and in his usual health, and all his wants shall be supplied without delay." This anonymous northern friend of the family of Robert Barnwell was offering not just the immediate solace of information but a promise to supplement the meager fare of Union prison camps for the duration of Nat's incarceration.

The *New York Daily News* ran regular columns of original notices and copied others from Richmond papers. In February 1864 William Racer of Madison County, Virginia, sought information that would "relieve the suspense of... [a] distressed father" about his son, who had been reported wounded at Gettysburg seven months before. Southerner William Smith responded to an inquiry from a northern relative that a Mobile paper had copied from the *New York Daily News*. "We are all well. Brother Sam died in Vicksburg the 17th of July, of a wound and typhoid fever. My love to all." Newspaper columns substituted for the personal letter that was unlikely to make its way through military lines. Ever hopeful, the "friends of Sergeant WALTER FARNAN, Jr., Company M. Fifteenth U.S. Infantry" sought an end to uncertainty by publishing a request to "THE AUTHORITIES At Richmond" to please confirm if he was indeed the W. Farnham reported to have died in a Virginia hospital two weeks before.[38]

Desperate families both North and South traveled by the hundreds to battlefields to search in person for missing kin. Observers described railroad junctions crowded with frantic relatives in pursuit of information about loved ones. When Oliver Wendell Holmes Sr. rushed to Maryland fearing his son dead after Antietam, he described the combination of hope and terror that must have been shared by many who traveled to the front in search of kin. When in spite of his worst fears he found the young captain alive, the father characterized his shifting expectations as in some profound sense a shifting reality: "Our son and brother was dead and is alive again, and was lost and is found." The boundary between life and death seemed at once permeable and infinite.[39]

Many of those who sought their fathers, brothers, husbands, and sons did not enjoy Holmes's happy outcome. Fanny Scott of Virginia began a search for her son Benjamin after more than three months of silence following the battle of Antietam in September 1862. She wrote to Robert E. Lee early in 1863. He forwarded her letter across the lines to Union general Joseph Hooker, who promised to have the U.S. surgeon general survey the hospital lists from Maryland. Lee enclosed Hooker's letter in a reply to Mrs. Scott and expressed his hopes "that you may hear good news of your son." But two months later Lee forwarded a letter sent him through a Flag of Truce that reported, "Diligent and careful inquiry has been made concerning the man referred to in the enclosure and no trace of him can be discovered in any hospital or among the records of the rebel prisoners." Within days Fanny Scott submitted to Lee a request for a pass through Union lines to herself search for Benjamin. But evidently the effort proved fruitless, for at the end of the war she was still seeking information. Union general E. A. Hitchcock, responsible for war-end exchanges of prisoners, gently responded to Scott's July 15, 1865, request: "From the length of time since the battle of Antietam and you not having heard from your son during all this time, I am very sorry to say that the presumption is that he fell a victim to that battle. If he were still living I cannot understand why he should not have found means of making the fact known to you."[40]

The Scott incident illustrates several significant aspects of the problem of the missing of the Civil War. First, it demonstrates the possibility of an individual's being entirely lost—a circumstance many civilians found difficult to fathom. As we have seen, the scale of the war presented unprecedented challenges of record keeping, so that undoubtedly many of those never identified were bodies that could not be connected with names. But another aspect of Civil War death contributed to the large numbers of unidentified—and would contribute even more dramatically to the nameless ranks of World War I dead. The Civil War sometimes obliterated not just names but entire bodies, often leaving nothing behind to identify or bury. A Union chaplain described in the aftermath of Gettysburg "little fragments so as hardly to be recognizable as any part of a man." Another soldier wrote in horror of comrades literally "blown to atoms." Many Civil War soldiers actually vanished, their bodies vaporized by the firepower of this first modern war. This may have been the fate of Benjamin Scott. Civilians found this outcome incomprehensible, but soldiers who had witnessed the destructiveness of battle understood all too well the reality of men instantly transformed into nothing. The implications of bodily disintegration for the immortality of both bodies and souls was troubling, and the disappearance of bodies rendered the search for names all the more important.[41]

Fanny Scott's story demonstrates as well the unifying power of death even amid the divisive forces of war. General Lee was not above concerning himself with the fall of an individual sparrow— though one assumes that Scott was no ordinary soldier but one whose family had some larger claims of class and connection on Lee's compassion. But the intimacy of this all-American war displays itself strikingly here, as Lee readily corresponded with his Yankee counterpart, who himself acted promptly and decisively to honor his enemy's request. Even as they contemplated the spring campaign that would produce their bloody confrontation at Chancellorsville, Lee and Hooker found themselves on the same side as Mrs. Fanny Scott in her desperate pursuit of information about her son. Killing enemy soldiers was the goal of both generals and both armies, yet bereavement could unite them in common purpose.[42]

Fanny Scott's 1865 request for information about a son who had by then been gone almost three years suggests the depth and tenacity of the need to secure accurate information about the fate of missing men. General Hitchcock's letter to Scott seems to reflect a certain incredulity that she had not yet resigned herself to a grim conclusion that he regarded as both undeniable and unavoidable. Yet Fanny Scott's story demonstrates not just the nationally unifying power of death but also the intensity and persistence of its hold upon the bereaved, especially in circumstances of continuing uncertainty. Nine years after the end of the war Mrs. R. L. Leach was still seeking information about what had happened to her son after he was sent to a hospital ship in Virginia. Unable to admit he must be dead, she confessed, "we think sometimes that he is in Some Insane Hospital." Without further information she lived in "suspense," even as she acknowledged "to know he was dead would be better." Jane Mitchell had received a letter after the Battle of Gettysburg from a soldier who described burying a corpse he found rolled in a blanket with her son's name pinned to it. But she never saw the body or found the grave and was never convinced it was really her son. "I would like to find that grave," she wrote. "It was years before I gave up the hope that he would some day appear. I got it into my head that he had been taken prisoner and carried off a long distance but that he would make his way back one day—this I knew was very silly of me but the hope was there nevertheless." The absence of identifiable bodies left these women with abiding uncertainty and fantastical hopes, illusions that for them made the world endurable.[43]

The power and longevity of hope manifested themselves dramatically in the responses that Union quartermaster general Montgomery Meigs received when he decided in 1868 to publish in northern magazines a drawing of a soldier who had died unidentified in a Washington military hospital in May 1864. The man had arrived too weak to give any information about himself and would have been quickly forgotten if he had not had in his possession the considerable sum of $360. The surgeon in charge of the hospital arranged to have him photographed after his death, and this likeness was copied by the press at the request of the War Department. The announcements seeking his identity also noted that the dead man had left an ambrotype of a child. Letters from women streamed into Meigs's office. While some may indeed have been fortune hunters seeking to claim the money, the great majority displayed what seems like such poignant desperation that it is difficult to doubt the sincerity of the wrenching tales they told. Mrs. Jenny McConkey of Illinois appeared to recognize the futility of her hopes when she wrote suggesting the unidentified man might be her son, whom she had last heard from in 1862. The photograph of the little boy was hard to explain, for her son was childless. But, she rationalized, he might have carried the portrait in any case "as he was very fond of children." A Pennsylvania woman whose husband had last been heard of in the infamous Confederate prison camp at Andersonville described her life as "one constant daze of anxiety" because of her inability to get any information about his fate. Martha Dort wrote explaining that her husband had reportedly been shot while being transferred from one prison to another in 1863, "but that may not be true. Mistakes do often occur." She was encouraged to hope by the report of

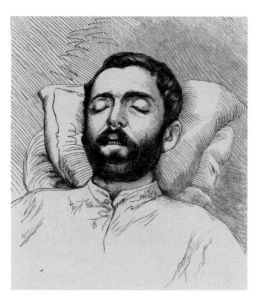

"An Unknown Soldier." Copied from a deathbed photograph and published in an effort to locate his survivors. Harper's Weekly, *October 24, 1868.*

the child's photograph, for her husband had carried an ambrotype of their son, aged three or four, in plaid pants with his hands in his pockets. She enclosed fifty cents for a copy of the photograph. Meigs's office returned the money, for the picture did not match her description.[44]

The mysterious soldier was never identified; the child in the ambrotype was never provided with the details of his father's death or with his $360 inheritance. But the unknown man had proved the catalyst for an outpouring of despair from women who represented the many thousands of loved ones left not just without their husbands, brothers, or sons but bereft of the kind of information that might enable them to mourn. It is chilling to recognize the very limited expectations of the many women who wrote to Meigs: the man they all sought to claim as their husband was quite dead; they were no longer looking to find a living person; the most they dared hope was for relief from the incapacitating uncertainty that controlled

Henry Clay Taylor.
Photographed on his twenty-fifth birthday.
Wisconsin Historical Society.

their lives. A professor at Gettysburg College who aided many civilians searching for kin after the battle there perceptively described "aching hearts in which the dread void of uncertainty still remained unsatisfied by positive knowledge." It was in some sense information as much as individuals that was "missing" in Civil War America. Those who had long since given up on reclaiming lost loved ones alive still sought eagerly for details of their lives, deaths, and burials.

J. M. Taylor of Fond du Lac, Wisconsin, was as assiduous and tenacious as Fanny Scott in search of information about his son, who was captured at Chickamauga in September 1863. Initially confined in Richmond's Libby Prison, twenty-five-year-old Henry Taylor managed to communicate with his parents by concealing miniature letters in buttons smuggled to the North. Early hopes for his return dimmed, for prisoner exchanges had been suspended, and Henry was transferred south. Months of confinement and scanty prison fare

"Libby Prison, Richmond Virginia, April 1865." Library of Congress.

took their toll, and he fell sick with diarrhea and consumption. By summer 1864 his parents learned he had entered a military hospital in Charleston. The irregular news they had received since his capture now almost ceased, until in October a fellow Union prisoner wrote from South Carolina that Henry could not recover. "I think it due you that you know the facts," the soldier explained. Taylor received the letter through the lines nine days later. "It makes a *child* of me," the father reported. He began a series of frantic inquiries, seeking to end the "painful suspense" with information from escaped and paroled prisoners and from military officials both North and South. In mid-November Taylor learned of two Union officers who were reported to have said they buried Henry. Now, assuming him dead, Taylor continued to write in pursuit of details: "Please bear in mind that the most trivial circumstances in regard to the last moments [and] death of *our loved* one will be of much interest to us." On December 27 Taylor received a letter from another former prisoner confirming that Henry had died at Charleston on October 3. But this was not the kind of official notification that would satisfy Taylor's longing to know everything possible about Henry's last days. Nor would it enable Taylor to, as he put it "settle my son's ac[counts] with the government." He continued to write to secure such evidence and to locate Henry's effects, "which will be preserved as relicks." Taylor was particularly concerned about the return of a twenty-five-dollar gold piece he had sent Henry just before his death and about remuneration for Henry's "servant . . . a negro by the name of Sam," who, Henry had reported in 1863, "thinks as much of me as *any* dog does of his master." As soon as Charleston fell into Union hands, Taylor began efforts to bring Henry's body home.[45]

Henry Taylor was one of the estimated 9 percent of Civil War dead who expired in prison camps. Like Henry, most of these men died in the years after the North's suspension of regular prisoner exchanges in mid-1863 in response to Confederate mistreatment of captured black soldiers. The North's numerical superiority made exchanges disadvantageous in what was fast evolving into a war of attrition, but Yankees and Confederates alike suffered in the harsh conditions that accompanied the rapid expansion of prison populations. Neither side had anticipated the need to hold so many men in captivity, and neither side had made adequate provision for supplying food, shelter, or medical care. In the course of the war 194,743 Union soldiers and 215,865 Confederates were held prisoner, and 30,218 northerners and 25,976 southerners died in captivity. Civil War prisons were indeed, as one inmate observed, "the closest existence to a hell on earth."[46]

In April 1895 J. M. Taylor received an answer to a letter he had recently sent one of Henry's old comrades. The veteran, who noted he was now gray-haired, confessed he could not recall enough about the layout of the Charleston hospital to answer Taylor's very specific inquiry about the circumstances of Henry's last days: "Maybe that some of the other boys may remember more about it." Thirty years might have led the soldier to put the war out of his mind, but the father could not. The consoling "facts" were still missing.[47]

Four years of Civil War propelled a remarkable shift in attitudes and behavior toward accounting for the dead. Military procedures themselves began to reflect this transformation, and in July 1864 the U.S. Congress passed an act that established a new organizational principle for handling casualties. This measure for the first time designated a special graves registration unit rather than, as had heretofore been the case, assuming that soldiers could simply be detailed from the line to carry out burial duties. When Confederate general Jubal Early attacked Fort Stevens near Washington, D.C., in 1864, this new unit, under Assistant Quartermaster James Moore, succeeded in identifying every Union body and recording every grave. But during the final operations of the war, men were not spared to serve in registration units, and the effort was abandoned. It represented nevertheless a new departure and, together with the establishment of the beginnings of the national cemetery system, marked a growing recognition of governmental responsibility for the remains—both bodies and names—of those who had perished in Civil War camps and battlefields.

The commitment to individual rights that emerged as such an important principle of the northern cause made attention to particular soldiers' fates and identities inescapable; honoring the dead became inseparable from respecting the living. But the strongest impetus for these changes was the anguish of wives, parents, siblings, and children who found undocumented, unconfirmed, and unrecognized loss intolerable. The Civil War took place in a newly and self-consciously humanitarian age. "The world is more easily moved by the spectacle of human misery than it ever has been," wrote a northern relief worker, explaining why "the Christian public either in this or any other country" would not allow soldiers to suffer as they had "in all previous wars." This was an age in which family ties were celebrated and sentimentalized, an age that believed, moreover, that it possessed the agency and responsibility, as well as the scientific expertise, to mitigate suffering.[48]

But the dimensions of Civil War loss did not yield to small-scale, individual intervention or even to entrepreneurial improvisations, and

Americans turned to the emerging philanthropic bureaucracies of the Sanitary and Christian commissions and ultimately to enhanced state power and responsibility. As Union victory became all but certain in the winter and early spring of 1864–65, the demands of the unnamed dead grew more pressing. At war's end, the United States would embark on a program of identification and reburial that redefined the nation's obligation to its fallen, as well as the meaning of both names and bodies as enduring repositories of the human self.

CHAPTER 5

REALIZING

Civilians and the Work of Mourning

"more trying than to face the battle's rage"
REUBEN ALLEN PIERSON

War victimized civilians as well as soldiers, and uncounted numbers of noncombatants perished as a direct result of the conflict. The war's circumstances created a variety of ways for ordinary Americans to die: from violence that extended beyond soldiers and battles, from diseases that spread beyond military camps, from hardships and shortages that enveloped a broad swath of the American—and especially the southern—population. It was, in Abraham Lincoln's words, a "people's contest," and the people suffered its cruelties.[1]

Civil War engagements respected no rigid delineation between home and battlefront but raged across farms and settlements, into Gettysburg's peach orchard and Sharpsburg's cornfield, as well as into countless churches and dwellings. At First Bull Run, Judith Henry, a bedridden eighty-five-year-old widow, was killed by an artillery shell. Twenty-year-old Jenny Wade of Gettysburg died from a rifle bullet that passed through her front door as she worked dough to make bread for wounded soldiers. Young Alvah Shuford, who lived near Antietam, died while playing with a shell he found on the field; another boy perished the same way after Gettysburg. An estimated twenty women were killed by artillery fire during the 1863 siege of Vicksburg, but one observer noted that citizens actually suffered much more from "scarcity of provisions than from the abundance of shells." Civilians died when Union gunboats fired on Natchez and Baton Rouge, when Union troops besieged Petersburg, when Yankees and Confederates struggled over the Shenandoah Valley—even in hand-to-hand combat in the streets of Martinsburg. In Richmond more than forty women working in an ordnance factory were killed in an explosion in 1863, and another fifteen died in similar circumstances in Jackson, Mississippi. Sherman's March targeted property rather than persons, but civilians died nonetheless, like the eighty-year-old man driving his mule who was shot when he refused to stop at a Union colonel's order. "That was one of the accidents of the war," a Yankee soldier nonchalantly reported. Noncombatants were caught up in almost every military action—collateral damage, as they might be designated today. Yet no one then or since has tried to make a systematic compilation or enumeration of such deaths. In an era when military record keeping was itself flawed and incomplete, no one thought to account for civilians. Their losses remain the stuff of anecdote and even legend—largely unacknowledged casualties of a war even more devastating than its official statistics imply.[2]

Disease as well as violence threatened civilians, who perished from the same illnesses that produced the preponderance of military deaths. The Civil War generated significant movements of peoples that served as deadly disease vectors. Contagions and epidemics that flourished in army camps spread to surrounding populations. Citizens of Danville, Virginia, for example, were certain that their debilitating "fevers" originated in the prisoner-of-war hospital located there. Philadelphia reported a smallpox epidemic that seemed closely connected to the numbers of soldiers stationed in the city who had succumbed to the disease. In the fall of 1862 nearly five hundred cases of yellow fever and malaria appeared in Wilmington, North Carolina, in part, local physicians believed, because the construction of army breastworks had increased the number of stagnant ponds around the city. After Antietam, Maryland families paid a price for their generosity in caring for the wounded. As a result of maintaining a hospital in his parlor throughout the fall of 1862, Adam Michael reported, "the disease ... has afflicted three of our family ... Mother died with this disease on the 25th day of November."[3]

African Americans in search of freedom frequently succumbed to illness as they fled northward. The Union army established what came to be known as "contraband camps" to help provide for the tens of thousands of slaves escaping into northern lines. Largely populated by women, children, and the elderly—often the families of black men who entered Union military service—these camps had extraordinarily high levels of mortality, due in considerable part to the conditions in which their residents were compelled to live. A Sanitary Commission observer described the camps as sites of "extreme destitution and suffering." At one camp near Nashville in 1864, 25 percent of the residents died in a single three-month period. Many who escaped to freedom never lived to enjoy it.[4]

Across the South white civilians remarked upon apparent increases in illness and mortality, due in part to the economic hardships mounting within the struggling Confederacy. "I never have heard of so many dying," a Virginia woman reported, as she sent news from home to her husband at the front. An 1864 appeal on behalf of refugee women and children near Nashville noted that "last spring the mortality among children was fearful," and expressed worries about a significant "decrease in the population of women and children." A petition to Jefferson Davis from forty-six citizens of Randolph County, Alabama, confirmed that by 1864 "deaths from starvation have absolutely occurred." Southerners acknowledged that both the physical and emotional pressures of war had taken their toll. A Virginia doctor, trying to give some measure of objective reality to his sense of sharply increased morbidity and mortality, estimated that "the average of deaths is 30 per ct greater among the non-combatant population than before the war." As a South Carolina woman remarked, "it is not strange that the body sometimes gives way when so much rests upon the mind."[5]

Even the most privileged and famous could not protect themselves from the reach of war-borne disease. William Tecumseh Sherman's nine-year-old son died of typhoid fever contracted on a visit to his father in camp; Confederate general James Longstreet lost both his young children when they moved to Richmond to join him and came down with scarlet fever soon after they arrived in the crowded wartime capital. Eleven-year-old Willie Lincoln died in 1862 from typhoid fever, the consequence, in all likelihood, of Washington's water supply, contaminated by the army camps stationed along the banks of the Potomac River.[6]

Hospitals were especially dangerous places, and nurses, matrons, and other medical workers often contracted illnesses from the patients they attended or from the polluted water supply they all shared. Union general Francis Barlow's wife, Arabella, died of typhus as a result of her service in the hospitals of the Army of the Potomac. In both North and South nurses—Louisa May Alcott prominent among them—regularly fell victim to typhoid, smallpox, and even heart failure brought on by the conditions and demands of their employment. When Wilmington, North Carolina, was taken by Union forces, prisoners released from Andersonville and Florence crowded its hospitals, spreading new waves of epidemic disease. Of five "lady nurses" from the North, three sickened and two died, along with a chaplain and other medical attendants. Residents of the long-suffering town cannot but have been affected as well. No statistics or systematic records document the impact of war-engendered disease on noncombatant populations, but citizens, especially in the South, had few doubts about its effects.[7]

The enormous battles—engagements like Shiloh, Antietam, Gettysburg, the Wilderness—that constituted the central theater and focus of war often overshadow the widespread and persistent small-scale encounters, guerrilla actions, and civic unrest that inevitably involved and threatened civilians. One set of such hostilities grew naturally out of the causes of the conflict. On farms and plantations across the South, the disruptions of war encouraged slaves to challenge their subordination as they witnessed erosions of white control and anticipated the possibility of freedom. Some masters died at the hands of slaves seeking vengeance or asserting a new sense of empowerment. Mary Chesnut described the horror that swept through the highest circles of South Carolina society when the elderly Betsey Witherspoon was smothered by her slaves. In Virginia a sixteen-year-old slave girl, determined not to be whipped, killed her mistress by hitting her with a fence rail and then choking her to death. As they struggled to maintain control, masters, in turn, killed slaves. Near Natchez anxious whites hanged thirty slaves suspected of using war's disruptions to plan an uprising against their owners. A northern woman working in the Nashville hospitals learned of a "negro boy of about nine years old who died from blows received from his mistress." She was beating him because of her "anger that his mother had run away in search of freedom." More commonly masters exacted retribution upon wives left behind by male slaves who had fled to join the Union army. Slaves suspected of helping the Yankees became particular targets of white southerners' wrath. A young slave girl in Darlington, South Carolina, was hanged for yelling, "Bless the Lord the Yankees have come!" when Sherman's troops arrived in town. Across the South slaves and masters battled over the future of the peculiar institution in a warfare, both overt and hidden, that yielded its own unacknowledged list of casualties.[8]

Racial violence was not confined to the South. Northern resentment at the human and financial cost of the war disturbed the public peace, most dramatically in the New York City riots that followed the introduction of a draft lottery in July 1863. White citizens were angry that the recently enacted federal conscription law would lead them off to battle in a war now explicitly committed to emancipation, and they expressed their fury in vicious attacks that were directed at first against government buildings but soon focused upon African American residents of the city. Five days of violence resulted in the burning of the Colored Orphan Asylum, the lynching of eleven black men, and more than one hundred deaths.[9]

Violence invaded everyday life in other parts of the nation as well, especially in locations where political loyalties divided the civilian population. East Tennessee, western North Carolina, southwest Virginia, and the Missouri borderlands were among the areas that

*"View of the Darlington Court-House and the Sycamore Tree Where
Amy Spain, the Negro Slave, Was Hung."* Harper's Weekly,
September 30, 1865.

experienced guerrilla conflict that made few distinctions between
combatants and noncombatants. In East Tennessee a Primitive Baptist minister of northern sympathies was killed in his house by secessionists; Unionists claimed that Confederates hanged several women
who had refused to reveal the whereabouts of their loyal husbands.
In Shelton Laurel, North Carolina, Confederates shot fifteen male citizens, including boys as young as thirteen. Confederate sympathizers
burned the town of Lawrence, Kansas, and the Union commander
retaliated by ordering houses in four counties vacated and destroyed.
In Missouri partisan rangers terrorized civilians and provided Jesse
James with a training ground for his violent postwar career.[10]

But for most civilians war's wounds proved less direct than they
were for a Judith Henry or a Jenny Wade or a victim of guerrilla violence or even epidemic disease. Most noncombatants felt war's cru-

elest impact not in their own illness or death but through the sufferings of the soldiers who were dear to them. The blow that killed a soldier on the field not only destroyed that man but also sent waves of misery and desolation into a world of relatives and friends, who themselves became war's casualties. In a poem, "Killed at the Ford," that represented a widely shared understanding of war's losses, Henry Wadsworth Longfellow dissolved the boundary between home and battlefront, between combatants and noncombatants, between war's physical and emotional wounds. The ball that killed the Yankee soldier in the South continued its trajectory of death:

> *That fatal bullet went speeding forth*
> *Till it reached a town in the distant North*
> *Till it reached a house in a sunny street*
> *Till it reached a heart that ceased to beat*
> *Without a murmur, without a cry*
>
> . . . .
>
> *And the neighbors wondered that she should die.*[11]

Some grieving survivors did indeed literally perish. Told that her husband had been killed, one Iowa woman declared she wished to see her mother and then die, and she proceeded to do just that. In South Carolina the parents of eighteen-year-old Oliver Middleton, killed in 1864, were perceived by their acquaintances to be unalterably transformed by the blow, and Oliver's despairing mother followed him in death in a little more than a year.[12]

But Longfellow's poem suggests the possibility of metaphorical death in his rendering of the unspecified—and thus generalized—wife, mother, or sister. Even without the actual demise of the body, the bereaved might suffer a living death of spirit, heart, and hope. Civil War fatalities belonged ultimately to the survivors; it was they who had to undertake the work not just of burial but also of consolation and mourning. This would be, as Louisiana soldier Reuben Allen Pierson wrote from the field in 1862, "more trying than to face the battle's rage."[13]

The notion of the Good Death, so often embodied in the condolence letter that bore "Aufaul knuse" from battle to home front, represented an initial collaboration between the dying and the living in managing death's terrors. The letter and the act of dying that it described affirmed a set of assumptions about death's meaning that established the foundations for the mourning to follow. A soldier's actual death comprised but a moment—"sudden and swift" like the subject of Longfellow's poem, even if it was preceded by lengthy struggle and agony. But for his survivors, his death was literally endless. His work was over, but theirs had just begun.

For many bereaved, even assimilating the fact of a loved one's death was difficult. Civil War letter and diary writers confronting news of loss repeatedly proclaimed their inability to "realize" a death—using the word with now antiquated precision to mean to render it real in their own minds. This word choice encompasses an important aspect of the process of grief as it has been described by psychologists and indeed observers through the ages. Freud, for example, contrasted mourning, a grief that understands that a loved object no longer exists, to melancholia, in which an individual "cannot see clearly what it is that has been lost" and thus remains mired in "profoundly painful dejection, cessation of interest in the outside world, loss of the capacity to love." Freud writes of "the work of mourning," defined by the effort to come to grips with the reality of loss and then to withdraw emotional investment from the departed. Mourning is a process with an end; melancholia a state, and, in Freud's terms, a pathology. The particular circumstances created by the Civil War often inhibited mourning, rendering it difficult, if not impossible, for many bereaved Americans to move through the stages of grief. In an environment where information about deaths was often wrong or entirely unavailable, survivors found themselves both literally and figuratively unable to "see clearly what . . . has been lost" and instead encouraged to deny it. In such conditions the temptation to distrust and resist bad news was all too alluring and the capacity for the genuine consolations of mourning severely compromised.[14]

Denial and numbness were, in fact, prominent means by which civilians—like soldiers—attempted to cope with war's losses. Abbie Brooks of Georgia confessed that sufferings had "purified and petrified me. I care very little for anybody or anything, am neither sorry nor glad, but passive." After her brother's death, Kate Foster of Mississippi felt emotionally altered: "My heart became flint. I am almost afriad to love too dearly anyone now." Kate Stone, who spent much of the war as a refugee from her Louisiana home, acknowledged that "death does not seem half so terrible as it did long ago. We have grown used to it." Cornelia Hancock, nursing in Union hospitals, felt the same as the young Confederate: "One can get used to anything." She had come to understand why hospital administrators so often failed to make the required list of fatalities: death had become too commonplace even to take note of. When she was told of the demise of a neighbor at home, Hancock confessed to her sister that a single death seemed not to mean "anything to me now." The young wife of a Confederate officer reported that some bereaved southerners became almost paralyzed by their losses, "stunned and stupefied . . . forever, and a few there were who died of grief." Mary Lee, living amid the constant battles over Winchester, agreed: "no one feels anything now." Such denial represented its own kind of loss, an abandonment of emotion and sensibility that was a death in itself, another dimension of war's dehumanization.[15]

Making a death real, feeling and accepting its certainty, required effort. After her brother James was killed at Second Bull Run, Sarah Palmer wrote in anguish to her sister Harriet, "I can't realize that I am never to see that dear boy again . . . it is too hard to realize." Death itself seemed impossible to understand, much less to connect with their vibrant young brother: "We have never known what death was before." Their mother, Esther, turned to fantasies of denial, trying to reject rather than embrace the reality of his loss, which she found unbearable. "I sometimes think he is not dead, it might have been a mistake," she wrote several weeks after he was killed. "I cannot begin to realize the death of my beloved brother," wrote another sister, Elizabeth. "I find myself continually thinking of him as alive."

Five months later Harriet still struggled to accept the fact of his loss. "It is very hard to believe that dear Jim is dead. Were it not for the cessation of those letters we used to hail with so much gladness... I could not realize it." Death seemed ineffable, a void that she could understand best through the physicality of the letters that came no more.[16]

Survivors sought material evidence that could convince their often "rebellious hearts" of the unfathomable and intolerable news that confronted them. Just two years after James's death another Palmer son and brother was killed. When bits of his clothing were forwarded to his family, his young widow, Alice, greeted them with relief: "The last lingering hopes have all been crushed. None of us could mistake those pieces of cloth. I thank God that he had on clothes that we knew. Otherwise we never would have felt sure that they were his precious remains."[17]

Alice Palmer was among the fortunate. Hundreds of thousands of wives, parents, children, and siblings of unidentified and missing men would never have what she called the "melancholy satisfaction" of irrefutable evidence to serve as a foundation for emotional acceptance of loss. The intensity with which Civil War Americans sought to retrieve the bodies of their slain kin arose in no small part from this need to make loss real by rendering it visible and tangible. A Union nurse described a young wife after Antietam "whose frantic grief I can never forget." Told that her husband had been buried two days before she arrived in search of him, she was "unwilling to believe the fact" and "insisted upon seeing him." His comrades kindly agreed to disinter the body. One glance quieted her frenzy as she sank beneath "the stern reality of this crushing sorrow" and made plans to take the body back to Philadelphia. The "stern reality" represented by a body succeeded in establishing "the fact" of death in her mind, and the new widow began to move from resistance to acceptance of her cruel fate and her new identity.[18]

To embody—quite literally—death was one way to make it real. But the effort to render death palpable included as well the creation of visible symbols of grief that could be used to rehearse and enact

John Saunders Palmer Jr. with his wife of less than a year,
Alice Ann Gaillard Palmer. South Caroliniana Library.

the new roles the bereaved now occupied. In the mid-nineteenth century respectable Americans, or those who aspired to be considered among their ranks, customarily observed a formal period of bereavement after the death of a spouse or relative. The first ladies of both North and South spent much of the war garbed in mourning, for each endured the loss of a young child, Mary Lincoln's Willie and Varina Davis's Joseph, who fell from the porch of the executive mansion in Richmond. Mary Lincoln remained in deep mourning for more than a year after Willie's death, dressing in black veils, black crape "without the gloss," and black jewelry. By 1863 she had progressed to half mourning and appeared in lavender, gray, and some

Half-mourning dress of Varina Howell Davis.
The Museum of the Confederacy.

purples, with a little white trim visible at the wrist. But after her husband's assassination, she returned to full mourning for the rest of her life. Men, too, wore tokens of mourning, armbands for lost kin, badges and rosettes, like those displayed by Virginia Military Institute cadets and officers for a month after Stonewall Jackson's death.[19]

By convention, a mother mourned for a child for a year, a child for a parent the same, a sister six months for a brother. A widow mourned for two and a half years, moving through prescribed stages and accoutrements of heavy, full, and half mourning, with gradually loosening requirements of dress and deportment. A widower, by contrast, was expected to mourn only for three months, simply by displaying black crape on his hat or armband. The work of mourning was largely allocated to women. The exigencies of war and, in the

South, shortages of clothing and money undermined the rigidity of these expectations. But war's changed circumstances prompted desire to replace necessity. Even as expectations loosened, women sought the solace they hoped the costumes and customs of mourning could provide. Many women struggled to find the garments that would enable them to participate in this rite of passage and display of respect. Formal observance of mourning created a sense of process, encouraging the bereaved to believe they could move through their despair, which might evolve through stages of grief represented by their changing clothing: from the flat black silks, veils, and crape of heavy mourning, to the white trim and collars acceptable in full mourning, to the grays and lavenders that half mourning introduced, until at last they returned fully to the world and their customary attire.[20]

In the South, where 18 percent of white males of military age perished in the war, death was omnipresent, and fabrics and fashions were scarce. As the *Daily South Carolinian* asked in 1864, "Who has not lost a friend during the war? We are literally a land of mourning." Confederate women, especially in cities and towns, seem to have done all they could to overcome obstacles to securing appropriate mourning dress, which promised the consolation of visibly shared misery. The southern death toll produced a uniformed sorority of grief. As Lucy Breckinridge of Virginia remarked, "There were so many ladies here, all dressed in deep mourning, that we felt as if we were at a convent and formed a sisterhood." When the Yankees entered Richmond in April 1865, a New York newspaperman observed, "the women are nearly all dressed in mourning."[21]

Teenaged Nannie Haskins of Tennessee was outraged when a visitor told her how well she looked in black after her brother's death. "Becomes me fiddlestick," she wrote. "What do I care whether it becomes me or *not*? I don't wear black because it becomes me ... I wear mourning because it corresponds with my feelings." Mourning garb was, to paraphrase language that Saint Augustine used to describe the Christian sacraments, an outward and visible sign of an inward invisible state.[22]

"Women in Mourning, Cemetery in New Orleans." Frank Leslie's
Illustrated Newspaper, *April 25, 1863.*

Susan Caldwell of Warrenton, Virginia, was eager to wear mourning after the death of her child in the fall of 1864. But her husband, Lycurgus, wrote from the army to forbid it. "You have too many things already to remind you of your bereavement and oppress your spirits—and our pecuniary circumstances will not permit it." Susan was not worried about being reminded of her grief; she was not likely to forget it, and she longed for a way to express her sorrow. She sadly but dutifully replied, "My dress at present corresponds but little with my mournful aching heart but I am willing to do as you wish me."[23]

Acquiring mourning apparel in the Civil War South required effort, even ingenuity, and often considerable expenditure. After receiving news of the death of her son Romulus in 1862, Margaret Gwyn of Georgia bought some "mourning goods" at the local store and began to sew a black dress. A woman of modest circumstances, she dyed other of her clothes to make them a suitable expression of

"View of the 'Burnt District,' Richmond, Va." Library of Congress.

her grief. As she worked, "my eyes was often filled with tears which is a relief to the troubled mind." A woman near Fredericksburg could not decide whether to don mourning in 1863, for she was "not willing to leave off col[ors], unless she can procure a handsome outfit in black, and that cannot be had though she is perfectly regardless of expense." Merchants in southern cities and towns announced successful acquisition of fabric and fashions in newspaper advertisements with a triumphant tone that reflected the scarcity of such goods. The *Daily South Carolinian* regularly carried notices when shipments arrived, often smuggled through the blockade. In "News for Ladies" the paper whetted appetites by describing in detail the elaborate mourning attire in fashion across the Atlantic.[24]

In the North, where the rate of death of men of military age was one-third that in the Confederacy, mourning was less universal, and the goods that made it possible proved more readily available.[25] Advertisements in northern papers announced far greater variety and availability of wares both in specialty stores and in more general establishments like New York's Lord & Taylor, which opened its own mourning department in April 1863. At Besson & Son, Mourning Store, at 918 Chestnut Street in Philadelphia, one could find in July 1863—just in time for Gettysburg—a veritable taxonomy of mourning fabrics all but unrecognizable by twenty-first-century Americans:

> Black Crape Grenadines
> Black Balzerines
> Black Baryadere Bareges
> Black Bareges
> Black Barege Hernani, Silk Grenadines, Challies,
>   Summer Bombazines, Mousseline de Laines,
>   Tamises, Mourning Silks, Lawns, Chintzes, Alpacas,
>   Barege Shawls, Grenadine Veils, English Crapes and
>   Veils, Collars, Sleeves &c, &c[26]

Godey's Lady's Book, the most popular American women's periodical and the nation's most important arbiter of fashion, regularly presented drawings of bonnets, collars, sleeves—even breakfast caps—suitable for half or full mourning, as well as illustrations of a variety of mourning dresses for all occasions. Mourning clearly did not dictate seclusion; the fashionable—and wealthy—bereaved woman sought appropriate attire for a wide range of social activities. In 1865 the magazine portrayed a "Promenade Suit for Second Mourning, From the celebrated establishment of Messrs. A T. Stewart & Co. of New York." The elaborate dress and shawl were of white organdy, dotted in black and violet and bordered in slightly different shades of the same. Each issue of *Godey's* featured a full-page hand-tinted portrait of a group of ladies, usually five, modeling a variety of the latest fashions—a "walking costume," a dinner dress, an evening dress, a "visiting dress," a "bridal toilet," or perhaps a "reception dress." One of these ladies was always dressed in mourning. In June 1862, for example, the figure at the far left of the illustration wore a black silk and French grenadine "costume for a watering-place, and suitable for

Lady on far left fashionably dressed in half mourning.
"Godey's Fashions for June 1862." Godey's Lady's Book
and Magazine, *June 1862.*

half mourning," together with a Leghorn hat, trimmed with black velvet and black plume, as she stood beside her companions in dinner dress, walking costume, and riding habit; May 1864 brought an evening dress for second mourning complemented by a coiffure adorned in black velvet and lavender daisies.[27]

Like the formal mourning period, the funeral provided the opportunity for survivors to enact—and thus in some measure assuage—their grief, as well as to honor the deceased. A community of friends and relatives shared this ritual affirmation of loss and marked the new status of each mourner, now deprived of husband, father, brother, or son. Many Civil War funerals were also occasions for displays of patriotism, especially during the early months of the conflict when soldiers' deaths were novel and often marked with elaborate public ceremony. In May 1861, Boston greeted three Massachusetts

"Women in Mourning at Stonewall Jackson's Grave, circa 1866."
Virginia Military Institute Archives.

soldiers killed in secessionist rioting in Baltimore with a procession to the Common, accompanied by a band and crowds of weeping citizens, men and women alike. When Charleston's dead were returned after First Bull Run in July 1861, business was suspended throughout the city, and three cavalry companies escorted the bodies from the railroad station to City Hall, where they lay in state until more than a thousand soldiers accompanied them first to St. Paul's Church for divine services and then to Magnolia Cemetery.[28]

Deaths soon became too numerous to warrant such public demonstrations for any but the most prominent figures. Stonewall Jackson's death in 1863, however, provided the occasion for an outpouring of grief across the Confederacy, for the combination of his legendary piety with his military successes rendered him the ideal embodiment of the Christian Soldier. Lee would indeed have reason to mourn his loss in the campaigns to come, but in marking his death the Confederate nation also asserted its claims to religious superiority. Such a man as Jackson, the observances underlined, would fight only for a cause that had God on its side. Jackson had died in Guiney's Station, Virginia, on Sunday, May 10, 1863, from pneumonia contracted after the amputation of his arm, injured by accidental fire from his own men a week before. Virginia's governor dispatched a railroad car to bring Jackson's remains to Richmond, forty-five miles away. Crowds gathered along the route, and all business in the Confederate capital was suspended. Black crape hung throughout the city; black even decorated the mastheads of the local newspapers; church bells tolled; and thousands assembled to accompany the coffin in a hearse pulled by two white horses to the governor's mansion. Jefferson Davis and other dignitaries paid their respects, though Lee dared not leave his post at the front. Later that night Jackson's body was embalmed and a death mask made of his face. The next day soldiers, Confederate statesmen and cabinet officials, judges, and additional crowds formed a funeral cortege that paraded two and a half miles through central Richmond before depositing Jackson's metal coffin in the Confederate House of Representatives, where twenty thousand filed past well into the night.

The next morning the trip to Jackson's home and burial site in Lexington, Virginia, began. Through two train trips and a final leg on a packet boat, the general's remains were greeted by artillery salutes, the tolling of church bells, garlands of spring flowers, and throngs of grieving admirers. Virginia Military Institute, where Jackson had taught before the war, was ready to receive its son, placing him to lie in state in his old lecture room, then honoring him with a parade of VMI cadets and faculty, local officials, recovering soldiers from a nearby hospital, religious worthies, and a squadron of Confederate cavalry who happened to be passing through town.

By this time, the ceremonies marking his death had gone on for so long that his imperfectly embalmed body began to show signs of deterioration, suggesting that a prompt end to the observances might be in order. The VMI cadet who served as officer of the day later remembered, "His body was said to be embalmed, but of no avail. Decomposition had already taken place, in consequence of which his face was not exposed to view as the features were said not to be natural." Brief funeral services were performed at the Presbyterian church where Jackson had been a deacon. His pastor, William White, offered a Bible reading and a sermon based on Corinthians 1:15: "O death where is thy sting? O grave where is thy victory?" The congregation sang "How Blest the Righteous When He Dies." For this Christian soldier, death was cast as his greatest triumph.[29]

Two springs later another outpouring of grief gripped a segment of Americans quite different from the white southerners who had mourned Jackson. Once again religion and patriotism united in the ritual observance of the passing of one who embodied popular hopes and sacrifices. Lincoln died on Good Friday, less than a week after Lee's surrender, just as the war's killing promised to end. His death was the ultimate death—and became in many ways emblematic of all the losses of the war. A national outpouring of grief represented an aggregation of the war's woe. It was, in the words of one popular song sheet, the "National Funeral." Lincoln's death was at once each soldier's death and all soldiers' deaths, but it also served purposes beyond catharsis. The parallels between Lincoln and Christ were powerful and unavoidable, reinforcing belief in the war's divine purpose, realized through the sacrifice of the one for the many. When Congregational clergyman Leonard Swain proclaimed in an Easter Sunday sermon in Providence that "one man has died for the people, in order that the whole nation might not perish," he invoked the Christian narrative of redemption as well as the very words of Lincoln himself, uttered two years earlier at Gettysburg. Lincoln's death had both broadly transcendent and specifically national significance, tying American purposes to those of God.[30]

Funeral observances for the president acknowledged and intensified his connection with the American people. Twenty-five thousand men and women filed by his open casket as it lay in state in the East Room of the White House. The service itself, by invitation only, was attended by six hundred, not including Mary Lincoln, who was too distraught to appear. A funeral procession of soldiers and dignitaries accompanied Lincoln's hearse, drawn by six gray horses, to the Capitol, where the president lay in state as lines of mourners passed. Across the nation a variety of observances marked the funeral day: a procession of twenty thousand in Memphis, a large gathering in San Francisco, an address by Ralph Waldo Emerson in Massachusetts, and throughout the northern states, as the *New York Herald* reported, "universal suspension of ordinary avocations and a closing of places of business."[31]

From the Capitol, Lincoln's body was taken to the railroad station to begin the seventeen-hundred-mile journey to Springfield, Illinois, and his grave. At each stop—Baltimore, Harrisburg, Philadelphia, New York, Albany, Buffalo, Cleveland, Columbus, Indianapolis, Chicago— mourners paid homage to the slain president. In Philadelphia his coffin lay in Independence Hall, while a column of people three miles long waited to view his remains. In New York the *Herald* estimated that 75,000 marched with his cortege while ten times that number watched from sidewalks and rooftops. Everywhere black Americans seemed to manifest particular sorrow—weeping along the routes of his cortege, marching in proud units of U.S. Colored Troops in processions that accompanied his hearse, writing poems and essays in the African American press, and proclaiming from the pulpit. "We, as a people," declared the pastor of the African Methodist Episcopal Church in Troy, New York, "feel more than all others that we are bereaved. We had learned to love Mr. Lincoln . . . We looked up to him as our saviour, our deliverer."[32]

By the time Lincoln reached Springfield on May 3, the shortcomings of contemporary embalming technology had become apparent, and his face took on a distorted, almost grotesque appearance. But the pageantry did not abate until May 4, when he was laid to rest in Oak Ridge Cemetery on the outskirts of the town he had left for Washington just a little more than four years earlier. A hymn composed for this final ceremony implored:

> *Grant that the cause, for which he died,*
> *May live forever more.*

"President Lincoln's Funeral—Citizens Viewing the Body at the City Hall, New York." Harper's Weekly, *May 6, 1865.*

Lincoln's death contained the redemptive promise of national immortality. But like Jackson's death, Lincoln's passing was marked by an irony that underscored the limitation and even futility of human powers. Jackson died close to the high-water mark of the Confederacy; Lincoln was assassinated just as victory proved firmly in Union grasp.

In the weeks after Lincoln's assassination, Walt Whitman composed three poems of mourning, meditations on the nation's grief. In "Hush'd Be the Camps To-day," written the very day of Lincoln's funeral, Whitman speaks as one of the people, leading the soldiers in mourning and urging the common men to whom he is so devoted to join him in tribute to "our dear commander."

> *Sing of the love we bore him—because you, dwellers in*
> *camps, know it truly.*
>
> *As they invault the coffin there,*
> *Sing...*
> *For the heavy hearts of soldiers.*[33]

"O Captain! My Captain," composed several months later during the summer of 1865, again invokes popular grief. It is, as literary scholar Helen Vendler explains, "a designedly democratic and populist poem," with a meter and refrain designed for public tastes. The regular rhythm and rhyme are uncharacteristic of Whitman's work, and "O Captain!" is probably the easiest of his poems to memorize and recite. In the voice of a young sailor, Whitman composed an elegy in "democratic style," speaking this time not for the collectivity of soldiers or for generalized sorrow but for the searing grief of a single man, in a representation of the individual pain of which the cumulative loss is constituted.[34]

> *Here Captain! Dear father*
> *The arm beneath your head!*
> *It is some dream that on the deck,*
> *You've fallen cold and dead.*[35]

In the third of these 1865 poems, "When Lilacs Last in the Dooryard Bloom'd," Whitman speaks as himself, of his own efforts to grapple with Lincoln's loss. The president's assassination is not explicitly mentioned; it is as if there is no need to specify the tragedy that occurred when lilacs last bloomed, for it is both known and common to all. The experiences of mourning have been shared as the coffin has journeyed "night and day" across the land. Like a series of photographs, the poem captures this experience, rendering the seventeen-hundred-mile funeral procession in scenes of lingering visual power.

> *Coffin that passes through lanes and streets,*
> *Through day and night with the great cloud darkening the*
> *   land,*
>
> . . . .
>
> *With processions long and winding and the flambeaus of the*
> *   night,*
> *With the countless torches lit, with the silent sea of faces and*
> *   the unbared heads,*
> *With the waiting depot, the arriving coffin, and the somber*
> *   faces,*
> *With the dirges through the night, with the thousand voices*
> *   rising strong and solemn . . .* [36]

The poem invokes no consoling Christian doctrines of immortality, and Whitman makes no reference to the pervasive contemporary imagery of Good Friday and the crucifixion. "Lilacs" suggests no promise of an afterlife beyond that of nature's own renewal. For Whitman, immortality rested, as he wrote in another poem, in mother earth's absorption of bodies and blood rendered "in unseen essence and odor of surface and grass, centuries hence." Dissenting from the comforting Christian redefinition of death into life, "Lilacs" embraces, in Vendler's words, "the value of acceptance, rather than denial, of the full stop of death." Yet for those who remain alive to mourn, death provides no full stop.

I saw the debris and debris of all the slain soldiers of
the war.

. . . .

They themselves were fully at rest, they suffer'd not,
The living remain'd and suffer'd, the mother suffer'd,
And the wife and the child and the musing comrade
suffer'd,
And the armies that remain'd suffer'd.[37]

In his 1865 Lincoln poems Walt Whitman served, as he had throughout the war, as the poet not just of death but of survival, of the suffering of the not-dead. Whitman's was the cultural work of mourning—on behalf of the nation and, in this instance, for its beloved leader. Yet he mourned, as he wrote in "Lilacs," "not for you, for one alone." He mourned for all the war's slain—for the "ashes of all dead soldiers South or North," for the "phantoms of countless lost" who "follow me ever—desert me not while I live." Lost yet not lost, absent yet ever present, these dead, these immortal phantoms with their unrelenting demands on mourners and survivors, became in Whitman's eyes the meaning and legacy of the war. Lincoln was but their finest exemplar.[38]

Perhaps the extravaganza of mourning that greeted the public commemorations of Jackson and Lincoln served in some way as a surrogate for all the funerals that citizens could not attend as their loved ones died unattended and far away. The many soldiers buried on the field received only the attention a chaplain and their harried comrades might afford, and as we have seen, tens of thousands of men were interred without either identities or ritual observances. Families fortunate enough to retrieve bodies and bring them home, however, honored their dead with services that varied according to status, circumstance, and religious affiliation. Mary Chesnut remarked that the sound of the funeral march seemed almost constant in South Carolina. Many small communities on the other side of the Mason-Dixon line found the same. In Dorset, Vermont, home of a quarry that provided thousands of tombstones for Gettysburg, 144 men volunteered and 28 died. Funerals in Dorset seemed never-ending and sometimes occurred in bunches when a unit with numbers of local men suffered heavy losses. In Worcester, Massachusetts, 4,227 men out of a total city population of 25,000 went to war, and 398 died. Nantucket received communications from the mainland only three times a week, when a steamer would arrive with its flag at half-mast if it brought news of casualties. Residents watching for the boat would be weeping before it even arrived at the dock. Seventy-three Nantucketers out of a population of about 6,000 died in the war, with 8 killed and 13 wounded at the Battle of Fredericksburg alone. When Lieutenant Leander Alley's body arrived home almost two weeks after the battle, "hundreds of people" called at his mother's house to view the body, which one of his commanding officers had paid to have embalmed before its shipment north. Schools and stores closed in his honor, and family and neighbors gathered for "impressive funeral services" and a lengthy procession to the Unitarian cemetery.[39]

In the Confederacy, Clark Stewart, a Presbyterian clergyman, divided his time between Virginia hospitals and his South Carolina home, where he traveled about visiting bereaved families and presiding over funerals of soldiers returned from the battlefield. In his journal he noted the biblical verse he selected for each occasion. "Funeral sermon for Robt Hellams who fell at Fburg John 14:18," his diary entry for January 18, 1863, read. "I will not leave you comfortless; I will come to you" was an especially appropriate text for this itinerant clergyman.[40]

The proffering of comfort was a key function of the sermons that served as the heart of almost every funeral service, however modest or extravagant. But the oration was intended to assist mourners in understanding as well as alleviating their grief. Funeral sermons usually attempted to define the meaning of the deceased's life and death, an effort that almost inevitably involved speculating on the nature of death itself. In both North and South many of these wartime sermons, as well as funeral biographies and memorials that grew out of them, appeared in print, ranging in size from a pamphlet of a few pages to full-sized octavos designed to serve as monuments to the dead and exhortations to the living. Almost without exception they drew explicitly upon details in the condolence letters that had announced the soldier's death in order to fashion a more formalized and self-conscious story of a life and its significance. In his funeral sermon for John W. Griffin, a young Confederate chaplain who died in 1864, for example, L. H. Blanton referred to reports of the deceased's last words and offered the consoling judgment that Griffin's "dying testimony was all that Christian friends or the Church of God could desire."[41]

The Good Death was the foundation for the process of mourning carried on by survivors who used the last words and moments of the dead soldier as the basis for broader evaluation of his entire life. More considered, more polished than condolence letters written from the front, the published funeral sermon was intended for distribution to a wider audience than simply next of kin or even those who might be able to attend a funeral service. The lost life, the soldier's death no longer belonged just to that individual and his family but was also to be understood and possessed by the community—even the nation— at large. The funeral sermon, like the ritual that surrounded it, was a memorial, not in granite, but in words; it sought, like the Good Death itself, to ensure that dying was not an end, not an isolated act, itself undertaken in isolation, but a foundation for both spiritual and social immortality—for eternal life and lasting memory.[42]

Dabney Carr Harrison of Virginia, shot through the lungs at Fort Donelson, reportedly murmured, "It is all right! I am perfectly willing to die." For Reverend William James Hoge, composing a sketch of Dabney's life, this phrase became the all-important message of Christian sacrifice, an emulation of the Savior himself: however bitter the cup of pain and grief put into his hands by his heavenly Father, he would still say as he drank, "It is all right." The entire life that Hoge recounted became a prelude to this final defining moment. Born on the Sabbath, Harrison died on the Sabbath, "his life bounded on either hand by the Day of God."[43]

Into the feelings of waste and futility represented by so many foreshortened young lives, funeral sermons injected the consolation of narrative, of a story with a purposeful trajectory and an ending that showed death was never premature but always came at exactly the right time in accordance with God's design. "The child of scarce unfolded piety, and the veteran Christian, alike yield up to God in death a mortality mysteriously compact," a New York sermon proclaimed, "the work both had to do on earth being as completely done, as if each had been assigned the longest period known to man." Reverend Philip Slaughter found in the life of Randolph Fairfax narrative continuities that might not have been evident before his heroic death. Slaughter noted that the dead Confederate always played fairly as a boy and obeyed his mother, had requested a Bible for his fourteenth birthday, and carried a New Testament in battle. When he was killed instantly by a shell at Fredericksburg, the testimony of his life served, in Slaughter's view, to provide the certainty of salvation that Fairfax himself had been unable to articulate. As Reverend Robert Dabney explained in a memorial to Lieutenant Colonel John Thornton, "he being dead, yet speaketh," through the "narrative of... [his] religious life." The dead carried a message from God, and in some sense were themselves that message, as Dabney made clear in another sermon, this one to honor Stonewall Jackson: "Our dead hero is God's sermon to us. His embodied admonition, His incorporate discourse."[44]

Soldiers remembered in published funeral sermons and biographies were usually individuals of considerable importance, with families of sufficient means to sponsor these memorials. Almost always they were officers. These soldiers were markedly less representative of the masses of Civil War armies than were the men whose deaths were reported in the stream of private condolence letters written by comrades to send news of particular deaths to loved ones at home. But the existence of these more polished and elaborated printed efforts to grapple with death and its meaning represent many more such sermons that never made their way into print. The cultural, emotional, spiritual, and ideological work that the privileged sought to accomplish with printed sermons was work that mourners from ordinary families would have needed to undertake as well—even if they lacked the resources to publish books and pamphlets that would be available to historians more than a century later. Beneath these countless historical silences, ordinary Americans were also struggling to come to terms with their losses.

How to mourn was often something that had to be learned, and the work of funeral sermons was to teach these lessons too. The orations of two clergymen, one northern, one southern, offer a primer in grief and consolation, articulating accepted understanding of what we today would call the psychology of loss, as well as the means of explaining and alleviating sorrow. At an upstate New York funeral service for Lieutenant Colonel James M. Green, whose body lay unidentified and unrecovered on Morris Island in South Carolina, Reverend Charles Seymour Robinson reminded the mourners that "time in a measure will help you." God's mercy had provided that "months and years" would lessen the "first violence of a sudden affliction." The bereaved would always feel their loss, he acknowledged, and always remember the departed with affection. But "you will," he assured them, "by and by be able to look calmly on these days of grief." Robinson listed three specific sources of consolation. "Patriotism," he declared, "will come in to aid in mitigating the sorrow. These times are historic." In a few years, he assured his listeners, they would look back and proudly recount the sacrifices of their dead, giving their lives for their country. A second source of comfort would be the sympathy of others. Shared mourning, he affirmed, was easier mourning. Finally, and "above all, the sublime hopes of the gospel will be a solace to you." The slain soldier, like Christ himself, would rise again. Robinson offered the distressed the healing forces of time, nation, community, and God.[45]

In the South, Joseph Cross of Tennessee chose to speak "On Grief" in his funeral oration for General Daniel Donelson. He began by assuring the mourners that sorrow was no sin. "There is no guilt in tears, if they are not tears of despair. It is no crime to feel our loss ... Religion," he explained, "does not destroy nature, but regu-

lates it, does not remove sorrow, but sanctifies it." Christian faith
and human psychology were in his view deeply intertwined, and
each supported and nourished the other. Cross enumerated biblical mourners—Abraham for Sarah, Joseph for Jacob, David for
Jonathan—to establish the history and legitimacy of grief. Acceptance of sorrow, he recognized, was a critical part of realizing death.
It was important to suffer in the face of loss, not to deny or suppress
it. "He that is not sensible of the affliction," Cross warned, "will continue secure in his sin." Survivors must feel "the stroke." Cross counseled the importance of what we of the twenty-first century would
call catharsis: "Grief must have vent, or it will break the heart . . . It is
cruel to deny one the relief of mourning when mourning is so often
its own relief." Like Robinson—and, indeed, like Freud—Cross understood mourning as a process and promised his congregation
progress through grief to some measure of recovery. Like Robinson
as well, Cross offered shared suffering as solace: "Sorrow calls for
sympathy. Compassion is better than counsel . . . Sympathy divides
the sorrow, and leaves but half the load."

But Cross worried about "excess of sorrow" and asked, "Where,
then, is the proper limit?" Sorrow, he posited, was "criminal" when it
obscured awareness of "remaining mercies." Things could always be
worse. Grief was excessive when it made the mourner forget the
afflictions of others or become "indifferent to the public welfare" or
neglectful of responsibilities to others or to personal health. Grief
was "excessive, and therefore criminal," he repeated, when it ignored
God's purposes and consolations. Like Robinson, Cross noted that
there was a contained "time for mourning," with a finite end, even
though the "inward sorrow . . . may last much longer than the outward show." The bereaved must work to alleviate their grief, attending to the solaces of friendship and religion. Robinson offered
sources of comfort and help; Cross included with his consolations a
series of warnings; both promised a gradual end to the agony of loss
to be achieved through the work of mourning.[46]

Some mourners reported quite explicitly their efforts to manage
grief, demonstrating a keen and self-conscious awareness of the pro-

cess both Robertson and Cross described. Henry Bowditch, father of Nathaniel, who was killed in Virginia in March 1863, kept a careful record of his experience of loss, from his physical reaction—"like a dagger in my heart"—to the news of his son's injury, to the consolations that ultimately liberated him from a world of pain.[47]

Bowditch "broke fairly down" when he was told of Nathaniel's death. But "almost immediately," he reported, "the divine influences of such a loss began to strive for mastery . . . & I thought that never was there a nobler cause for which he could have died." Henry Bowditch assured himself that Nat, described to him as "brave and conscious to the last," had indeed experienced a Good Death, had repeatedly professed his Christian faith and willingness to die during the three days after he was wounded. Nathaniel had certainly "died happily," a fellow soldier assured the father. Bowditch embraced the very consolations that the *ars moriendi* offered and that Robinson had prescribed. From Nat's death, he explained to his wife, he would derive even greater commitment to the doctrines of immortality, and these would sustain him in his loss. Just a day after Nat died, Bowditch wrote from Virginia of his determination "after as short a delay as possible" to "return to life & (made—oh! how blank!) to my accustomed work." The very phrase displayed the difficulty he faced: the sober dedication to reasoned self-control and to a swift resumption of normal existence, interrupted by the powerful emotions of emptiness and loss that undermined his rational intentions.[48]

Bowditch was not prepared for the force of grief that overtook him. In Virginia to retrieve Nat's body he sought "concealment" from others lest they witness the feelings he could not hide. He judged himself "ill fitted to see anyone" and was distressed by his "display of unmanliness." In its implications of loss of control and of weakness, grief seemed to challenge and erode masculinity. Men would find it especially difficult to acknowledge their sorrow and truly mourn.[49]

When the solace Bowditch sought in faith and nation proved insufficient to mitigate his sorrow, he seemed bewildered that he was unable to contain his grief. With tears as "my constant companion," he confessed, "my heart seems almost breaking." But, he wondered,

Henry Ingersoll Bowditch at the time of the
Civil War. Harvard University Archives.

"why do I complain?" There could not have been "a more noble life
or a more noble death." What more could he have hoped for? But
this knowledge was not enough. "My whole nature yearns to see &
hear him once again." For months, Bowditch found, "the full force
of . . . affliction would press itself forwards and my first sorrow would
return." It was in vain that he sought refuge in "other sustaining
thoughts" of God and country. Grief was so overpowering that his
resolution to return promptly to regular life and work proved impossible. "For months at times I have been unable to work at all."[50]

Bowditch found his feelings reflected in a poem entitled "My
Child," by John Pierpont, a fellow abolitionist, a Unitarian clergyman, and a friend. The poem, Bowditch wrote, "tells the tale far better than I can in prose the real story of my constant thought of my
soldier boy"; it represented the kind of sharing of sorrow Robinson

and Cross had advised, and it offered as well a narrative of redemption from suffering and from death. The poet, like Bowditch, could not believe—could not "realize"—this son's death. "I cannot make him dead!" the first line proclaimed. He saw his "fair sunshining head," heard his footfall, expected his arrival, but "he is not there!" Like Bowditch yearning with his whole nature to see his son again, the poet at last accepts his child's absence and then is free to ask the question that will lead to an alleviation of his pain: "Where is he?" The poem ends with the assurance that "we all live to God!," that we all will meet "in the spirit land," and "twill be our heaven to find that—he is there!" Accepting a son's terrestrial death was the first step toward denial of his death in another realm, a sustaining affirmation that elsewhere he was still alive. Pierpont's poem aided Bowditch in his effort to move to "Hope rather than Mourning."[51]

At the same time Bowditch was struggling spiritually to deal with Nat's loss, he also undertook actions within the world to express and relieve his grief, as well as to ensure Nat's continuing presence in memory. Arranging for the body to be embalmed so that "it may be seen on my return to Boston" by Nat's mother, fiancée, siblings, and friends, who were also in need of solace, Bowditch shared his sorrow with the dozens of mourners who attended Nat's funeral. "You have not lost him," Reverend James Freeman Clarke's sermon comforted them; he was "not dead but alive with a higher life"; he was "just the other side of the veil," where "he says . . . I wait for you all."[52]

Bowditch supplemented the formal rituals of religion with rituals of his own. From a ring given Nat by his fiancée together with a "cavalry button cut from his blood-stained vest," Bowditch fashioned an amulet that he attached to his watch: "There I trust they will remain until I die." For Nat's grave at Mount Auburn Cemetery, Bowditch designed another embodiment of his life, exactly copying his sword in stone to serve as a monument. Unable to overcome his preoccupation with his dead son, Bowditch turned his distress into consoling activity, compiling elaborate memorial volumes and scrapbooks that traced Nat from birth to death, a "collation of the letters, journals &c

illustrative of his dear young life." Bowditch did not complete this extensive and therapeutic effort until 1869. "The labor was a sweet one. It took me out of myself." Coping with Nat's death required a transcendence and transformation of self.[53]

Henry Bowditch undertook another action in relief of his own suffering and in honor and memory of his son. His preoccupation with Nat would serve as a lever at last to get, as he put it, "out of myself" and out of his grief in order once again to embrace his reformist commitments: he made Nat's death, and the long abandonment on the battlefield without medical care that preceded it, a cause célèbre in the effort to establish adequate ambulance service in the Union army, a goal that was achieved in the last year of the war. Bowditch transformed Nat's suffering into the salvation of others.

In the twenty-first century Americans considering the impact of death regularly invoke the notion of "closure," the hope and anticipation of an end to the disruption of loss. Civil War Americans expected no such relief. For hundreds of thousands, the unknown fate of missing kin left a "dread void of uncertainty" that knowledge would never fill. Even for those who had detailed information or, better still, the consolation of a body and a grave, mourning had no easy or finite end. Many bereaved spent the rest of their lives waiting for the promised heavenly reunion with those who had gone before. Wives, parents, children, and siblings struggled with the new identities—widows, orphans, the childless—that now defined their lives. And they carried their losses into the acts of memory that both fed on and nurtured the widely shared grief well into the next century.

But if such devastating loss could not be denied, if it was "realized" and acknowledged, it had to be explained. The Civil War's carnage required that death be given meaning.

CHAPTER 6

BELIEVING AND DOUBTING

"What Means this Carnage?"

"How does God have the heart to allow it?"
SIDNEY LANIER

W hat is Death?" Reverend John Sweet asked "a large assemblage" of mourners dressed in "somber black" who had gathered at services for Edward Amos Adams of the 59th Massachusetts in July 1864. Adams had died ten days after being wounded at Petersburg, a victim in the series of bloody assaults that Grant had launched in the effort to dislodge Lee's army from its position some twenty miles south of Richmond. Age twenty-four, a member of Billerica's Baptist church, a seaman turned teacher, Adams took his place in a long line of losses suffered by his community and his state. "Once again," Sweet observed, "we are in the house of mourning." Another soldier killed; another family bereaved; another funeral observed: "There is not a household exempt from the universal lamentation which ascends from a grief stricken people." More than three years into the conflict Sweet turned to what had become a central question, even preoccupation, for many Americans of both North and South. Where had all those young men gone? Friends and relatives who rushed to battlefields in the effort to locate their bodies undertook what was in some sense just the first step in the search for the missing. Even if their material remains could be retrieved and decently buried, the fate of the self and the soul, as well as the meaning of the departed life, remained unknown. Survivors like those gathered on a

New England midsummer's day in 1864 asked with new war-born urgency what happened when life on earth ceased.[1]

Americans on the eve of civil war found their traditional systems of belief both powerfully challenged and fervently reaffirmed. Although the United States had been established as a secular state by founders wary of religious influences upon government, religion defined the values and assumptions of most mid-nineteenth-century Americans. Nearly four times as many attended church every Sunday in 1860 as voted in that year's critical presidential election. Overwhelmingly Christian and Protestant, Americans were also increasingly evangelical, committed to the hope of salvation, and eager to seize their own responsibility for any future beyond the grave. Calvinist notions of predestination that had characterized much of American Christianity in the colonial era had yielded to waves of nineteenth-century revivals, culminating in widespread religious enthusiasm in the 1850s. Historian Richard Carwardine has concluded that by midcentury "over 10 million Americans, or about 40 percent of the population, appear . . . to have been in close sympathy with evangelical Christianity. This was the largest, and most formidable, subculture in American society." With its concerted attention to salvation, evangelicalism made the afterlife the focus of American religious belief and practice.[2]

Still, reflective Christians in this nineteenth-century age of progress faced troubling questions about the foundations of their faith. New historical and philological scholarship and new forms of textual criticism had raised doubts about the literal truth of the Bible. As southerners amassed evidence of scriptural support for slavery, antislavery northerners sought and found different meanings. These divisions in interpretation marked more than just sectional disagreement; they represented a new uncertainty about the undisputed and indisputable power of the Bible itself, an unsettling contingency that struck at the very bases of conviction.

Even more disturbing than issues of biblical interpretation were the questions that science posed for religious belief. Geological discoveries about the vast age of the Earth discredited scriptural accounts of creation, suggesting a much diminished and distanced role for any divine creator. Charles Lyell's *Principles of Geology,* published in the early 1830s, challenged the veracity of Genesis by demonstrating that the Earth was millions of years old, not the six or seven thousand postulated by Scripture. Darwin's theories of evolution, shared and discussed in preliminary form with American scientists well before the publication of *The Origin of Species* in 1859, further challenged biblical literalism and replaced notions of divine teleology and benevolence with the heartless mechanisms of natural selection.[3]

Nevertheless, traditional religious arguments from design, which understood God to be the prime mover behind all scientific processes, rationalized persisting faith in a divine presence; most Americans continued to regard science and religion as in alliance rather than in conflict well into the late nineteenth century. But this reconciliation required intellectual effort and left its adherents with a universe in which the place of both humans and God had changed. The possibility and plausibility of scientific explanation strengthened the claims of the rational and worldly against the force of the transcendent. Humans had been moved into the realm of animals, and God threatened a distressing indifference to the fall of every sparrow.[4]

Rather than emphasizing the compatibility of new discoveries with older beliefs, some Americans sought to fuel skepticism about revealed religion. The intellectual ferment of New England Transcendentalism challenged many accepted religious truths. As early as the 1830s Ralph Waldo Emerson announced in a lecture at Harvard Divinity School that he no longer believed in the divinity of Christ. "I regard it as the irresistible effect of the Copernican astronomy to have made the theological *scheme of Redemption* absolutely incredible." Freethinkers like Robert Owen and Fanny Wright argued for a materialism that reduced human consciousness to nothing more than brain function, a position reinforced by widely hailed, if still controversial, neurological discoveries about cerebral localization. Phrenology, the belief that character and personality could be derived from the shape and contours of the head, brought these ideas to a wide popular audience. Poet James Russell Lowell described how this growing materialism had begun to define the age:

> *This nineteenth century with its knife and glass*
> *That make thought physical.*

Uncertainty about the relationship of biology and consciousness, of body and soul, troubled even the most devout, who speculated about the definition of the human spirit and the justification for belief in immortality.[5]

Into this environment of cultural ferment, the Civil War introduced mass death. For an increasingly humanitarian age, such suffering could not help but raise disturbing questions about God's benevolence and agency. But this was more than an abstract intellectual issue for the hundreds of thousands of Americans bereaved by the war. Loss demanded an explanation that satisfied hearts as well as minds.

Religion remained the most readily available explanatory resource, even as it was challenged by rapid cultural and intellectual change. Reverend John Sweet's all-too-timely query, "What is Death?" had long served as a foundation and central concern of Christian doctrine. Sweet's answer, "It is the middle point between two lives," reveals much of the substance and the solace of belief. In the face of war's slaughter, mid-nineteenth-century religion promised that there need be no death. Only a willful failure to believe could bring humans to the dread "second death" that cast them into hell. "Turn ye! Turn ye! for why will ye die?" a chaplain's powerful sermon demanded of Confederate soldiers; "Why Will You Die?" a widely distributed Confederate tract reiterated. Death was a matter of choice and could be consciously rejected in favor of immortality. Soldiers need not be victims; even if their earthly destiny was beyond their control, they remained the masters of their more important eternal fate.[6]

Such convictions, as we have seen in the ritual of the Good Death, made both dying and mourning easier. Some historians have argued that, in fact, only the widespread existence of such beliefs made acceptance of the Civil War death tolls possible, and that religion thus in some sense enabled the slaughter. Confidence in immortality could encourage soldiers to risk annihilation. Civil War Americans themselves would not have questioned what one Confederate chaplain called the *"military power of religion."* It is hard to imagine today a letter like the one a northern nurse sent from the front to a friend in 1864: "I should hardly think it worthwhile," she remarked, "for Rebecca to grieve much for a dead person for she certainly will soon be with them in heaven." Firm conviction could yield confidence that bordered on heartlessness and, in some cases, behavior that approached recklessness. But the long tradition of Christian soldiery would have cast religion's contributions to war more positively, emphasizing faith as a fundamental motivation to religious and patriotic duty. Evangelical tracts and preachers, for example, repeatedly invoked the word "efficiency" in their communications to the troops. The Christian soldier, these preachers and exhorters explained, would be an efficient soldier because he would execute his obligations "conscientiously" and would not be afraid to die.[7]

Thomas B. Hampton of southwest Virginia became an exemplar of such a man, filling his letters to his wife, Jestin, with professions of his steadily growing religious faith as his regiment passed through the trials of Chickamauga, Resaca, and Atlanta. When the Confederate army was convulsed by religious revivals from the fall of 1862 onward, Hampton increasingly looked toward refuge in a "heaven where wars & rumors of wars are no more." His company, he reported, held prayer meetings "nearly every night . . . a beautiful and sublime sight." War, he found, was weaning him "from the things of this world." His anticipations of death as relief from the horrors of battle focused his mind on what preachers like John Sweet offered as a second life beyond the grave: "although I may fall by the sword or by the missiles of the enemy I will fear no evil for I verily believe that my sole will be loosed from this prision of mortality to traverse the regions of the celestial skies of Glory I may fall by some of the monsters Disease of camp but still I will put my trust in the Lord for he knoweth all things and doth all things aright."[8]

For hundreds of thousands of soldiers, some believers before their enlistment but many converted by revivals that swept armies of both North and South, death became a fixation. But often it was not so much as a fear but as a promise—of relief, of salvation from war and suffering, and of an escape into a better world. "I rather believe," Thomas Hampton wrote, "if my friends knew the hardships that is incumbent on a soldier that they would scarsely begrudge a withdrawal from this Tabernacle of Mortality to that of Immortal Glory for which I often long to see." Death offered these devout men a "change" but not an ending; the celestial skies of Glory became more alluring than the bloody fields of Georgia or Virginia. Spared the direct experience of combat, civilians were less likely to acknowledge death's attractions, but they too found in religious doctrine the means to diminish its horror and to manage the losses war inflicted upon them. As Hampton's wife explained, "I suffer all the time about you. Not half So much as I should if I knew you were not prepared. That is the greatest comfort of all believing if you fall by the hand of the enemy or disease you will rest in heaven . . . if it was not for the great hope I have I never could bear up under the present distress."[9]

Thomas Hampton survived until the very last month of the war, when he was mortally wounded near Bentonville, North Carolina. His obituary reported that he died "in the full triumphs of faith." Hampton sent word to Jestin "not to greave for him for he was going to be far better off than . . . in this troublesome world." He would see her again in "Bright mansions above."[10]

There has been much discussion in our own time of the denial of death, of the refusal of contemporary American culture to confront or discuss it. In widely read books and essays published in the 1970s and early 1980s, historian Philippe Ariès accused Western Europe and the United States of making death "invisible." Modern dying, he argued, had been medicalized; mourning was regarded as "indecent." Death had become as unmentionable as pornography.[11] In the Civil War death was hardly hidden, but it was nevertheless, seemingly paradoxically, denied—not through silence and invisibility but through an active and concerted work of reconceptualization that rendered it a cultural preoccupation. Redefined as eternal life, death was celebrated in mid-nineteenth-century America. But its centrality, in popular culture as well as religious discourse, suggested that great effort was required to control and repudiate its terrors. Songs, poems, and stories struggled to answer the same question Reverend Sweet had posed to his afflicted congregation. "My God! What is all this For?" the title on one songsheet demanded:

> *"Oh great god! What means this carnage,*
> *Why this fratricidal strife,*
> *Brethren made in your own image*
> *Seeking for each other's life?"*

> *Thus spoke a dying Federal soldier,*
> *Amid the clash of arms he cried;*
> *With hope he fixed his eyes on heaven,*
> *Then bid adieu to earth—and died.*[12]

These verses left their own question unanswered, with heaven only a hope, but other songs promised that an afterlife would "turn our mourning into joy" and assured, "Mother, I die happy," for "I see the angels coming, / With bright garlands for my brow." To a chorus that asked, "Shall we know each other, shall we know each other, shall we know each other there?" a ballad published in New York confirmed that "Ye shall join the loved and lost ones / In the land of perfect day . . . 'We shall know each other there.' "[13]

Heaven would re-create earthly ties in a realm of perfection and joy. Death as termination of life simply did not exist. A July 1863 poem in a popular Philadelphia magazine decisively erased death, even as more than six thousand soldiers were expiring in a Pennsylvania town little more than a hundred miles away.

There is no Death! The stars go down
　To rise upon some fairer shore;
And bright in heaven's jeweled crown
　They shine forevermore.

. . . .

And ever near us, though unseen,
　The dear, immortal spirits tread;
For all the boundless Universe
　Is Life—There are no Dead.[14]

The prominence of heaven in the discourse about Civil War death derived in part from the attractive place it had gradually become during the preceding century. The publication of Emanuel Swedenborg's *Heaven and Hell* in 1758 marked the origins of an important movement away from a conception of heaven as forbiddingly ascetic, distant from earth and its materiality, and highly theocentric. Instead, a more modern notion of heaven began to emerge as a realm hardly separate or different—except in its perfection—from Earth itself. "Man after death," wrote Swedenborg, "is as much man as he was before, so much so as to be unaware that he is not still in the former world ... Death is only a crossing." At the same time, hell became less and less a subject for worry or dread.[15]

Swedenborgianism as an organized denomination never came to hold more than a marginal place within American religious life. But Swedenborg's ideas attracted widespread attention in the United States, and Americans from Johnny Appleseed to Ralph Waldo Emerson, Henry Ward Beecher and Henry James Sr. cited its influences. "This age is Swedenborg's," Emerson proclaimed in 1858. Swedenborgian thought made a significant mark upon Transcendentalism and encouraged tendencies toward a softening view of heaven across American religious denominations. As historian James H. Moorhead has demonstrated, the second half of the nineteenth century witnessed a muting of the "negative images traditionally associated with life's end." A new eschatology that influenced nearly all of Protestant thought "sought to narrow the distance between this world and the next, even to annex heaven as a more glorious suburb of the present life."[16]

But this transition remained incomplete as the Civil War opened. Emily Dickinson was not alone in the concerns she voiced about the forbidding nature of the afterlife in her wartime poetry and letters: "Heaven is so cold!"; "I don't like Paradise—Because it's Sunday—all the time." The transformation of heaven intensified as war made questions about immortality more immediate and more widely shared. Historians Colleen McDannell and Bernhard Lang have noted that more than fifty books on heaven were published in the United States between 1830 and 1875, but this total does not include fictional works, or the dozens of Civil War funeral sermons appearing as printed pamphlets that made heaven a central theme, or the many periodical and newspaper articles with titles like "Heaven, the House of God" (which appeared in the columns of the *Daily South Carolinian* in 1864), or popular poetry that addressed the nature of the afterlife in rhyme (like "Hereafter" or "Up to the Hills," from *Harper's New Monthly Magazine*). In 1863 *Harper's Weekly* announced a second edition of William Branks's *Heaven Our Home* as a promising "New Source of Consolation" and reported it to be "having a large sale." It was one of three titles Branks produced about heaven during these years. Historian Phillip Shaw Paludan counts nearly a hundred books on heaven in the decade after the war alone. The geography and society of the afterlife persisted as widespread concerns, for even when the slaughter had ceased, loss and grief remained.[17]

An issue of particular focus in this literature, and in the struggle to come to terms with death, was the fate of human relationships in the afterlife. If death was no longer to be an ending, it would also no longer be a parting. Earlier visions of heaven had focused almost exclusively on the connection between God and man within the heavenly kingdom, even to the point of denying the persistence of earthly ties of family and friendship. But Swedenborg and thinkers influenced by his views created the foundation for what now came to seem a necessary component of an adequately consoling portrait of paradise.

Presbyterian Robert Patterson acknowledged in his *Visions of Heaven for the Life on Earth,* published a decade after the war, that earlier conceptions of heaven that had excluded the continuation of love and friendship were "very chilling." The era of Victorian domesticity could not tolerate the obliteration of these cherished ties of home and family. The widespread assumption among Civil War Americans that they would one day be reunited with lost kin was fundamental to the solace of religious faith. When *Harper's Weekly* published its notice of the best-selling *Heaven Our Home,* the aspect of the book it found most worthy of comment was that its author supported "the comforting belief of the recognition of friends in Heaven, which to him is a *home,* with a great, and happy and loving family in it." Seven of the book's chapters were specifically devoted to "Recognition of Friends in Heaven." If soldiers needed to be assured they would not really die, survivors yearned to know their loved ones were not—even if they were missing or unknown— forever lost. "They will not leave us long," one South Carolina woman affirmed. They were "only gone before." Jews as well as Christians invoked these consolations. Rebecca Gratz comforted her brother Ben about his son's death in 1861 by reassuring him "they shall be reunited in another world." The Civil War made urgent the transformation of heaven into an eternal family reunion, encouraging notions of an afterlife that was familiar and close at hand, populated by loved ones who were just "beyond the veil."[18]

Many bereaved Americans, however, were unwilling to wait until their own deaths reunited them with lost kin, and they turned eagerly to the more immediate promises of spiritualism. A series of spirit rappings in upstate New York in the late 1840s had intensified spreading interest in the apparent reality of communication between the living and the dead. To an age increasingly caught up in the notion of science as the measure of truth, spiritualism offered belief that seemed to rely on empirical evidence rather than revelation and faith. If the dead could cause tables to rise, telegraph messages from the world beyond, and even communicate in lengthy statements through spirit mediums, an afterlife clearly must exist. Here was, in the words of one popular spiritualist advocate, "proof palpable of immortality."[19]

Men and women began to participate in regular spirit circles in hopes of communicating with the dead. By 1853 one spiritualist estimated that thirty such groups met regularly in the city of Philadelphia alone, and that thirty thousand mediums were operating across the country. The *Spiritualist Register* reported that just before the outbreak of war 240,000 inhabitants of New York State—6 percent of its total population—were spiritualists. Strongest in the Northeast, where it often attracted abolitionists, feminists, and adherents of other radical social movements, spiritualism had its southern disciples as well, an estimated 20,000 in Louisiana, for example, and 10,000 in Tennessee. In the mid-1850s South Carolina planter and politician James Henry Hammond and author William Gilmore Simms, both vigorous proslavery advocates, explored spiritualism as an alternative to what they regarded as the unconvincing tenets of revealed religion. Simms believed he had successfully communicated with his dead children, and Hammond developed a series of questions for the dead that Simms posed to a medium on a visit to New York.[20]

By the time war broke out, spiritualist notions were sufficiently common to influence and engage even those who were not formal adherents, and the war made spiritualist doctrines increasingly attractive. Mary Todd Lincoln sought regularly to communicate with her dead son Willie. She sponsored a number of séances at the White House, some of which the president himself was said to have attended. Henry Bowditch was no spiritualist but found deep comfort after Nathaniel's death in the explicitly spiritualist outlook of the author of the poem "My Child." John Pierpont, fellow New Englander and fellow abolitionist, offered Bowditch

> *The promise That in the spirit-land,*
> *Meeting at thy right hand,*
> *'Twill be our heaven to find that—he is there!*

Bowditch's struggle to grapple with—to "realize"—the loss of his son was made considerably easier by Pierpont's assurance that he was only invisible, that he lived on in another, only temporarily inaccessible world. Swedenborg's comforting ideas about heaven were central to spiritualist ideology and spiritualism's appeal, and such sentiments played a prominent place in Nathaniel's funeral sermon as well, which assured mourners that "he is just the other side of the thin veil . . . He stands there, waiting till you come."[21]

In New Orleans an officer of the Native Guard led an active spiritualist circle called the Grandjean Séance. Within weeks of André Cailloux's death, the group made contact with their departed hero. "They thought they had killed me but they made me live," Cailloux reported from the afterlife. "It will be I who receive you into our world if you die in the struggle, so fight!" He consoled his black comrades that "there must be victims to serve as stepping stones on the path to liberty."[22]

Extensive marketing of the planchette, precursor of the Ouija board, during the 1860s, and especially in the years immediately following the war, offered everyone the opportunity to be a medium and turned spiritualist exploration into a parlor game. A heart-shaped piece of wood on three legs, the planchette was believed to move in response to spiritual forces passing through the hands that rested upon it. The device, often equipped with a pencil, could point to letters of the alphabet or actually write out messages from the dead. In the North planchettes were available in a variety of woods and decorative styles; they transformed spiritual communication into a fashionable and "novel amusement."[23]

Spiritualists held their first national convention in Chicago in 1864, marking a growing prominence and self-consciousness that extended well beyond the realm of popular amusement. "Virtually everyone," historian R. Laurence Moore has observed, "conceded that spirit communication was at least a possibility." Amid a war that was erasing not only lives but identities, the promise, as one spiritualist spokesman wrote, of the "imperishability of the individual and the continuation of the identical Ego" after death was for many irresistible. "And you will never lose your identity," John Edmonds and George T. Dexter assured readers of *Spiritualism,* first published in 1853 and then reprinted throughout the rest of the century. "Physical death does not affect the identity of the individual."[24]

Spiritualism responded to a question of pressing importance to the soldier and his kin. As an 1861 article in the spiritualist newspaper *Banner of Light* posed it, "he desires to know what will become of himself after he has lost his body. Shall he continue to exist?—and, if so, in what condition?" Each issue of the paper provided a chorus of answers, a "Message Department" of "Voices from the Dead" transmitted through "Mrs. J. H. Conant, while in a condition called the Trance." Confederates and Yankees alike chimed in; soldiers of all ranks and origins reported that they had died well, that they had met relatives in heaven, and that, as one voice declared, "death has taken nothing from me, except my body." Stonewall Jackson weighed in to defend his actions ("I adopted the course I took because I felt it was right for me to"), and Willie Lincoln sent regular communications.[25]

Philip Gregg, a Confederate killed three months before his appearance in print in April 1862, observed that "the emotions of the returning soldier, who has yielded up his life upon the battle-field, can be scarcely imagined." Those who indeed found the notion of posthumous emotions too much to imagine were presented with his vivid description, although Gregg cut the rendering of his feelings short, concluding, "What I would say to my family the world has no right to hear."[26]

Many messages contained the kind of information found in condolence letters written to inform relatives about the deaths of kin in hospital or battle: affirmations of a Good Death and of the principles of the *ars moriendi.* Whether or not Mrs. Conant was able to communicate with the dead, she certainly channeled the concerns of the living. Lieutenant Gilbert Thompson asked "as a favor of you to-day, that you will inform my father, Nathaniel Thompson of Montgomery, Alabama, if possible, of my decease. Tell him I died ... eight days ago, happy and resigned." Leander Bolton wanted to "give my mother a little sketch of the manner of my death." Charlie Hiland reported, "I lost my life in your Bull Run affair, and the folks want to know how I died and what became of me after death . . . I should like to inform them." Families were promised relief from that "dread void of uncertainty" about both the earthly and spiritual fate of their sons and brothers.[27]

Caleb Wilkins, private of the 11th Indiana, described from his own experience how bodies persist into the afterlife. At the same time he offered an explanation of a puzzle that had tormented thousands of wounded men: why amputated limbs so often continued to hurt. "I can understand some things now that I couldn't before death," he confirmed. Wilkins reported that his leg had been amputated and that several days later he had bled to death. ("The surgeons did n't tie the arteries well.") When Caleb met his brother in heaven and took a look at himself, he declared, "that aint my body . . . I lost a leg, and this body is perfect."[28]

His brother, already practiced in death, explained that Caleb was looking at his spiritual body. His "spirit foot and leg" were perfect, and the pain he had felt after his amputation in his absent foot had been a consequence of the separation of his material from his spiritual appendages. "The sudden severing of the mortal from the spirit leg caused pain, which lasted some minutes after the material leg had been amputated." His amputation had been a kind of pre-death, a forerunner of the disjunction of material body and spirit yet to come. Wilkins and his brother helpfully provided readers with an explanation of the relationship of body and soul, as well as the assurance that no man, and indeed not even any leg, was truly lost.[29]

There is no Caleb Wilkins of Indiana, or Gilbert Thompson of Alabama, or Leander Bolton of Pennsylvania in the database of 6.3 million records of 3.5 million soldiers that the National Park Service has compiled with the assistance of the tools of our computerized age. The *Banner of Light* did not present the story of any reader's actual kin; it did not provide accurate details of deaths and burials, the kind of information families sought as they flocked to battlefields or inundated the Sanitary Commission's Hospital Directory with tens of thousands of anxious inquiries. The consolation of spiritualism lay in its promise that there could and would be answers to these questions, even if it did not itself immediately provide them. There would be an ending to uncertainty—perhaps through contact with the spirit world but certainly through reunion in the world beyond. The unfinished narratives of so many lives would ultimately have a conclusion.[30]

The Message Department of the *Banner of Light,* which continued to carry communications from dead soldiers for more than a decade after the war, affirmed for its community of readers that individual soldiers were neither dead nor lost. They were still their definable and particular selves—still, as they described themselves, eighteen- or twenty-two- or twenty-four-year-olds, still men of six feet or five foot six or five foot eight inches tall, still northerners or southerners, still black or white, each still possessing his own identity and name. And they were struggling to reach out to those they had left behind in order to console them with the reassurance at spiritualism's core: "I Still Live."

Tellingly, Reverend John Sweet had used this very same phrase to explain death's meaning to the Baptist congregation mourning Edward Amos Adams. Adams was not sending spiritualist messages from the world beyond, and Sweet, a devout Baptist pastor, was no medium. But Sweet still designated Adams as one of the "speaking dead," a man whose life and death in themselves—"a life and character that still moves and acts among us"—represented certain immortality. "They whom we call dead have voices for us" and "speak to us by the lives which they have lived." Like the spiritualist dead, Sweet affirmed, Edward Amos Adams too "still lives." Mainstream denominations shared many of spiritualism's consoling tenets and its promise that the dead remained, in important ways, still with them.[31]

The reassurances of spiritualism reached their broadest audience through popular fiction. After *Uncle Tom's Cabin,* the best-selling book of the nineteenth century was Elizabeth Stuart Phelps's *The Gates Ajar.* If Stowe's novel, as Lincoln reportedly remarked to its author, helped to cause the war, Phelps's work dealt with the war's consequences. Within twenty years of its 1868 publication, *The Gates*

Ajar had been reprinted fifty-five times. Enterprising marketers even devised *Gates Ajar* funeral wreaths, cigars, and patent medicines.

Phelps began to write the book in 1864, when she was just twenty years old, at a time, she said, when the "country was dark with sorrowing women." A soldier with whom she was in love had been killed at Antietam, but she recognized that her own personal grief was simply part of an inescapable "material miasma" of loss and pain. Phelps wrote in order to "say something that would comfort some few . . . of the women whose misery crowded the land." Looking back thirty years later, Phelps remembered that she had not "thought so much about the suffering of men—the fathers, the brother, the sons." The mourners she sought to console were the women, "the helpless, outnumbering, unconsulted women; they whom war trampled down, without a choice or protest." Men had fought and died, but now they were beyond help. It was the victimization and sacrifice of the women who continued to suffer that attracted her concern. After her book appeared, these women wrote her by the thousands. "For many years," Phelps reported, "I was snowed under by those mourners' letters . . . signs of human misery and hope."[32]

The Gates Ajar is structured as the journal of Mary Cabot, a young woman who has just learned that her brother Roy has been "shot dead." Unable to reconcile herself to his loss or resign herself to God's will, she is near despair when her aunt Winifred arrives for an unexpected visit. A widow with a young child, fittingly named Faith, Winifred offers Mary a new understanding of heaven, together with the assurance that she will be reunited with Roy, "not only to look at standing up among the singers," as an angel with a harp, but "close to me; somehow or other to be as near as—to be nearer than—he was here—*really* mine again."[33]

Mary's pastor has provided her only an unsatisfactory vision of a place dedicated to "harping and praying" and to endless glorifying of God, a place that would "crowd out all individuality and human joy," a place beyond any special personal human attachments. "He gave me glittering generalities, cold commonplace, vagueness, unreality, a God and a future at which I sat and shivered." Mary is clear-sighted about what she needs to believe. "I wanted something actual, something pleasant, about this place into which Roy has gone."[34]

Winifred readily offers it. Harps, choirs, white robes, pearl gates, she explains, are all just symbols, not the reality of heaven at all. Instead the future life is very like Earth at its most ideal, with trees and mountains, with houses filled with books, pianos, and pictures, and with individuals preserved as themselves, looking as they did in life, maintaining their own bodies and identities. Roy is, Winifred assures Mary, "*only, out of sight . . .* not lost, nor asleep, nor annihilated," but continuing to love those from whom he has departed.[35]

Phelps, speaking through Winifred, stumbles a bit on the question of the body and its fate after death. "A little complication there!" Winifred admits. Deferring to the realities of science, she acknowledges that "popular notions of resurrection are simply physiological impossibilities," and she cites as an example the problem of the material destiny of "two Hottentots, one of whom has happened to make a dinner of the other one fine day." But without resolving these intractable complexities, which were all too relevant in a war in which amputation was so widespread, Phelps simply affirms that a real body that can be heard and touched and kissed will be preserved. To try to "speculate" exactly how, she concludes, is "a waste of time."[36]

The authority on which Winifred and Phelps rest their claims for the afterlife is not that of Scripture or science but of distress and desire. What humans most need is what a benevolent God would want to provide for them. Most important in Phelps's vision of the future is the continuation of the self, of an identity that is defined by a body and by a set of relationships that seem to include both people and domestic objects. These are the essence of what the heaven of *The Gates Ajar* promises to restore to the bereaved. Heaven is reconceived as a more perfect Earth: Victorian family and domesticity are immortalized, and death all but disappears.

But many bereaved sufferers could not duplicate Mary Cabot's escape from despair to certainty. The "rebellious state of mind" in which Mary found herself at the outset of the novel, the firm declaration "I am *not* resigned," echoed the diaries and letters of real-life mourners who found themselves unable to understand why a benevolent God would afflict them—and indeed the world—with such suffering. As Confederate poet and novelist Sidney Lanier wondered, "How does God have the heart to allow it?" The venerable problem of theodicy—of how and why God permits evil—presented itself forcefully to those witnessing the devastation of civil war. One solution to the dilemma was to discount or dismiss evil, and that indeed was the strategy of those who denied death's horrors and focused on the attractions of a highly Earth-like heaven. If death was to be not dreaded but welcomed, it need not challenge God's fundamental goodness.[37]

But many were unable to console themselves with a vision of heaven that transcended war's afflictions, and they instead confronted doubts about the very foundations of their faith. In the Confederacy, where one in five white men of military age would die in the war, mounting death tolls brought widespread and all but unbearable suffering. Catherine Edmondston of North Carolina understood the meaning of the summer of Gettysburg and Vicksburg firsthand, when in September 1863 she called at the houses of eight neighbors and found each one in mourning for a lost husband, brother, or son. Accepting such loss began to seem impossible, especially to women for whom the imperatives of family conventionally took precedence over those of politics. It was increasingly hard to simply murmur, "God's will be done." Susan Caldwell of Warrenton, Virginia, a town located at the very seat of war, anguished over the "loss of our brave and gallant men" on the battlefields all around her and found herself unable "to gain power over my own rebellious heart . . . Oh! how hard to be submissive." War-weary Americans invoked the trials and patience of Job, reminded themselves that the Lord "doeth all things well," and dutifully and almost ritually affirmed, "Thou he slay me, yet I will trust in him." But like Susan Caldwell, many feared they could not "stand a great deal more."[38]

For some, consolation derived not just from assurances of a close and comfortable heaven but also from visions of transformations on

Earth. Death would be not just easy but purposeful. Southerners and northerners alike elaborated narratives of patriotic sacrifice that imbued war deaths with transcendent meaning. Soldiers suffered and died so that a nation—be it the Union or the Confederacy—might live; Christian and nationalist imperatives merged in a redemptive vision of political immortality.

Lincoln's Gettysburg Address is perhaps the best-known example of such an explanation and justification of war's carnage. Determined that "these dead shall not have died in vain," Lincoln hallowed and sacralized a nation and its purposes with biblical cadences—even as he scarcely mentioned God. In the address the dead themselves become the agents of political meaning and devotion; they act even in their silence and anonymity. Lincoln immortalized them as the enduring inspiration for an immortal nation. Unlike the "honored dead," the Union would not "perish from the earth." Soldiers' deaths, like Christ's sacrifice, become the vehicle of salvation, the means for a terrestrial, political redemption.[39]

Lincoln's providential view of the war and its carnage appeared with perhaps even greater force a year and a half later, as both the conflict and his life neared conclusion. In the Second Inaugural of March 1865 Lincoln again offered an explanation for wartime slaughter, but this time it was God, not man, who gave it meaning. An Old Testament God of justice is avenging the sins of slavery. The Civil War and its deaths are not so much sacrifice as atonement. "Yet if God wills that it continue until every drop of blood drawn with the lash, shall be paid by another drawn with the sword, as was said three thousand years ago, so still it must be said, 'the judgments of the Lord are true and righteous altogether.' "[40]

Providential views of the war had abounded from the earliest days of the conflict, when North and South competed to claim God for their side. The Confederacy, as one southern clergyman declared, would be the "nation to do His work upon earth." *Deo Vindice,* with God as vindicator, the official Confederate seal proclaimed. But only as the enormous cost in lives became clear did it seem imperative explicitly to link providentialist notions to war's losses, to impart to these deaths both transcendence and meaning. As Georgia bishop Stephen Elliott explained this necessity in an 1864 sermon, "To shed such blood, as we have spilled in this contest for the mere name of independence, for the vanity or the pride of having a separate national existence, would be unjustifiable before God and man. We must have higher aims than these." War's dead and war's cost were changing and amplifying the understanding of its ends.[41]

But as Lincoln's Second Inaugural, delivered on the eve of victory, insisted, God "has his own purposes" and makes his own judgments. He, and neither Yankees nor Confederates, would define the reach of his providence. Both sides in the terrible conflict "read the same Bible and pray to the same God, and each invokes his aid against the other ... The prayers of both could not be answered." Northern success and southern defeat necessarily altered providential explanations of war and its carnage. Northerners were reinforced in their conviction that lives had not been lost in vain and were encouraged in their sense of national mission; Confederates confronted what for many became a profound test of faith.[42]

A little more than three months after Appomattox, northern clergyman and theologian Horace Bushnell celebrated northern victory by placing the dead and their sacrifice at the center of war's accomplishment. The slain, he declared, were "the price and purchase-money of our triumph." You get what you pay for, his oration implied; only war's cost had ensured its transformative impact. Bleeding, he asserted, was necessary to God's expansive—and expensive—purposes for America, and "in this blood our unity is cemented and forever sanctified." The Christian narrative of redemption through suffering and sacrifice framed Bushnell's rendering of the war and its meaning. Death was not loss, but both the instrument and the substance of victory.[43]

Early in the conflict, on the Sunday after the Union defeat at First Bull Run in 1861, Bushnell had delivered a sermon entitled "Reverses Needed," calling for the nation's resolve and devotion to be tested. Four years later he could affirm that America had passed its trial. The war's suffering had guaranteed that "we are not the same people that we were, and never can be again." A new understanding of nationhood as the incarnation of God's design had been purchased by "our acres of dead." Because, like Christianity, history "must feed itself on blood," the United States now "may be said to have gotten a history." The nation was "no more a mere creature of our human will, but a grandly moral affair." Its purposes were now God's purposes. "Hallowed" by "rivers of blood," the United States claimed its place as the redeemer nation. "Government is now become Providential." The "mournful offering" of war's deaths had "bought a really stupendous chapter of history." And the blood that had been shed to achieve God's design of freedom, emancipation, and inspired nationhood, he explicitly recognized, was black as well as white, sacrificed at Fort Pillow and Fort Wagner as well as at Fredericksburg, Gettysburg, and Shiloh.[44]

Bushnell closed his oration by invoking a manifest destiny of national expansion, impelled in no small part by the need to compensate for war's cost. There was a need, Bushnell emphasized, "to wind up and settle this great tragedy in a way to exactly justify every drop of blood that has been shed in it." Like Confederate bishop Stephen Elliott, he too sought still "higher aims" to balance the flow of "such blood." War's destructiveness called for broadened purposes. "Ours be it also, in God's own time," he concluded, "to champion . . . the right of this whole continent to be an American world, and to have its own American laws, liberties, and institutions."[45]

Bushnell spoke as a victor. One also suspects that he could talk so enthusiastically about blood because he had spent the war in Connecticut, distant from the battlefields "black with dead" that he described. But Providence had favored him, and he could thus claim its purposes as his own. His dead, the northern dead, could be explained as part of a larger purpose and grander plan. But for the defeated South, war's terrible losses could only seem meaningless.[46]

As Confederate fortunes faltered, some white southerners "plainly indicated," one woman reported, "that if our cause failed, they would lose all faith in a prayer answering God." Confederate poet Henry Timrod had in fact suggested in "Ethnogenesis," his 1861 celebration of the southern nation's birth, that "to doubt the end were want of trust in God." What then did it mean actually to see the end and to face defeat? What then of God's trustworthiness? Surrender made war's sacrifices seem purposeless; losses would remain unredeemed; southern fathers, brothers, and sons had not died that a nation might live.[47]

Even the most devout struggled to reconcile themselves to defeat and to find meaning for the slaughter. The Presbytery of South Carolina observed in the fall of 1865 that "the faith of many a Christian is shaken by the mysterious and unlooked-for course of divine Providence." Baptist leader Samuel Ford recognized that " 'Where is God' seemed to be the anxious questioning of each heart...Is there a God? many *many* asked." Virginian Mary Lee felt herself "like a ship without a pilot or compass." She could see no God at the helm.[48]

Some believers, like the Presbyterian editor John Adger, reminded their fellow southerners, as clergy had indeed reiterated throughout the trials of four years of war, that God chastened those he loved. Defeat was simply another burden to be borne with the unwavering patience that Job had exhibited in the face of divine affliction. "Yes! The hand of God, gracious though heavy, is upon the South for her discipline." In Richmond, Reverend Moses Drury Hoge confessed that defeat "enwraps me like a pall." But he determined not to "murmur" at God and instead would "await the development of his providence."[49]

Many felt they had endured enough. After Appomattox Grace Elmore of South Carolina wrote in despair, "I know not how to bear it. I cannot be resigned." She acknowledged that "hard thoughts against my God will arise." She had lost two cousins to the war, had dealt with Yankee invaders in her own house, and had lived through the burning of Columbia with "flames before, behind and around us." She struggled to fit her experience into Christian narratives of suffering and redemption, but with the resurrection of the Confederate state all but impossible, she saw little hope of salvation. "Night and day in every moment of quiet," she wrote, "I am trying to work out the meaning of this horrible fact, to find truth at the bottom of this impenetrable darkness . . . Has God forsaken us?" Widowed, homeless, and destitute, Cornelia McDonald of Virginia shared Elmore's feelings of abandonment. She described lying immobile on a sofa through "dreadful hours of unbelief and hopelessness." But gradually memories of God's mercies crept over her, and she resolved once again to trust in him despite her afflictions.[50]

Like McDonald, most former Confederates would suppress their doubts and return to religious belief and observance. Churches grew dramatically in the South in the years after the Civil War, setting the stage for the region's emergence as the Bible Belt in the twentieth century. But many white southerners remained bewildered, as Mary Lee put it, by God's mysterious ways in subjecting them to the anguishing losses of war. The cult of the Lost Cause and the celebration of Confederate memory that emerged in the ensuing decades were in no small part an effort to affirm that the hundreds of thousands of young southern lives had not, in fact, been given in vain.

The victors' providential view of the conflict and of Union and emancipation offered white northerners and African Americans throughout the nation a consoling narrative of divine purpose and sacrifice. But not all Americans were satisfied with such a justification of war's cost. The horrors of battle and the magnitude of the carnage were difficult to put aside. The force of loss left even many believers unable to abandon lingering uncertainties about God's benevolence. Doubters confronted profound questions not just about God but about life's meaning and the very foundations of both belief and knowledge.

In his study of a group of prominent mid-nineteenth-century intellectuals clustered around Harvard, Louis Menand has argued that the Civil War not only "discredited the beliefs and assumptions of the era that preceded it"; it destroyed "almost the whole intellectual culture of the North." Oliver Wendell Holmes Jr., whose father had rushed to find him after he was wounded at Antietam, was one of these men, and Menand believes he never recovered from the mental impact of his experiences. The younger Holmes had volunteered to fight, Menand explains, because of certain moral principles, but "the war did more than make him lose those beliefs. It made him lose his belief in beliefs." This was more than just a loss of faith; it was an issue of both epistemology and sensibility, of how we know the world and how we envision our relationship to it.[51]

One product of the horror of the Civil War was the proliferation of irony, of a posture of distance and doubt in relation to experience. Literary scholar Paul Fussell has written that wars always beget irony because intentions are so often overturned by circumstance; war's outcomes are so much more terrible than we can ever anticipate. Certainly this was true of the American Civil War, which began with statesmen assuring one another of all but bloodless victory. But the predominant response to the unexpected carnage was in fact a resolute sentimentality that verged at times on pathos. Songs abounded in which soldiers entreated their mothers to "come, Your Boy is Dying," to "bless me . . . ere I die," or "kiss me once before I go," or "make me a child again just for tonight." Novels and stories shared the enthusiastic earnestness of *The Gates Ajar.* But another, contrasting sensibility emerged in the course of the war as well, often appearing in direct reaction to the gap between the conventions of Victorian sentimentality and the reality of modern industrialized warfare.[52]

Parody was one mode for this response. In the realm of popular song, "Mother Would Comfort Me" was countered by "Mother Would Wallop Me," a quite different take on the nature of domesticity. One lyricist mocked the countless ballads on motherhood by linking more than a dozen titles together to create the words to "Mother on the Brain," to be sung to the tune of "The Bonnie Blue Flag."

> *"It was my Mother's customs," "My gentle Mother dear";*
> *"I was my Mother's darling," for, I loved my lager beer.*
> *"Kiss me good-night, Mother," and bring me a Bourbon*
> *   plain—*
> *"Mother dear, I feel I'm dying," with Mother on the brain.*[53]

Published by Chas Magnus, 12 Frankfort St. N.Y.

THE DYING SOLDIER.

"OH! DO NOT BUREY ME HERE!"

"Air—Dearest May."

By E. Walter Lowe, 19. N. Y. Cavalry.

Oh! bury me not 'neath foreign skies,
  Where nought is bright to see,
So far from home, from those whose eyes
  Are filled with tears for me;
But bear my body to the spot,
  Near where the primrose smiled,
When I play'd 'round our little cot,
A merry, happy child.

Chorus:

Oh! do not bury me here, where all is dark and drear,
  But make my grave
  Where the willows wave,
  And friends can drop a tear.

When first the cry of War arose,
  How fast our ranks did swell;
And not a friend did then suppose,
  'Twould be the last "farewell:"
Friends pressed me as I took the train,
  Tears stood in many an eye:
I thought I'd see Estelle again,
  But Oh! I've got to die!

Chorus:

Could I but live to hear it said,
  That our blest Flag once more
Waved "Peace" o'er every patriot's head,
  And streamed from every shore:
But Oh! life's sun is waning fast,
  Death's hand is on my brow,
Farewell, loved ones, each hope is past—
  I feel I'm going now!

Chorus:

500 Illustrated Ballads, lithographed and printed by CHARLES MAGNUS, No. 12 Frankfort Street, New York. Branch Office: No. 520 7th St. Washington, D. C.

"The Dying Soldier." Song sheet.
The Library Company of Philadelphia.

Mark Twain took on *The Gates Ajar* in a "burlesque" entitled "Extract from Captain Stormfield's Visit to Heaven." Although he showed a version of it to William Dean Howells in the early 1870s, he dared not publish it until after the turn of the century and the death of his disapproving wife. Twain complained that Phelps's novel "had imagined a mean little ten-cent heaven about the size of Rhode Island—a heaven large enough to accommodate about a tenth of one percent of the Christian billions who had died in the past nineteen centuries." Twain's hero had trouble managing his angel wings and flew so badly that he regularly collided with others. Stormfield was also startled to discover that the overwhelming proportion of American angels were in fact Indians, not white men, for Indians had been dying in the New World and accumulating in the American section of heaven for centuries. The combination of his poor aeronautic abilities and his minority status rendered Stormfield less than entirely comfortable in paradise. Twain reduced Phelps's lugubrious earnestness to comic absurdity.[54]

Ambrose Bierce styled himself a wit, not a humorist, emphasizing the sardonic and cutting intent of his newspaper columns and stories. "Humor is tolerant, tender ... its ridicule caresses. Wit stabs, begs pardon—and turns the weapon in the wound." Raised on a midwestern farm where, as he later described it, "we had to grub out a very difficult living," Bierce was the tenth of thirteen children—all given names beginning with A—born to parents he seems to have despised. He enlisted in the Union army when he was only eighteen. The most significant and prolific American writer actually to fight in the Civil War, Bierce saw nearly four years of combat and won multiple commendations for bravery before receiving a serious head wound at Kennesaw Mountain in 1864. After the war he moved to San Francisco, where he worked as a journalist. Haunted all his life by what he described as persisting "visions of the dead and dying," Bierce began in the 1880s to publish both fiction and nonfiction based on his military experiences. His writings about the war are often cited as the beginnings of modern war literature and as a major influence upon both Stephen Crane and Ernest Hemingway. Bierce

crafted unromanticized depictions of battle that reflected his fundamental approach to both writing and to life: "Cultivate a taste for distasteful truths. And ... most important of all, endeavor to see things
as they are, not as they ought to be."[55]

The yawning discrepancy between the hopes that inaugurated the
war and the experience of its horrors deeply affected Bierce's subsequent view of the world. Surviving the war left him tormented by the
"phantoms of that blood-stained period" and by a bitterness that
derived not just from his own loss of innocence in war but from his
sense that he was among the few truly to admit war's terror and its
price. He felt both isolated and angered by the denial and repression
of loss that characterized the postwar world. Organized religion,
which he believed to be filled with hypocrisy and self-delusion, was
his particular bugbear; he defined it in his *Devil's Dictionary* as "a
daughter of Hope and Fear, explaining to Ignorance the nature of the
Unknowable."[56]

Bierce's writings about the war are preoccupied with the gruesome and the macabre and display what seems almost an eagerness
to transgress proprieties of thought and representation. In "What I
Saw of Shiloh," published in December 1881, Bierce offers his memories of the battle—explicitly partial and personal rather than heroic
and sweeping. His work contrasted sharply with the celebratory *Century Magazine* series on "Battles and Leaders," which had just begun
in the early 1880s to engage a wide popular audience in Civil War
reminiscence and hagiography. Bierce's essay contains one of the
most graphic presentations of war death ever written, juxtaposing its
sensory and moral horrors. He describes coming upon the site of the
previous day's fighting and finding

Men? There were men enough; all dead, apparently, except one,
who lay near where I had halted my platoon...—a Federal
sergeant, variously hurt, who had been a fine giant in his time. He
lay face upward, taking his breath in convulsive, rattling snorts,
and blowing it out in sputters of froth which crawled creamily
down his cheeks, piling itself alongside his neck and ears. A bullet

had clipped a groove in his skull, above the temple; from this the brain protruded in bosses, dropping off in flakes and strings. I had not previously known one could get on, even in this unsatisfactory fashion, with so little brain. One of my men, whom I knew for a womanish fellow, asked if he should put his bayonet through him. Inexpressibly shocked by the cold-blooded proposal, I told him I thought not; it was unusual, and too many were looking.[57]

The particulars and the pain of death are unrelieved here; but convention prohibits mercy—"too many were looking"—and renders true compassion "cold blooded"; the notion of a Good Death is made oxymoronic. "Death was a thing to be hated," Bierce wrote elsewhere. "It was not picturesque, it had no tender and solemn side—a dismal thing, hideous in all its manifestations and suggestions."[58]

Deaths—executions, suicides, battle casualties—constitute the central theme of Bierce's war writing, and indeed he saw death, not glory or political purpose, as the fundamental reality of war itself. As Edmund Wilson observed in *Patriotic Gore,* death was Bierce's "only real character." A soldier was, in Bierce's view, essentially an "assassin," a man "in the business of killing his fellow-men." Yet Bierce's bitterness was hardly a manifestation of lack of feeling, as his at once chilling and deeply sympathetic description of the dying sergeant at Shiloh suggests.[59]

One of the most powerful of Bierce's war stories portrays the night-long encounter of a "brave and efficient" young second lieutenant with a dead body. Assigned to guard the nearby Union encampment while his comrades sleep, Brainerd Byring finds himself alone in the woods with a Confederate corpse. A sensitive man, he has always appreciated the "exhilaration of battle," but he possesses a particular loathing for "the sight of the dead, with their clay faces, blank eyes and stiff bodies, which when not unnaturally shrunken were unnaturally swollen." As the night wears on, the body seems to begin to move. "What does it want?" the soldier demands. "It did not appear to be in need of anything but a soul," the narrator wryly observes.[60]

Byring invokes the certitudes of fact and reason to combat growing anxiety about his dead companion. He rehearses in his mind all he knows about the history of attitudes toward the dead, about burial customs from ancient Europe and central Asia, and about the surprising cultural persistence of belief in the supernatural, which he does not share. "I suppose it will require a thousand ages—perhaps ten thousand—for humanity to outgrow this feeling. Where and when did it originate?" he muses in the effort to gain control of his intensifying feelings of dread. But his philosophizing cannot calm him; it is death, not he, that is in control. Even as he reassures himself that notions of the "malevolence of the dead body" are simply the vestige of antiquated myth, he sees that the body is "visibly moving!" The story ends with the discovery the next day by a Federal captain and surgeon of two dead bodies—one Confederate, already rotting, "frightfully gashed and stabbed" but with bloodless wounds; the second a young Federal officer with his own sword thrust through his chest. Confronted by a corpse, Byring is driven to try to annihilate both death and himself, embracing death as the only means to overcome his fear of it.[61]

Bierce, too, found the role of survivor troubling. The war had left him, he observed, "sentenced to life," and the war dead haunted him and his prose, just as the Confederate corpse so disturbed Brainerd Byring. The line between battle's survivors and battle's dead is blurred for Bierce. "When I ask myself," he once remarked, "what has happened to Ambrose Bierce the youth, who fought at Chickamauga, I am bound to answer that he is dead." Rather than the purposeful and providential Christian death, Biercean death is often a surprise, sprung on the reader, as in the story of Byring, as it is on its victim—even, paradoxically, when it is suicide. The notion of death involving human preparation or agency, the central tenets—and hope—of the *ars moriendi,* is entirely alien in Bierce's world. It is instead death that possesses agency—like the apparently moving corpse—to exert its claim upon the living, and it is in this sense that it becomes, as Wilson remarked, Bierce's central character.[62]

Bierce's best-known story, "An Occurrence at Owl Creek Bridge," exemplifies death's surprise and man's futility in its depiction of a southern spy about to be hanged. Peyton Farquhar seems to have escaped his fate when the rope snaps and plunges him into the creek, permitting him to flee the Yankees and return home to his wife. But his escape proves a fantasy in which the reader too has been fooled. The story ends with Farquhar swinging from Owl Creek Bridge. The power of Bierce's irony derives from his insertion not just of the main character but of the reader into the gap he creates between appearance and actuality. Like Farquhar, his startled reader is left hanging.[63]

Dissenting from his era's romanticization of death, fully embracing Darwinian notions of "nature red in tooth and claw," mocking the doctrines and authority of organized religion, Bierce had little faith in any afterlife. In his *Devil's Dictionary* he defined the Dead with rhymed irreverence:

> *Done with the work of breathing; done*
> *With all the world; the mad race run*
> *Through to the end; the golden goal*
> *Attained and found to be a hole!*[64]

The afterlife for which so many Americans avidly searched was not heaven but simply the void of the grave. Death was "hideous," and it was complete in itself; it was not a passage to another life; it was not the embodiment or instrument of patriotic or religious purpose. But Bierce was moved as well as horrified by the dead, which was why they continued to haunt him. Both the Confederate and the Yankee slain deserved reverent attention; just as death defined life, the dead represented the real meaning of the war. "We know we live, for with each breath / We feel the fear and imminence of death."[65]

Herman Melville did not share Bierce's extensive military experience, but he did understand the loss of innocence that rendered initial expectations absurd. Forty-two years old at the time of Fort Sumter, Melville spent most of the war on a Massachusetts farm, struggling to recover from what seemed to him the demise of his literary ambition in his critical and commercial failures of the 1850s. But the participation of close relatives in the army gave him a window into the conflict, and in the spring of 1864, on the eve of the Wilderness campaign, he undertook a tour of Virginia battlefields. He managed to secure an audience with Grant and to join a three-day excursion with a band of soldiers in search of Confederate partisan John Mosby. By the time of the southern surrender the following spring, Melville was launched on a new literary venture in an unfamiliar form. War would be his subject, and poetry his genre. His *Battle-Pieces and Aspects of the War,* published in 1866, presents the conflict in a collection of glimpses and fragments, not in the novelistic form of his most important earlier work. The choice reflected his judgment that "none can narrate that strife," and even "entangled rhyme / But hints at the maze of war." Melville recognized the momentousness of the nation's experience; the conflict had been "an upheaval affecting the basis of things," and those things included literary form and language as well as human purposes and values.[66]

The poems are arranged in a chronology, not of their composition but of the war itself, beginning with John Brown and the "Conflict of Convictions" that resulted in secession and continuing through Fort Donelson, Shiloh, Antietam, Stones River, Gettysburg, Chattanooga, the Wilderness, the March to the Sea, the fall of Richmond, and the surrender at Appomattox. The volume opens with the "expectancy" of ignorant youth marching joyously off to battle. But Melville delineates the dashing of these hopes, the harsh education of these young who "perish, enlightened by the vollied glare." As it does for Bierce, death comes with the irony of surprise. A glorious adventure undertaken with the enthusiasm and pleasure of "a berrying party" becomes a burying party of a quite different sort. War's young soldiers had not "dreamed what death was—thought it mere / Sliding into some vernal sphere." In their anticipations they had "leaped the grief" of war, but battle and Melville restore it.[67]

At the heart of Melville's poetic inquiry rests "the riddle of death," a question with which he had been personally much concerned before war propelled it to the center of national consciousness. Like

so many other Americans of his era, Melville struggled to overcome his doubts about Christian doctrine in order to find a plausible
foundation for reassuring faith in immortality. His friend Nathaniel
Hawthorne had reported in 1856 that Melville "can neither believe,
nor be comfortable in his unbelief," but had out of frustration with
his indecision "pretty much made up his mind to be annihilated."
The issue remained far from settled for Melville, however, when the
outbreak of war gave death new prominence in both private and
public life. Literary critic Daniel Aaron has judged *Battle-Pieces* to be
Melville's continuing inquiry into this question, "a sustained debate
between belief and disbelief."[68]

Annihilation took on a different meaning after 1861, and Melville
rendered the texture of war's destructiveness unblinkingly: the soldiers in the Wilderness meet "skull after skull" and green and rotting
"shoes full of bones," the remains of the dead still unburied from the
previous year's campaigns. "Few burial rites shall be," as even the
dignifying rituals of death are abandoned to the grim necessities of
military slaughter. Glory, plumes, sashes, banners have become irrel-
evant; men are but operatives, cogs in a machinery of destruction, for
war itself has been modernized and industrialized, as the ascendancy
and "anvil-din" of the war's ironclad warships vividly symbolize.

> *No passion; all went on by crank,*
> *Pivot and screw,*
> *And calculations of caloric.*[69]

Death itself becomes war's end, the product of its industrialized
machinery; there is no more transcendent or glorious purpose;
northerners and southerners lie mingled together, "fame or country
least their care." But they now understand what in their youthful zeal
for battle they did not—"What like a bullet can undeceive!"—for the
pieties and pomposities of war have dissolved. The dead have discovered as well the answer to the riddle that Melville cannot know,
the riddle "of which the slain / Sole solvers are." Beginning in such

Skulls and bones left unburied on the field. "Battle-field of Gaines Mill, Virginia." Library of Congress.

innocence, they are brought by war to an ultimate knowledge that even their survivors lack. The living remain captured in uncertainty.[70]

In Amherst, Massachusetts, where she rarely left her father's house, Emily Dickinson lived even more removed from the war than Melville. But she too displayed a sense of the ironic disjunction between reality and appearance, expectation and experience. "Could Prospect taste of Retrospect," Emily Dickinson wrote at the end of the war, echoing the notion of dark enlightenment that structured Melville's *Battle-Pieces.*

> *My Triumph lasted till the Drums*
> *Had left the Dead alone*

And then I dropped my Victory
And chastened stole along
To where the finished Faces
Conclusion turned on me
And then I hated Glory
And wished myself were They.

"A Bayonet's contrition / Is nothing to the dead," the poem ends. Conclusion repudiates anticipation; regret cannot recuperate what is "finished" and rendered irreversible—what in another poem she describes as the "Repealless—list" of the fallen. Dickinson decries the incommensurability of victory and its human cost. Sentenced, like Bierce, to both survivor's guilt and survivor's glory, she cannot escape either. Irony rests in death's destruction of the innocence and ignorance of prospect, as well as in the very notion of loss itself as irremediable annihilation rather than the redemptive sacrifice of Christian promise.[71]

Emily Dickinson is renowned as a poet preoccupied with death. Yet curiously any relationship between her work and the Civil War was long rejected by most literary critics, even though she wrote almost half her oeuvre, at a rate of four poems a week, during those years. Dickinson has been portrayed as a recluse, closeted from the real world and its tribulations. But her work is filled with the language of battle—the very vocabulary of war that she would have encountered in the four newspapers regularly delivered to the Dickinson house. Campaigns, cannons, rifle balls, bullets, artillery, soldiers, ammunition, flags, bayonets, cavalry, drums, and trumpets are recurrent images in her poetry.[72]

During the second year of the war Dickinson began a correspondence that would prove one of the most important of her life, with a man she came to call her "preceptor," Thomas Wentworth Higginson. She had inaugurated the exchange in response to an essay he published about aspiring writers in the *Atlantic Monthly* of April 1862. But Higginson was more than a man of letters. Long an abolitionist, he accepted command of a regiment of black soldiers and early in 1863 departed for South Carolina. Although she would not actually meet him until 1870, Dickinson feared the grief his loss in battle would bring. "Could you, with honor, avoid death, I entreat you, sir—It would bereave Your Gnome"[73]

Dickinson understood loss, for citizens of her tight-knit Massachusetts town had already been claimed by war. The death of Frazer Stearns, son of the Amherst College president, at New Berne, North Carolina, in March 1862 had cast the whole community into mourning. Emily described her brother Austin as "stunned completely" by the news of his friend's demise. She had seen young Stearns ride through Amherst with his sword and comrades at his side, and now "crowds came to tell him goodnight, choirs sang to him, pastors told how brave he was . . . And the family bowed their heads, as the reed the wind shakes." Her fears about Higginson's fate grew out of very direct experience with war's cost.[74]

Emily Dickinson may have been preoccupied with the theme of death well before the outbreak of conflict, but national conflagration gave her a new language and a new context in which to contemplate its meaning. In writing to Higginson of the war, she herself acknowledged that the loss of friends to death that struck "sharp and early" had created in her "a brittle love—of more alarm, than peace." And she understood that war placed her own despair in a new relationship to the afflictions of others around her. "Sorrow seems more general than it did, and not the estate of a few persons, since the war began; and if the anguish of others helped one with one's own, now would be many medicines." War provided Dickinson with inexhaustible material for her metaphysical speculations. The worth and meaning of human life were for her defined by death's cost and promise, just as the war itself constantly demanded a balance sheet of loss and purpose. Her poetry uses the deaths of war to ask timeless questions, but her speculations at the same time engage more timely issues that also tormented her far less gifted contemporaries. She too sought to understand the meaning of war's carnage, the price of victory and defeat, and the implications of Civil War slaughter for the Christian faith that shaped how most Americans lived their lives.[75]

Dickinson dwelled, as she wrote, "in Possibility." In the face of doubt, she searched for "Paradise," for firm foundations for belief, for signs of immortality to relieve her deep uncertainty. She felt herself isolated from the community of believers and once described her family to Higginson as "religious, except me." Like so many reflective Americans of her time, she grappled with the contradictions of spirit and matter and with their implications for heaven and for God. Death seemed a "Dialogue between the Spirit and the Dust," an argument left painfully unresolved. Dickinson wondered where she might find heaven ("I'm knocking everywhere") and what an afterlife might be ("Is Heaven a place—a Sky—a Tree?"). She speculated too on the possibility of corporeal immortality: "I felt my life with both my hands / To see if it was there." But she could not resolve her uncertainty and found no sure comfort in a "religion / that doubts as fervently as it believes." Death remained inexorable.[76]

> *All but Death, can be Adjusted—*
>
> . . . .
>
> *Death—unto itself—Exception*
> *Is exempt from Change.*[77]

Ironically, it was death, not life, that seemed eternal, for it "perishes—to live anew . . . Annihilation—plated fresh / With Immortality." No terrestrial justifications, no military or political purposes balance this loss; victory cannot compensate; it "comes late" to those already dead, whose "freezing lips" are "too rapt with frost / to take it." Dickinson permits herself no relief or escape into either easy transcendence or sentimentality. Instead she faces death in its horror, as "Piles of solid Moan," and explores how death challenges God's presence and benevolence, as it raises questions about her own worth and destiny. "It feels a shame to be Alive— / When Men so brave—are dead." She, like Bierce, finds herself "sentenced to life."

Dickinson makes clear that the soul's internal battle is "of all the battles prevalent— / By far the Greater One—." But the circumstances of national conflict illustrated and objectified her inner turmoil and encouraged four years of extraordinary poetic productivity.[78]

Critics writing about Dickinson, Bierce, and Melville have identified in each of them characteristics associated with "modernity." The challenge to certainty is an important dimension of this designation; each of these writers grapples with religious doubt, and all adopt an irony that reflects anxiety about deception and delusion. All three seek, to borrow Melville's word, to "undeceive." But their doubts affect the form as well as the substance of their work. Melville resorts to poetry from the impossibility of narrative. As Helen Vendler has written, Melville recognizes that the war requires "a new sort of language and rhyme." No comprehensive understanding is possible; any vantage offers, as he writes in "Armies of the Wilderness," only "glimpses" and only "hints at the maze of war."[79]

Bierce similarly eschews any effort at synthesis or claim to omniscience. He writes only of what "I saw" at Shiloh, offers just "A Little of Chickamauga"—once again "what I saw of it." He trusts his knowledge only of what he has directly experienced. His short stories are like snapshots. War cannot be understood or communicated as a grand panorama. It is real only in the context of individual lives—and deaths. This individualization undermines war's coherence and ignores any larger purpose. Bierce's *Devil's Dictionary* represents yet another presentation of fragments, within a form that undermines the very essence of its genre. Instead of a compilation of ordered meanings, Bierce offers definitions that challenge—even reject— meaning, with mockery and irony.

Dickinson's poetry was revolutionary in its departure from the order and logic of prevailing poetic form.

> *The thought behind, I strove to join*
> *Unto the thought before—*
> *But Sequence ravelled out of Sound*
> *Like Balls—upon a Floor,*

she wrote in 1864. Marked by discontinuities, her poems were assailed after their posthumous publication by critics who deplored their travesties of grammar and syntax. But contemporary critics see in these attributes the embodiment of Dickinson's doubts about the foundations of understanding and coherence. Shira Wolosky has argued that Dickinson's poetry challenges "the whole question of linguistic meaning and of meaning in general." This is a crisis of language and epistemology as much as one of eschatology; it is about not just whether there is a God and whether we can know him but whether we can know or communicate anything at all.[80]

Dickinson's poems did not appear in print for three decades after the Civil War; Melville's *Battle-Pieces,* published in 1866, sold about five hundred copies; Bierce was well known as a journalist but did not begin to publish his writings about the war until nearly twenty years after Appomattox. The significance of these authors' understanding of war's destruction does not lie in their influence upon popular thought. Nor can they be seen as representative of widely held views. Their writings instead provide access into one point on the spectrum of possible reactions to the crisis of belief that war presented to mid-nineteenth-century America. Dickinson, Melville, and Bierce transformed the need to grapple with the meaning of national conflagration into broad and lasting questions about the foundations of religion and of human understanding. Each of these authors has been regarded as a way station on the route to the modernist disillusion that would be associated with the even more destructive war that erupted in 1914. That very connection with the future suggests the tenuous relationship that each writer had with the prevailing assumptions and outlook of an earlier time. But the Civil War contributed to the ability of each of these authors to see the world in the framework and images that made his or her work possible. And in mapping the contours of doubt, Dickinson, Melville, and Bierce helped delineate the broader topography of belief and unbelief that grew from the war. It is, in fact, striking to see that their sense of a failure of knowledge and understanding was widely articulated by ordinary Americans.

Oliver Wendell Holmes Jr. called the experience of war "incommunicable." Fellow soldiers felt the same and filled their letters and diaries with declarations of their inability to describe what they had seen. "Language would in no way express the true picture as it really was," Confederate Reuben Allen Pierson wrote his father after Gaines Mill in 1862, emphasizing in his redundancy both the power and the inaccessibility of his experience. A depiction of Chickamauga, James Suiter of the 84th Illinois wrote in his diary, "would be an absolute impossibility." Daniel Holt, a Union surgeon, proclaimed battle "indescribable" in its horror. John Casler of the Stonewall Brigade struggled for words to tell his parents about his first experience of combat: "I have not power to describe the scene. It beggars all description." Like Melville, the soldiers found war beyond narration.[81]

Women nurses and relief workers responded to the suffering they witnessed at the front with a similar sense of verbal incapacity. In 1862, Cordelia Harvey wrote home from Tennessee to Madison's *Wisconsin State Journal,* "There are times when the meaning of words seem to fade away; so entirely does our language fail to express the reality. This fact I never so fully realized as when attempting to depict the suffering, both mental and physical, which I have witnessed within the last ten days." Confederate Kate Cumming reacted to her entry onto the wards in almost identical terms. "I do not think that words are in our vocabulary expressive enough to present to the mind the realities of that sad scene." Suffering exceeded language and understanding.[82]

But even if they could not explain the experience of war, they could not escape it. "A battle is indescribable," a Union chaplain wrote after Fredericksburg, "but once seen it haunts a man till the day of his death." Like Bierce, who declared himself possessed "by visions of the dead and dying," many witnesses to the Civil War could not exorcise the phantoms of war by transforming them into reassuring religious or patriotic narratives of redemptive sacrifice. They remained glimpses, fragments, "visions," sights not stories, visual rather than explanatory in their effect.[83]

Civil War carnage transformed the mid-nineteenth century's growing sense of religious doubt into a crisis of belief that propelled many Americans to redefine or even reject their faith in a benevolent and responsive deity. But Civil War death and devastation also planted seeds of a more profound doubt about human ability to know and to understand. In an environment in which man seemed already increasingly undifferentiated from animals, the failure of the uniquely human capacity of language represented another assault upon the foundations of the self. The Civil War compelled Americans to ask with intensified urgency, "What is Death?" and in answering to find themselves wondering why is death, what is life, and can we ever hope to know? We have continued to wonder ever since.

CHAPTER 7

ACCOUNTING

"Our Obligations to the Dead"

"Such a consecration of a nation's power and resources
to a *sentiment,* the world has never witnessed."

EDMUND B. WHITMAN

Only a little more than three months had passed since Appomattox when Horace Bushnell addressed the annual reunion of Yale alumni in July 1865. Asked to honor those Yale graduates who had lost their lives in the conflict, Bushnell insisted he could not and should not distinguish fellow collegians from the legions of those who had perished. Instead he spoke of all the Union dead, calling for the nation to acknowledge its debt to the fallen. Bushnell's oration, "Our Obligations to the Dead," sought to define the war's meaning as inseparable from its human cost. In effect, he submitted to the reunited nation a bill on behalf of those who had paid the ultimate price during four years of conflict. In a language of gain and loss, of earning, buying, paying, and owing, Bushnell called Americans to account, demanding that the hundreds of thousands of lives lost be rendered purposeful, worth their expense of blood and suffering.[1]

Bushnell was far from alone in invoking and extolling the dead in the weeks after southern surrender. Just a few days before Bushnell's Yale oration, for example, James Russell Lowell had stood before a parallel gathering of Harvard graduates in Cambridge to read a lengthy ode—more than four hundred lines—written to commemorate lost classmates. Twentieth-century novelist and critic Richard Marius once remarked that "on a hot summer day in Cambridge, this wretched poem must have been only slightly less painful than battle itself." Romantic, sentimental, replete with rhetorical flourishes and classical and biblical references, Lowell's ode hailed northern victory and mourned those missing from the assembly of graduates. "In these brave ranks I only see the gaps, / Thinking of dear ones whom the dumb turf wraps, / Dark to the triumph which they died to gain." But Lowell's empyrean salute to the "sacred dead" contrasted sharply with Bushnell's pragmatic recognition that the living bore specific obligations to those who had perished. Bushnell's remarks appealed to a widespread desire to translate commemoration into concrete action and to address what were seen as the enduring needs of the slain.[2]

The war's work of killing was complete, but the claims of the dead endured. Many soldiers lay unburied, their bones littering battlefields across the South; still more had been hastily interred where they fell, far from family and home; hundreds of thousands remained unidentified, their losses unaccounted for. The end of combat offered an opportunity to attend to the dead in ways war had made impossible. Information could now flow freely across North and South; military officials would have time to augment and scrutinize incomplete casualty records; bodies scattered across the defeated Confederacy could be located and identified; the fallen could be honored without encroaching on the immediate and pressing needs of the living.

Clara Barton eagerly embraced these new possibilities. The necessities of war seemed to her to evolve logically into the demands of peace. Her care for wounded soldiers had always included supplying information to families about the men she treated at the front, and the end of hostilities seemed to bring only an increase in the numbers of letters she received in search of lost husbands and sons. Deeply sympathetic to "the distressed class of sufferers all through our land waiting, fearing, hoping, watching day by day for some little tidings of the loved and lost," Barton determined to develop a way to relieve what she described as the "intense anxiety ... amounting in many instances almost to insanity" of these petitioners.[3]

In the spring of 1865 she founded the Office of Correspondence with the Friends of the Missing Men of the United States Army to serve as an information clearinghouse. Bypassing the tangled federal bureaucracy, she turned directly to the soldiers themselves for information about their slain or surviving friends. She would publish the names submitted by those in search of kin in hopes of soliciting news about them. As she explained at the top of one printed list: "I appeal to you to give such facts relative to the fate of these men as you may recollect or can ascertain. They have been your comrades on march, picket or raid, or in battle, hospital, or prison; and, falling there, the fact and manner of their death may be known *only* to you." Within days of her announcement Barton had received several hundred letters, and communications soon poured in by the thousands to the tiny third-floor room at Seventh and E streets in Washington that served, as its sign announced, as the "Missing Soldiers Office." Lincoln had endorsed her efforts before his death, and in response to her persistent inquiries, President Andrew Johnson agreed to subsidize the dissemination of her lists. By mid-June she had published the names of 20,000 men; by the time she finally closed the office in 1868, she reported that it had received and answered 68,182 letters and had secured information about 22,000 missing soldiers.[4]

For the military, war's end permitted the systematic assessment of losses that the unrelenting pressures of conflict had prohibited. In July 1865 Quartermaster General Montgomery Meigs ordered every Union commander to submit a report of "all interments registered during the war." These records became the basis for the *Roll of Honor,* lists of names and burial places of "soldiers who died in defence of the American Union" that Meigs would print in twenty-seven installments, constituting eight bound volumes, as officers executed his order over the course of the next six years. But wartime records listed only 101,736 registered burials, fewer than a third of the estimated total of Union fatalities. It was clear that hundreds of thousands of northern soldiers lay in undocumented locations, their remains untended and even unmarked, their deaths unknown to their families as well as to military record keeping.[5]

Official policy toward the dead evolved slowly over the next sev-

Clara Barton, circa 1865. Photograph by Mathew Brady.
Clara Barton National Historic Site/National Park Service.

eral years, but immediate action seemed imperative, as a matter of
both decency and expediency. The longer bodies were left without
proper burial, the more vulnerable they became to depredation and
the less likely they were to be identifiable. Military commanders
improvised in the face of need and opportunity. In June 1865 Captain
James Moore, an assistant quartermaster who had been active in
fledgling graves registration efforts during the war, was ordered to
the Wilderness and Spotsylvania "for the purpose of superintending
the interments of the remains of Union soldiers yet unburied and
marking their burial-places for future identification." Moore found
hundreds of unmarked graves, as well as skeletons that had been left
for more than two years without the dignity of burial. "By exposure
to the weather," he reported, "all traces of their identity were entirely
obliterated." Summer heat and "the unpleasant odor from decayed
matter" prevented him from removing all bodies to a central loca-

tion, but he made sure all were carefully interred, with remains appropriately "hidden from view." On these two fields he estimated that he oversaw the burial of fifteen hundred men, although the scattering of so many bones made an exact count impossible. Soldiers of the U.S. Colored Troops, not yet mustered out of service, did the often repellent work. Moore reported that 785 tablets were erected over named graves, and he submitted a list of the officers and men he had identified.[6]

As soon as Moore completed this assignment, he was ordered to the site of the notorious Confederate prison at Andersonville, Georgia, where so many Union soldiers had perished. Officially named Camp Sumter, Andersonville had held 45,000 Union soldiers between its opening in February 1864 and the end of the war. Known for its especially brutal conditions, it comprised little more than a stockade surrounding twenty-five acres of ground on which men crowded together without shelter or adequate food, polluting the stream that provided the camp's only drinking water. The death rate from disease and violence reached nearly 30 percent, and the prison's commander, Captain Henry Wirz, would hang in November 1865 for war crimes.[7]

In late June 1865 a former Andersonville prisoner named Dorence Atwater contacted Clara Barton, offering to help identify men on her published lists. A Connecticut soldier who had been confined at the camp for almost its entire existence, Atwater had been assigned to maintain a record of the dead. Determined to document the horror he had witnessed, he had kept a hidden copy for himself. This enumeration corresponded with numbered graves, offering the possibility of identifying a great many who had endured the camp's extreme conditions. When he learned of the existence of the list, Secretary of War Edwin Stanton authorized an expedition to Andersonville under Captain Moore's command and invited Clara Barton to participate. Moore, Barton, Atwater, forty laborers and craftsmen, and seven thousand "unlettered headboards" departed from Washington by boat on July 8, 1865. Vying for preeminence—Barton insisted the expedition was her idea—Moore and Barton quickly grew to resent

"*A Burial Party on the Battle-field of Cold Harbor, Virginia,
April 1865.*" *A part of the Federal reinterment effort under the
command of James Moore. Negative by John Reekie; print and
caption by Alexander Gardner. Library of Congress.*

and even detest each other. Moore was overtly hostile, in part to the
very presence of a woman on an official military expedition, and he
reportedly declared at the outset of the trip, "God damn it to hell!
Some people don't deserve to go anywhere. And what in hell does
she want to go for?" Upon her return Barton formally complained to
Stanton about Moore's behavior.[8]

The insalubrious conditions that had tormented the prisoners also
took their toll. The summer heat was almost unbearable—often well
over a hundred degrees—and a number of laborers became ill, including a "letterer" assigned to paint headboards, who died of typhoid—
the "last martyr of Andersonville," Barton noted in her diary. The
expedition nevertheless documented 13,363 bodies and succeeded in

identifying 12,912. All were reinterred in marked graves, and on August 17 their resting place was dedicated as the Andersonville National Cemetery. Barton was honored to raise the Stars and Stripes where "the flag of the country" had not "floated in four dark years."[9]

In the western theater similar efforts were under way. On June 23, 1865, Major General George H. Thomas, commander of the Department of the Cumberland, had ordered Chaplain William Earnshaw to identify and reinter soldiers scattered around Murfreesboro, Tennessee, in the Stones River National Cemetery, established in 1864 to commemorate the bloody battle that had taken place there two years before. Earnshaw began searches of the surrounding area, investigating old sites of camps and garrisons within a radius of nearly a hundred miles.

In the summer of 1865 the ultimate intentions of the federal government toward the war dead were not yet clear, and officers acted in response to circumstances in the field. Moore had at first thought that he would move all the bodies he found on the Virginia battlefields to a central cemetery, but summer weather changed his plan. His activities came to focus on the effort just to provide decent burial for remains that were either still above ground or were buried so shallowly as to invite destruction by hogs or vandals. Ordered to attend to the Union dead, Moore also interred many Confederates in order simply to clean up the littered Virginia fields. In the West Earnshaw undertook a wider and more systematic search, with the definite purpose of transferring Union bodies to an already existing national cemetery. It was, he declared, "our solemn duty to find every solitary Union soldier's grave that marked the victorious path of our men in pursuit of the enemy." Indeed, by the time he was finished, he believed that within his assigned area "not more than 50 Union soldiers still sleep outside our beautiful cemetery."[10]

Only gradually in the years following southern surrender did a general sense of obligation toward the dead yield firm policy. Only slowly did the orders of individual military commanders combine with legislative authorization and funding to create an enormous and comprehensive postwar reburial program intended to locate every

"Miss Clara Barton Raising the National Flag, August 17, 1865,"
at Andersonville. Sketched by I. C. Schotel. Harper's Weekly,
October 7, 1865.

Union soldier across the South and inter all within a new system of
national cemeteries. But this was not the goal at the outset. Widespread and continuing public discussion about the dead gradually
articulated a set of principles that influenced military and legislative
policy. The experience of federal officials assigned, like James Moore,
to begin the interment and identification of the slain shaped attitudes
as well, as the actual conditions of wartime graves and burials became known. The transcendent ideals of citizenship, sacrifice, and

national obligation united with highly practical and ever-growing concerns about southern mistreatment of gravesites and bodies to result in what was arguably the most elaborate federal program undertaken in nearly a century of American nationhood.

In October 1865, sobered by the difficulties already encountered in the attempt to compile reliable lists of the dead, Quartermaster General Montgomery Meigs issued another general order, calling upon officers to provide a survey of cemeteries containing Union soldiers. He requested details about the location and condition of graveyards, the state of relevant records, and officers' recommendations for the protection and preservation of remains. He asked specifically for an evaluation of the appropriateness of each site and a judgment as to whether bodies should be left in place or removed to a "permanent cemetery near." After interruptions necessitated by summer heat, Moore in the East and Earnshaw in the West resumed their efforts under these new guidelines, and on December 26 Edmund B. Whitman, chief quartermaster of the Military Division of the Tennessee, was relieved of his regular duties and assigned responsibility "to locate the scattered graves of Union soldiers" across a wide area of Kentucky, Tennessee, Georgia, Mississippi, and Alabama. Whitman had served in the Quartermaster Corps during the war, enlisting from his home in Kansas soon after the opening of hostilities. A Harvard College graduate of the Class of 1838 and a New England schoolteacher, he had emigrated to Kansas in 1855 as one of a number of abolitionists committed to preventing the permanent establishment of slavery in that strife-torn and "bleeding" territory. Now, a decade later, he embarked on an expedition to locate and honor those who had perished in the cause for which he had fought so long.[11]

As he contemplated his assignment, Whitman concluded that *"a knowledge and a record of every grave"* must be *"in the possession of some living person."* Like Clara Barton, he sought surviving witnesses who alone had the information necessary to enable him to locate and identify the dead. Whitman composed a circular entitled "Important Information Wanted," addressed to "Surgeons, Chaplains, Agents of Sanitary and Christian Commissions, Quartermasters, Officers or

Soldiers," and forwarded it to three hundred newspapers and periodicals for publication. Announcing that the United States Quartermaster General had ordered the preparation of a "record ... of all Union soldiers who have been buried in the Rebel States," Whitman requested assistance in locating the fallen. Whitman later reflected, after completion of the assignment, how important this circular had proved not simply in generating information but in engaging the broader public. His communication, he judged, had proved critical in creating a "sympathetic chord" and had "exerted an influence in the creation of the public sentiment which justified and sustained the subsequent measures adopted."[12]

The circular provoked an outpouring of responses. Relatives begged Whitman to find the remains of lost kin; other correspondents furnished "drawings and descriptions" indicating the exact spot where a friend or comrade had been buried. Often, Whitman reported, these proved "so minute and accurate in the details, that any person could proceed with unerring certainty to the very grave." A letter from A. T. Blackmun, for example, explained that his brother had been buried in a cemetery five miles east of Vicksburg, in an orchard near the railroad. "The grave is under & to the South side of the fourth apple tree, in the third row of trees, counting from the side nearest Vicksburg." Pencil marks on Blackmun's letter indicate that these detailed directions served their purpose and that his brother was indeed found. Isaac Weightman of the 29th Pennsylvania, killed in battle in Georgia, was buried "on the left side of the Railroad going towards Atlanta about a mile off along a small creek near the Breastworks of the rebels ... by a big tree," reported a letter written by a neighbor on his mother's behalf. A fellow soldier had sent the bereaved woman information about her son's death and burial, but she had not been able to visit or reclaim his body. A piece of cracker box inscribed with lead pencil marked his grave; his body was buried in only his trousers. "Any information will be a great solace to his mother who has given three (3) sons and (3) sons in law to the armies of our country."[13]

Chaplains wrote to Whitman with complete lists of regimental dead and their places of burial. One clergyman who had returned home to New Bedford, Massachusetts, provided documentation for two hundred graves in Tullahoma, Tennessee. Many soldiers seemed to have "whiled away boredom copying names from graves," lists that they eagerly forwarded in response to Whitman's request. Surgeons sent plans of hospital burial grounds with numbered graves and rolls of names. Officers who had been in charge of burial parties on the field had sometimes prepared plots of interments. "In the case of the 46 Ohio Regiment," Whitman reported, "such a paper, stained and soiled at the time of burial," would lead "to the identification after the lapse of more than 4 years of the entire group of dead from that regiment on the Shiloh battlefield."[14]

Whitman's circular served as Gabriel's trumpet, summoning the names and memories of the dead, raising them from neglect and anonymity, and ultimately returning hundreds of thousands of them to the nation. Whitman's trumpet summoned another band, arousing the living as well. His request for information uncovered an army of record keepers, waiting to be asked for the details they had carefully gathered and preserved, even without any clear notion of their purpose. They had documented identities and gravesites, had spent spare hours copying names and regiments from headboards, in hopes that this information might someday and somehow assist in the return of a body or the commemoration of a grave. They had compiled their lists and drawn their maps as acts of respect and reverence in and of themselves, as a small personal statement of opposition to the war's erasure of human life. Whitman's appeal invited them to connect their individual efforts to the policies and actions of the state. The federal government had provided Gabriel with his horn.

On March 1, 1866, a day he described as fine, cold, and windy, Whitman left Nashville on his mission, heading first to the site of the battle at Fort Donelson with a party of ten clerks and soldiers, as well as a cook and a mule handler. He would later add three more clerks and eight more soldiers to manage the work he found. The "entire country over which the war has extended its ravages," he soon recognized, "composes one vast charnel house of the dead." Whitman approached his work with the system and organization that marked him as an experienced quartermaster. In each locality he first visited battlefields, then the sites of former military hospitals, then private cemeteries. He devised a memorandum of eleven points "for guidance in exploring for Graves," a kind of checklist of matters to be considered, beginning with locating and counting graves, characterizing their condition, then listing inscriptions on headboards, identifying individuals who might have relevant information, and finally making suggestions for permanent cemeteries. He strove above all to be thorough, for he was committed to the importance of every Union body and every soldier's grave.[15]

Whitman proceeded with a sense of growing urgency, recognizing that information and even the bodies themselves were highly vulnerable to both human and natural forces. News abounded of distressing incidents of vandalism of Union graves and bodies. Accounts reached Whitman of corpses thrown naked and facedown into pits, of a body left lying to rot with a pitchfork still impaled in its back, and of the "constant depredation of headboards" in battlefield burial grounds. When he pursued a father's request that his son be moved from where he had fallen on the field in Georgia to the national cemetery in Chattanooga, Whitman learned that the body had already been claimed by local men "for the purposes of studying anatomy." Only two small arm bones, one hand bone, and his clothing remained in Oliver Barger's ransacked grave. Whitman received numerous reports of violence perpetrated against those who dared to care for Union bodies or graves. In Kentucky a man had even been killed for permitting two Yankees to be buried in his yard. A "constant depredation of Headboards and other trespasses and defilements, are constantly occurring," Whitman's superior officer in Nashville informed the quartermaster general in Washington.[16]

In February 1866 Major General George Thomas issued a general order forbidding desecration of Union graves and directing specifically that they must not be mutilated or obliterated in the course of the spring plowing season, which was about to begin for the first time since the end of the war. By April concerns about vandalism had reached Washington, and Congress passed a joint resolution requiring the secretary of war "to take immediate measures to pre-serve from desecration the graves of the soldiers of the United States who fell in battle or died of disease... and secure suitable burial places in which they may be properly interred." Now the legislative branch joined the military in the disposition of the Union dead.[17]

Whitman's superiors delivered elaborate orders about his respon-sibilities and their goals: "so far as practicable every Union soldier in the Milt Div of the Tennessee, shall finally rest in a well enclosed and decent ground, with a neat index to his grave, and with an accessible record of his final resting place." On "battle fields of national inter-est," where the northern public might be enlisted to support the "work of ornamentation," or where graves were "scattered and unprotected," it would be advisable to collect the bodies together in one place. But if remains lay peaceably in a churchyard or cemetery, "it is not desirable to incur an increase of expense to remove them, *simply* to carry out a general scheme." Whitman was to locate graves, mark and protect isolated burial spots, and "form some plans" about graves that should be moved and about sites to which they might be relocated. Whitman's superiors insisted that bodies that had been decently interred should be left where they lay except when "a sav-age and vindictive spirit of the part of the disloyal inhabitants" sug-gested "a disposition to molest the remains." Increasingly, Whitman was coming to regard such vengefulness as less the exception than the rule.[18]

In the year since Appomattox the defeated white South had moved from stunned disbelief to a posture of growing defiance. Encouraged by President Andrew Johnson's sympathy, former Con-federates tested the limits of northern will, challenging Yankee claims to the fruits of victory. In the summer of 1865 southern legis-latures passed restrictive and discriminatory Black Codes, designed to reestablish slavery in all but name; in the fall the recently rebel-lious states elected former Confederate military officers and politi-cians to represent them in Washington; throughout the South white southerners perpetrated and tolerated relentless violence against freedpeople. The hundreds of thousands of Union bodies in their midst provided an irresistible target for southern rage as well as a means to express the refusal to accept Confederate defeat. It had proved impossible to overcome a live Union army, but bitter Confederates could still wage war against a dead one.[19]

A particularly virulent outbreak of white violence in fact served as a direct cause of intensified congressional interest in Union graves. During the first four days of May 1866, Memphis erupted in what were generally designated as riots, although the death toll of forty-six blacks and two whites suggests that those who wrote of a "massacre" were more accurate. Ninety-one houses, all but one occupied by African Americans, four churches, and twelve schools were destroyed. Fear became so widespread among African Americans in the area that Whitman reported he was for some time unable to persuade black laborers to continue to work for him. Congress promptly dispatched a committee of three members of the House of Representatives to investigate causes of the disturbance. Ultimately the legislators made recommendations about controlling white defiance that played a significant role in the movement toward Radical Reconstruction. But the assistant quartermaster of the Division of the Tennessee, George Marshall, seized the opportunity provided by the congressmen's presence in Memphis to impress upon them the importance of the effort to bury the Union dead and the danger in which many soldiers' bodies lay. A delegation including Chaplain William Earnshaw, who had been overseeing reinterments at Stones River, convinced the congressmen that a comprehensive reburial program was imperative. The committee chair, Representative Elihu Washburne of Illinois, was particularly moved by the account of Union dead scattered across the South, and Whitman believed that this meeting led directly to the National Cemeteries Act that passed, along with a fifteenfold increase in appropriation, in the next Congress. But even before the bill became law, it was clear that after the discussion in Memphis the reinterment effort would assume a new and enhanced scope and importance.[20]

As spring unfolded, Whitman proceeded through the battlefields of Tennessee: Fort Donelson, Fort Henry, and then Shiloh. There, at the site of the battle that had first intimated the scale of slaughter to come, he encountered human bones scattered in "large quantities," and he learned from nearby inhabitants that their hogs, customarily left free to forage, were no longer fit to be eaten "on account of their living off the dead." Sweeping the field "deployed in the manner of a skirmish line," Whitman and his men sought to cover every foot of terrain involved in the battle. A list of 315 gravesites that had been compiled by a Sanitary Commission agent just after the fighting proved of critical assistance, and Whitman's party recorded and marked by compass points 178 different areas containing graves, including 21 burial trenches that held, he estimated, 250 bodies. Hundreds of men, he reported, seemed to have been "buried indiscriminately"—Yankees and rebels together—but Whitman was deeply moved by finding many soldiers in regimental groups, obviously carefully interred at the end of the battle by their comrades. These would be kept together when they were later removed to the national cemetery. In all Whitman discovered 1,874 Union dead, of whom 620 were identified by headboards or other inscriptions. About 200, he estimated, had been removed by relatives or friends. Keeping in mind the idea of siting national cemeteries at points of great historical interest, Whitman selected a potential spot on the Shiloh field.[21]

Near Memphis, Whitman encountered a road built over Union graves that had been all but destroyed by teams and carts, and he wrote sadly of 810 neglected Union graves in a cemetery three miles from the city. Nine hundred rebel graves in the same burial ground were carefully tended, with identities listed in a sexton's book. The "Association of Southern Mothers," he learned, had assumed responsibility for these Confederate dead, while their victorious Union counterparts lay dishonored beside them.[22]

Locating the many graves scattered beyond actual battlefields—casualties from skirmishes, or wounded men who died on the march, or men who succumbed to disease—required Whitman to seek information from local citizens who might have seen or heard of buried soldiers or even assisted in their interments. "As a rule," he later remembered, "no residence or person was to be passed without the inquiry. 'Do you know, or have you heard of any graves of Union soldiers in this neighborhood?' " When he arrived in Oxford, Mississippi, Whitman called upon the town postmaster, a federal employee after all, who might be expected to be both knowledgeable and helpful to a Union official. Whitman received not assistance but a warning. The postmaster declared that he would not dare tell a Yankee soldier about Union graves, even if he knew of them. Since the postmaster had taken the loyalty oath to qualify for his position at the end of the war, all his friends, cultivated during nineteen years of residence in the town, had abandoned him. He had even been asked to cease attending his church. "I am informed," Whitman wrote his commanding officer, "that a disposition has been shown in this vicinity to obliterate and destroy all traces of the graves union soldiers find scattered in the country."[23]

Farther south the Union dead seemed to be in even more distressing circumstances. Whitman discovered "immense numbers" of bodies in the area between Vicksburg and Natchez—perhaps, he thought, as many as forty thousand. These corpses were in every imaginable place and condition: buried on river embankments and then wholly or partially washed away (there were even reports of coffins floating like little boats down the Mississippi toward the sea), or abandoned in "ravines and jungles and dense cane brakes" and never buried at all. A farmer named Linn, who wanted to extend his cotton fields, had plowed up about thirty Union skeletons and then delivered the bones *"in bulk"* to the Vicksburg city cemetery. Not far away a Union graveyard had been leveled entirely to make way for a racecourse.[24]

As Whitman pursued his explorations, three hundred black soldiers at the Stones River National Cemetery continued to collect and rebury Union bodies from the wide surrounding area at the rate of fifty to a hundred a day. Stones River represented a pioneering example of the comprehensive reburial effort that by the summer of 1866 had come to be seen as necessary across the South. It also represented the critical role that African Americans had come to play in honoring the Union dead. Almost invariably units of U.S. Colored Troops were assigned the disagreeable work of burial and reburial, and Whitman's own exploration party included several soldiers from U.S. Colored regiments. Individual black civilians also proved critical to Whitman's effort to locate corpses and graves.[25]

"Justice to the race of freedmen," Whitman reported to headquarters, demands "a tribute of grateful mention." Rebuffed in his search for information by whites like the Mississippi postmaster, Whitman learned to turn to black southerners for help as he traversed the South in the spring and fall of 1866. "Most all the information gained" at one Georgia location, he reported to his journal, "was from negroes, who, as I was told ... *pay more attention to such matters than the white people.*" There was a good deal more at issue here, Whitman soon recognized, than just attentiveness. Black southerners cared for the Union dead as a gesture of political assertiveness as well as a demonstration of gratitude and respect.[26]

During the war African Americans had risked their lives burying Union soldiers and trying to preserve both their names and their graves. About two miles from Savannah, in a corner of "the Negro Cemetery," lay seventy-seven "graves of colored soldiers" in four neat rows. All but three were identified, all in "very good condition," and all marked with "good painted headboards." This was the last resting place of the dead of a unit of U.S. Colored Troops, carefully buried and tended by the freedpeople of the area. Whitman encountered other sites where former slaves had interred Yankees and still watched over their graves. Behind an African Colored Church near Bowling Green, Kentucky, for example, 1,134 well-tended graves sheltered both black and white Union soldiers. A black carpenter nearby was able to provide the most useful information about the area because he had made coffins and helped to bury many of the Union dead himself.[27]

Freedmen provided Whitman with assistance and information throughout his travels. Moses Coleman, "an intelligent negro," sought Whitman out to tell him about the graves of nine Union soldiers who had been shot by Confederate cavalry after being taken prisoner: "one of whom he saw shot after being compelled to climb a tree." A freedman eagerly offered the names and locations of two soldiers he had buried more than a year before; another former slave reported his employer's desecration of soldiers' graves and offered to identify thirty on his plantation that still remained undefiled.[28]

Such concern on the part of African Americans was hardly limited to Whitman's experiences in the Military Division of the Tennessee. At the very end of the war, for example, African Americans in Charleston had tended the graves of more than two hundred Union captives who had died while confined in a makeshift prison on the city racecourse. Enclosing the burial ground and mounding and planting the graves, the freedmen painted a sign over the entryway inscribed "Martyrs of the Race Course." On May 1, 1865, the African American population of the city, under the protection of a full brigade of Union infantry, including three regiments of U.S. Colored Troops, honored the federal dead with flowers, processions, and oratory in what historian David Blight has argued was the first Decoration Day. In the warfare over the disposition of the dead, black southerners showed little hesitation in choosing sides.[29]

At the end of June Whitman proposed sites for national cemeteries at Fort Donelson, Pittsburgh Landing, Corinth, Memphis, and Vicksburg and presented his views about the future to the chief quartermaster of the Military Division of the Tennessee. Whitman affirmed his "conviction, which seems to have impressed itself in some degree upon all," of the government's "duty" toward the remains of those who "have died in so noble a service." The experiences of the preceding months, he reported, had produced a "daily deepening in my own mind" of the importance of this federal obligation, as he had witnessed the "total neglect" or "wanton desecration" of Union graves by a southern population whose "hatred of the dead" seemed to exceed their earlier "abhorrence of the living."[30]

Whitman's travels across what he described as the "vast charnal house" of the South had, he confessed, "awakened a feeling of deep personal interest" in an undertaking that was "technically official."

He urged that in spite of the concerns his superiors had expressed about scope and cost, *"the work be well and thoroughly done, with a true conception of its magnitude and significance."* Arguing that the federal government stood "in loco parentis" toward the Union dead, Whitman displayed a growing emotional engagement that was evident in his eloquent plea, phrased, like Bushnell's oration, in the language of debt and obligation. The government, he insisted, held "a stewardship, the account of which must be rendered to the spirit of humanity and Christian patriotism, to the friends of republican liberty and of human freedom and progress throughout the world, to the free people of the North, whose dearest sons have been sacrificed to the demon of slavery and whose choicest treasures have been poured out." Those who had fallen were not "hireling mercenaries" but citizens of a "Republican America where every man is himself a constituent and integral part of the Government."[31]

The understanding of governmental obligation to the dead that Whitman advanced—"a stewardship, the account of which must be rendered"—was not his alone. By the middle of 1866 a chorus of voices in the North had begun to advocate policies toward the fallen that reflected fundamental assumptions about the principles for which the war had been fought. With the passage of conscription legislation in 1863, the nation had, for the first time in its history, mandated the obligation of the citizen to fight in its defense; it had mobilized millions of volunteers; now it had an obligation to those who had served. Citizenship represented a contract in which the state and the individual both assumed certain rights and duties, for which either could be called to account.

Clara Barton embraced these principles in her insistence that the work of naming the dead be regarded as a governmental responsibility. Late in 1865 she had explained her position in a letter to Secretary of War Edwin Stanton seeking federal support in the search for missing men. "The true patriot," she declared,

> willingly loses his life for his country—these poor men have lost not only their lives, but the very record of their death. Common

humanity would plead that an effort be made to restore their identity... As call after call for "three hundred thousand more" fell upon their stricken homes, the wife released her husband and the mother sent forth her son, and they were nobly given to their country for its necessities: it might take and use them as the bonded officer uses the property given into his hands; it might if needs be use up or lose them and they would submit without complaint, but never... has wife or mother agreed that for the destruction of her treasures no account should be rendered her. I hold these men in the light of Government property unaccounted for.[32]

Like Bushnell, Barton wrote of accounts and treasures; like Whitman, she called for federal engagement with the care of Union dead. She explored basic notions of human rights, of the mutual obligations that bind state and citizens. Significantly, at the end of a war about slavery, she situated her discussion in concepts of property in persons. But this was not the property of slavery; this was citizenship, not bondage. Here the individual freely acted as his own agent, as a true patriot "willingly" ceding control over his life. And here, again in contrast to an institution that tore families asunder, the wife and mother consented to give up her husband and son "to their country for its necessities."

But this cession of rights, of property in person, remains incomplete. It is, in effect, a contract in which the state must in return accept certain obligations—in Barton's view, to provide a record of death, an accounting for the destruction of human treasure. And tellingly, in Barton's rendering, it is undertaken between women and the state. Women, legally denied the right to make contracts in most of pre–Civil War America, here claim new rights of personhood and citizenship that derive from their wartime sacrifice. An accounting for the dead is an accounting to the bereaved. As she affirmed the individual's right to identity and humanity even in death, Clara Barton articulated a notion of citizenship founded in the nation's experience of civil war and in the suffering of both soldiers and civilians. The war that freed the slaves established broad claims to rights—for

*"The Soldier's Grave," by Currier and Ives, a lithograph
that families could inscribe with details of a lost loved one.
For those who had no actual grave to mark, this
could serve as a substitute. Library of Congress.*

blacks as well as whites, for women as well as men, for both the living and the dead. But as Clara Barton certainly recognized, the soldier dead were all men. Survivors had not made the ultimate sacrifice; their claims upon the state would not have the same force as those of the soldiers who had suffered and perished. The rhetoric of Clara Barton's letter to Stanton sought to minimize and even erase a gendered divide and a gendered hierarchy that Civil War death had only rendered more profound. But it was no accident that when the nation, however fleetingly, sought to expand its polity in the years immediately following the war, it was black men, who had served and died in such significant numbers, and neither white nor black women, whom the Fifteenth Amendment welcomed as newly enfranchised citizens.[33]

In August 1866, as reburial efforts in the South slowed in response to summer heat, *Harper's New Monthly Magazine* published an article calling for a comprehensive system of national cemeteries to include all Union dead. Building on notions of federal obligation that Bushnell, Barton, and Whitman had already articulated, James F. Russling defined treatment of the fallen as the sign and test of democracy, as well as the indicator of progress and modernity.

Except for "Republican Athens," Russling argued, no people or nation had ever designated a burial place for the common soldier. He has "been overlooked, as if too humble to be taken into account." But this was "a new era," determined to "elevate our common humanity." And perhaps even more important, the United States was a nation that had newly displayed its dedication to the proposition of human equality.

> A Democratic republic like ours, based on the equality of the race, and affirming justice for all that knows or professes to know only excellence and worth wherever found, can not afford to pass by unheeded, however humble, those who have proven themselves by fierce and sturdy warfare in its behalf at once its best citizens and brave defenders.

The purposes of the war and the treatment of the dead were inextricable. Urging that the bodies of all Union soldiers should be disinterred and "brought speedily together into great national cemeteries," Russling emphasized the mutuality of obligation between citizen and state.[34]

> *Dulce et decorum est pro patria mori* is a good sentiment for soldiers to fight and die by. Let the American Government show, first of all modern nations, that it knows how to reciprocate that sentiment

by tenderly collecting, and nobly caring for, the remains of those who in our greatest war have fought and died to rescue and perpetuate the liberties of us all.[35]

In its invocation of modernity, in its reference to the "greatest war," in its citation of a line from Horace that became the title of World War I's most famous poem, Russling's words almost seem to look to another Great, and yet more bloody, War, one that would install mass carnage at the core of existence in the twentieth century. That dying for one's country is sweet and proper becomes for Wilfred Owen by 1917 "the old Lie." But a half century earlier it remained for Russling "a good sentiment"—one that he believed should animate national policy toward the Civil War dead.[36]

Russling's prescriptions soon became settled policy. Even before Congress passed formal legislation in February 1867, the effort to bury every Union soldier within the safe confines of a national cemetery began. During the summer of 1866 Whitman made plans for "commencement of the general work of disinterment" in the cooler weather of fall, designing record-keeping forms that would minimize errors, mapping routes, and gathering needed labor and supplies. Whitman was acutely aware of both the dangers and the opportunities in relocating so many bodies. Moving a grave could mean losing an identity tied to a place or circumstance of burial; it might also provide a final chance to discover a name. He and his superiors were sensitive, too, to the implications of this unprecedented extension of governmental responsibility into the intimate and domestic arena of death. Brevet Major General J. L. Donaldson, chief quartermaster of the Military Division of the Tennessee, introduced an uncharacteristically personal tone into the customary formality of general orders when he emphasized in an August directive that "the Government in assuming to perform a work, which belongs as a special right only to kindred and friends of the deceased, demands of its Agents to discharge the duty, with the delicacy and tenderness of near and dear friends." Later in the month Donaldson issued a circular addressed to "Friends of Deceased Union Soldiers" announcing to the general public that disinterment of all bodies in his Military Division would begin in October. He invited those who wished to be present at exhumations in hope of identifying lost kin to contact Whitman for an exact schedule of localities. The national government had assumed the unprecedented role of the citizen's friend.[37]

In early September Whitman set forth on his explorations once more, moving through Kentucky from the Tennessee line to the Ohio River, embarking again in late October to Chattanooga and Chickamauga, then along the route of Sherman's March, and back through Macon and Andersonville at the close of the year. By the end of his journey, Whitman estimated he had traveled thirty thousand miles in his search for the dead. Increasing local violence, resulting from the growing national conflict over Reconstruction, made Union bodies and graves, not to mention his own mission, ever more vulnerable. "The country in that section," Whitman wrote from Lexington, Kentucky, in late September 1866, "is in a very unsettled state and the lives of Union men are unsafe." Whitman kept a careful eye out for land that might be suitable for permanent cemeteries, recording details about plots, owners, and purchase options. His reports to headquarters, he later remembered, called regular attention to "the wretched condition of the graves and burial places of the dead and to their miscellaneous and universal distribution throughout the entire country that had been the seat of war." Collectively his communications powerfully reinforced "the necessity of . . . universal disinterment and collection of the scattered remains into permanent National Cemeteries."[38]

In early 1867 Whitman's position was at last enshrined in law, as well as War Department policy. With "A bill to establish and protect national cemeteries," passed by Congress in February 1867, and the creation of seventeen additional cemeteries in the course of that year, the federal government legally signaled its acceptance of responsibility for those who had died in its service. The locating and recording of graves that Whitman had undertaken in his 1866 expedition would be transformed into a comprehensive program of reburial,

combined with acquisition of land for a system of government cemeteries adequate to hold hundreds of thousands of soldiers' remains.[39]

Across the Military Division of the Tennessee Whitman reaped
what he described as a "Harvest of Death," reporting that by 1869 he
had gathered 114,560 soldiers into twenty national cemeteries within
his assigned territory. Each body was placed in a separate coffin, its
original burial site recorded and its final destination documented by
cemetery section and grave number. Reinterments cost an average of
$9.75 a body, with $2 to $3 of this for the coffin. Ultimately each
reburied soldier would also be marked by a name—if it was in fact
known—for in 1872 Congress at last yielded to Quartermaster General Montgomery Meigs's insistence upon such commemoration. In
December 1868, Meigs had written to the secretary of war in terms
that suggested the growing importance of public opinion—the sentiment of the "friends" of the fallen—in shaping governmental policy
toward the dead. "I do not believe," Meigs declared, "that those who
visit the graves of their relatives would have any satisfaction in finding them ticketed and numbered like London policemen, or con-
victs. Every civilized man desires to have his friend's name marked
on his monument." And every citizen deserved to be remembered as
an individual and identifiable human self.[40]

As Whitman supervised the removal of tens of thousands of bodies to national cemeteries in the Division of the Tennessee, so the
work begun in 1865 by Moore and Earnshaw continued in other
parts of the South. Charged with responsibility for burials in Virginia,
Maryland, and Washington, D.C., Moore collected more than fifty
thousand bodies into national cemeteries. Near Petersburg, Virginia,
for example, he directed a force of one hundred men, forty mules,
and twelve horses that over a three-year period relocated 6,718 bodies killed in the final campaigns of the war to the new Poplar Grove
National Cemetery. The dead were gathered from more than ninety-
five different sites in nine different counties, and only 2,139 of them
could be positively identified, even though bounties were offered to
local citizens for information about bodies. In the cemetery at Seven

Pines, about seven miles east of Richmond, 1,202 of 1,356 dead soldiers remained unknown.[41]

At Antietam Moore oversaw units of the U.S. Burial Corps as they gathered what they expected to be about eight thousand soldiers from within a twenty-mile radius. Their goal was to complete the work in time for the fifth anniversary of the battle in September 1867. Some of the bodies—especially those with red hair, it seemed to one curiously analytic observer—remained "in an almost perfect state of preservation," facilitating recognition, while others could be identified only if distinctive objects had been interred with them. The comrades who had buried a soldier with a sealed bottle containing his name, address, and details of death had ensured that William Stickney of the Seventh Maine Volunteers would not be counted among the unknown.[42]

Overall the rate of identification proved rather better than at Poplar Grove. When the reinterment program was completed in 1871, 303,536 Union soldiers had been buried in seventy-four national cemeteries, and the War Department had expended $4,000,306.26 on the effort to gather the dead. Quartermaster General Meigs reported that 54 percent of the men had been identified as a result of careful attention to the bodies and their original graves, as well as extensive research in military hospital records, muster rolls, casualty reports, and even documentation gathered by the Sanitary Commission about deaths and burials. Some thirty thousand of these dead were black soldiers; they were buried in areas designated "colored" on the drawings that mapped the new national cemeteries and were enumerated in columns marked "black" on the forms officially reporting the progress of interments. Separated into units of U.S. Colored Troops in life, these soldiers were similarly segregated in death, and only about a third of them were identified. The notions of equality of citizenship that animated the reburial program clearly had their limits, despite the critical role African Americans had played in the identification and interment of the war's dead.[43]

The reburial program represented an extraordinary departure for the federal government, an indication of the very different sort of nation that had emerged as a result of civil war. The program's extensiveness, its cost, its location in national rather than state government, and its connection with the most personal dimensions of individuals' lives all would have been unimaginable before the war created its legions of dead, a constituency of the slain and their mourners, who would change the very definition of the nation and its obligations. "Such a consecration of a nation's power and resources to a *sentiment*," Whitman observed, "the world has never witnessed."[44]

But this transformative undertaking included only Union soldiers. These were the staunch defenders the nation sought to honor; these were the bodies imperiled by vengeful former Confederates; these were the men whose survivors bombarded the War Department with petitions for information about deaths and burials. The absence of official concern for the Confederate dead stood in stark contrast, even in the eyes of some northerners. John Trowbridge, a New Englander writing for the *Atlantic Monthly*, traveled through Virginia battlefields in 1865 soon after Moore had completed the initial phase of his work. Accompanied by a local resident, Trowbridge stumbled upon the unburied remains of two soldiers at the Wilderness. He was, he reported, "appalled," because he had heard—and had hoped—that the work of reinterment "was faithfully done." His Virginia guide examined the uniform buttons fallen from the clothing of the rotted corpses and informed Trowbridge, "They was No'th Carolinians; that's why they didn't bury 'em." Trowbridge was still more horrified to learn that the bodies had been left to rot as a matter of policy rather than simple negligence: "I could not believe that the true reason why they had not been decently interred."[45]

Trowbridge's sense that federal burial efforts should include the Confederate dead placed him in a minority, especially as Congress and the North assumed an increasingly radical position in regard to Reconstruction. In early 1868 the *New York Times* documented a dispute among three northern politicians on the question of the rebel dead. Governor Reuben Fenton of New York had counseled humanity in the treatment of slain Confederates and had in vain urged their inclusion in the Antietam Cemetery dedicated in 1867 and in the national reburial program more generally. But Governor John White Geary of Pennsylvania, who had fought for the Union and whose soldier son had died in his arms, and Pennsylvania's Radical Republican congressman John Covode, who lost two sons in the war, embraced no such generosity, insisting on the "personal guilt of the individual soldiers of the rebel army." Quartermaster General Meigs, responsible for executing federal policy on graves and interments, was himself bitterly angry at what he believed to have been the "murder" of his son John, who was shot in 1864 after he surrendered to Confederate soldiers in Virginia's Shenandoah Valley. Most veterans were more forgiving of their former enemies, recognizing the ties of duty that bind any soldier. But they had just waged a long and destructive struggle against these rebellious southerners; it seemed unimaginable that those who had tried to destroy the Union should be accorded the same respect as those who had saved it.[46]

This differential treatment of the dead had powerful, and seemingly unanticipated, effects. Southern civilians, largely women, mobilized private means to accomplish what federal resources would not. Their efforts to claim and honor the Confederate dead—and the organizations they spawned—became a means of keeping sectionalist identity and energy not just alive but strong. It did not pass unnoticed in the impoverished postwar South that during the five years that followed Appomattox, more than $4 million of public funds would be expended exclusively on dead northerners.

The April 1866 joint congressional resolution proposing the national cemetery system provoked an outraged response from white Virginians. Northerners were wrong, the *Richmond Examiner* proclaimed, to think that the Confederate was "the less a hero because he failed." Calling upon Richmond's churchwomen to assume responsibility for Virginia's fallen, the paper underscored the irony of defining southerners as outside a nation with which they had been forcibly reunited. If the Confederate soldier "does not fall into the category of the 'Nation's Dead' he is *ours*—and shame be to us if we do not care for his ashes."[47]

On May 3, 1866, a group of Richmond women responding to the *Examiner*'s call gathered to found the Hollywood Memorial Association of the Ladies of Richmond, recognizing both the obligation and the challenge before them. As Mrs. William McFarland, newly installed association president, acknowledged, the former Confederate capital was "begirt with an army of Confederate dead." Thousands of men lay in neglected graves in Hollywood Cemetery or in Oakwood, its counterpart on the eastern edge of the city, conveniently close to the site where Chimborazo, the South's largest military hospital, had stood. Tens of thousands more lay scattered on the many battlefields that surrounded the city. Mrs. McFarland believed that these soldiers belonged not just to Richmond but to the South, and it was to the Women of the South that she directed her appeal. In "dying," she proclaimed, Confederates "left us the guardianship of their graves." Every southerner, she insisted, held an obligation to the fallen, out of gratitude for their "noble deeds," as much as in sorrow at their loss. And every southerner was connected to these men, for although Confederate families suffered differing "degrees of affliction and bereavement, none are without sorrow and grief."[48]

The association began repair of the eleven thousand soldiers' graves dug at Hollywood during the war. Nearly all needed remounding and returfing, and few had adequate markers. The ladies worried too about the bodies scattered through the countryside, which they believed should be gathered, like the Union dead, into hallowed and protected ground. With the help of farmers from battle sites on the outskirts of the city, the association arranged for the transfer of hundreds of bodies to new graves in the Richmond cemetery during the summer and fall of 1866.

Across town the Ladies Memorial Association for the Confederate Dead of Oakwood, led by an executive council representing seven different Christian denominations, determined to mark and turf the sixteen thousand graves in its care. In early June the association received proposals for headboards, at costs ranging from forty cents to a dollar each. By mid-month they had submitted an order for an initial thousand. By summer 1867 the committee on headboards reported that the work was accomplished. In the course of the year a Hebrew Ladies Memorial Association was established as well, its members dedicated to caring for the graves of thirty Jewish Confederates buried in the soldiers' section of the city's Hebrew Cemetery.[49]

The ladies of Richmond supported their efforts through private donations, through contributions from the legislatures of other former Confederate states whose soldiers lay on Virginia soil, and through fund-raising activities that involved the broader community—and all its religious denominations—in the care of the dead. In the spring of 1867 the Hollywood Association sponsored a two-week-long bazaar that included the sale of such items as ink-stands carved from the bones of horses killed in the war and the raffling of Stonewall Jackson's coat buttons. But commercialization had its limits; both the Hollywood and Oakwood associations "respectfully declined" the offer of a Mr. Webb to produce a memorial soap to be sold on their behalf.[50]

The honoring of Confederate dead in the months after Appomattox quite naturally included decoration of graves with seasonal flowers. By the following spring these tributes had become more formal, often involving some combination of prayers, music, and oratory. Henry Timrod, poet laureate of the Confederacy, who had hailed its birth in "Ethnogenesis," now marked its demise in a eulogy to the dead that was sung to accompany the decoration of graves in Charleston's Magnolia Cemetery in 1867. "There is no holier spot of ground," he affirmed,

> *Than where defeated valor lies;*
> *By mourning beauty crowned.*

Different locations across the South scheduled the ritual for different days: May 10, the anniversary of Jackson's death; or April 26, the day Johnston surrendered to Sherman and the war truly ended; or May 30 or 31, when flowers promised to be abundantly available; or June 3, Jefferson Davis's birthday. Northerners, too, frequently chose a spring day for formal commemoration of the dead, and in 1868 General John Logan, commander in chief of the Grand Army of the Republic, issued a general order designating May 30 for the purpose of "strewing with flowers or otherwise decorating the graves of comrades who died in defense of their country during the late rebellion." The South, charged in Logan's order with "rebellious tyranny," continued its separate observances until after the First World War. Even today many southern states recognize Confederate Memorial Day on a different date from the nationwide holiday. More than two dozen cities and towns North and South claim to have invented Decoration Day, as Memorial Day was originally called, but these observances seem instead to have grown up largely independently and, for at least a half century after the Civil War, to have continued to reflect persisting sectional divisions among both the living and the dead.[51]

The northern reburial movement was an official, even a professional effort, removed by both geography and bureaucracy from the lives of most northern citizens; it was the work—and expense—of the Quartermaster Corps, the U.S. Army, and the federal government. In the South care for the Confederate dead was of necessity the work of the people, at least the white people; it became a grassroots undertaking that mobilized the white South in ways that extended well beyond the immediate purposes of bereavement and commemoration.

Winchester, in the northernmost part of Virginia, had been a site of almost unrelieved military activity, including three major Battles of Winchester, one each in 1862, 1863, and 1864; the town was said to have changed hands more than seventy times in the course of the war. The dead surrounded Winchester as they did Richmond, and women organized similarly to honor them. Fanny Downing, who assumed the presidency of the Ladies Association for the Fitting Up of Stonewall Jackson Cemetery, issued an "Address to the Women of the South" that echoed Richmond's Mrs. William McFarland. "Let us remember," her broadside cried, "that we belong to that sex which was last at the cross, first at the grave ... Let us go now, hand

*"Hollywood Cemetery, Richmond, Virginia—Decorating the Graves of
the Rebel Soldiers."* Harper's Weekly, *August 17, 1867.*

in hand, to the graves of our country's sons, and as we go let our
energies be aroused and our hearts be thrilled by this thought: *It is
the least thing we can do for our soldiers.*"[52]

Downing invoked the long tradition of female responsibility for
mourning, but her profession of allegiance to a country that had sup-
posedly surrendered its existence suggested a second motivation for
women's leadership of the southern reburial effort. To respectfully
bury one's neighbors and kin was a personal and private act; to
honor those who had risen up in rebellion against the national government was unavoidably public and political. Yet women were
regarded in mid-nineteenth-century America as apolitical in their
very essence; their aggressions and transgressions could be—and
largely had been—ignored during the war. Even amid the escalating
conflicts of Reconstruction, their gender would provide them with
wide leeway as they enacted a role they had played since they took
Jesus from the Cross. Mrs. Charles J. Williams, secretary of the Georgia Ladies Memorial Association, clearly understood the nature of

this gendered claim. "Legislative enactment may not be made to do honor to [Confederate] memories," as it had to those of the Union dead, "but the veriest radical that ever traced his genealogy back to the deck of the Mayflower, could not refuse us the simple privilege of paying honor to those who died defending the life, honor and happiness of the Southern women." But the "simple privilege" of memorializing the Confederate dead—like so many women's actions during the war itself—was in fact highly political; honoring the slain offered women a claim to both prominence and power in the new postwar South. Ensuring the immortality of the fallen and of their memory became a means of perpetuating southern resistance to northern domination and to the reconstruction of southern society.[53]

On October 25, 1866, a crowd five thousand strong gathered to dedicate Winchester's Stonewall Cemetery, graveyard for 2,494 Confederate soldiers who had been collected from a radius of fifteen miles around the town. Eight hundred twenty-nine of these bodies remained unknown and were buried together in a common mound surrounded by 1,679 named graves. General Turner Ashby, a dashing cavalry commander and local hero who had been killed in 1862, served as the ranking officer among the dead, as well as a focus of the day's ceremonies. His old mammy was recruited to lay a wreath on his grave in a pointed celebration of the world for which the Confederacy had fought. The American flag flying in the adjoining national cemetery, where five thousand Union soldiers had already been interred, provoked a "good deal of rancor" from the crowd, and the members of the U.S. Burial Corps, caring for the Federal dead, were jeered and insulted. Twenty-five hundred Confederates on one side; five thousand Yankees on the other: perhaps this was the Fourth Battle of Winchester, the one in which the soldiers were already dead.[54]

Women founded memorial associations almost everywhere there were concentrations of Confederate bodies. In Nashville an association of women purchased land in an existing cemetery to establish a Confederate Circle into which fifteen hundred bodies from nearby battlefields were moved. In Vicksburg the Ladies Confederate Cemetery Association oversaw the reinterment of sixteen hundred soldiers from the Vicksburg campaign at "Soldier's Rest," within an existing city cemetery. The Confederate Memorial Association of Chattanooga, under the leadership of Mrs. J. B. Cooke, acquired a site in 1867 in which to reinter Confederates from the surrounding area. In Atlanta, Mary Cobb Johnson "personally superintended" the removal of the dead from a radius of ten miles around the city. In some trenches she found as many as ninety bodies, wrapped in blankets, their hands folded across their chests, their hats over their faces. In Marietta the Georgia Memorial Association added bodies gathered from the battlefields around Chickamauga and Ringgold to a wartime cemetery for a total of three thousand Confederate graves. A local Unionist had suggested burying Yankees and Confederates together in the national cemetery established at Marietta, but women of the area were horrified and insisted that the Confederate dead be "protected from a promiscuous mingling with the remains of their enemies." In all of these cemeteries soldiers were grouped by state, in lasting tribute to the principles for which the conflict had been fought.[55]

Across Virginia women responded to Mrs. McFarland's call. The Ladies Memorial Association of Appomattox, founded like so many of its sister organizations in the spring of 1866, gathered the bodies of nineteen southern soldiers from the war's last campaign into a Confederate cemetery. The Petersburg Ladies Memorial Association oversaw the reinterment of thirty thousand dead Confederates in the Blanford Cemetery. The entire population of Petersburg in 1860 had been only 18,266, 50 percent of whom were black. The Spotsylvania Ladies Memorial Association procured five and a half acres of ground about a half mile northeast of Spotsylvania Court House for more than five hundred Confederates who lay scattered across the field of the 1864 battle. In Fredericksburg the Ladies Memorial Association (which is still thriving at the outset of the twenty-first century) acquired land on which they reinterred 3,553 Confederates from fourteen states. They were inspired in these efforts by a poem penned in their honor by Father Abram Ryan, author of the popular Lost Cause ballad "The Conquered Banner," who urged them to

Gather the corpses strewn
O'er many a battle plain;
From many a grave that lies so lone,
Without a name and without a stone,
Gather the Southern slain.

They had fallen, Ryan insisted, in a "cause, though lost, still just."[56]

For all the politics that inevitably surrounded the care and reinterment of the Confederate dead, the movement was also profoundly personal, for it provided bereaved families with bodies and graves on which to fix their sorrow. John Palmer of South Carolina had lost the first of two sons to die in the war at Second Bull Run in 1862. In the summer of 1869 he began a correspondence with Mary J. Dogan of the Manassas Memorial Association, who had identified James Palmer's grave near those of thirteen comrades. She wished to remove it to what became the Groveton Confederate Cemetery, where 266 southern soldiers are buried.

John Palmer readily forwarded funds for a walnut coffin and a four-foot marble stone—$32 to acquire and $1.86 to haul and install—inscribed with the details of his son's life and death. "The mere removal of the body will cost nothing," Dogan assured him, as that would be the responsibility of the association. In James's original grave Dogan had found a cross and a locket, and she removed the "fatal ball," now readily visible beneath his breastbone. Knowing the Palmers would value these relics "very highly," she shipped them to South Carolina. John Palmer carried the bullet with him for the rest of his life.[57]

Dogan expressed her condolences and wished "that all who have friends buried on this field could as easily and surely identify the spot where they be as you could that of your beloved son. But, alas, so few comparatively could." James Jerman Palmer's grave is one of only two at Groveton that are identified. The project on which the Manassas Association had embarked was daunting, and Dogan confessed to Palmer in 1871 that "I feel very much discouraged at times in regard to our accomplishing our objective of burying all our dead but yet hope when the spring opens we may be able to resume the work and if possible finish it this summer."[58]

In the early 1870s the attention of a number of southern memorial associations turned to the thousands of Confederate soldiers who still lay neglected on northern soil. Gettysburg seemed particularly critical, not just as the supposed "high-water mark" of Confederate fortunes. A sizable number of southern dead were scattered in unprotected and unmarked locations throughout the Pennsylvania countryside, subject to desecration by northerners hostile to the South. Several southern legislatures offered funds for moving bodies to the South, and memorial associations urged prompt action. Warning that yet another spring plowing might entirely destroy the bodies of Georgians still buried in Pennsylvania, the Savannah Memorial Association, for example, called for "her sister associations in the State to come forward at once and assist her in removing these remains."[59]

At Gettysburg, Samuel Weaver, who had supervised reinterments at the national cemetery, had come into possession of lists of Confederate burials compiled both by soldiers and by local residents. Although he died in 1871, his son Rufus, a young physician beginning a medical career in Philadelphia, was persuaded to respond to the entreaties of the ladies associations for aid. "If all could see what I have seen," he wrote, "and know what I know, I am sure there would be no rest until every Southern father, brother and son would be removed from the North." Weaver seemed to place little trust in the benevolence of his fellow Pennsylvanians toward these Confederate graves.[60]

During the spring and summer of 1871 Weaver disinterred and shipped 137 Confederates to Raleigh, 101 to Savannah, and 74 to Charleston, where they were greeted with an elaborate ceremony of orations, hymns, and prayers at Magnolia Cemetery. In the fall the Hollywood Memorial Association contacted Weaver, first about the Virginia dead, then with a request that all remaining Confederates be sent to Richmond. For the next two years Weaver worked exhuming bodies, forwarding groups in periodic shipments to the South. By the end of 1873 he had sent 2,935 Confederates to the Hollywood Association.[61]

The city of Richmond met their arrival with solemn pageantry; a cortege that included more than a thousand former Confederate soldiers and four Confederate generals accompanied the dead down Main Street to the cemetery. But the association struggled to raise the funds to reimburse Weaver for his efforts, and he never received at least $6,000 that was owed him. Despite his lists of burials and despite the newspaper advertisements Weaver had placed appealing for information about Confederate graves, a few southerners remained to be discovered even into the last decade of the twentieth century—by surprised citizens gathering herbs in 1888, macadamizing a road in 1895, digging trenches for water lines in 1938, planting a garden for the Eisenhowers in the 1950s, and simply walking near a railroad cut after a heavy rain in 1996. The goal of returning every southern soldier to the South was never realized. But the ladies memorial associations led a voluntary, improvisational, decentralized effort that overcame extraordinary obstacles—of organization, funding, and logistics—to bring tens of thousands of soldiers into cemeteries where they, like their Union counterparts, could be recognized for their valor and sacrifice.[62]

Some historians have argued that memorial activities in the immediate postwar South did not possess the explicitly partisan intentions of later commemorations, those that occurred after the founding of the United Confederate Veterans and the Daughters of the Confederacy in the last decade of the nineteenth century. Tied to that era's virulent politics of Jim Crow, disfranchisement, and states' rights, Confederate memory became in the 1890s a force that effectively undermined the emancipationist, nationalist, and egalitarian meaning of the war. But the earlier activities of the ladies memorial associations, undertaken in considerable measure as a direct response to the exclusion of Confederates from congressional measures establishing national cemeteries, were themselves explicitly sectional, intended to proclaim continuing devotion to the Confederacy, as well as to individual husbands, fathers, brothers, and sons. The Reverend John L. Girardeau, a Presbyterian theologian and the featured orator at the 1871 ceremony marking the reinterment of the Gettysburg dead at Charleston's Magnolia Cemetery, made the political nature of the gathering clear when he insisted that "we are not here simply as mourners for the dead." The occasion addressed "living issues," he explained, not just the past; "gigantic problems affecting our future" involved "the principles which led to our great struggle," principles, in his words, like states' rights and opposition to "Radicalism" and to racial "amalgamation." The living, he noted, confronted a compelling and unavoidable question: "Did these men die in vain?" Honor to the dead required the continuing defense of Confederate principles, which had been "defeated, not necessarily lost." Only vindication of the original purposes of the conflict could ensure the meaning of so many men's sacrifice. The Confederacy would not live on as a nation, but its dead would in some sense become its corporeal and corporate representation, not only a symbol of what once was but a summons to what must be.

Neither northern nor southern participants in the commemoration and reburial movement were "simply . . . mourners for the dead." Instead, they became in a very real sense the instruments of the dead's immortality. Gathered together in mass cemeteries with graves marshaled in ranks like soldiers on the field of battle, the dead became a living reality, a force in their very presence and visibility. They were also, paradoxically, a force in their anonymity. The postwar burial movements in both North and South made it possible for many bereaved families to identify kin and to visit or ornament graves, as did the Palmers of South Carolina or the many petitioners whom Whitman and Moore were able to assist. These reunions of the living with their dead were, of course, about ending anonymity, restoring names, and marking them on stones and monuments for posterity. But the lack of individuality of the Civil War dead had its powerful significance as well. Civil War cemeteries—both national and Confederate—were unlike any graveyards that Americans had ever seen. These were not clusters of family tombstones in churchyards, nor garden cemeteries symbolizing the reunion of man with

Ranks of soldier dead. "Confederate Cemetery of Vicksburg."
Photo by David Butow, 1997.

nature. Instead the Civil War cemetery contained ordered row after row of humble identical markers, hundreds of thousands of men, known and unknown, who represented not so much the sorrow or particularity of a lost loved one as the enormous and all but unfathomable cost of the war.[63]

The establishment of national and Confederate cemeteries created the Civil War Dead as a category, as a collective that represented something more and something different from the many thousands of individual deaths that it comprised. It also separated the Dead from the memories of living individuals mourning their own very particular losses. The Civil War Dead became both powerful and immortal, no longer individual men but instead a force that would shape American public life for at least a century to come. The reburial movement created a constituency of the slain, insistent in both its existence and its silence, men whose very absence from American life made them a presence that could not be ignored.

CHAPTER 8

NUMBERING

"How Many? How Many?"

"What imagination can reach the fearful aggregate of woe?"
HARPER'S WEEKLY, MAY 24, 1862

As Americans like Edmund Whitman and James Moore and Clara Barton and Mary Dogan and Mrs. William McFarland worked to name and bury the fallen, they counted: 13,363 at Andersonville, with 12,912 identified; 6,718 at Poplar Grove, with 2,139 identified; 2,935 Confederates from Gettysburg reinterred at Hollywood; 303,536 Union soldiers buried in national cemeteries. In face of the inadequacy of words, counting seemed a way to grasp the magnitude of sorrow, to transcend individual bereavement in order to grapple with the larger meaning of loss for society and nation. Counting helped shift focus from individual to total, from death to the Dead.

"How many homes have been made desolate," a young South Carolina woman had demanded in 1863, seeking not just a count of the dead but an accounting for death's impact. "How many Mothers and Sisters and Wives have been made to mourn since this war has been sent upon us [?] Numbers on top of numbers and we are not yet through." When at last the war was over, the nation demanded the answer to her plea.[1]

Counting had grown in importance in the decades that preceded the war. A population that had been largely innumerate—basic arithmetic was not even required for entrance to Harvard until 1803— began to count and calculate, to teach mathematics in schools, to regard numbers as a tool of mastery over both nature and society. The American Statistical Association, founded in 1839 by five Bostonians, grew within months into a nationwide organization with a constitution, bylaws, and regular publications. Americans had by the middle of the nineteenth century entered into what historian Patricia Cline Cohen has called an "infatuation with numbers."[2]

As the very term itself implies, statistics emerged in close alliance with notions of an expanding state, with the assessment of its resources, strength, and responsibilities. Often this quantification focused on censuses, on demography, and on mortality records, the very questions of life and death that took on new salience with the outbreak of war. Americans confronted the conflict and its death tolls predisposed to seek understanding in quantitative terms. In the face of the war's scale and horror, statistics offered more than just the possibility of comprehension. Their provision of seemingly objective knowledge promised a foundation for control in a reality escaping the bounds of the imaginable. Numbers represented a means of imposing sense and order on what Walt Whitman tellingly depicted as the "countless graves" of the "infinite dead."[3]

But it was as difficult to count the dead as to name them—and for the same reasons. Whitman wrote both literally and figuratively in calling them "countless." Just as Civil War armies lacked procedures for accurate identification of dead and wounded, so too structures for ensuring accurate reports of numbers of casualties after each battle did not exist. Army regulations had required military commanders to submit lists of captured, killed, wounded, and missing with the official description of each engagement. Hundreds of these handwritten lists are crammed into boxes at the National Archives, but they represent a highly problematic record, as E. B. Whitman discovered when he turned to them as part of his effort to identify and reinter thousands of Union dead. At the end of an engagement, commanders usually had more compelling concerns than compiling lists of casualties. If reports were made close in time to a battle, the number of deaths was understated, not just because of incomplete information but because many of the wounded who would soon die still clung to life. However, a lengthy interval between battle and casualty report—and this interval sometimes stretched as long as months—produced other sorts of errors.

Contemporaries readily admitted the shortcomings in official casualty data. William F. Fox, a Union lieutenant colonel who devoted his postwar years to trying to document the numbers of war deaths, found officers' reports a poor source. "After a hard fought battle," Fox remembered, "the regimental commander would, perhaps, write a long letter to his wife detailing the operations of his regiment, and some of his men would send to their village paper an account of the fight, but no report would be forwarded officially to head quarters. Many colonels regarded the report as an irksome and unnecessary task." Mass modern warfare had not brought with it the bureaucratic apparatus appropriate to its unanticipated scale. "What may be called the book-keeping of our volunteer army," former Union colonel Thomas Higginson wrote, as he tried to compile data on Massachusetts soldiers, "was borrowed from the book-keeping of our little regular army. It had suddenly to be expanded from thousands to millions." The duty of keeping records, he observed, tended to fall either to a man of military experience "without training in red tape," or to a "man of red tape without any training . . . as a soldier. In either case confusion resulted." History, Higginson concluded, was necessarily "an inexact science."[4]

The military's purposes in counting the dead had also influenced the reliability of military records. Casualty lists were not compiled because of concern about accounting for the individual lives lost, as the absence of any formal procedure for notifying kin made apparent. Counting the dead had been largely an issue of assessing military resources, of seeing who was left alive to fight. A commander needed to know his military strength. Union general George McClellan had been famously obsessed with both his own numbers and those of his enemy, consistently overestimating the number of Confederates arrayed against him by two- or threefold and essentially incapacitating himself through this statistical fixation. For William Tecumseh Sherman, a man of action and decision rather than crippling reflection, numbers became a language in which to express and assess battle's challenges and achievements. In his postwar memoirs he accompanied his description of each engagement with a summary of losses presented in the form that the War Department had prescribed for casualty reports. After his discussion of the Battle of Atlanta, for example, Sherman filled several pages with detailed numbers of losses and concluded, "I have no doubt that the Southern officers flattered themselves that they had killed and crippled of us two and even six to one ... but they were simply mistaken, and I herewith submit official tabular statements made up from the archives of the War Department, in proof thereof." For Sherman, as literary scholar James Dawes has observed, counting represented "the epistemology of war." He could best understand the war and explain his military virtuosity by translating his experience into numbers of dead.[5]

But if a general needed to know his own strength, so too he hoped to conceal it from the enemy, and these tactical misrepresentations could distort the permanent historical record. In May 1863 General Robert E. Lee had issued a general order criticizing prevailing custom in reporting casualties for encouraging "our enemies, by giving false impressions as to the extent of our losses." Inflated estimates and a tendency to report minor wounds as casualties, he believed, had resulted from commanders' pride in losses as "an indication of the service performed or perils encountered." After Gettysburg Lee himself pursued quite a different strategy but one equally inimical to the accurate reporting of losses: he seems to have quite systematically and intentionally undercounted his casualties in order to conceal the battle's devastating impact on his army.[6]

After the war, as the immediacy of death receded, the pride in sacrifice that Lee had identified as a source of dangerously inflated numbers grew even stronger. "Claims to gallant conduct," William Fox complained, "are very apt to be based upon the size of the casualty list." Regiments competed for having sustained the greatest losses and thus, by implication, for having exhibited the greatest valor. Fox found that "there have been too many careless, extravagant statements made regarding losses in action. Officers have claimed losses for their regiments, which are sadly at variance with the records which they certified as correct at the close of the war." In this postwar battle for glory, deaths became a measure not of defeat but of victory.[7]

The effort to compile definitive death statistics became a preoccupation in the years after Appomattox. But as with the reinterment movement, Yankees and Confederates possessed very different resources to direct to the task. Northerners would employ the expanding bureaucracy of the triumphant nation-state not just to rebury the dead but to count them. The census of interments requested by the quartermaster general at the end of the war made its contribution, ultimately resulting, as we have seen, in the reburial movement and in the twenty-seven installments of the *Roll of Honor,* which in their enumerations of graves provided one approximation of the totals of Union dead. Military officials had also ordered that before disbanding each Union regiment submit a "muster-out" roll including the name and fate—wounded, killed, died of disease, deserted, captured, discharged—of every man who had served at any point during the conflict. The War Department supplied large sheets, one yard square, printed with appropriate headings to be completed in multiple copies. William Fox largely relied on these documents for his compilation of casualties, and he believed they showed "clearly and accurately the mortuary losses of the regiments to which they pertain."[8]

Union officer–turned–writer John W. De Forest suggests reason for some skepticism. In his popular 1867 novel *Miss Ravenel's Conversion from Secession to Loyalty,* he provided a vivid portrait of the challenges one officer faced in completing the muster rolls at the end of the war. Dulled by "clouds of fever and morphine" and confronted by "a mass of company records," Captain Edward Colbourne nevertheless struggles to do his assigned duty within the three days allotted before the troops disband. He is, he observes, the only man in his unit who has been present since its origin and thus is the only one with the requisite memory. At the end of a long night of labor, he submits the completed document to others to copy, faints, and is confined to bed for forty-eight hours. One cannot but wonder if William Fox ever read De Forest's novel or recognized that his own data rested on such contingencies of memory and circumstance.[9]

Between 1865 and 1870 the War Department acknowledged the deficiencies in its records, issuing reports that presented three different—and ever-increasing—numbers of Union losses. In 1866 the *Final Report of the Provost Marshal General to the Secretary of War* counted 279,689 dead, but in early 1869 the adjutant general revised that number to 294,416 and then a year later, in response to an inquiry from the surgeon general, reported a total of 303,504. In 1885 Joseph Kirkley, who held the newly established post of statistician of the War Department, offered a further revision, reporting 359,528 Union deaths. A small subsequent adjustment, deriving from new information about deaths in Confederate prisons, added 694 to this sum, yielding what has come to be the most widely accepted count of 360,222.[10]

These constant revisions resulted in large part from information gradually brought forward by individuals seeking back pay of deceased kin or applying for federal pension and survivors' benefits, which were established in 1862 and expanded steadily through the rest of the century. The creation of this extensive pension system for Union veterans made systematic and accurate data about military service necessary. The array of muster rolls, strength reports, hospital records, and casualty lists kept during the war did not create a coherent personnel record for any individual soldier and thus left no easily accessible file to support a pension claim. To rectify this situation, the federal government worked to create from the mass of wartime documentation a set of records that would detail the experiences of individual men. These came eventually to be known as the Compiled Military Service Records, and after 1903 they included Confederate as well as Union soldiers. Ultimately nearly thirty million northern and more than six million southern entries—each documenting the appearance of a name on a muster roll, a hospital census, a casualty list, or other official form—were inscribed on index cards and sorted into individual soldiers' files. The scale of the effort required a small army of clerks, and the literal weight of this history inflicted its own postwar casualties. In 1893 the overcrowding of workers and documents in offices in the ill-fated Ford's Theatre—the site of Lincoln's assassination twenty-eight years earlier—caused two floors to collapse and kill twenty-two employees.[11]

But both public and private efforts to account for the dead preceded and paralleled those specifically related to pension claims. Almost every state in the North and many in the South had endeavored to produce counts and rosters well before expanding pension provisions required substantial federal involvement. Even during the conflict, individual states had authorized "Rolls of Honor" and other lists of names of those who had served and died. Many of these efforts foundered amid wartime exigencies, but in the years after Appomattox nearly every northern state renewed its effort to produce a roster.

The Pennsylvania legislature, for example, had authorized the creation of a comprehensive roster of soldiers in 1864, but the project was not launched until 1866. Samuel Bates, Pennsylvania state historian, found his assignment no easy task, at first locating only a partial file of muster rolls in the state adjutant general's office as a basis for his work. His "only recourse," he recognized, was to contact individual officers and interrogate them about the history of their units.[12]

Massachusetts made two separate efforts to assemble a complete list of soldiers' service and their fates. Rosters kept by the state adjutant general's office were printed in 1868 and 1869, but twenty years later the legislature created the post of State Military and Naval Historian and directed its first incumbent, Thomas Wentworth Higginson, to compile an index list of Massachusetts soldiers and sailors that would incorporate the more accurate information that had been collected by the federal pension office. Together with lists of men, Higginson published statistical summaries of casualties by unit and engagement. Massachusetts, he concluded, had sent 113,835 men to the war and had lost a total of 13,498. Higginson's skepticism about history's precision seems to have been well founded: a 1997 compilation of Massachusetts soldiers based on records in the National Archives counts 146,738.[13]

Confederates, who after 1865 had no nation-state, no government bureaucracy, and no expectation of federal pensions, turned state and private resources to a similar effort to document and honor soldiers' lives and deaths. But the incompleteness of Confederate records posed special challenges. The figure of 258,000 Confederate military deaths commonly cited by historians today can at best be regarded as an educated guess. The disintegration of the Confederate army made the collection of comprehensive data at war's end impossible, and the movement of the Confederate Archives between the evacuation of Richmond, their capture in Charlotte, North Carolina, and their eventual acquisition by the U.S. War Department meant that a significant number of regimental casualty lists and other official records are missing. There are, for example, almost no muster rolls at all of Alabama troops, and all records after the end of 1864 are very fragmentary. Nevertheless, in the South as well as the North, most states tried to compile and publish rosters of those who had served and those who had died, and these volumes continued to appear into the second decade of the twentieth century.[14]

In 1862 the South Carolina legislature had passed a measure calling for a comprehensive Record Book "as a token of respect" to Carolina's dead. The report that resulted was riddled with errors. In 1864 Professor William Rives of South Carolina College was appointed to undertake a second effort, and he struggled with military devastation, interruptions of mail service, and inadequate financial support. By advertising in newspapers for information, scanning obituaries, interviewing veterans, enlisting the help of tax collectors, and filling notebooks of "coarse brown paper" with data, he had by 1870 collected the names of twelve thousand South Carolina soldiers who had died in Confederate service. But, he stated, "I could not complete the work to my satisfaction." In 1912 the Historical Commission of South Carolina took up the task once again, and A. S. Salley, commission secretary, published three volumes covering five infantry regiments in 1913.[15]

In North Carolina, John W. Moore overcame obstacles presented by the incomplete and erroneous data available within the state by turning to Confederate records that were in the hands of the U.S. War Department. But he found these official reports inadequate as well. "Scarcely one had full account of the casualties," he wrote. "Unlettered orderly sergeants" produced "spelling that was really wonderful" although likely, he feared, to astonish those whose names were so creatively rendered. Nevertheless, Moore was confident that the four volumes he published in 1882 represented the most accurate presentation of North Carolina statistics possible.[16]

Other southern initiatives extended beyond individual states and addressed explicitly sectionalist purposes. The newly formed Southern Historical Society, established in 1869 and committed to "vindicate the truth" of Confederate history, sought to provide an accurate count of southern losses. In 1869 its secretary, the distinguished physician Joseph Jones, shared his estimate of casualties with the former Confederate adjutant general Samuel Cooper. Jones believed that one-third of all men actively engaged on the southern side had died in the conflict. Cooper affirmed that these numbers were "nearly . . . correct" but believed that a fuller search of Confederate records now in the hands of the federal government would provide greater detail and accuracy. For both Cooper and Jones, establishing the totals of troops North and South and documenting the extensive Confederate losses promised to provide an explanation—and justification—for the defeat as well as irrefutable evidence of the Confederate soldier's "resolution, unsurpassed bravery and skill."[17]

Private citizens in the North also set to counting wartime casualties and deaths. Frederick Phisterer, a German immigrant who had received the Medal of Honor for heroism at Stones River in 1862, published a *Statistical Record of the Armies of the United States* in 1883 as a supplement to Scribner's popular series of thirteen volumes entitled *Campaigns of the Civil War.* Phisterer's work included chapters on "Losses" and "Officers Deceased While in Service." William Fox claimed that his monumental *Regimental Losses in the American Civil War,* published in 1889, offered "full and exhaustive" numbers from both Union and Confederate units. Thomas Livermore, who had served as a major in the New Hampshire volunteers, attempted to amplify and correct Fox's conclusions in *Numbers and Losses in the Civil War in America,* which grew from an essay read before the Military History Society of Massachusetts in 1897 into a book that appeared in 1900. Frederick Dyer undertook an even more comprehensive effort in what became his 1908 *Compendium of the War of the Rebellion* in 1,796 pages, based, he assured his readers, on "authentic information from all reliable and available sources." The government's *Official Records of the War of the Rebellion,* begun in 1874 and ultimately published in 128 volumes, was, Dyer proclaimed, "woefully deficient," thus rendering his work imperative. Dyer's first volume opens with a summary of Union enlistments and losses that lists the number of those killed in action and those dying of wounds, disease, suicide, and even sunstroke. But Dyer perpetuated errors in government data that Fox had corrected nearly two decades earlier.[18]

Americans North and South, in official capacities and as private citizens, proliferated enumerations of the war dead but remained far from establishing a definitive count. The specificity, rather than the accuracy, of these totals attracted Americans seeking consolation in the comprehensive and comprehensible character of numbers. A figure might begin to grasp the entirety of so many dead and communicate the enormity of war's toll.

Yet even as they counted, Americans speculated about what the numbers they so eagerly amassed actually meant. Joseph Jones counted soldiers and their deaths both to demonstrate southern valor and to explain the defeat of the hopelessly outnumbered Confederacy. Regimental commanders counted to tell the story of "how well [their unit had] stood" and to be remembered among those whose losses, and thus whose courage, was greatest. States in both North and South enumerated the dead to honor the slain. A name upon a list was like a name upon a grave, a repository of memory, a gesture of immortality for those who had made the supreme sacrifice. And the hundreds of thousands of Civil War dead who remained unnamed could at least be counted. Names might remain unknown, but numbers need not be.[19]

Americans counted in order to define the emerging notion of the Civil War Dead as a describable and shared national loss that transcended individual bereavements. They counted to establish the dimensions of the war's sacrifice and the price of freedom and national unity. They counted because numbers offered an illusion of certitude and control in the aftermath of a conflict that had transformed the apparent limits of human brutality. They counted, too, because there were just so many bodies to count. Numbers seemed the only way to capture what was most dramatically new about this war: the very size of the cataclysm and its human cost.

But as numbers solved some problems of understanding, so they presented others. William Fox worried that the sheer magnitude of the war's death toll rendered it incomprehensible. "As the numbers become great," he wrote, "they convey no different idea, whether they be doubled or trebled." His proffered solution was to reduce the numbers to what he regarded as a more human scale, by considering casualties on the level of the regiment. "It has a well known limit of size, and its losses are intelligible." Fox urged his readers not to "grow impatient at these statistics." The numbers, he assured them, were not "like ordinary figures" but instead were "statistics every unit of which stands for the pale, upturned face of a dead soldier." These were not cold abstractions but numbers that literally, he argued, possessed a human face.[20]

The muster roll that served as the source for his statistical analysis was an aggregation, but its lists, Fox found, offered far more than just numbers. Its brief entries invoked "sad pictures" of individual deaths and lives. A world lay behind every name. "There are no war stories that can equal the story of the muster-out roll," he insisted:

"Killed, May 3, 1863 at Marye's Heights;" and the compiler lays down his pencil to dream again of that fierce charge which swept upward over the sloping fields of Fredericksburg.

"Wounded and missing, May 6, 1864, at the Wilderness," sug-

gests a nameless grave marked, if at all, by a Government head-
stone bearing the short, sad epitaph, "Unknown."

"Killed at Malvern Hill, July 1, 1862;" and there rises a picture of
an artilleryman lying dead at the wheels of his gun . . .

"Died of fever at Young's Point, Miss.," reminds one of the campaigns in the bayous and poisonous swamps, with the men falling in scores before a foe more deadly and remorseless than the
bullet.[21]

Fox offered his readers some of the most "curious" of his discoveries from the rolls, demonstrating the startling variety of ways soldiers
managed to die: Lorenzo Brown of the 112th Illinois, "kicked to
death by a mule"; J. A. Benedict, Fifth New York Cavalry, "died from
amputation resulting from the bite of a man on his thumb"; Jacob
Thomas of the 38th Ohio, "killed . . . by the falling of a tree";
A. Lohman of the Eighth New York, "died of poison while on picket,
by drinking from a bottle found at a deserted house." With this list of
curiosities, Fox demonstrated that behind the "full and exhaustive
statistics" of *Regimental Losses* lay the highly particular—and even
peculiar—deaths of hundreds of thousands of individual men.[22]

Fox articulated a dilemma that lay at the heart of the effort to
understand Civil War death: how to grasp both the significance of a
single death and the meaning of hundreds of thousands. Joseph
Stalin would later remark, with both experience and insight, "One
death is a tragedy; a million is a statistic." A half century earlier Fox
made a similar observation. "It is hard," he wrote, "to realize the
meaning of the figures . . . It is easy to imagine one man killed; or ten
men killed; or, perhaps, a score of men killed . . . but even . . . [the vet-
eran] is unable to comprehend the dire meaning of the one hundred
thousand, whose every unit represents a soldier's bloody grave. The
figures are too large." Yet understanding the vastness of what had
happened in those four years of war seemed imperative.[23]

Walt Whitman engaged this same tension. He was fascinated with
the war's magnitude, which was for him one measure of its democratic reach. Statistics offered a vivid means of displaying the con-

flict's dimensions and impact, and it was to numbers that he readily turned to present the war "summ'd up" when the fighting ceased. He defined his own experience by estimating the sick and wounded he had visited ("80,000 to 100,000"). But to capture and characterize the war, he invoked the numbers of the dead: conjecturing how many lay entirely unburied, how many in "hitherto unfound localities," and finally, and most important, how many gravestones carried "the significant word Unknown." Even as he tried to imagine these "countless" dead—"The Million Dead," he designated them—he claimed each one as his own. They were at once "infinite" and intimate: "all, all, all, finally dear to me." Every soldier was to Whitman "a man as divine as myself"; each was *my loving comrade,* even if he lay unheralded and unknown. These singular soldiers represented for Whitman "the real war," the true meaning of the devastating conflict. His abstraction from the one to the many and his embodiment of the many in the one served as both political and poetical synecdoche. To understand even "an inkling of this War," Whitman believed, it was necessary to try always to "multiply . . . by scores, aye hundreds," the particular "hell scenes" of battle and the individual soldiers he had watched suffer and die.[24]

This problem of the one and the many challenged northerners and southerners alike and served as a central theme in the war's popular culture. How could the meaning of so many deaths be understood? And conversely, how could an individual's death continue to matter amid the loss of so many? "All Quiet Along the Potomac Tonight," a song claimed and sung by both Union and Confederacy, focused with irony upon the dismissal of a single soldier's death as unworthy of notice. "'Tis nothing," it said, in the face of the lengthy casualty lists that have become commonplace: "a private or two now and then will not count in the news of the battle." Yet the work of the song was to reclaim the importance of this individual life, the husband and father who was just as dead in this night of "quiet" as if he were one of the thousands who had perished in the din of dramatic battle. He was a man, the song insisted, who counts, even if he was not counted.[25]

Walt Whitman. Photograph by Mathew Brady.
Library of Congress.

An 1862 story in *Harper's Weekly* entitled "Only One Killed" echoed the same theme and served as a gesture of popular resistance to the insignificance of an individual death amid what the writer called "a fearful aggregate of woe." The story's main character blithely responds to a report of "one killed" by declaring the news so insignificant as to be "hardly worth the cost of a telegram." The "pair of sober gray eyes" of a man sitting nearby offer a "silent rebuke" to this heartlessness, and indeed subsequent information reveals that the slain soldier is this man's only son. "Only one killed!" the narrator exclaims. "How differently the fact impressed me now! It was no longer an unrealized newspaper announcement, but a present stern reality." The problem of the one and the many was central to the problem of "realizing" with which Americans struggled. "One, two, three hundred killed or mangled. It is awful to contemplate; and yet we must come down to the single cases to get at the heart of this fearful matter," the writer explained, having in his story tried to do exactly that. A soldier from New York, Charles Lewis, chose almost the same language as the *Harper's* author after his brigade was reported to have lost "but one" in an engagement. "We say 'but one,' never thinking that that one was somebody's all perhaps. Had a million been slain, it would have been 'only one' in a million homes."[26]

Like the effort to identify the dead, poems, songs, and stories—with titles like "One of Many," "Only a Private Killed," "Only One Killed," or just "Only"—sought to preserve the meaning of the individual amid the multitude. Numbers complicated this understanding. On the one hand, counting equalized; rank and distinction disappeared in the totals of war dead. But at the same time numbers undermined the individuality that was tied closely to equality's purposes and to the democratic imperatives of the war. Naming individualized the dead; counting aggregated them; the two impulses served opposite yet coexisting needs, marking the paradox inherent in coming to terms with Civil War death.[27]

The distance, the discrepancy between the one and the many juxtaposed and reinforced two modes of understanding that emerged from the Civil War experience. Sentimentality and irony grew side by side in Americans' war-born consciousness. The sentimental drew its strength from the need to resist the unintelligibility of mass death by focusing on the singularity of each casualty, the tragedy of each loss. Sentimentality served as a weapon against the force of numbers, against the statistical homogenization and erasure of individuals. Irony, by contrast, emerged from acknowledgment of this fundamental tension, the admission of the almost unspeakable possibility that the individual might not, in this juggernaut of modern mass warfare, actually matter. "All Quiet Along the Potomac" managed, like Civil War America more generally, to be at once sentimental and ironic in its treatment of the dead soldier who was simultaneously all and "nothing."[28]

The effort to count the Civil War dead was only in part about numbers and casualty reports, only in part about the duties of a nation to its citizens. Numbering the dead was also about more transcendent questions that extended beyond the state and its policies and obligations. As William Fox observed, "Every story, even a statistical one, has a moral." The rhetoric of Civil War mortality statistics provided the language for a meditation on the deeper human meaning of the conflict and its unprecedented destructiveness, as well as for the exploration of the place of the individual in a world of mass—and increasingly mechanized—slaughter. It was about what counted in a world transformed.[29]

SURVIVING

Then with the knowledge of death as walking one side of me,
And the thought of death close-walking the other side of me,
And I in the middle, as with companions, and as holding the hand
of companions . . .

WALT WHITMAN, "WHEN LILACS LAST IN
THE DOORYARD BLOOM'D"

John Palmer carried the bullet that killed his son with him to the grave; Henry Bowditch habitually wore a watch fob fashioned from his fallen son's uniform button; Mary Todd Lincoln dressed in mourning till she died; Walt Whitman believed the war had represented the "very centre, circumference, umbilicus" of his life; Ambrose Bierce felt haunted by "visions of the dead and dying"; Jane Mitchell continued to hope for years after Appomattox that her missing son would finally come home; J. M. Taylor was still searching for details of his son's death three decades after the end of the war; Henry Struble annually laid flowers on the grave that mistakenly bore his name. Civil War Americans lived the rest of their lives with grief and loss.[1]

More than 2 percent of the nation's inhabitants were dead as a direct result of the war—the approximate equivalent of the population in 1860 of the state of Maine, more than the entire population of Arkansas or Connecticut, twice the population of Vermont, more than the whole male population of Georgia or Alabama. These soldiers had experienced what many Americans called "the great change," the uncharted passage from life to death. No longer fathers or brothers or sons, they had become corpses and memories, in hundreds of thousands of cases without even identifiable graves.

But the fallen had solved the riddle of death, leaving to survivors the work of understanding and explaining what this great change had meant. And the living had been changed too, by what they had seen and done, what they had felt, and what they had lost. They were, like Bierce, "sentenced to life" and to making sense of how Civil War death had redefined what life might be. Sidney Lanier, Confederate poet who had fought in the bloody Seven Days Battles in 1862 and later suffered in a Union prison camp, commented in 1875 that for most of his "generation in the South since the War, pretty much the whole of life has been not-dying."[2]

Managing Civil War death was made all the more difficult by the mystery that so often surrounded it. Nearly half the dead remained unknown, the fact of their deaths supposed but undocumented, the circumstances of their passage from life entirely unrecorded. Such losses remained in some sense unreal and thus "unrealized," as the bereaved described them, recognizing the inhibition of mourning that such uncertainty imposed. The living searched in anxiety and even "phrensy" to provide endings for life narratives that stood incomplete, their meanings undefined.[3]

This crisis of knowledge and understanding extended well beyond the problem of the unidentified dead to challenge, in Melville's words, "the very basis of things." Individuals found themselves in a new and different moral universe, one in which unimaginable destruction had become daily experience. Where did God belong in such a world? How could a benevolent deity countenance such cruelty and such suffering? Doubt threatened to overpower faith—faith in the Christian narrative of a compassionate divinity and a hope of life beyond the grave, faith in the intelligibility and purpose of life on Earth. Language seemed powerless to explain, humans unable to comprehend what their deaths—and thus their lives—could mean.[4]

Man had been at once agent and victim of war's destruction. Both as butcher and butchered, he had shown himself far closer to the beasts than to the angels. The vaunted human soul had seemed to count for little in the face of war's fearsome physicality, its fundamental economy of bodies, of losses and casualties, of wounding and killing. Mutilated and nameless corpses challenged notions of the unity and integrity of the human selves they once housed, for by the tens of thousands these selves had fragmented and disappeared. Death without dignity, without decency, without identity imperiled the meaning of the life that preceded it. Americans had not just lost the dead; they had lost their own lives as they had understood them before the war. As Lucy Buck of Virginia observed, "We shall never any of us be the same as we have been."[5]

The nation was a survivor, too, transformed by its encounter with death, obligated by the sacrifices of its dead. The war's staggering human cost demanded a new sense of national destiny, one designed to ensure that lives had been sacrificed for appropriately lofty ends. So much suffering had to have transcendent purpose, a "sacred significance," as Frederick Douglass had insisted in the middle of the war. For him, such purpose was freedom, but this would prove an unrealized ideal in a nation unwilling to guarantee the equal citizenship on which true liberty must rest. Slavery had divided the nation, but assumptions of racial hierarchy would unite whites North and South in a century-long abandonment of the emancipationist legacy.[6]

Instead, the United States' new and elevated destiny became bound up with the nation itself: its growing power, its wealth, its extent, its influence. Debates about nationalism had caused the war; national might had won the war; an expanded nation-state with new powers and duties emerged from war's demands. And both the unity and responsibilities of this transformed nation were closely tied to its Civil War Dead.

The meaning of the war had come to inhere in its cost. The nation's value and importance were both derived from and proved by the human price paid for its survival. This equation cast the nation in debt in ways that would be transformative, for executing its obligations to the dead and their mourners required a vast expansion of the federal budget and bureaucracy and a reconceptualization of the government's role. National cemeteries, pensions, and records that preserved names and identities involved a dramatically new understanding of the relationship of the citizen and the state. Edmund

Whitman had observed with pride after his years living among the dead that the reinterment program represented a national commitment to a "sentiment." In acknowledging that decent burial and identifiable graves warranted such effort and expense, the United States affirmed its belief in values that extended beyond the merely material and instrumental. Soldiers were not, as Melville articulated and so many Americans feared, "operatives," simply cogs in a machinery of increasingly industrialized warfare. Citizens were selves—bodies and names that lived beyond their own deaths, individuals who were the literal lifeblood of the nation.[7]

Without agendas, without politics, the Dead became what their survivors chose to make them. For a time they served as the repository of continuing hostility between North and South, but by the end of the century the Dead had become the vehicle for a unifying national project of memorialization. Civil War death and the Civil War Dead belonged to the whole nation. The Dead became the focus of an imagined national community for the reunited states, a constituency all could willingly serve—"the dead, the dead, the dead—*our* dead—or South or North, ours all (all, all, all, finally dear to me)," Walt Whitman chanted.[8]

In 1898 President William McKinley announced to the South, in a much-heralded speech in Atlanta, that "the time has now come in the evolution of sentiment and feeling under the providence of God, when in the spirit of fraternity we should share with you in the care of the graves of the Confederate soldiers." The sons and grandsons of "these heroic dead" had in the preceding year risked their lives in a new American war; the brave Confederates should be officially honored alongside their Union counterparts.[9]

To Frederick Douglass's despair, the reasons for which men had died had been all but subsumed by the fact of their deaths. "Death has no power to change moral qualities," he insisted in a Decoration Day speech in 1883. "Whatever else I may forget," the aging abolitionist declared, "I shall never forget the difference between those who fought for liberty and those who fought for slavery." But many even of those who had fought felt otherwise. "The brave respect the brave. The brave / Respect the dead," Ambrose Bierce wrote in a poem chiding one "Who in a Memorial Day oration protested bitterly against decorating the graves of Confederate dead."

> *Remember how the flood of years*
> *Has rolled across the erring slain;*
> *Remember, too, the cleansing rain*
> *Of widows' and of orphans' tears.*
>
> *The dead are dead—let that alone:*
> *And though with equal hand we strew*
> *The blooms on saint and sinner too,*
> *Yet God will know to choose his own.*
>
> *The wretch, whate'er his life and lot,*
> *Who does not love the harmless dead*
> *With all his heart and all his head—*
> *May God forgive him, I shall not.*[10]

And Oliver Wendell Holmes Jr., who had as a young soldier facing death so resolutely rejected the solace of Christianity, came to embrace war's sacrifice as the one foundation for truth. His "Soldier's Faith" speech, delivered on Memorial Day 1895, became emblematic of the elegiac view of the war that hailed death as an end in itself. "I do not know the meaning of the universe," Holmes baldly declared. "But in the midst of doubt, in the collapse of creeds," he had found one certainty: "that the faith is true and adorable which leads a soldier to throw away his life in obedience to a blindly accepted duty, in a cause which he little understands, in a plan of campaign of which he has no notion, under tactics of which he does not see the use." The very purposelessness of sacrifice created its purpose. In a world in which "commerce is the great power" and the "man of wealth" the great hero, the disinterestedness and selflessness of the soldier represented the highest ideal of a faith that depended on the actions not of God but of man. "War, when you are at it," Holmes admitted, "is horrible and dull. It is only when time has passed that you see that its message was divine." War may have shattered the young Holmes's beliefs, but for the old man, war became the place where man's confrontation with annihilation had made him "capable of miracle, able to lift himself by the might of his own soul." Man's ability to choose death became for both Holmes and Bierce the most important experience and memory of the war.[11]

We still live in the world of death the Civil War created. We take for granted the obligation of the state to account for the lives it claims in its service. The absence of next-of-kin notification, of graves registration procedures, of official provision for decent burial all seem to us unimaginable, even barbaric. The Civil War ended this neglect and established policies that led to today's commitment to identify and return every soldier killed in the line of duty.

But even as the Civil War brought new humanity—new attentiveness to "sentiment"—in the management of death, so too it introduced a level of carnage that foreshadowed the wars of the century to come. Even as individuals and their fates assumed new significance, so those individuals threatened to disappear into the bureaucracy and mass slaughter of modern warfare. We still struggle to understand how to preserve our humanity and our selves within such a world. We still seek to use our deaths to create meaning where we are not sure any exists. The Civil War generation glimpsed the fear that still defines us—the sense that death is the only end. We still work to live with the riddle that they—the Civil War dead and their survivors alike—had to solve so long ago.

Notes

The following acronyms are used in the notes to refer to archives:

BHL   Bentley Historical Library, University of Michigan, Ann Arbor
CAH   The Center for American History, The University of Texas, Austin
ESBL Eleanor S. Brockenbrough Library, Museum of the Confederacy,
      Richmond, Va.
LC   Library of Congress, Washington, D.C.
LCP   The Library Company of Philadelphia
MAHS Massachusetts Historical Society, Boston
MOHS Missouri Historical Society, St. Louis
NARA National Archives and Records Administration, Washington, D.C.
NYHS New-York Historical Society, New York City
NYPL Manuscripts and Archives Division, New York Public Library, Astor,
      Lennox, and Tilden Foundations, New York City
PAHRC Philadelphia Archdiocesan Historical Research Center,
      Wynnewood, Pa.
RBMSC Rare Book, Manuscript, and Special Collections Library, Duke
      University, Durham, N.C.
SCHS South Carolina Historical Society, Charleston
SCL   South Caroliniana Library, University of South Carolina, Columbia
SHC   Southern Historical Collection, Wilson Library, University of North
      Carolina, Chapel Hill
VHS   Virginia Historical Society, Richmond
VMIA Virginia Military Institute Archives, Lexington
WFCHS Winchester-Frederick County Historical Society, Winchester, Va.
WHS   Wisconsin Historical Society Archives, Madison

PREFACE

1. [Stephen Elliott], *Obsequies of the Reverend Edward E. Ford, D.D., and Sermon by the Bishop of the Diocese* . . . (Augusta, Ga.: Augusta Chronicle and Sentinel, 1863), p. 8.
2. James David Hacker, "The Human Cost of War: White Population in the United States, 1850–1880," Ph.D. diss. (University of Minnesota, 1999), pp. 1, 14.

Hacker believes that Civil War death totals may be seriously understated because of inadequate estimates of the number of Confederate deaths from disease. Civil War casualty and mortality statistics are problematic overall, and the incompleteness of Confederate records makes them especially unreliable. See Chapter 8 of this book. Maris A. Vinovskis concludes that about 6 percent of northern white males between ages thirteen and forty-five died in the war, whereas 18 percent of white men of similar age in the South perished. But because of much higher levels of military mobilization in the white South, mortality rates for southern soldiers were twice, not three times, as great as those for northern soldiers. James McPherson cites these soldiers' death rates as 31 percent for Confederate soldiers, 16 percent for Union soldiers. Gary Gallagher believes Vinovskis's overall death rate for the South is too low; he estimates that closer to one in four rather than one in five white southern men of military age died in the conflict. I have cited the more conservative total. See Vinovskis, "Have Social Historians Lost the Civil War?" in Maris A. Vinovskis, ed., *Toward a Social History of the American Civil War: Exploratory Essays* (New York: Cambridge University Press, 1990), pp. 3–7; James M. McPherson, personal communication to author, December 27, 2006; Gary Gallagher, personal communication to author, December 16, 2006.

3. James M. McPherson, *Crossroads of Freedom: Antietam* (New York: Oxford University Press, 2002), pp. 3, 177, n. 56.

4. [Francis W. Palfrey], *In Memoriam: H.L.A.* (Boston: Printed for private distribution, 1864), p. 5; Richard Shryock, "A Medical Perspective on the Civil War," *American Quarterly* 14 (Summer 1962): 164; H. Clay Trumbull, *War Memories of an Army Chaplain* (New York: C. Scribner's Sons, 1898), p. 67. Vital statistics for this period are very scarce, and the most complete cover only Massachusetts. I am grateful to historical demographer Gretchen Condran of Temple University for discussing these matters with me. See U.S. Bureau of the Census, *Historical Statistics of the United States, Part I* (Washington, D.C.: Government Printing Office, 1975), pp. 62–63. On the "untimely death of an adult child" as "particularly painful" in mid-nineteenth-century England, see Patricia Jalland, *Death in the Victorian Family* (New York: Oxford University Press, 1996), p. 39.

5. One notable appearance of the image of a harvest of death is in the title given Timothy O'Sullivan's photograph of a field of bodies at Gettysburg in Alexander Gardner, *Gardner's Photographic Sketchbook of the War* (1866; rpt. New York: Dover, 1959), plate 36; Kate Stone, *Brokenburn: The Journal of Kate Stone, 1861–1868*, ed. John Q. Anderson (Baton Rouge: Louisiana University Press, 1955), p. 264; C. W. Greene to John McLees, August 15, 1862, McLees Family Papers, SCL.

6. [Frederick Law Olmsted], *Hospital Transports: A Memoir of the Embarkation of the Sick and Wounded from the Peninsula of Virginia in the Summer of 1862* (Boston: Ticknor & Fields, 1863), p. 115.

7. The general literature on death is immense and rich. A few key texts not cited elsewhere in this volume include Thomas Lynch, *The Undertaking: Life Studies from the Dismal Trade* (New York: W. W. Norton, 1997); Thomas Lynch, *Bodies in*

Motion and at Rest: On Metaphor and Mortality (New York: W. W. Norton, 2000); Sandra Gilbert, *Death's Door: Modern Dying and the Way We Grieve* (New York: W. W. Norton, 2006); Paul Monette, *Borrowed Time: An AIDS Memoir* (San Diego, Calif.: Harcourt Brace Jovanovich, 1988); Paul Monette, *Last Watch of the Night* (New York: Harcourt Brace, 1994); Jessica Mitford, *The American Way of Death* (New York: Simon & Schuster, 1963); Sherwin B. Nuland, *How We Die: Reflections on Life's Final Chapter* (New York: Alfred A. Knopf, 1994); Maurice Bloch and Jonathan Parry, eds., *Death and the Regeneration of Life* (New York: Cambridge University Press, 1982); Peter Metcalf and Richard Huntington, *Celebrations of Death: The Anthropology of Mortuary Ritual,* 2nd ed. (New York: Cambridge University Press, 1991).

8. Mrs. Carson to R. F. Taylor, September 14, 1864, Carson Family Papers, SCL. On changing notions of the self, see Charles Taylor, *Sources of the Self: The Making of Modern Identity* (Cambridge, Mass.: Harvard University Press, 1989), and Jerrold Seigel, *The Idea of the Self: Thought and Experience in Western Europe Since the Seventeenth Century* (New York: Cambridge University Press, 2005).

9. *New York Times,* October 20, 1862. See William A. Frassanito, *Antietam: The Photographic Legacy of America's Bloodiest Day* (New York: Charles Scribner's Sons, 1978); Franny Nudelman, *John Brown's Body: Slavery, Violence and the Culture of War* (Chapel Hill: University of North Carolina Press, 2004), pp. 103–31; and Alan Trachtenberg, *Reading American Photographs: Images as History, Mathew Brady to Walker Evans* (New York: Hill & Wang, 1989). Even as we acknowledge the impact of Civil War photography, it is important to recognize how few Americans would actually have seen Brady's or other photographs of the dead. Newspapers and periodicals could not yet reproduce photographs but could publish only engravings derived from them, like the many *Harper's Weekly* illustrations included in this book.

10. Maude Morrow Brown Manuscript, z/0907.000/S, Mississippi Department of Archives and History, Jackson, Miss.; on nineteenth-century science and the changed meaning of death, see Adam Phillips, *Darwin's Worms: On Life Stories and Death Stories* (New York: Basic Books, 2000).

CHAPTER I. DYING

1. Chesnut cited in James Shepherd Pike, *The Prostrate State* (New York: D. Appleton, 1874), pp. 74–75.

2. Letter to Mattie J. McGaw, May 5, 1863, McGaw Family Papers, SCL. For a consideration of the size of the Revolutionary army and its mortality, see Charles H. Lesser, *The Sinews of Independence* (Chicago: University of Chicago Press, 1976), pp. 84–86, and Howard H. Peckham, *The Toll of Independence* (Chicago: University of Chicago Press, 1974). On the size of Civil War armies, see James M. McPherson, *Battle Cry of Freedom* (New York: Oxford University Press, 1988), p. 306n.

3. Alonzo Abernethy, "Incidents of an Iowa Soldier's Life, or Four Years in Dixie," *Annals of Iowa,* 3rd ser. 12 (1920): 411; William A. Hammond, "Medical Care, Bat-

tle Wounds, and Disease," online at www.civilwarhome.com/civilwarmedicine
.htm; George Worthington Adams, *Doctors in Blue: The Medical History of the
Union Army in the Civil War* (New York: H. Schuman, 1952), pp. 222, 242, 125.
On diarrhea and dysentery in the Confederate army, see Horace Cunningham,
Doctors in Gray: The Confederate Medical Service (Baton Rouge: Louisiana State
University Press, 1958), p. 185; Paul E. Steiner, *Disease in the Civil War: Natural
Biological Warfare in 1861–1865* (Springfield, Ill.: Charles C. Thomas, 1968), p. 14.
Camp Sink quote in U.S. Sanitary Commission, *Two Reports on the Condition of
Military Hospitals* (New York: W. C. Bryant, 1862), p. 6. See also Joseph Janner
Woodward, *Outlines of the Chief Camp Diseases of the United States Armies as
Observed During the Present War* (Philadelphia: J. B. Lippincott, 1863); Robert E.
Denney, *Civil War Medicine: Care and Comfort of the Wounded* (New York: Ster-
ling, 1994); John W. Schildt, *Antietam Hospitals* (Chewsville, Md.: Antietam Pub-
lications, 1987); Frank R. Freemon, *Gangrene and Glory: Medical Care During the
American Civil War* (Urbana: University of Illinois Press, 1998); James I. Robert-
son Jr., *Soldiers Blue and Gray* (Columbia: University of South Carolina Press,
1988), pp. 145–69. See also Lisa Herschbach, "Fragmentation and Reunion:
Medicine, Memory and Body in the American Civil War," Ph.D. diss. (Harvard
University, 1997).

4. *The Sentinel: Selected for the Soldiers* No. 319 (Petersburg, Va.: n.p., 1861), p. 1.

5. E. G. Abbott to Mother, February 8, 1862, Abbott Family, Civil War Letters, MS
    Am 800.26(5), Houghton Library, Harvard University, Cambridge, Mass.

6. A. D. Kirwan, ed., *Johnny Green of the Orphan Brigade: The Journal of a Confeder-
    ate Soldier* (Lexington: University of Kentucky Press, 1956), p. 93.

7. John Weissert to Dearest wife and children, October 17, 1862, Box 1, Corre-
    spondence Sept.–Oct. 1862, John Weissert Papers, BHL.

8. Jeremy Taylor, *The Rule and Exercises of Holy Dying* (London: R. Royston, 1651);
    Jeremy Taylor, *The Rule and Exercises of Holy Living* (London: Francis Ash,
    1650); Sister Mary Catherine O'Connor, *The Art of Dying Well: The Development
    of the Ars Moriendi* (New York: Columbia University Press, 1942), pp. 11, 208.
    See also L. M. Beier, "The Good Death in Seventeenth Century England," in
    Ralph Houlbrooke, ed., *Death, Ritual and Bereavement* (New York: Routledge,
    1989); Ralph Houlbrooke, *Death, Religion, and the Family in England, 1480–1750*
    (Oxford: Clarendon Press, 1998); Ralph Houlbrooke, "The Puritan Death-Bed,
    c. 1560–c. 1600," in C. Durston and J. Eales, eds., *The Culture of English Puri-
    tanism, 1560–1700* (New York: St. Martin's, 1996), pp. 122–44; M. C. Cross, "The
    Third Earl of Huntingdon's Death-Bed: A Calvinist Example of the Arts
    Moriendi," *Northern History* 21 (1985): 80–107; R. Wunderle and G. Broce, "The
    Final Moment Before Death in Early Modern England," *Sixteenth Century Jour-
    nal* 20 (1989): 259–75; David Cressy, *Birth, Marriage and Death: Ritual, Religion
    and the Life-Cycle in Tudor and Stuart England* (New York: Oxford University
    Press, 1997).

9. Frances Comper, ed., *The Book of the Craft of Dying and Other Early English Tracts
    Concerning Death* (London, 1917); Nancy Lee Beaty, *The Craft of Dying: A Study
    in the Literary Tradition of the Ars Moriendi in England* (New Haven: Yale Univer-

sity Press, 1970); Jeremy Taylor, *The Rule and Exercises of Holy Dying* (London: R. Royston, 1651). At least eight editions of *Holy Dying* appeared in London in the first half of the nineteenth century; editions were printed in Boston in 1864 and 1865; in Philadelphia in 1835, 1859, 1869; New York, 1864. On conceptions of *ars moriendi* included in advice and conduct books, see Margaret Spufford, *Small Books and Pleasant Histories: Popular Fiction and Its Readership in Seventeenth Century England* (Athens: University of Georgia Press, 1981), pp. 200–208. For an example of a sermon, see Eleazer Mather Porter Wells, *Preparation for Death... Trinity Church, Boston* (n.p., 1852). On popular health, see the many American editions of John Willison, *The Afflicted Man's Companion* (Pittsburgh: Luke Loomis & Co., 1830), which was reprinted again by the American Tract Society of New York in 1851. So popular was Dickens's serialized *The Old Curiosity Shop* that New Yorkers lined the quay for the arrival of the installment that would reveal Little Nell's fate. Harriet Beecher Stowe's *Uncle Tom's Cabin* was the best-selling American book of the nineteenth century. Charles Dickens, *The Old Curiosity Shop* (London, 1841); William Makepeace Thackeray, *The Newcomes* (London: Bradbury & Evans, 1844–45); Harriet Beecher Stowe, *Uncle Tom's Cabin* (Boston: John P. Jewett, 1851). See also the rendition of death in Samuel Richardson's *Clarissa, or, the History of a Young Lady* (London: Published for S. Richardson, 1748).

10. William Corby, *Memoirs of Chaplain Life* (Notre Dame, Ind.: Scholastic Press, 1894), p. 184. Memorials to this moment are located at Notre Dame and on the field at Gettysburg. It has been estimated that Catholics constituted about 7 percent of Union armies. They would have been a far smaller percentage of Confederate soldiers. See Randall M. Miller, "Catholic Religion, Irish Ethnicity, and the Civil War," in Randall M. Miller, Harry S. Stout, and Charles Reagan Wilson, eds., *Religion and the American Civil War* (New York: Oxford University Press, 1998), p. 261.

11. Bertram Korn, *American Jewry and the Civil War* (Philadelphia: Jewish Publication Society of America, 1951), p. 59; D. DeSola Pool, "The Diary of Chaplain Michael M. Allen, September 1861," *Publications of the American Jewish Historical Society* 39 (September 1949): 177–82; L. J. Lederman, letter to parents of David Zehden upon his death, quoted in Mel Young, *Where They Lie: The Story of the Jewish Soldiers...* (Lanham, Md.: University Press of America, 1991), p. 149; Rebecca Gratz, *Letters of Rebecca Gratz*, ed. Rabbi David Philipson (Philadelphia: Jewish Publication Society of America, 1929), pp. 426–27. See *From This World to the Next: Jewish Approaches to Illness, Death and the Afterlife* (New York: Jewish Theological Seminary of America, 1999), and Jack Riemer, ed., *Jewish Insights on Death and Mourning* (New York: Schocken Books, 1995), pp. 309–53. On ecumenism see Korn, *American Jewry and the Civil War*, p. 59; Warren B. Armstrong, *For Courageous Fighting and Confident Dying: Union Chaplains in the Civil War* (Lawrence: University Press of Kansas, 1998), pp. 53–54; Kurt O. Berends, " 'Wholesome Reading Purifies and Elevates the Man': The Religious Military Press in the Confederacy," in Miller, Stout, and Wilson, eds., *Religion and the American Civil War*, pp. 134, 157; Peter Paul Cooney, "The War Letters of

Father Peter Paul Cooney of the Congregation of the Holy Cross," ed. Thomas McAvoy, *Records of the American Catholic Historical Society* 44 (1933): 223, 164; Louis-Hippolyte Gache, *A Frenchman, a Chaplain, a Rebel: The War Letters of Louis-Hippolyte Gache* (Chicago: Loyola University Press, 1991), pp. 176–77, 118–19; Sara Trainer Smith, ed., "Notes on Satterlee Hospital, West Philadelphia," *Records of the American Catholic Historical Society* 8 (1897): 404. On limitations to that ecumenism, see Gache, *Frenchman*, pp. 190–91.

12. *Once to Die* (Richmond, Va.: Presbyterian Committee of Publication, 186–), p. 3; see also Karl S. Guthke, *Last Words: Variations on a Theme in Cultural History* (Princeton: Princeton University Press, 1992), p. 36.

13. Confederate States Christian Association for the Relief of Prisoners (Fort Delaware), Minutes, March 31, 1865, Francis Atherton Boyle Books, 1555 Southern Historical Collection, University of North Carolina, Chapel Hill (hereafter SHC); James Gray to Sister, June 12, 1864, in Mills Lane, ed., *Dear Mother: Don't Grieve About Me. If I Get Killed, I'll Only Be Dead: Letters from Georgia Soldiers in the Civil War* (Savannah, Ga.: Beehive Press, 1990), p. 300. See also William Stilwell to Molly, September 18, 1862, in Lane, *Dear Mother*, p. 185; letter to Mollie J. McGaw, May 5, 1863, McGaw Family Papers, SCL; Desmond Pulaski Hopkins Papers, July 17, 1862, CAH. Statistics on locations of deaths from Robert V. Wells, *Facing the "King of Terrors": Death and Society in an American Community* (New York: Cambridge University Press, 2000), p. 195.

14. [Frederick Law Olmsted], *Hospital Transports* (Boston: Ticknor & Fields, 1863), p. 80. Disruptions of African American family ties through the slave trade to the southwestern states was, of course, another matter—in its coerciveness, in its permanence. See Michael Tadman, *Speculators and Slaves: Masters, Traders and Slaves in the Old South* (Madison: University of Wisconsin Press, 1989).

15. Patricia Jalland, *Death in the Victorian Family* (New York: Oxford University Press, 1996), p. 2. The English queen's own lengthy bereavement after Albert's death in 1861 focused additional attention on death as a defining element in Anglo-American family and cultural life.

16. *The Dying Officer* (Richmond, VA.: Soldiers' Tract Society, Methodist Episcopal Church, South, 186–), p. 6; Hiram Mattison quoted in Michael Sappol, *"A Traffic in Dead Bodies": Anatomy and Embodied Social Identity in Nineteenth-Century America* (Princeton: Princeton University Press, 2002), p. 31. See statement on meaning of last words in Susie C. Appell to Mrs. E. H. Ogden, October 20, 1862, Sarah Perot Ogden Collection, GLC 6556.01.106, Gilder Lehrman Collection, The Gilder Lehrman Institute of American History, NYHS. Materials quoted courtesy of the Gilder Lehrman Institute may not be reproduced without written permission. See discussion of significance of last words in *Frank Leslie's Illustrated Weekly*, December 7, 1861, p. 44.

17. See Gregory Coco, *Killed in Action: Eyewitness Accounts of the Last Moments of 100 Union Soldiers Who Died at Gettysburg* (Gettysburg, Pa.: Thomas Publications, 1992); Gregory Coco, *Wasted Valor: The Confederate Dead at Gettysburg* (Gettysburg, Pa.: Thomas Publications, 1990); Warren B. Armstrong, *For Courageous*

Fighting and Confident Dying: Union Chaplains in the Civil War (Lawrence: University Press of Kansas, 1998).

18. "Reminiscence of Gettysburg," *Frank Leslie's Illustrated Newspaper,* January 2, 1864, p. 235. On photographs see Steve R. Stotelmyer, *The Bivouacs of the Dead: The Story of Those Who Died at Antietam and South Mountain* (Baltimore: Toomey Press, 1992), p. 6; *Godey's Lady's Book,* March 1864, p. 311; Mark H. Dunkelman, *Gettysburg's Unknown Soldier: The Life, Death, and Celebrity of Amos Humiston* (Westport, Conn.: Praeger, 1999); William Stilwell to Molly, September 18, 1862, in Lane, ed., *Dear Mother,* p. 186.

19. Clara Barton, Lecture Notes [1866], Clara Barton Papers, LC.

20. Elmer Ruan Coates, "Be My Mother Till I Die" (Philadelphia: A. W. Auner, n.d.), Wolf 115; "Bless the Lips That Kissed Our Darling: Answer to: Let Me Kiss Him for His Mother" (Philadelphia: Auner, n.d.); J. A. C. O'Connor, "Bless the Lips That Kissed Our Darling" (New York: H. De Marsan, n.d.), Wolf 115. See also George Cooper, "Mother Kissed Me in My Dream" (Philadelphia: J. H. Johnson, n.d.), Wolf 1468. All these song sheets are in the American Song Sheet Collection, LCP.

21. William J. Bacon, *Memorial of William Kirkland Bacon: Late Adjutant of the Twenty-sixth Regiment of New York State Volunteers* (Utica, N.Y.: Roberts Printer, 1863), p. 50.

22. On condolence letters, see Michael Barton, "Painful Duties: Art, Character, and Culture in Confederate Letters of Condolence," *Southern Quarterly* 17 (1979): 123–34; and Barton, *Goodmen: The Character of Civil War Soldiers* (University Park: Pennsylvania State University Press, 1981), pp. 57–62. See also William Merrill Decker, *Epistolary Practices: Letter Writing in America Before Telecommunications* (Chapel Hill: University of North Carolina Press, 1998); Janet Gurlin Altman, *Epistolarity: Approaches to a Form* (Columbus: Ohio State University Press, 1982). For contemporary guidebooks for letter writers, see *The American Letter-Writer and Mirror of Polite Behavior* (Philadelphia: Fisher & Brother, 1851), and *A New Letter-Writer, for the Use of Gentlemen* (Philadelphia: Porter & Coates, 1860). For an acknowledgment of the ritual of the condolence letter in Civil War popular culture, see the *Daily South Carolinian,* February 26, 1864; see also June 22, 1864, and the song by E. Bowers, "Write a Letter to My Mother!" (Philadelphia: n.p., [1860s]), Wolf 2677, LCP.

23. Williamson D. Ward diary quoted in Joseph Allan Frank and George A. Reaves, *"Seeing the Elephant": Raw Recruits at Shiloh* (Westport, Conn.: Greenwood Press, 1989), p. 98; Minutes, July 1864–June 1865, Confederate States Christian Association for the Relief of Prisoners (Fort Delaware), Francis Atherton Boyle Books, 1555 SHC.

24. W. J. O'Daniel to Mrs. [Sarah A.] Torrence, quoted in Haskell Monroe, ed., "The Road to Gettysburg: The Diary and Letters of Leonidas Torrence of the Gaston Guards," *North Carolina Historical Review* 36 (October 1959): 515; William Fields to Mrs. Fitzpatrick, June 8, 1865, Maria Clopton Papers, Medical and Hospital Collection, ESBL; I. G. Patten to Mrs. Cadenhead, August 5, 1864, in I. B.

Cadenhead, "Some Letters of I. B. Cadenhead," *Alabama Historical Quarterly* 18 (1956): 569; Henry E. Handerson, *Yankee in Gray: The Civil War Memoirs of Henry E. Handerson with a Selection of His Wartime Letters* (Cleveland: Case Western Reserve University Press, 1962), p. 62.

25. William Fields to Mrs. Fitzpatrick, June 8, 1865, Maria Clopton Papers, Medical and Hospital Collection, ESBL; Clara Barton, Manuscript Journal, 1863, Clara Barton Papers, LC. See also Elizabeth Brown Pryor, *Clara Barton: Professional Angel* (Philadelphia: University of Pennsylvania Press, 1987), pp. 94, 148; "Our Army Hospitals," unidentified and undated newspaper clippings, Louis C. Madeira Civil War Scrapbooks, vol. A, pp. 111–26, LCP. For an example of a nurse cueing a soldier to leave a message for his wife, see William H. Davidson, ed., *War Was the Place: A Centennial Collection of Confederate Soldier Letters* (Chattahoochie Valley Historical Society, Bulletin no. 5 [November 1961]): 115. On the important role of hospital personnel in a Good Death, see Gary Laderman, *The Sacred Remains: American Attitudes Toward Death, 1799–1883* (New Haven: Yale University Press, 1996), p. 131; Gerald Linderman, *Embattled Courage: The Experience of Combat in the American Civil War* (New York: Free Press, 1987), p. 29; Corby, *Memoirs of Chaplain Life*, p. 93. See also Jestin Hampton to Thomas B. Hampton, January 25, 1863, Thomas B. Hampton Papers, CAH; S. G. Sneed to Susan Piper, September 17, 1864, Benjamin Piper Papers, CAH.

26. *Christian Recorder*, November 12, 1864.

27. Richard Rollins, ed., *Pickett's Charge!: Eyewitness Accounts,* (Redondo Beach, Calif.: Rank & File Publications, 1994), p. 96.

28. James R. Montgomery to A. R. Montgomery, May 10, 1864, CSA Collection, ESBL; John M. Coski, "Montgomery's Blood-Stained Letter Defines 'The Art of Dying'—and Living," *Museum of the Confederacy Magazine* (Summer 2006): 14.

29. Coski, "Montgomery's Blood-Stained Letter."

30. Contrast this "checklist" with the "stock messages" that Jay Winter describes from British officers in World War I informing relatives of a soldier's death: he was loved by his comrades, was a good soldier, and died painlessly. This is a remarkably secular formula in comparison to the Civil War's embrace of the *ars moriendi* tradition. See J. M. Winter, *Sites of Memory, Sites of Mourning: The Great War in European Cultural History* (Cambridge and New York: Cambridge University Press, 1995), p. 35. For a Civil War condolence letter written almost in the form of a checklist—indentations and all—see John G. Barrett and Robert K. Turner Jr., *Letters of a New Market Cadet: Beverly Stannard* (Chapel Hill: University of North Carolina Press, 1961), pp. 67–68. For a Catholic example, see Cooney, "War Letters of Father Peter Paul Cooney," pp. 153–54. Much of the "checklist" had its origins in the deathbed observers' search for reassurance that the dying person was successfully resisting the devil's characteristic temptations: to abandon his faith, to submit to desperation or impatience, to demonstrate spiritual pride or complacence, to show too much preoccupation with temporal matters. See Comper, *Book of the Craft of Dying*, pp. 9–21. For a brief discussion of consolation letters, see Reid Mitchell, *The Vacant Chair: The Northern Soldier Leaves Home* (New York: Oxford University Press, 1993), pp. 84–86.

31. Edwin S. Redkey, ed., *Grand Army of Black Men: Letters from African American Soldiers in the Union Army* (Cambridge and New York: Cambridge University Press, 1992), p. 67. Preparation constituted a significant dimension of the Good Death for Jewish soldiers as well. Note the emphasis of Albert Moses Luria's family on his preparedness and note his epitaph: "He went into the field prepared to meet his God." See Mel Young, ed., *Last Order of the Lost Cause: The True Story of a Jewish Family in the Old South* (Lanham, Md.: University Press of America, 1995), p. 147. See also, on sudden death, W. D. Rutherford to Sallie F. Rutherford, June 23, 1864, W. D. Rutherford Papers, SCL; Houlbrooke, *Death, Religion and the Family*, p. 208.

32. Letter to Mrs. Mason, October 3, 1864, 24th Reg. Virginia Infantry, CSA Collection, ESBL.

33. Alexander Twombly, *The Completed Christian Life: A Sermon Commemorative of Adjt. Richard Strong* (Albany, N.Y.: J. Munsell, 1863), p. 10; David Mack Cooper, *Obituary Discourse on Occasion of the Death of Noah Henry Ferry, Major of the Fifth Michigan Cavalry* (New York: J. F. Trow, 1863), p. 30.

34. Bacon, *Memorial of William Kirkland Bacon*, p. 57. On presentiment see also Alonzo Abernethy, "Incidents of an Iowa Soldier's Life, or Four Years in Dixie," *Annals of Iowa*, 3d ser. 12 (1920): 408. For a Jewish example, see the report of the death of Gustave Poznanski in *Charleston Daily Courier*, June 18, 1862. On presentiment and on soldiers' deaths more generally, see James M. McPherson, *For Cause and Comrades: Why Men Fought in the Civil War* (New York: Oxford University Press, 1997), pp. 63–70. See also Reid Mitchell, *Civil War Soldiers* (New York: Viking, 1988), pp. 63–64; L. L. Jones to Harriet Beach Jones, Herbert S. Hadley Papers, MOHS; W. D. Rutherford to Sallie Fair, July 26, 1861, W. D. Rutherford Papers, SCL. See also E. S. Nash to Hattie Jones, August 19, 1861, Herbert S. Hadley Papers, MOHS; Wells, *Facing the "King of Terrors,"* pp. 162–63.

35. J. C. Curtwright to Mr. and Mrs. Lovelace, April 24, 1862, in Lane, ed., *Dear Mother*, p. 116. T. Fitzhugh to Mrs. Diggs, June 23, 1863, Captain William W. Goss File, 19th Virginia Infantry, CSA Collection, ESBL; Sallie Winfree to Mrs. Bobo, October 9, 1862, Henry Bobo Papers, CSA Collection, ESBL.

36. T. J. Hodnett quoted in Davidson, ed., *War Was the Place*, pp. 80, 76–77; Walter Pharr, *Funeral Sermon on the Death of Capt. A. K. Simonton* (Salisbury, N.C.: J. J. Bruner, 1862), p. 11; Elijah Richardson Craven, *In Memoriam, Sermon and Oration . . . on the Occasion of the Death of Col. I. M. Tucker* (Newark, N.J.: Protection Lodge, 1862), pp. 5–6.

37. James B. Rogers, *War Pictures: Experiences and Observations of a Chaplain in the U.S. Army, in the War of the Southern Rebellion* (Chicago: Church & Goodman, 1863), p. 182; Guy R. Everson and Edward W. Simpson Jr., *Far, Far from Home: The Wartime Letters of Dick and Talley Simpson, 3rd South Carolina Volunteers* (New York: Oxford University Press, 1994), p. 287; J. Monroe Anderson to the Sisters of Gen. Gregg, January 9, 1863, Maxcy Gregg Papers, SCL; John Weissert to Dearest Wife and Children, October 17, 1862, John Weissert Papers, Box 1, Correspondence Sept.–Oct. 1862, BHL. For a Catholic example of reading the body for signs of the state of the soul, see Sister Catherine to Father Patrick Reilly,

December 5, 1862, Patrick Reilly Papers, PAHRC, which describes the death of Sister Bonaventure "with sweet peace and joy" and reports "the peace and calm of her soul was evident on her countenance."

38. L. S. Bobo to Dear Uncle, July 7, 1862, August 14, 1862, Bobo Papers, CSA Collection, ESBL; Cadenhead, "Some Confederate Letters of I. B. Cadenhead," p. 568; E. and E. Nash to Respected Nephews in Camp, November 11, 1862, Alpheus S. Bloomfield Papers, LC.

39. Frank Perry to J. Buchannon, September 21, 1862, in Lane, ed., *Dear Mother,* p. 189.

40. Frank Batchelor to Dear Wife, in *Batchelor-Turner Letters: 1861–1864: Written by Two of Terry's Texas Rangers,* annotated by H. J. H. Rugeley (Austin, Tex.: Steck Co., 1961), p. 80.

41. Sanford Branch to his mother, July 26, 1861, in Lane, *Dear Mother,* p. 36; Coco, *Killed in Action,* p. 91; Alonzo Hill, *In Memoriam. A Discourse . . . on Lieut. Thomas Jefferson Spurr* (Boston: J. Wilson, 1862); Davidson, ed., *War Was the Place.* Chaplain Corby observed that nearly all men called to their mothers as they lay dying. This was enshrined in Civil War popular song: see, for example, Thomas MacKellar, "The Dying Soldier to His Mother" (New York: Charles Magnus, n.d.) Wolf 551, and C. A. Vosburgh, "Tell Mother, I Die Happy" (New York: Charles Magnus, n.d.), Wolf 2290. For a southern example, see Charles C. Sawyer, "Mother Would Comfort Me!" (Augusta, Ga.: Blackmar & Bro., 186–). There were so many songs written as messages to Mother from the battlefield that they began to generate parodies and satirical responses. See John C. Cross, "Mother on the Brain" (New York: H. De Marsan, n.d.), Wolf 1470, and Cross, "Mother Would Wallop Me" (New York: H. De Marsan, n.d.), Wolf 1437. All of these songs, except the southern example, are in the American Song Sheet Collection, LCP. See Chapter 6.

42. William W. Bennett, *A Narrative of the Great Revival Which Prevailed in the Southern Armies* (Philadelphia: Claxton, Remsen & Haffelfinger, 1877), pp. 243–44. T. Fitzhugh to Mrs. Diggs, June 23, 1863, Captain William W. Goss File, 19th Virginia Infantry, CSA Collection, ESBL. For a letter in almost identical language, see E. W. Rowe to J. W. Goss, December 16, 1863, CSA Collection, ESBL.

43. Oliver Wendell Holmes Jr., *Touched with Fire: Civil War Letters and Diary of Oliver Wendell Holmes, Jr., 1861–1864,* ed. Mark DeWolfe Howe (New York: Da Capo Press, 1969), p. 27; Holmes, Civil War Diary, Harvard Law School Library, Harvard University.

44. A. D. Kirwan, ed., *Johnny Green of the Orphan Brigade: The Journal of a Confederate Soldier* (Lexington: University of Kentucky Press, 1956), p. 37; David Cornwell, quoted in Earl J. Hess, *The Union Soldier in Battle: Enduring the Ordeal of Combat* (Lawrence: University Press of Kansas, 1997), p. 143.

45. *Army and Navy Messenger,* April 1, 1864, quoted in Berends, "Wholesome Reading," p. 154. See also Fales Henry Newhall, *National Exaltation: The Duties of Christian Patriotism* (Boston: John M. Hewes, 1861); William Adams, *Christian Patriotism* (New York: A. D. F. Randolph, 1863); Joseph Fransioli, *Patriotism: A*

Christian Virtue (New York: Loyal Publication Society, 1863). The last of these works is Catholic. Note the disapproval of Sister Matilda Coskey of the father who refuses to permit his wounded son to be baptized, arguing "he has served his country, fought her battles & that is enough—he has nothing to fear for his soul." Sister Matilda Coskey to Father Patrick Reilly, October 18, 1864, Patrick Reilly Papers, PAHRC.

46. William Preston Johnston to Wade Hampton, November 3, 1864; James Connor to Wade Hampton, November 6, 1864, Wade Hampton Papers, ESBL; N. A. Foster to William K. Rash, 52nd North Carolina, CSA Collection, ESBL. For another discussion of gallantry, see Eleanor Damon Pace, ed., "The Diary and Letters of William P. Rogers, 1846–1862," *Southwestern Historical Quarterly* 32 (April 1929): 299.

47. George Barton, *Angels of the Battlefield* (Philadelphia: Catholic Art Publishing Co., 1897), p. 181.

48. Linderman makes this point about compulsion in *Embattled Courage*, p. 30; Smith, ed., "Notes on Satterlee," pp. 433–34; Berends, "Wholesome Reading," p. 137.

49. Hugh McLees to John, December 20, 1863, John McLees Papers, SCL; Berends, "Wholesome Reading," p. 139, n21; Gache, *Frenchman*, 164. On bad deaths, see also Ralph Houlbrooke, *Death, Religion and the Family*, p. 207.

50. Laderman, *Sacred Remains*, p. 99; Robert I. Alotta, *Civil War Justice: Union Army Executions Under Lincoln* (Shippensburg, Pa.: White Mane Press, 1989); *Charleston Mercury*, September 18, 1863; John Ripley Adams, *Memorial and Letters of John R. Adams, D.D.* (Cambridge, Mass.: Harvard University Press, 1890), p. 123; letters from Guilburton, September 4, 1863, and from Henry Robinson to his wife, both in Lane, ed., *Dear Mother*, pp. 263–64, 107.

51. Corby, *Memoirs*, p. 248; Frances Milton Kennedy Diary, M-3008, entry for September 26, 1863, SHC. For examples of descriptions of executions, see Cooney, "War Letters of Father Peter Paul Cooney," p. 57. On dying badly, see Edward Acton, " 'Dear Mollie': Letters of Captain Edward Acton to His Wife, 1862," ed. Mary Acton Hammond, *Pennsylvania Magazine of History and Biography* 89 (January 1965): 28.

52. Robert Kenzer, "The Uncertainty of Life: A Profile of Virginia's Civil War Widows," in Joan E. Cashin, *The War Was You and Me: Civilians in the American Civil War* (Princeton: Princeton University Press, 2002), p. 120; Clarke County Will Book E, 1860–67, pp. 129–30, Clarke County Courthouse, Berryville, Va.; Lane, ed., *Dear Mother*, 108. See N. Crosby, Financial Plans in Case of Death, GLC 03046. N. Crosby to son, April 23, 1862, Gilder Lehrman Collection, The Gilder Lehrman Institute of American History, NYHS.

53. John Edwards, Noncuptative Will, April 3, 1862, dictated to Hill at the hospital of the 53rd Virginia Infantry regiment at Suffolk, VHS. Thanks to Frances Pollard for drawing my attention to this document.

54. Burns Newman to Mr. Shortell, May 24, 1864, Michael Shortell Papers, WHS. See also Disposition of Personal Effects of Dead Wisconsin Soldiers, 1863, Wisconsin Governor's Papers, WHS.

55. *Daily South Carolinian,* May 29, 1864. For other examples, see obituaries of W. W. Watts, August 23, 1864; H. L. Garlington, August 13, 1864; Milton Cox, August 9, 1862; Joseph Friedenberg, September 15, 1862, all in *Daily South Carolinian;* George Nichols in *Richmond Daily Whig,* December 24, 1862; Walter Matthews in *Richmond Daily Dispatch,* December 25, 1862; Isaac Valentine in *Charleston Daily Courier,* June 18, 1862; Thomas B. Hampton [March 1865] in Thomas B. Hampton Papers, CAH.

56. Roland C. Bowen to Friend Ainsworth, September 28, 1862, in Gregory A. Coco, ed., *From Ball's Bluff to Gettysburg . . . and Beyond: The Civil War Letters of Private Roland E. Bowen, 15th Massachusetts Infantry, 1861–1864* (Gettysburg, Pa.: Thomas Publications, 1994), p. 124.

57. Washington Davis, cited in Linderman, *Embattled Courage,* p. 241. On numbness see Drew Gilpin Faust, *"A Riddle of Death": Mortality and Meaning in the American Civil War,* 34th Annual Robert Fortenbaugh Memorial Lecture (Gettysburg, Pa.: Gettysburg College, 1995), p. 21.

58. Herman Melville, "The Armies of the Wilderness," in Melville, *Battle-Pieces and Aspects of the War* (New York: Harper & Brothers, 1866), p. 103.

CHAPTER 2. KILLING

1. Tolstoy quoted in Lieutenant Colonel Dave Grossman, *On Killing: The Psychological Cost of Learning to Kill in War and Society* (Boston: Little, Brown, 1995), p. ix; Orestes Brownson, *The Works of Orestes Brownson,* ed. Henry F. Brownson (Detroit: T. Nourse, 1882–87), vol. 17, p. 214.

2. Grossman, *On Killing,* p. xiv. See also Joanna Bourke, *An Intimate History of Killing: Face-to-Face Killing in Twentieth-Century Warfare* (New York: Basic Books, 1999).

3. Theophilus Perry, quoted in Randolph B. Campbell, *A Southern Community in Crisis: Harrison County, Texas, 1850–1880* (Austin: Texas State Historical Press, 1983), p. 239; [Mrs. Frances Blake Brockenbrough,] *A Mother's Parting Words to Her Soldier Boy* (Petersburg, Va.: Evangelical Tract Society, 186–), p. 3; *Confederate Baptist,* December 3, 1862; Knox Mellon Jr., ed., "Letters of James Greenalch," *Michigan History* 44 (June 1960): 198–99; *Christian Recorder,* October 18, 1864.

4. Scott quoted in *Frank Leslie's Illustrated Newspaper,* August 3, 1861, p. 178; T. Harry Williams, "The Military Leadership of the North and the South," U.S. Air Force Academy, Harmon Memorial Lecture no. 2, 1960, p. 6, online at www .au.af.mil/au/awc/awcgate/usafa/harmon02.pdf.

5. *Frank Leslie's Illustrated Newspaper,* May 18, 1861, p. 3. On baptism of fire, see also Joseph Allan Frank and George A. Reaves, *"Seeing the Elephant": Raw Recruits at the Battle of Shiloh* (New York: Greenwood Press, 1989). The language of virginity was also often used to describe initiation into battle. See, for example, Creed Davis Diary, entry for May 11, 1864, VHS. On soldiers, killing, and religion, see also Reid Mitchell, *Civil War Soldiers* (New York: Viking, 1988), pp. 138–39.

6. Hugh McLees to John McLees, March 18, 1864, McLees Family Papers, SCL; Oliver Norton quoted in James I. Robertson Jr., *Soldiers Blue and Gray* (Columbia: University of South Carolina Press, 1988), pp. 220–21.

7. "Sensations Before and During Battle," clipping in George Bagby Scrapbook, 3:149, VHS; Charles Royster, *The Destructive War: William Tecumseh Sherman, Stonewall Jackson, and the Americans* (New York: Alfred A. Knopf, 1991), p. 279.

8. Byrd Charles Willis Journal, August 25, 1864, Diary Collection, ESBL. See T. I. McKenny to Earl Van Dorn, March 9, 1862, for description of federal dead being tomahawked and scalped in *The War of the Rebellion: A Compilation of the Official Records of the Union and Confederate Armies* (Washington, D.C.: Government Printing Office, 1883–1901), ser. I, vol. 8, p. 194; see report of Thomas Livermore of the Fifth New Hampshire at Antietam ordering his men to put on paint and leading them with a war whoop, James M. McPherson, *Crossroads of Freedom: Antietam* (New York: Oxford University Press, 2002), p. 123.

9. Osmun Latrobe Diary, October 16, 1862, May 10, 1863, transcript at VHS, original in Latrobe Papers, MS 526, Maryland Historical Society, Baltimore. Redman quoted in Kent Masterson Brown, *Retreat from Gettysburg: Lee, Logistics, and the Pennsylvania Campaign* (Chapel Hill: University of North Carolina Press, 2005), p. 234. On love of killing, see Theodore Nadelson, *Trained to Kill: Soldiers at War* (Baltimore: Johns Hopkins University Press, 2005), p. 72; Drew Gilpin Faust, " 'We Should Grow Too Fond of It': Why We Love the Civil War," *Civil War History* 50 (December 2004): 368; William Broyles, "Why Men Love War," *Esquire*, November 1984, pp. 54–65; Bourke, *Intimate History of Killing*, p. 31; Earl J. Hess, *The Union Soldier in Battle: Enduring the Ordeal of Combat* (Lawrence: University Press of Kansas, 1997), pp. 92–93.

10. John W. De Forest, *A Volunteer's Adventures: A Union Captain's Record of the Civil War* (New Haven: Yale University Press, 1946), pp. 111–12; Mills Lane, ed., *"Dear Mother: Don't Grieve About Me. If I Get Killed, I'll Only Be Dead": Letters from Georgia Soldiers in the Civil War* (Savannah, Ga.: Beehive Press, 1990), p. 156; Robertson, *Soldiers Blue and Gray*, 220; William White, July, 13, 1862, William White Collection, PAHRC.

11. Henry Matrau, February 27, 1862, in Marcia Reid-Green, ed., *Letters Home: Henry Matrau of the Iron Brigade* (Lincoln: University of Nebraska Press, 1993), p. 20.

12. Bagby Scrapbook, vol. 2, p. 55, VHS. On comradeship as motivation to fight, see James M. McPherson, *For Cause and Comrades: Why Men Fought in the Civil War* (New York: Oxford University Press, 1997).

13. Some historians cite the range of the new rifle as up to a thousand yards, but Gary W. Gallagher of the University of Virginia believes three hundred yards of effective use is a more accurate way to understand its capacities. My thanks to him for his help on this question. James M. McPherson estimates that 20 percent of the Confederate army and 8 percent of the Union army were draftees and substitutes. McPherson, *Ordeal by Fire: The Civil War and Reconstruction* (New York: Alfred A. Knopf, 1982), pp. 182–83.

14. Grossman, *On Killing*, pp. 24–25. Debate has raged about soldiers' firing rates

since the work of S. L. A. Marshall on nonfirers in World War II. See Grossman's response to these debates on p. 333. See also S. L. A. Marshall, *Men Against Fire: The Problem of Battle Command in Future War* (New York: Morrow, 1947), and John Keegan, *The Face of Battle* (New York: Viking Press, 1976).

15. Val C. Giles, *Rags and Hope: The Recollections of Val C. Giles, Four Years with Hood's Brigade, Fourth Texas Infantry, 1861–1865,* ed. Mary Lasswell (New York: Coward-McCann, 1961), p. 208.

16. S. H. M. Byers, "How Men Feel in Battle: Recollections of a Private at Champion Hills," *Annals of Iowa* 2 (July 1896): 449; Henry Abbott, July 6, 1863, in Robert Garth Scott, ed., *Fallen Leaves: The Civil War Letters of Major Henry Livermore Abbott* (Kent, Ohio: Kent State University Press, 1991), p. 188; Hess, *Union Soldier in Battle*, pp. 55, 52. On wounds, see George Worthington Adams, *Doctors in Blue: The Medical History of the Union Army in the Civil War* (New York: Henry Schuman, 1952), p. 113.

17. Kenneth Macksey and William Woodhouse, eds., *The Penguin Encyclopedia of Modern Warfare: 1850 to the Present Day* (London: Penguin, 1991), p. 111. On the changing nature and size of battle, see also John Keegan, *The Face of Battle* (New York: Viking, 1976), pp. 285–336. On tactics, see James M. McPherson, *Battle Cry of Freedom* (New York: Oxford University Press, 1988), pp. 474–76, and Brent Nosworthy, *The Bloody Crucible of Courage: Fighting Methods and Combat Experience of the Civil War* (New York: Carroll & Graf, 2003).

18. William Drayton Rutherford to Sallie F. Rutherford, June 23, 1864, William Drayton Rutherford Papers, SCL. On requirements, see Gerald Smith, "Sharpshooters," in David and Jeanne Heidler, eds., *Encyclopedia of the Civil War* (Santa Barbara, Calif.: ABC Clio, 2000), vol. 4, p. 1743. "To the Sharp Shooters of Windham County," August 19, 1861 (Bellows Falls, Vt.: Phoenix Job Office, 1861), reproduced in *Letters from a Sharpshooter: The Civil War Letters of Private William B. Greene, 1861–1865,* transcribed by William H. Hastings (Belleville, Wis.: Historic Publications, 1993), p. 4.

19. Isaac Hadden to Brother, Wife and All, June 5, 1864, and June 12, 1864, Misc. Mss. Hadden, Isaac, NYHS; Henry Abbott to J. G. Abbott, July 6, 1863, in Scott, ed., *Fallen Leaves* p. 184. On snakes, see Richard Pindell, "The Most Dangerous Set of Men," *Civil War Times Illustrated,* July–August 1993, p. 46.

20. Petersburg paper quoted in William Greene to Dear Mother, June 26, 1864, in *Letters from a Sharpshooter,* p. 226; De Forest, *Volunteer's Adventures,* p. 144. On sharpshooters see also Hess, *Union Soldier in Battle,* pp. 106–7, and Michael Walzer, *Just and Unjust Wars* (New York: Basic Books, 1977), p. 140. On sharpshooting and its very personal nature, see "On the Antietam," *Harper's Weekly,* January 3, 1863, reprinted in Kathleen Diffley, ed., *To Live and Die: Collected Stories of the Civil War* (Durham, N.C.: Duke University Press, 2002), pp. 128–32. On changing technology of sharpshooting, see Ron Banks, "Death at a Distance," *Civil War Times Illustrated,* March–April 1990, pp. 48–55.

21. Howell Cobb to James A. Seddon, January 8, 1865, in *War of the Rebellion,* ser. 4, vol. 3, pp. 1009–10; Mary Greenhow Lee Diary, April 3, 1864, WFCHS.

22. Thomas R. Roulhac quoted in McPherson, *Battle Cry of Freedom,* p. 566; *Arkansas*

Gazette quoted in Gregory J. W. Urwin, " 'We Cannot Treat Negroes . . . as Prisoners of War': Racial Atrocities and Reprisals in Civil War Arkansas," *Civil War History* 42 (September 1996): 202–3; W. D. Rutherford to Sallie F. Rutherford, May 2, 1864, William D. Rutherford Papers, SCL; Urwin, "We Cannot Treat Negroes," pp. 197, 203. Whether or not Fort Pillow was a massacre has been debated since the day after the event itself. Recent historical work has established persuasively that it was. See John Cimprich, *Fort Pillow: A Civil War Massacre and Public Memory* (Baton Rouge: Louisiana State University Press, 2005); John Cimprich and Robert C. Mainfort Jr., "The Fort Pillow Massacre: A Statistical Note," *Journal of American History* 76 (December 1989): 831–33; and Andrew Ward, *River Run Red: The Fort Pillow Massacre in the American Civil War* (New York: Viking, 2005). For casualty statistics, see Cimprich, *Fort Pillow,* app. B, pp. 130–31, and table 7, p. 129. See also the official federal investigation: U.S. Congress, *House Report* (serial 1206), "Fort Pillow Massacre," 38th Cong., 1st sess., no. 63, 1864. On killing black soldiers, see also Gary W. Gallagher, ed., *Fighting for the Confederacy: The Personal Recollections of General Edward Porter Alexander* (Chapel Hill: University of North Carolina Press, 1989), pp. 462, 465, 487.

23. George Gautier, *Harder Than Death: The Life of George Gautier, an Old Texan* (Austin, Tex.: n.p., 1902), pp. 10–11.

24. John Edwards cited in Urwin, " 'We Cannot Treat Negroes,' " p. 205; Henry Bird to fiancée, August 4, 1864, Bird Family Papers, VHS, quoted in Chandra Miller Manning, "What This Cruel War Was Over: Why Union and Confederate Soldiers Thought They Were Fighting the Civil War," Ph.D. diss. (Harvard University, 2002), p. 27.

25. Seddon quoted in John David Smith, "Let Us All Be Grateful That We Have Colored Troops That Will Fight," in John David Smith, ed., *Black Soldiers in Blue: African American Troops in the Civil War Era* (Chapel Hill: University of North Carolina Press, 2002), p. 45. See Kirby Smith to Samuel Cooper, in *War of the Rebellion,* ser. 2, vol. 6, pp. 21–22.

26. William Marvel, *Andersonville: The Last Depot* (Chapel Hill: University of North Carolina Press, 1994), p. 155.

27. *Christian Recorder,* July 30, 1864, p. 121; April 30, 1864, p. 69; August 22, 1863, p. 133.

28. W. E. B. DuBois, *Black Reconstruction in America* (1935; rpt. New York: Atheneum, 1969), p. 110; *Christian Recorder,* August 1, 1863, p. 126; Letter from Henry Harmon, *Christian Recorder,* November 7, 1863, p. 177; Alice Fahs, *The Imagined Civil War: Popular Literature of North and South, 1861–1865* (Chapel Hill: University of North Carolina Press, 2001), p. 175. See Andrew K. Black, "In the Service of the United States: Comparative Mortality Among African-American and White Troops in the Union Army," *Journal of Negro History* 79, no. 4 (Autumn 1994): 317–27.

29. *Christian Recorder,* August 15, 1863, p. 131. On Cailloux, see "The Funeral of Captain Andre Cailloux," *Harper's Weekly,* August 29, 1863; "Funeral of a Negro Soldier", *Weekly Anglo-African* (New York), August 15, 1863; James G. Hol-

landsworth Jr., *Louisiana Native Guards: The Black Military Experience During the Civil War* (Baton Rouge: Louisiana State University Press, 1995); Stephen J. Ochs, *A Black Patriot and a White Priest: Andre Cailloux and Claude Paschal Maistre in Civil War New Orleans* (Baton Rouge: Louisiana State University Press, 2000).

30. "The Funeral of Captain Andre Cailloux," *Harper's Weekly*, August 29, 1863, p. 551; see also *Weekly Anglo-African*, August 15, 1863.

31. George E. Stephens in Donald Yacovone, ed., *A Voice of Thunder: The Civil War Letters of George E. Stephens* (Urbana: University of Illinois Press, 1997), p. 203.

32. "The Two Southern Mothers," in *Weekly Anglo-African*, November 7, 1863.

33. David W. Blight, *Frederick Douglass' Civil War: Keeping Faith in Jubilee* (Baton Rouge: Louisiana State University Press, 1989), pp. 113, 115. The Covey story is in Douglass, *My Bondage and My Freedom* (1855; rpt. New York: Dover, 1969), pp. 246–49.

34. *Christian Recorder*, February 20, 1864, p. 29; December 19, 1863, p. 203.

35. Cordelia A. Harvey to Governor James Lewis, April 24, 1864, Cordelia A. Harvey Papers, Wisconsin Historical Society, Madison.

36. *Christian Recorder*, April 30, 1864, p. 69; July 9, 1864, p. 110; February 4, 1865, p. 18.

37. Abraham Lincoln, "Second Inaugural Address," in *Lincoln: Speeches, Letters and Miscellaneous Writings, Presidential Messages and Proclamations* (New York: Library of America, 1989), pp. 686–87.

38. Aunt Aggy tells this story to Mary Livermore in Livermore, *My Story of the War* (Hartford, Conn.: A. D. Worthington, 1889), p. 261. On black vengeance, see also Louisa May Alcott, "The Brothers," *Atlantic Monthly*, November 1863, in Diffley, ed., *To Live and Die*, pp. 191–208, and "Buried Alive," *Harper's Weekly*, May 7, 1864, in Diffley, *Live and Die*, pp. 284–88.

39. Daniel M. Holt, *A Surgeon's Civil War: The Letters and Diary of Daniel M. Holt, M.D.*, ed. James M. Greiner, Janet L. Coryell, and James R. Smither (Kent, Ohio: Kent University Press, 1994), p. 188; Howells quoted in Gerald Linderman, *Embattled Courage: The Experience of Combat in the American Civil War* (New York: Free Press, 1987), p. 128; James Wood Davidson to C. V. Dargan, August 6, 1862, Clara Dargan MacLean Papers, RBMSC; Charles Kerrison to his cousin, July 19, 1862, Kerrison Family Papers, SCL; statistics from "Bull Run, First Battle of," in Heidler and Heidler, eds. *Encyclopedia of the Civil War*, vol. 1, p. 316, "Shiloh, Battle of," vol. 4, p. 1779, and "Casualties," vol. 1, pp. 373–74. See also James McDonough, *Shiloh: In Hell Before Night* (Knoxville: University of Tennessee Press, 1977), and Larry Daniel, *Shiloh: The Battle That Changed the Civil War* (New York: Simon & Schuster, 1997). On Confederate losses, see *The War of the Rebellion*, ser. 2, vol. 27, pp. 338–46; Kent Masterson Brown, *Retreat from Gettysburg: Lee, Logistics and the Pennsylvania Campaign* (Chapel Hill: University of North Carolina Press, 2005), p. 2. Lee's losses at Gettysburg, which he systematically understated, can only be estimated. John W. Busey and David G. Martin conjecture 23,231 in *Regimental Strengths and Losses at Gettysburg*, 4th ed. (Hightstown, N.J.: Longstreet House, 2005), p. 258; James M. McPherson sug-

gests between 24,000 and 28,000; personal communication to the author, December 27, 2006.

40. Colonel Luther Bradley to My dear Buel, January 5, 1863, letter in possession of Robert Bradley, Somerville, Mass.; Frank, *"Seeing the Elephant,"* p. 120; Henry C. Taylor to Father and Mother, October 1863, Henry C. Taylor Papers, WHS.

41. William Stilwell to his Wife, September 18, 1862, in Mills Lane, ed., *"Dear Mother: Don't Grieve About Me. If I Get Killed, I'll Only Be Dead": Letters from Georgia Soldiers in the Civil War* (Savannah, Ga.: Beehive Press, 1990), pp. 184–85. Indiana soldier quoted in Hess, *Union Soldier in Battle,* p. 119; James B. Sheeran, *Confederate Chaplain: A War Journal,* ed. Joseph T. Durkin (Milwaukee: Bruce Publishing Co., 1960), pp. 88–89; W. D. Rutherford to Sallie Rutherford, July 3, 1862, SCL; Robert Goldthwaite Carter, *Four Brothers in Blue: or, Sunshine and Shadows of the War of the Rebellion* (Austin: University of Texas Press, 1978), p. 325; James Wood Davidson to C. V. Dargan, August 6, 1862, Clara Dargan MacLean Papers, RBMSC; George G. Benedict, *Army Life in Virginia: Letters from the Twelfth Vermont Regiment* (Burlington, Vt.: Free Press Association, 1891), pp. 190–91.

42. *Frank Leslie's Illustrated Weekly Newspaper,* May 24, 1862, p. 98; Ulysses S. Grant, *Personal Memoirs* (1885; rpt. New York: Library of America, 1990), p. 238; L. Minor Blackford, *Mine Eyes Have Seen the Glory: The Story of a Virginia Lady* (Cambridge, Mass.: Harvard University Press, 1954), p. 213. On stepping on bodies, see *Christian Recorder,* July 18, 1863; L. S. Bobo to A. Bobo, July 7, 1862, Bobo Papers, CSA Collection, ESBL; Mary A. Newcomb, *Four Years of Personal Reminiscences of the War* (Chicago: H. S. Mills, 1893), p. 43; John Driscoll to Adelaide, April 18, 1862, Gould Family Papers, WHS; Alexander G. Downing, *Downing's Civil War Diary* (Des Moines: Historical Department of Iowa, 1916), p. 325.

43. John O. Casler, *Four Years in the Stonewall Brigade* (Guthrie, Okla.: State Capital Printing Co., 1893), p. 29; Thompson in Gregory A. Coco, *A Strange and Blighted Land: Gettysburg, the Aftermath of a Battle* (Gettysburg, Pa.: Thomas Publications, 1995), p. 54; Chauncey Herbert Cooke, *A Soldier Boy's Letters to His Father and Mother, 1861–1865* (Independence, Wis.: News-Office, 1915), p. 97; Pierce in Gregory A. Coco, *Killed in Action: Eyewitness Accounts of the Last Moments of 100 Union Soldiers Who Died at Gettysburg* (Gettysburg, Pa.: Thomas Publications, 1992), p. 112; Walker Lee to Dear Mother, June 15, 1862, in Laura Elizabeth Lee Battle, *Forget-Me-Nots of the Civil War* (St Louis: A. R. Fleming Printing Co., 1909), p. 355.

44. *Southern Churchman,* June 26, 1862; John Weissert to Dearest Mother and Children, December 14, 1862, John Weissert Papers, Box 1, Correspondence Nov.–Dec. 1862, BHL; Henry L. Abbott to J. G. Abbott, October 17, 1863, in Scott, ed., *Fallen Leaves,* pp. 223–24; "Indifference of Soldiers to Death," *Christian Recorder,* November 14, 1863, p. 184; Surgeon [name illegible] to Reverend Patrick Reilly, June 25, 1862, Patrick Reilly Papers, PAHRC; Henry Clay Trumble, *War Memories of an Army Chaplain* (New York: C. Scribner's Sons, 1898), pp. 158, 39; Isaac Hadden to his Kate, May 24, 1864, Misc. Mss. Hadden, Isaac,

NYHS; Charles Wainwright in Allan Nevins, ed., *A Diary of Battle: The Personal Journals of Colonel Charles S. Wainwright, 1861–1865* (New York: Harcourt Brace & World, 1962), p. 56; Wilbur Fisk quote in Reid Mitchell, *The Vacant Chair: The Northern Soldier Leaves Home* (New York: Oxford University Press, 1993), p. 157.

45. Weymouth Jordan, ed., "Hugh Harris Robison Letters," *Journal of Mississippi History* 1 (January 1939), p. 54; Elijah P. Petty, *Journey to Pleasant Hill: The Civil War Letters of Captain Elijah P. Petty, Walker's Texas Division, CSA*, ed. Norman D. Brown (San Antonio: University of Texas, Institute of Texan Cultures, 1982), p. 304; Angus Waddle to My dear Sister, March 6, 1862, Ellen Waddle McCoy Papers, MOHS; Katharine Prescott Wormeley, *The Other Side of War: With the Army of the Potomac: Letters from the Headquarters of the United States Sanitary Commission During the Peninsular Campaign in Virginia in 1862* (Boston: Ticknor & Co., 1889), p. 114.

46. Daniel E. Sutherland, *Seasons of War: The Ordeal of a Confederate Community, 1861–1865* (New York: Free Press, 1995), p. 163; Casler, *Four Years in the Stonewall Brigade*, p. 89; *Soldiers' Almanac* (Richmond, Va.: MacFarlane & Fergusson, 1863).

CHAPTER 3. BURYING

1. Board of Trustees of the Antietam National Cemetery, *History of Antietam National Cemetery* (Baltimore: J. W. Woods, 1869), p. 5.

2. [Henry Raymond], "Editor's Table," *Harper's New Monthly Magazine* 8 (April 1854): 690, 691.

3. Ibid., pp. 691, 693. On body and death, see Caroline Bynum, *The Resurrection of the Body in Western Christianity* (New York: Columbia University Press, 1995), and Bynum, *Fragmentation and Redemption: Essays on Gender and the Human Body in Medieval Religion* (New York: Zone Books, 1991).

4. Daniel E. Sutherland, *Seasons of War: The Ordeal of a Confederate Community, 1861–1865* (New York: Free Press, 1995), p. 274; Gage in Gregory A. Coco, *Wasted Valor: The Confederate Dead at Gettysburg* (Gettysburg, Pa.: Thomas Publications, 1990), p. 137; Wirt Armistead Cate, ed., *Two Soldiers: The Campaign Diaries of Thomas J. Key, C.S.A., December 7, 1863–May 17, 1865 and Robert J. Campbell, U.S.A., January 1, 1864–July 21, 1864* (Chapel Hill: University of North Carolina Press, 1938), p. 182; *Frank Leslie's Illustrated Newspaper*, August 16, 1862, p. 334.

5. Sutherland, *Seasons of War*, p. 76.

6. A. P. Meylist to Edmund B. Whitman, June 10, 1868, Edmund B. Whitman, Letters and Reports Received, Record Group 92 E A1–397A, NARA; H. Clay Trumbull, *War Memories of a Chaplain* (New York: C. Scribner's Sons, 1898), p. 209. See especially "Soldiers Graves and Soldier Burials," pp. 203–32.

7. *General Orders of the War Department, Embracing the Years 1861, 1862 & 1863* (New York: Derby & Miller, 1864), vol. 1, pp. 158, 248. See also James E. Yeatman, [Sanitary Commission,] "Burial of the Dead," printed circular, September 20, 1861, William Greenleaf Eliot Collection, MOHS; Erna Risch, *Quartermaster*

Support of the Army: A History of the Corps, 1775–1939 (Washington, D.C.: United States Army, 1989), p. 464.

8. Horace H. Cunningham, *Field Medical Services at the Battles of Manassas* (Athens: University of Georgia Press, 1968), p. 48; *Regulations for the Army of the Confederate States, 1862* (Atlanta: James McPherson & Co., 1862).

9. Report of Colonel Henry A. Weeks, 12th New York Infantry, May 28, 1862, *The War of the Rebellion: A Compilation of the Official Records of the Union and Confederate Armies* (Washington, D.C.: Government Printing Office, 1884), ser. 1, vol. 11/1, p. 725; *Frank Leslie's Illustrated Newspaper,* February 28, 1863, p. 366; *Christian Recorder,* May 21, 1864, p. 83; Richard F. Miller and Robert F. Mooney, *The Civil War: The Nantucket Experience: Including the Memoirs of Josiah Fitch Murphey* (Nantucket: Wesco Publishing Co., 1994), p. 107.

10. Many descriptions of Antietam assert that the dead were buried by the 21st, but Holt's observations contradict this. Daniel M. Holt, *A Surgeon's Civil War: The Letters and Diary of Daniel M. Holt, M.D.,* ed. James M. Greiner, Janet L. Coryell, and James R. Smither (Kent, Ohio: Kent State University Press, 1994), p. 28; Mrs. H. [Anna M. E. Holstein], *Three Years in Field Hospitals in the Army of the Potomac* (Philadelphia: J. B. Lippincott, 1867), p. 11.

11. James M. McPherson, *Crossroads of Freedom: Antietam* (New York: Oxford University Press, 2002), p. 4; W. D. Rutherford to Sallie Rutherford, May 21, 1864, William Drayton Rutherford Papers, SCL. (This example is not from Antietam, as are all others in this section, but from Spotsylvania in 1864.) See also Steven R. Stotelmyer, *The Bivouacs of the Dead: The Story of Those Who Died at Antietam and South Mountain* (Baltimore: Toomey Press, 1992), p. 10.

12. Stotelmyer, *Bivouacs of the Dead,* pp. 9, 5.

13. Gregory A. Coco, *A Strange and Blighted Land: Gettysburg, the Aftermath of a Battle* (Gettysburg, Pa.: Thomas Publications, 1995), p. 313; Gerard A. Patterson, *Debris of Battle: The Wounded of Gettysburg* (Mechanicsburg, Pa.: Stackpole Books, 1997), p. 28; Coco, *Strange and Blighted Land.,* pp. 60, 64. On lack of tools, see also Richard Coolidge to Major General W. A. Hammond, September 4, 1862, Papers of George A. Otis, RG 94 629A, NARA.

14. W. B. Coker to his Brother, July 28, 1861, in Mills Lane, ed., *"Dear Mother: Don't Grieve About Me. If I Get Killed, I'll Only Be Dead": Letters from Georgia Soldiers in the Civil War* (Savannah, Ga.: Beehive Press, 1990), p. 40; *Official Records,* ser. 1, vol. 27, p. 79, cited in Gerard A. Patterson, *Debris of Battle: The Wounded of Gettysburg* (Mechanicsburg, Pa.: Stackpole Books, 1997), p. xi; Theodore Fogel to his parents, September 28, 1862, in Lane, ed., *Dear Mother,* p. 190.

15. John A. Wyeth, *With Sabre and Scalpel: The Autobiography of a Soldier and Surgeon* (New York: Harper & Brothers, 1914), p. 254; *Frank Leslie's Illustrated Newspaper,* November 14, 1863, p. 124; Frank Oakley's reactions described in Cynthia to My Dear Father, August 22, 1862, Frank Oakley Papers, WHS.

16. Quotes from Joseph Allan Frank and George A. Reaves, *"Seeing the Elephant": Raw Recruits at the Battle of Shiloh* (New York: Greenwood Press, 1989), p. 122.

17. Coco, *Strange and Blighted Land,* p. 89; Stotelmyer, *Bivouacs of the Dead,* p. 4; Frank and Reaves, *"Seeing the Elephant,"* 123; Coco, *Strange and Blighted Land,*

p. 127; Earl J. Hess, *The Union Soldier in Battle: Enduring the Ordeal of Combat* (Lawrence: University Press of Kansas, 1997), p. 41; Cyrus F. Boyd, *The Civil War Diary of Cyrus F. Boyd, Fifteenth Iowa Infantry 1861–1863*, ed. Mildred Throne (Millwood, N.Y.: Kraus Reprint Co., 1953), pp. 41–42; H. Clay Trumbull, *War Memories of an Army Chaplain* (New York: C. Scribner's Sons, 1898), p. 209; Robert Zaworski, *Headstones of Heroes: The Restoration and History of Confederate Graves in Atlanta's Oakland Cemetery* (Paducah, Ky.: Turner Publishing Co. 1997), p. 7.

18. *New York Herald,* September 7, 1862; James Eldred Phillips Diary, entry for May 1863, p. 16, VHS. On hogs see for example Sutherland, *Seasons of War,* pp. 193, 228; William D. Rutherford to Sallie Fair, August 26, 1861, Rutherford Papers, SCL.

19. "Burials," *Sanitary Commission Bulletin* 1, no. 20 (August 15, 1864): 623; R. A. Wilkinson to M. F. Wilkinson, July 8, 1862, Wilkinson-Stark Family Papers (mss. 255), The Historic New Orleans Collection, New Orleans; Hardin quoted in Frank and Reaves, *"Seeing the Elephant,"* p. 122.

20. William Corby, *Memoirs of Chaplain Life: Three Years Chaplain in the Famous Irish Brigade, "Army of the Potomac"* (Notre Dame, Ind.: Scholastic Press, 1894), p. 91; Coco, *Strange and Blighted Land,* p. 119; Wyeth, *With Sabre and Scalpel,* p. 248; Holt, *Surgeon's Civil War,* pp. 190, 103.

21. William Gore, February 25, 1865, BV Gore, William B., NYHS. Edgar Allan Poe wrote frequently about the fear of being buried alive in his widely popular short stories. See, for example, "The Premature Burial" and "The Fall of the House of Usher," in Stephen Peithman, ed., *The Annotated Tales of Edgar Allan Poe* (Garden City, N.Y.: Doubleday, 1981). See also Timothy Trend Blade, "Buried Alive!" *American Cemetery,* September 1991, pp. 34–54.

22. Gregory A. Coco, *Killed in Action: Eyewitness Accounts of the Last Moments of 100 Union Soldiers Who Died at Gettysburg* (Gettysburg, Pa.: Thomas Publications, 1992), p. 34.

23. Cate, ed., *Two Soldiers,* p. 93; Houghton quoted in Coco, *Killed in Action,* pp. 44–45; Fannie A. Beers, *Memories: A Record of Personal Experience and Adventure During Four Years of War* (Philadelphia: J. B. Lippincott, 1888), p. 83.

24. Trumbull, *War Memories of a Chaplain,* p. 219.

25. J. W. McClure to My Dearest Kate, August 17, 1864, McClure Family Papers, SCL.

26. Sutherland, *Seasons of War,* pp. 160–61; Charles Kerrison to My Dear Sister, May 19, 1864, Kerrison Family Papers, SCL; George R. Gauthier, *Harder Than Death: The Life of George R. Gauthier, an Old Texan* (Austin, Tex.: n.p., 1902), p. 15; Oliver Wendell Holmes, "My Hunt After 'The Captain,'" *Atlantic* 10 (December 1862), p. 743.

27. *Narrative of Privations and Sufferings of United States Officers and Soldiers While Prisoners of War in the Hands of Rebel Authorities, Being the Report of a Commission of Inquiry, Appointed by the United States Sanitary Commission* (Philadelphia: King & Baird, 1864), p. 159; Holt, *Surgeon's Civil War,* p. 63.

28. Coco, *Strange and Blighted Land,* p. 49. On death and Civil War horses, see Drew Gilpin Faust, "Equine Relics of the Civil War," *Southern Cultures* 6 (Spring 2000): 23–49.

29. Hollywood Cemetery, Records, 1847–1955, VHS; Mary H. Mitchell, *Hollywood Cemetery: The History of a Southern Shrine* (Richmond: Virginia State Library, 1985), p. 48.

30. Benedict Anderson, *Imagined Communities: Reflections on the Origin and Spread of Nationalism* (New York: Verso, 1991).

31. John Thompson, "The Burial of Latané," online at www.civilwarpoetry.org/confederate/officers/latane.html. See Drew Gilpin Faust, "Race, Gender and Confederate Nationalism: William D. Washington's *Burial of Latané*," in Faust, *Southern Stories: Slaveholders in Peace and War* (Columbia: University of Missouri Press, 1992), pp. 148–59.

32. Faust, "Race, Gender and Confederate Nationalism," pp. 149–51.

33. *Harper's Weekly*, October 11, 1862, p. 655; Coco, *Strange and Blighted Land*, p. 11; John W. Schildt, *Antietam Hospitals* (Chewsville, Md.: Antietam Publications, 1987), p. 14.

34. Flora McCabe to Dearest Maggie, January 26, 1862, Flora Morgan McCabe Collection, LC. On fear of getting the wrong body, see also Friedrich Hartmann to Sarah Ogden, September 10, 1863, Sarah Ogden Correspondence and Ephemera, GLC6559.01.114, Gilder Lehrman Collection, The Gilder Lehrman Institute of American History, NYHS.

35. Patterson, *Debris*, p. 173; see also, "Yorktown," *New York Herald*, April 30, 1862; Robert E. Denney, *Civil War Medicine: Care and Comfort of the Wounded* (New York: Sterling Publishers, 1994), p. 58; W. White to Dear Parents, June 21, 1862, William White Papers, PAHRC.

36. See Pennsylvania State Agency, December 10, 1863, Record Book, November 1863–December 1864, NYHS; New England Soldiers Relief Association Papers, RG 94, p. 800, NARA. On Central Association, see T. N. Dawkins to J. W. McClure, December 4, 1864, McClure Papers, SCL; *Louisiana Soldiers Relief Association and Hospital* (Richmond, Va.: Enquirer Book and Job Office, 1862), p. 30. On support from a single community, see Robert V. Wells, *Facing the "King of Terrors": Death and Society in an American Community, 1750–1990* (New York: Cambridge University Press, 2000), p. 129.

37. On the U.S. Sanitary Commission, see "Burials," *Sanitary Commission Bulletin* 1, no. 20 (August 15, 1864): 623; "Rev. Mr. Hoblitt on Nashville Hospitals," *Sanitary Reporter*, 1, no. 5 (July 15, 1863): 34; "The Commission on the James River and the Appomattox," *Sanitary Commission Bulletin* 1, no. 18 (July 15, 1864): 567. On Sanitary Commission and burials, see [Holstein], *Three Years in Field Hospitals*, p. 71; J. S. Newberry, "Report of the Hospital Directory," *Sanitary Reporter* 1, no. 11 (October 15, 1863): 81.

38. Chattanooga, Tenn., Disinterments from March to September 1864, Telegrams from January to July 1864, ms. vol. bd., Box 284.1, folder 3, p. 119, U.S. Sanitary Commission Records, NYPL.

39. Mary C. Brayton, October 15, 1864, J. S. Moore, November 2, 1864, Chattanooga, Tenn., Orders for Disinterment and Removal of Bodies, September 1864–February 1865, Box 284.1, folder 5, U.S. Sanitary Commission Records, NYPL.

40. "Soldiers' Cemetery at Belle Plain Va May 23 1864," Box 192.3, folder 4; "Plot of Soldiers' Cemetery, Port Royal Va 28 May 1864," Box 192.3, folder 5, U.S. Sanitary Commission Records, NYPL.

41. Cornelius quoted in Christine Quigley, *The Corpse: A History* (Jefferson, N.C.: McFarland & Co., 1963), p. 55. See Cain and Cornelius Ledger, 1859, 1862, RBMSC.

42. "The Terrible Telegram," March 18, 1863; Henry I. Bowditch to My Own Sweet Wife [Olivia Yardley Bowditch], March 19, 1863, both in Manuscripts Relating to Lieutenant Nathaniel Bowditch, vol. 2, pp. 98, 92, Nathaniel Bowditch Memorial Collection, MAHS.

43. Henry I. Bowditch, *A Brief Plea for an Ambulance System for the Army of the United States* (Boston: Ticknor & Fields, 1863), pp. 6, 15.

44. Coco, *Strange and Blighted Land,* pp. 114–15, 110; order in *Christian Recorder,* August 1, 1863, p. 1.

45. Alexander quoted in Kent Masterson Brown, *Retreat from Gettysburg: Lee, Logistics and the Pennsylvania Campaign* (Chapel Hill: University of North Carolina Press, 2005), p. 50; see also pp. 371–72, 381.

46. Receipt, August 15, 1862, Goodwin Family Papers, MAHS; Alvin F. Harlow, *Old Waybills: The Romance of the Express Companies* (New York: D. Appleton-Century, 1934), p. 299. See also Stillman King Wightman, "In Search of My Son," *American Heritage* 14 (February 1963), pp. 64–78.

47. Stotelmyer, *Bivouacs of the Dead,* p. 15.

48. Staunton Transportation Company, "Transportation of the Dead!" (Gettysburg, Pa.: H. J. Stahle, 1863), broadside, LCP.

49. Robert W. Habenstein and William M. Lamers, *The History of American Funeral Directing* (Milwaukee: Bulfin Printers, 1955), pp. 330–35.

50. On Ellsworth, see *Frank Leslie's Illustrated Magazine,* June 1, 1861, pp. 40–41. On embalming, see also Michael Sappol, *A Traffic of Dead Bodies: Anatomy and Embodied Social Identity in Nineteenth-Century America* (Princeton: Princeton University Press, 2002).

51. Charlotte Elizabeth McKay, *Stories of Hospital and Camp* (Philadelphia: Claxton, Remsen & Haffelfinger, 1876), p. 47.

52. *Richmond Enquirer,* June 2, 1863, p. 2; December 4, 1863, p. 3; Charles R. Wilson, "The Southern Funeral Director: Managing Death in the New South," *Georgia Historical Quarterly* 67 (Spring 1983): 53.

53. Habenstein and Lamers, *History of American Funeral Directing,* pp. 330, 334. See also Gary Laderman, *The Sacred Remains: American Attitudes Towards Death, 1799–1883* (New Haven: Yale University Press, 1996), and Karen Pomeroy Flood, "Contemplating Corpses: The Dead Body in American Culture, 1870–1920," Ph.D. diss. (Harvard University, 2001).

54. George A. Townsend, *Rustics in Rebellion: A Yankee Reporter on the Road to Richmond, 1861–1865* (Chapel Hill: University of North Carolina Press, 1950), pp. 121–22, 153–54.

55. Hardie to Provost Marshal General, City Point, November 23, 1864, M619, 2195, S1864 Roll 309, NARA; Turner and Baker Files, November 8, 1864, 363-B,

M797, Roll 130, NARA; R. Burr to Brig. Gen. M. R. Patrick, November 21, 1864, M619 2195 S1864 Roll 309, NARA.

56. War Department, Quartermaster General's Office, *Compilation of Laws, Orders, Opinions, Instructions, Etc. in Regard to National Military Cemeteries* (Washington, D.C.: Government Printing Office, 1878), p. 5. See also Monro MacCloskey, *Hallowed Ground: Our National Cemeteries* (New York: Richard Rosens Press, 1968), p. 24.

57. Garry Wills, *Lincoln at Gettysburg: The Words That Remade America* (New York: Simon & Schuster, 1992).

58. Trumbull, *War Memories of a Chaplain*, p. 209.

59. Bowditch, *Brief Plea*, p. 15.

CHAPTER 4. NAMING

1. Walt Whitman, *Specimen Days* (1882; rpt. Boston: David Godine, 1971), p. 60.

2. Caroline Alexander, "Letter from Vietnam: Across the River Styx," *New Yorker*, October 25, 2004, p. 44. See also Michael Sledge, *Soldier Dead: How We Recover, Identify, Bury, and Honor Our Military Fallen* (New York: Columbia University Press, 2004).

3. Mark Crawford, *Encyclopedia of the Mexican-American War* (Santa Barbara, Calif.: ABC-Clio, 1999), p. 68, cites 13,768 U.S. deaths out of 104,556 who served. Only one in eight of these deaths was battle-related; the others were from disease.

4. U.S. War Department, *General Orders of the War Department* (New York: Derby & Miller, 1864), vol. 1, pp. 158, 248; "Return of Deceased Soldiers" and "Field Returns," paras. 451, 452, 453, in *Regulations for the Army of the Confederate States, 1862* (Atlanta: James McPherson & Co., 1862); Samuel P. Moore, August 14, 1862, in Wayside Hospital, Charleston, Order and Letter Book, SCL; *Charleston Mercury*, January 27, 1864; Edward Steere, *The Graves Registration Service in World War II*, Quartermaster Historical Studies no. 21, Historical Section, Office of the Quartermaster General (Washington, D.C.: Government Printing Office, 1951), pp. 4–5. On inadequacies of Confederate casualty reporting in the Peninsula Campaign, see *The War of the Rebellion: A Compilation of the Official Records of the Union and Confederate Armies* (Washington, D.C.: Government Printing Office, 1880–1901) ser. 1, vol. 11, pt. 2, pp. 559, 760, 775, 501–2.

5. Sarah J. Palmer to Harriet R. Palmer, September 5, 1862, Palmer Family Papers, SCL; F. S. Gillespie to Mrs. Carson, July 5, 1864, Carson Family Papers, SCL.

6. Elvira J. Powers, *Hospital Pencillings: Being a Diary While in Jefferson General Hospital* (Boston: Edward L. Mitchel, 1866), p. 19. On chaplains, see Warren B. Armstrong, *For Courageous Fighting and Confident Dying: Union Chaplains in the Civil War* (Lawrence: University Press of Kansas, 1998), p. 134n98, quoting an 1864 order from the assistant medical director of the Department of the Cumberland. Chaplain figures in Steven E. Woodworth, *While God Is Marching On: The Religious World of Civil War Soldiers* (Lawrence: University Press of Kansas, 2001), p. 148.

7. *Daily South Carolinian*, June 16, 1864.

8. *Daily South Carolinian*, July 22, 1863; F. S. Gillespie to Mrs. Carson; Mathew Jack

Davis Narrative, "War Sketches," CAH; Joseph Willett to Dear Sister, June 6, 1864, Misc. Mss. Cummings, NYHS; Henry W. Raymond, ed., "Extracts from the Journal of Henry J. Raymond II," *Scribner's Monthly* 19 (January 1880): 419–20; Steven R. Stotelmyer, *The Bivouacs of the Dead* (Baltimore: Toomey Press, 1992), p. 17.

9. On mail see W. D. Rutherford to Sallie Fair Rutherford, June 5, 1864, William Drayton Rutherford Papers, SCL.

10. J. W. Hoover to Mr. Kuhlman, September 8, 1864, J. W. Hoover Papers, WHS; Reverend Lemuel Moss, *Annals of the United States Christian Commission* (Philadelphia: J. B. Lippincott, 1868), pp. 411, 506. On letters after Gettysburg, see Andrew Boyd Cross, "The Battle of Gettysburg and the Christian Commission," in Daniel J. Hoisington, ed., *Gettysburg and the Christian Commission* ([Roseville, Minn.]: Edinborough Press, 2002), p. 59. A quire is a set of twenty-four or twenty-five sheets of paper of the same size and stock.

11. Moss, *Annals,* pp. 512, 487–88, 563, 475. See U.S. Christian Commission, Record of Letters Written for Soldiers, Army of the Potomac, 1865, RG 94 E 746, and U.S. Christian Commission, Abstracts of Letters Written for Sick and Wounded Soldiers, Army of the Potomac, 1864–65, RG 94 E745, NARA.

12. Moss, *Annals,* pp. 409, 439–40. See U.S. Christian Commission, Letters Received, Individual Relief Department, 1864–65 RG 94 E748, NARA; U.S. Christian Commission, Record of Inquiries, Central Office, 1864–65 RG 94 E743, NARA.

13. U.S. Christian Commission, Death Register, 1864–65, October 6, 1864; October 9, 1864; October 8, 1864; September 19, 1864; October 3, 1864; November 3, 1864; October 18, 1864, RG 94 E797, NARA.

14. Moss, *Annals,* pp. 508, 439. U.S. Christian Commission, *Record of the Federal Dead Buried from Libby, Belle Isle, Danville and Camp Lawton Prisons and at City Point and in the Field Before Petersburg and Richmond* (Philadelphia: J. B. Rodgers, 1866). See U.S. Christian Commission, Correspondence Concerning "Record of the Federal Dead," RG 94 E795, NARA.

15. Charles J. Stillé, *History of the United States Sanitary Commission* (New York: Hurd & Houghton, 1868), p. 451; George M. Fredrickson, *The Inner Civil War: Northern Intellectuals and the Crisis of the Union* (New York: Harper & Row, 1965), chap. 7; Judith Ann Giesberg, *Civil War Sisterhood: The U.S. Sanitary Commission and Women's Politics in Transition* (Boston: Northeastern University Press, 2000); Jeanie Attie, *Patriotic Toil: Northern Women and the American Civil War* (Ithaca, N.Y.: Cornell University Press, 1998); William Quentin Maxwell, *Lincoln's Fifth Wheel: The Political History of the United States Sanitary Commission* (New York: Longmans, Green & Co., 1956).

16. Stillé, *History of Sanitary Commission,* pp. 287, 308.

17. Ibid., p. 309; John Herrick to Frederick Law Olmsted, December 14, 1862, Washington Hospital Directory Archives, Letters of Inquiry, Box 192.2, folder 3, U.S. Sanitary Commission Records, NYPL.

18. *Sanitary Reporter,* January 15, 1864, p. 135.

19. Stillé, *History of Sanitary Commission,* p. 309; Howard A. Martin to H. A. de France, July 4, 1863, John Bowne to H. A. de France, July 9, 1863, July 16, 1863, and July 21, 1863, Philadelphia Agency, Hospital Directory Correspondence,

vol. 1, Box 596, U.S. Sanitary Commission Records, NYPL; H. A. de France to Jos. P. Holbrook, July 27, 1863 and July 18, 1863, Washington Hospital Directory Archives, Box 195.1, U.S. Sanitary Commission Records, NYPL.

20. Richard Deering, June 13, 1864, Louisville Hospital Directory Archives, Chattanooga, Special Inquiries, April 8, 1864, to August 25, 1864, Box 284.2, folder 1, p. 58; Report of Hospital Directory, July 9, 1864, Washington Hospital Directory Archives, Box 192.3, folder 12, U.S. Sanitary Commission Records, NYPL; "The Hospital Directory," *Sanitary Commission Bulletin* 1 (December 15, 1863): 109.

21. Report of Hospital Directory, July 9, 1864, Washington Hospital Directory Archives, Box 192.3, folder 12, U.S. Sanitary Commission Records, NYPL. For casualty numbers, see James McPherson, *Battle Cry of Freedom: The Civil War Era* (New York: Oxford University Press, 1988), p. 742.

22. Peter Williams to Dear Sir, March 28, 1863, Philadelphia Agency, Hospital Directory Correspondence, vol. 1, Box 596, U.S. Sanitary Commission Records, NYPL. Susannah Hampton to Dear Sir, September 14, 1863, Philadelphia Agency, Hospital Directory Correspondence, vol. 2, Box 597, U.S. Sanitary Commission Records, NYPL.

23. Mrs. Biddy Higgins to Sir, December 16, 1863, Philadelphia Agency, Hospital Directory Correspondence, vol. 2, Box 597, U.S. Sanitary Commission Records, NYPL.

24. John Bowne to John W. Wilson, December 17, 1863, Philadelphia Agency, Hospital Directory Correspondence, vol. 2, Box 597, U.S. Sanitary Commission Records, NYPL.

25. Stillé, *History of Sanitary Commission,* pp. 310, 309.

26. *Louisiana Soldiers' Relief Association and Hospital in the City of Richmond, Virginia* (Richmond, Va.: Enquirer Book and Job Press, 1862), p. 30; Kurt O. Berends, " 'Wholesome Reading Purifies and Elevates the Man': The Religious Military Press in the Confederacy," in Randall M. Miller, Harry S. Stout, and Charles Reagan Wilson, eds., *Religion and the American Civil War* (New York: Oxford University Press, 1998), p. 147.

27. P. Hunter to Oliver H. Middleton, July 27, 1864; Henry W. Richards to Oliver H. Middleton, December 19, 1864; E. W. Mikell to Colonel B. H. Rutledge, June 21, 1864, all in Middleton-Blake Papers, SCHS.

28. *Harper's Weekly,* September 3, 1864, p. 576.

29. W. H. Fowler, *Guide for Claimants of Deceased Soldiers* (Richmond, Va.: Geo. P. Evans & Co., 1864), pp. 66, 17; Megan McClintock, "Civil War Pensions and the Reconstruction of Union Families," *Journal of American History* 83 (September 1996): 456–80; Theda Skocpol, *Protecting Soldiers and Mothers: The Political Origins of Social Policy in the United States* (Cambridge; Mass.: Harvard University Press, 1992), pp. 106–7.

30. *Daily South Carolinian,* May 17, 1864; W. D. Rutherford, telegram to Sallie F. Rutherford, July 6, 1862, William Drayton Rutherford Papers, SCL.

31. Gregory Coco, *Killed in Action: Eyewitness Accounts of the Last Moments of 100 Union Soldiers Who Died at Gettysburg* (Gettysburg, Pa.: Thomas Publications, 1992), p. 76; *Harper's Weekly,* August 1, 1863, p. 495, and September 3, 1864,

p. 576. Murphey quoted in Richard F. Miller, and Robert F. Moore, *The Civil War: The Nantucket Experience, Including the Memoirs of Josiah Fitch Murphey* (Nantucket, Mass.: Wesco Publishing, 1994), p. 80.

32. Louis Menand, *The Metaphysical Club: A Story of Ideas in America* (New York: Farrar, Straus & Giroux, 2001), p. 41.

33. Katharine Prescott Wormeley, *The Other Side of War: With the Army of the Potomac. Letters from the Headquarters of the United States Sanitary Commission During the Peninsular Campaign in Virginia in 1862* (Boston: Ticknor & Co. 1889), p. 145; Clara Barton, Journal, 1863, Clara Barton Papers, LC; T. J. Weatherly Diary, 1864–65, SCL.

34. Walt Whitman, *Memoranda During the War* (1875; rpt. Bedford, Mass.: Applewood Books, 1993), p. 5; Edwin Haviland Miller, ed., *Walt Whitman: The Correspondence* (New York: New York University Press, 1961), vol. 1, p. 59; Walt Whitman, "A Sight in Camp in the Daybreak Gray and Dim," *Civil War Poetry and Prose* (New York: Dover, 1995), p. 16; Whitman, *Memoranda*, p. 36; M. Wynn Thomas, "Fratricide and Brotherly Love: Whitman and the Civil War," in Ezra Greenspan, ed., *The Cambridge Companion to Walt Whitman* (Cambridge: Cambridge University Press, 1995), p. 35.

35. *Times* quoted in Thomas, "Fratricide and Brotherly Love," pp. 32–33; James Perrin Warren, "Reading Whitman's Postwar Poetry," in Greenspan, ed., *Cambridge Companion to Whitman*, p. 46; Whitman, *Memoranda*, pp. 65–67; Miller, ed., *Whitman: Correspondence*, vol. 1, p. 259.

36. Walt Whitman, "Come Up from the Fields Father," in *Civil War Poetry and Prose*, pp. 12–14. See also Walt Whitman, *The Wound Dresser*, ed. Richard Maurice Bucke (Boston: Small Maynard & Co., 1898); John Harmon McElroy, ed., *The Sacrificial Years: A Chronicle of Walt Whitman's Experiences in the Civil War* (Boston: David Godine, 1999); Roy Morris Jr., *The Better Angel: Walt Whitman in the Civil War* (New York: Oxford University Press, 2000).

37. O'Neal quoted in Gregory A. Coco, *Gettysburg's Confederate Dead* (Gettysburg, Pa.: Thomas Publications, 2003), p. 15.

38. *Daily South Carolinian*, July 21, 1864. These were copied by the *Carolinian* "from the Richmond papers." *New York Daily News*, February 5, 1864, February 4, 1864, January 8, 1864.

39. Oliver Wendell Holmes, "My Hunt After 'The Captain,'" *Atlantic Monthly* 10 (December 1862): 764.

40. Robert E. Lee to Joseph Hooker, February 14, 1863; Joseph Hooker to Robert E. Lee, February 16, 1863; Robert E. Lee to Fanny Scott, February 18, 1863; Charles S. Venable to Fanny Scott, April 1, 1863; William Alexander Hammond to Robert E. Lee, March 23, 1863; Thomas M. R. Talcott to Fanny Scott, April 18, 1963; E. A. Hitchcock to Fanny Scott, July 25, 1865, all in Scott Family Papers, VHS. See Mrs. T. B. Hurlbut to Clara Barton, September 26, 1865, Clara Barton Papers, LC, for a description of Confederate general James Longstreet's comparable aid to a northern woman searching for her son.

41. Coco, *Strange and Blighted Land*, p. 48; Robert G. Carter, *Four Brothers in Blue* (Austin: University of Texas Press, 1978), pp. 324–25.

42. On the unifying power of death, see David Blight, *Race and Reunion: The Civil War in American Memory* (Cambridge, Mass.: Harvard University Press, 2001), and Drew Gilpin Faust, "The Civil War Soldier and the Art of Dying," *Journal of Southern History* 67 (February 2001): 5.

43. Mrs. R. L. Leach to Clara Barton, March 28, 1874, Clara Barton Papers, LC; Gregory Coco, *Wasted Valor: The Confederate Dead at Gettysburg* (Gettysburg, Pa.: Thomas Publications, 1990), p. 141. Sébastien Japrisot's novel and the film based on it, *A Very Long Engagement*, explore this fantasy of a lost soldier found with amnesia in the setting of the First World War.

44. Quartermaster General Montgomery C. Meigs to Surgeon General, September 19, 1868, Office of the Quartermaster General, Consolidated Correspondence File, 1794–1915, Portrait of Unknown Soldier, RG 92, Box 1173, NARA, Mrs. Jenny McConkey to Meigs, November 4, 1868; Ellen Hardback to Meigs, October 26, 1868; Mrs. J. P. Coppersmith to Meigs, November 30, 1868; James M. Truitt to Meigs, November 6, 1868, all ibid. See "An Unknown Soldier," *Harper's Weekly,* October 24, 1868, p. 679.

45. Charles H. Morgan to J. M. Taylor, October 2, 1864; J. M. Taylor to Doct. J. F. Walton, October 12, 1864; J. M. Taylor to Lieutenant Colonel W. F. Bennett, October 30, 1864; J. M. Taylor to Captain Vliet, November 17, 1864; J. M. Taylor to Captain R. H. Spencer, November 22, 1864; Captain N. M. Clark to J. M. Taylor, December 27, 1864; J. M. Taylor to Captain H. K. Edwards [December 1864]; J. M. Taylor to L. F. Davis, February 5, 1865; Henry C. Taylor to Alonzo Taylor, August 16, 1863, all in Henry Clay Taylor Papers, WHS.

46. Lonnie R. Speer, *Portals to Hell: Military Prisons of the Civil War* (Mechanicsburg, Pa.: Stackpole Books, 1997), p. 16. For statistics, see James M. McPherson, personal communication to the author, December 27, 2006. See also *Narrative of Privations and Sufferings of United States Officers and Soldiers While Prisoners of War in the Hands of Rebel Authorities* (Philadelphia: King & Baird, 1864); James Canon, Diary, WHS; William Best Hesseltine, *Civil War Prisons: A Study in Psychology* (Columbus: Ohio State University Press, 1930); Charles W. Sanders, *While in the Hands of the Enemy: Military Prisons of the Civil War* (Baton Rouge: Louisiana State University Press, 2005).

47. Bob to J. M. Taylor, April 3, 1895, Henry Clay Taylor Papers, WHS.

48. "The Sanitary Movement in European Armies," *Sanitary Commission Bulletin* 1 (April 15, 1864): 354, 353. On this emerging humanitarianism, see more generally David Brion Davis, *The Problem of Slavery in the Age of Revolution* (Ithaca, N.Y.: Cornell University Press, 1975), and David Brion Davis, *Slavery and Human Progress* (New York: Oxford University Press, 1984).

CHAPTER 5. REALIZING

1. Abraham Lincoln, "Special Session Message, July 4, 1861," in James D. Richardson, ed., *Compilation of the Messages and Papers of the Presidents* (New York: Bureau of National Literature and Art, 1908), vol. 6, p. 30.

2. On Gettysburg, see Margaret Creighton, *The Colors of Courage: Gettysburg's For-*

gotten History: Immigrants, Women, and African Americans in the Civil War's Defining Battle (New York: Basic Books, 2005), pp. 121–22. Kathleen Ernst, *Too Afraid to Cry: Maryland Civilians in the Antietam Campaign* (Mechanicsburg, Pa.: Stackpole Books, 1999), p. 186; Albertus McCreary, "Gettysburg: A Boy's Experience of the Battle," *McClure's Magazine* 33 (July 1909): 243–53; Gregory A. Coco, *A Strange and Blighted Land: Gettysburg: The Aftermath of a Battle* (Gettysburg, Pa.: Thomas Publications, 1995), p. 338 (number of Vicksburg deaths). On Baton Rouge, see Sarah Morgan Dawson, *A Confederate Girl's Diary: Sarah Morgan Dawson* (Boston: Houghton, Mifflin & Co, 1913), p. 51. On Natchez see Mel Young, *Where They Lie: The Story of the Jewish Soldiers of the North and South* (Lanham, Md.: University Press of America), p. 28. For the Vicksburg quote, see John T. Trowbridge, *The South: A Tour of Its Battlefields and Ruined Cities* (Hartford, Conn.: L. Stebbins, 1866), p. 358. See also Willene Clark, ed., *Valleys of the Shadow: The Memoir of Confederate Captain Reuben G. Clark* (Knoxville: University of Tennessee Press, 1994), p. 16. On the shelling of Petersburg, see J. W. McClure to My dearest Kate, J. W. McClure Papers, SCL. On ordnance explosion, see *Richmond Enquirer*, March 17, 1863. For the Yankee soldier quote, see Oscar O. Winter, ed., *With Sherman to the Sea: Civil War Letters, Diaries and Reminiscences of Theodore F. Upson* (Baton Rouge: Louisiana State University Press, 1943), p. 144.

3. Petition of Citizens of Danville, Virginia, to the Confederate Secretary of War, February 1, 1864, quoted in Robert E. Denney, *Civil War Medicine: Care and Comfort of the Wounded* (New York: Sterling, 1994), p. 5; *Report of the Board of Health of the City and Port of Philadelphia to the Mayor for 1861* (Philadelphia: James Gibbons, 1862), p. 10; William T. Wragg, "Report on the Yellow Fever Epidemic at Wilmington, N.C., in the Autumn of 1862," *Confederate Medical and Surgical Journal* 1 (February 1864): 17–18; Ted Alexander, "Destruction, Disease and Death: The Battle of Antietam and the Sharpsburg Civilians," *Civil War Regiments* 6, no. 2 (1998): 158. See also J. Matthew Gallman, *Mastering Wartime: A Social History of Philadelphia During the Civil War* (New York: Cambridge University Press, 1990), and Frank H. Taylor, *Philadelphia in the Civil War 1861–1865* (Philadelphia: The City, 1913).

4. Gaines Foster, "The Limitations of Federal Health Care for Freedmen, 1862–1868," *Journal of Southern History* 48 (August 1982), pp. 353 (quote), 356–67 (estimate). See also Thavolia Glymph, " 'This Species of Property': Female Slave Contrabands in the Civil War," in Edward D. C. Campbell and Kym S. Rice, eds., *A Woman's War: Southern Women, Civil War, and the Confederate Legacy* (Charlottesville: University Press of Virginia, 1996), pp. 55–71.

5. Jestin Hampton to Thomas B. Hampton, October 8, 1862, Thomas B. Hampton Papers, CAH; Caleb Cope et al., "An appeal in behalf of the Refugee Woman and Children concentrating in and about Nashville, Tennessee, December 23, 1864" (Philadelphia, 1864), printed circular, Civil War Miscellanies (McA 5786.F), McAllister Collection, LCP; Randolph County petition in Ira Berlin et al., eds., *Free At Last: A Documentary History of Slavery, Freedom, and the Civil War* (New York: New Press, 1992), p. 150; Mary H. Legge to Harriet Palmer, July 3, 1863,

Palmer Family Papers, SCL; Charles Royster, *The Destructive War: William Tecumseh Sherman, Stonewall Jackson, and the Americans* (New York: Alfred A. Knopf, 1991), p. 247.

6. Paul E. Steiner, *Disease in the Civil War: Natural Biological Warfare in 1861–1865* (Springfield, Ill.: C. C. Thomas, 1968), p. 35; Mary H. Mitchell, *Hollywood Cemetery: The History of a Southern Shrine* (1985; rpt. Richmond: Library of Virginia, 1999), p. 50; Doris Kearns Goodwin, *Team of Rivals: The Political Genius of Abraham Lincoln* (New York: Simon & Schuster, 2005), p. 419.

7. "IN MEMORIAM," *Sanitary Commission Bulletin* 1 (August 15, 1864): 615; Frank Moore, *Women of the War: Their Heroism and Self-Sacrifice* (Hartford, Conn.: S. S. Scranton, 1867), pp. 390, 53; Mary Denis Maher, *To Bind Up the Wounds: Catholic Sister Nurses in the U.S. Civil War* (New York: Greenwood Press, 1989).

8. Mary Boykin Chesnut, *Mary Chesnut's Civil War*, ed. C. Vann Woodward (New Haven: Yale University Press, 1981), pp. 199, 209–11; Daniel E. Sutherland, *Seasons of War: The Ordeal of a Confederate Community, 1861–1865* (New York: Free Press, 1995), p. 73; Winthrop D. Jordan, *Tumult and Silence at Second Creek: An Inquiry into a Civil War Slave Conspiracy* (Baton Rouge: Louisiana State University Press, 1993); Elvira J. Powers, *Hospital Pencillings* (Boston: Edward L. Mitchell, 1866), p. 71; Kym S. Rice and Edward D. C. Campbell, "Voices from the Tempest: Southern Women's Wartime Experiences," in Campbell and Rice, eds., *A Woman's War*, pp. 103–6.

9. Leslie M. Harris, *In the Shadow of Slavery: African Americans in New York City, 1626–1863* (Chicago: University of Chicago Press, 2003), pp. 279–88; Iver Bernstein, *The New York City Draft Riots* (New York: Oxford University Press, 1990). Adrian Cook, *The Armies of the Streets: The New York City Draft Riots of 1863* (Lexington: University Press of Kentucky, 1974), lists the dead and wounded on pp. 213–32.

10. Noel C. Fisher, *War at Every Door: Partisan Politics and Guerrilla Violence in East Tennessee, 1860–1869* (Chapel Hill: University of North Carolina Press, 1997), pp. 85, 74; Phillip Paludan, *Victims: A True Story of the Civil War* (Knoxville: University of Tennessee Press, 1981); Michael Fellman, *Inside War: The Guerrilla Conflict in Missouri During the Civil War* (New York: Oxford University Press, 1989); Daniel E. Sutherland, ed., *Guerrillas, Unionists, and Violence on the Confederate Homefront* (Fayetteville: University of Arkansas Press, 1999).

11. Henry Wadsworth Longfellow, "Killed at the Ford," *Atlantic* 17 (April 1866): 479.

12. Marjorie Ann Rogers, "An Iowa Woman in Wartime," *Annals of Iowa* 36 (Summer 1961): 31; Oliver Hering Middleton Family Correspondence, SCHS.

13. Reuben Allen Pierson, August 3, 1862, in Thomas W. Cutrer and Michael Parish, eds., *Brothers in Gray: The Civil War Letters of the Pierson Family* (Baton Rouge: Louisiana State University Press, 1997), p. 110.

14. Sigmund Freud, "Mourning and Melancholia," in James Strachey, ed., *The Standard Edition of the Complete Psychological Works of Sigmund Freud* (London: Hogarth Press, 1957), vol. 14, pp. 245, 244. See also Martin Jay, *Force Fields: Between Intellectual History and Cultural Critique* (New York: Routledge, 1993), p. 93. See Mary Louise Kete, *Sentimental Collaborations: Mourning and Middle-Class Identity*

in Nineteenth-Century America (Durham, N.C.: Duke University Press, 2000). See also contemporary mourning manuals: Daniel C. Eddy, *The Angel's Whispers; or, Echoes of Spirit Voices* (Boston: Horace Wentworth, 1866), and Emily Thornwell, *The Rainbow Around the Tomb; or, Rays of Hope for Those Who Mourn* (New York: Derby & Jackson, 1857).

15. Abbie Brooks Diaries, April 4, 1865, Mss 39f, Keenan Research Center, Atlanta History Center, Atlanta, Ga.; Kate Foster Diary, November 15, 1863, RBMSC; Kate Stone, *Brokenburn: The Journal of Kate Stone, 1861–1868*, ed. John Q. Anderson (Baton Rouge: Louisiana State University Press, 1955), p. 258; Cornelia Hancock, *South After Gettysburg: Letters, 1863–1868* (New York: T. Y. Crowell, 1956), pp. 67, 15; Myrta Lockett Avary, ed., *A Virginia Girl in the Civil War, 1861–1865* (New York: D. Appleton, 1903), p. 41; Mary Greenhow Lee Diary, July 24, 1863, WFCHS.

16. Louis P. Towles, ed., *A World Turned Upside Down: The Palmers of South Santee, 1818–1881* (Columbia: University of South Carolina Press, 1996), pp. 341, 348, 342, 359.

17. J. Michael Welton, ed., *"My Heart Is So Rebellious": The Caldwell Letters, 1861–1865* (Warrenton, Va.: Fauquier National Bank, 1991); Towles, ed., *World Turned Upside Down*, p. 404.

18. Towles, ed., *World Turned Upside Down*, p. 404; Mrs. H. [Anna Morris Ellis Holstein], *Three Years in Field Hospitals of the Army of the Potomac* (Philadelphia: J. B. Lippincott, 1867), p. 13.

19. Jean H. Baker, *Mary Todd Lincoln: A Biography* (New York: W. W. Norton, 1987), p. 216; Major General F. H. Smith, Superintendent, Virginia Military Institute, General Orders no. 30, May 13, 1863, VMIA, online at www.vmi.edu/archives/Jackson/cwjacksn.html.

20. On mourning garb, see "Fashionable Mourning," *Christian Recorder,* September 19, 1863; Katherine Basanese, "Victorian Period Mourning," *The Courier: The Official Newsletter of the American Civil War Association* 1 (May 1995): 5–7; "The Fashion of Mourning," *Godey's Lady's Book* 54 (March 1857): 286. See also Joan L. Severa, *Dressed for the Photographer: Ordinary Americans and Fashion, 1840–1900* (Kent, Ohio: Kent State University Press, 1995).

21. Mary D. Robertson, ed., *Lucy Breckinridge of Grove Hill: The Journal of a Virginia Girl, 1862–1864* (Kent, Ohio: Kent State University Press, 1979), pp. 80–81. *Daily South Carolinian,* February 26, 1864. Patricia Loughridge and Edward D. C. Campbell Jr., *Women in Mourning* (Richmond, Va.: Museum of the Confederacy, 1985), p. 24.

22. Margaret Gwyn Diary, April 22 and 29, 1862, Special Collections, RBMSC; Nannie Haskins Diary, March 3, 1863, Tennessee State Library and Archives, Nashville.

23. Welton, *"My Heart Is So Rebellious,"* p. 239.

24. Kate Corbin to Maggie Tucker, April 21, 1863, manuscripts in possession of David Eilenberger, Chapel Hill Rare Books, Chapel Hill, N.C. See also Lila to Willie Chunn, September 21, 1863, William Augustus Chunn Papers, Emory University, Atlanta; *Daily South Carolinian,* March 10, 1864.

25. *Philadelphia Inquirer,* July 3, 1863; *Richmond Enquirer,* April 25, 1861, p. 3; *New York Times,* May 31, 1863, p. 6.

26. *Godey's Lady's Book* 71 (August 1865): 106; 64 (June 1862): 617; 68 (May 1864): 498.

27. Mary D. Robertson, ed., *Lucy Breckinridge of Grove Hill: The Journal of a Virginia Girl, 1862–1864* (Kent, Ohio: Kent State University Press, 1979), pp. 80–81; *Daily South Carolinian,* February 26, 1864; Patricia Loughridge and Edward D. C. Campbell Jr., *Women in Mourning* (Richmond, Va.: Museum of the Confederacy, 1985), p. 24.

28. "The Massachusetts Dead Returned from Baltimore," *Frank Leslie's Illustrated Newspaper,* May 11, 1861, p. 410; *Christian Recorder,* May 11, 1861; John Marszalek, ed., *The Diary of Miss Emma Holmes, 1861–1866* (Baton Rouge: Louisiana State University Press, 1979), pp. 69–70. In early months of the war funerals received attentive press coverage that soon disappeared as they became commonplace. See, for example, "The Funeral Ceremonies in Honor of Addison Whitney and Luther C. Ladd at Lowell, Mass. On Monday, May 6," *New York Illustrated News,* May 25, 1861, p. 43; "Funeral of Colonel Vosburgh," *New York Illustrated News,* June 8, 1861, p. 75; "The Late Captain Ward," *Frank Leslie's Illustrated Newspaper,* July 13, 1861, p. 133.

29. George Skoch, "A Lavish Funeral for a Southern Hero: 'Stonewall' Jackson's Last March," *Civil War Times Illustrated,* May 1989, pp. 22–27; Samuel B. Hannah, May 17, 1863, Death of Stonewall Jackson, VMIA; online at www.vmi.edu/archives/jackson/tjjhanna.html. See also *Lexington Gazette,* May 20, 1863, Funeral of Stonewall Jackson, VMIA, online at www.vmi.edu/archives/jackson/tjjobit.html; Daniel Stowell, "Stonewall Jackson and the Providence of God," in Randall M. Miller, Harry S. Stout, and Charles Reagan Wilson, *Religion and the American Civil War* (New York: Oxford University Press, 1998), pp. 187–207; Charles Royster, *The Destructive War: William Tecumseh Sherman, Stonewall Jackson, and the Americans* (New York: Alfred A. Knopf, 1991), pp. 193–231. See also "Funeral of Gen. Maxcy Gregg," newspaper clipping, December 22, 1862, Maxcy Gregg Papers, SCL; "Funeral of General Winthrop," clipping, 1864, Frederick Winthrop Papers, MAHS.

30. Rev. T. H. Stockton, "Hymn for the National Funeral" (Philadelphia: A. W. Auner, [1865]); Swain quoted in David B. Chesebrough, *"No Sorrow Like Our Sorrow": Northern Protestant Ministers and the Assassination of Lincoln* (Kent, Ohio: Kent State University Press, 1994), p. 88.

31. *New York Herald,* April 20, 1865; Merrill D. Peterson, *Lincoln in American Memory* (New York: Oxford University Press, 1994), pp. 15–22.

32. *New York Herald,* April 26, 1865; Jacob Thomas quoted in Chesebrough, *"No Sorrow Like Our Sorrow,"* p. 187. See also *Christian Recorder,* April 22, 1865, May 6, 1865.

33. Walt Whitman, "Hush'd Be the Camps To-Day," in *Walt Whitman: Civil War Poetry and Prose* (New York: Dover, 1995), pp. 34–35.

34. Helen Vendler, "Poetry and the Mediation of Value: Whitman on Lincoln," Tanner Lecture on Human Values delivered at the University of Michigan,

October 29 and 30, 1999, online at www.tannerlectures.utah.edu/lectures/
Vendler_01.pdf, pp. 147–48. I am deeply indebted to Professor Vendler for sharing thoughts about Whitman with me.

35. Whitman, "O Captain! My Captain," in *Civil War Poetry and Prose,* p. 34.

36. Whitman, "When Lilacs Last in the Dooryard Bloom'd," in *Civil War Poetry and
Prose,* pp. 27–28.

37. Whitman, "Pensive on Her Dead Gazing," in *Civil War Poetry and Prose,* p. 38;
Vendler, "Poetry and the Mediation of Value," pp. 155–56; Whitman, "When
Lilacs Last in the Dooryard Bloom'd," pp. 27–28, 33.

38. Whitman, "When Lilacs Last in the Dooryard Bloom'd," p. 28; Whitman,
"Ashes of Soldiers," in *Civil War Poetry and Prose,* pp. 36, 37.

39. Tyler Resch, *Dorset: In the Shadow of the Marble Mountain* (Dorset, Vt.: Dorset
Historical Society, 1989), pp. 141, 174; *Nantucket Weekly Mirror,* December 27,
1862, quoted in Richard F. Miller and Robert F. Mooney, *The Civil War: The
Nantucket Experience* (Nantucket, Mass.: Wesco, 1994), p. 137.

40. Reverend Clark B. Stewart, Journal-Diary, 1859–1865, Works Progress Administration typescript, SCL.

41. L. H. Blanton, *"Well Done Thou Good and Faithful Servant," Funeral Sermon on the
Death of Rev. John W. Griffin, Chaplain of the 19th Va. Regt., August 1, 1864* (Lynchburg, Va.: Power-Press Book & Job Office, 1865), p. 8.

42. On funeral sermons, see Robert V. Wells, *Facing the "King of Terrors": Death and
Society in an American Community, 1750–1990* (New York: Cambridge University
Press, 2000), pp. 54–56.

43. William J. Hoge, *Sketch of Dabney Carr Harrison, Minister of the Gospel and Captain in the Army of the Confederate States of America* (Richmond, Va.: Presbyterian
Committee of Publication of the Confederate States, 1862), pp. 50, 51–52, 53.

44. Alexander Twombly, *The Completed Christian Life: A Sermon Commemorative of
Adjutant Richard M. Strong, 177th N.Y.S.V.* (Albany, N.Y.: J. Mussell, 1863), p. 7;
Philip Slaughter, *A Sketch of the Life of Randolph Fairfax, A Private in the Ranks of
the Rockbridge Artillery* (Richmond, Va.: Tyler, Allegre and McDaniel, 1864), pp.
6, 8, 35, 39; R. L. Dabney, *A Memorial of Lieut. Colonel John T. Thornton of the
Third Virginia Cavalry, C.S.A.* (Richmond, Va.: Presbyterian Committee of Publi-
cation of the Confederate States), pp. 6, 8; Robert Lewis Dabney, *True Courage:
A Discourse Commemorative of Lieutenant General Thomas J. Jackson* (Richmond,
Va.: Presbyterian Committee of Publication of the Confederate States, 1863),
p. 4.

45. Charles Seymour Robinson, *A Memorial Discourse: Occasioned by the Death of
Lieutenant James M. Green, 4th N.Y.S.V.* (Troy, N.Y.: Daily Times Printing, 1864),
pp. 14, 15.

46. Joseph Cross, "On Grief: A Funeral Service Oration for General Daniel Donelson," in *Camp and Field: Papers from the Portfolio of an Army Chaplain* (Columbia,
S.C.: Evans & Cogswell, 1864), pp. 68, 69, 71.

47. Henry I. Bowditch, "Memorial of Lt. Nathaniel Bowditch," p. 1015, Nathaniel
Bowditch Memorial Collection, MAHS.

48. Ibid., pp. 1015, 1048; Henry I. Bowditch to My Own Sweet Wife [Olivia Yardley

Bowditch], March 19, 1863, "Manuscripts Relating to Lieutenant Nathaniel Bowditch," vol. 2, p. 98, Nathaniel Bowditch Memorial Collection, MAHS.

49. Henry I. Bowditch to Darling [Olivia Yardley Bowditch], March 21, 1863, "Manuscripts Relating to Lieutenant Nathaniel Bowditch," vol. 2, p. 98, Nathaniel Bowditch Memorial Collection, MAHS; Bowditch, "Memorial," p. 1019. On the unmanliness of grief, see also H. L. Abbott to J. G. Abbott, in Robert Garth Scott, ed., *Fallen Leaves: The Civil War Letters of Major Henry Livermore Abbott* (Kent, Ohio: Kent State University Press, 1991), p. 140; W. D. Rutherford to Sallie Fair Rutherford, June 12, 1862, William D. Rutherford Papers, SCL.

50. Henry I. Bowditch to My Darling, March 19, 1863, "Manuscripts," vol. 2, pp. 98–100; Bowditch, "Memorial," p. 1015.

51. Bowditch, "Memorial," p. 1015; Memorials of Lieut. Nathaniel Bowditch A.A.A.G., 1st Cavalry Brigade, Second Division, Army of the Potomac, title page, Nathaniel Bowditch Memorial Collection, MAHS. "My Child" was originally published in *Monthly Miscellany* 3 (October 1840): 193–94, with the title "He is Not There." The poem was "addressed by the writer to a clerical friend, on the death of his only son." See also Louis Harmon Peet, *Who's the Author?: A Guide to the Authorship of Novels, Stories, Speeches, Songs and General Writings of American Literature* (New York: Thomas Y. Crowell, 1901), p. 169, and Henry I. Bowditch, "The Celebration of John Pierpont's Centennial Birthday," *Reminiscences* (Boston: n.p., 1885).

52. Bowditch to My Darling, March 19, 1863; Nat's Funeral, Rev. James Freeman Clarke's Remarks, both in "Manuscripts," vol. 2, pp. 97, 160–64, Nathaniel Bowditch Memorial Collection, MAHS.

53. Bowditch, "Memorial," p. 1015; Henry I. Bowditch, *A Brief Plea for an Ambulance System for the Army of the United States, as Drawn from the Extra Sufferings of the Late Lieutenant Bowditch and a Wounded Comrade* (Boston: Ticknor & Fields, 1863).

CHAPTER 6. BELIEVING AND DOUBTING

1. John D. Sweet, *The Speaking Dead. A Discourse Occasioned by the Death of Serg't Edward Amos Adams* (Boston: Commercial Printing House, 1864), pp. 6, 4, 5.

2. Carwardine quote and church statistics in Mark A. Noll, *The Civil War as a Theological Crisis* (Chapel Hill: University of North Carolina Press, 2006), p. 12.

3. Charles Lyell, *Principles of Geology* (London: John Murray, 1830–33); Charles Darwin, *On the Origin of Species by Means of Natural Selection* (London: John Murray, 1859). On biblical criticism, see Jerry Wayne Brown, *The Rise of Biblical Criticism in America, 1800–1870: The New England Scholars* (Middletown, Conn.: Wesleyan University Press, 1969); Hans W. Frei, *The Eclipse of Biblical Narrative: A Study in Eighteenth and Nineteenth Century Hermeneutics* (New Haven: Yale University Press, 1974); James Turner, *Without God, Without Creed: The Origins of Unbelief in America* (Baltimore: Johns Hopkins University Press, 1985). Lyell published another devastating work in the midst of the Civil War itself. See *The Geological Evidences of the Antiquity of Man, with Remarks on Theories of the Origin of Species by Variation* (London: John Murray, 1863).

4. On the argument from design, the classic text was William Paley's *Natural Theology* (1802). For two efforts to reconcile the science of Darwin and Lyell with religious belief, published during the Civil War, see Reverend Edward F. Williams, "On the Origin of Species," *Evangelical Quarterly Review* 16 (January 1865): 11–23, and Daniel R. Goodwin, "The Antiquity of Man," *American Presbyterian and Theological Review* 6 (April 1864): 233–59.

5. Louis Menand, *The Metaphysical Club* (New York: Farrar, Straus & Giroux, 2001), p. 18. See also Robert C. Albrecht, "The Theological Response of the Transcendentalists to the Civil War," *New England Quarterly* 38 (March 1965): 21–34.

6. Sweet, *Speaking Dead*, p. 7; A. M. Poindexter, *Why Will Ye Die?* (Raleigh, N.C.: n.p., 186–); G. A. A. Riggs, Diary, August 14, 1864, CAH.

7. See Mark Schantz, "The American Civil War and the Culture(s) of Death," unpublished paper; W. H. Christian, *The Importance of a Soldier Becoming a Christian* (Richmond, Va.: Soldiers' Track Association, [186–]), p. 3; Mrs. Hancock, in *North Carolina Presbyterian,* August 4, 1862 p. 149; Drew Gilpin Faust, "Christian Soldiers," in Faust, *Southern Stories: Slaveholders in Peace and War* (Columbia: University of Missouri Press, 1992), pp. 98–99.

8. Jestin Hampton to Thomas B. Hampton, July 7, 1864; Thomas B. Hampton to Jestin Hampton, August 9, 1863, July 17, 1863, May 27, 1863, all in Thomas B. Hampton Papers, CAH.

9. Thomas B. Hampton to Jestin Hampton, October 15, 1863; Jestin Hampton to Thomas B. Hampton, April 24, 1864; both in Thomas B. Hampton Papers, CAH.

10. A. S. Collins and H. Collins to Jestin Hampton, March 21, 1865; Thomas B. Hampton Obituary [March 1865]: both in Thomas B. Hampton Papers, CAH.

11. Philippe Ariès, *The Hour of Our Death*, trans. Helen Weaver (New York: Alfred A. Knopf, 1981), pp. 557–601; Philippe Ariès, *Western Attitudes Toward Death: From the Middle Ages to the Present*, trans. Patricia M. Ranum (Baltimore: Johns Hopkins University Press, 1974).

12. "My God! What Is All This For?," Wolf C116, American Song Sheets Collection, LCP.

13. Captain Edson Gerry, "Battle of Winchester," Wolf 108, online at musicanet.org/robokopp/usa/harkthem.htm; "Tell Mother, I Die Happy," words by C. A. Vosburgh, music by Jabez Burns (New York: Charles Magnus, n.d.), Wolf 2290. See also "Shall We Know Each Other There?," Wolf 2081, "Our Southern Dead," Wolf C130, E. Walter Lowe, "The Dying Soldier" (New York: Charles Magnus, n.d.), Wolf 5486; L. Katzenburger, "The Dying Confederate's Last Words," Wolf C49, "Oh! Bless Me, Mother, Ere I Die," Wolf 1653, all in American Song Sheet Collection, LCP.

14. J. L. M'Creery, "There Is No Death," *Arthur's Home Magazine* 22 (July 1863): 41.

15. Swedenborg quoted in Colleen McDannell and Bernhard Lang, *Heaven: A History* (New Haven: Yale University Press, 1988), p. 186. See Erland J. Brock, ed., *Swedenborg and His Influence* (Bryn Athyn, Pa.: Academy of the New Church, 1988). My thanks to James Kloppenberg and Trygve Throntveit for help on Swedenborg. On heaven see also Jeffrey Burton Russell, *Paradise Mislaid: How*

We Lost Heaven and How We Can Regain It (New York: Oxford University Press, 2006).

16. James H. Moorhead, " 'As Though Nothing At All Had Happened': Death and Afterlife in Protestant Thought, 1840–1955," *Soundings* 67, no. 4 (1984): 458–59. Ralph Waldo Emerson, "Swedenborg; or, the Mystic," in Robert E. Spiller, ed., *Selected Essays, Lectures and Poems of Ralph Waldo Emerson* (New York: Washington Square Press, 1965), p. 155.

17. Emily Dickinson to Fanny Norcross and Loo Norcross, April 1861, in Mabel Todd Loomis, ed., *Letters of Emily Dickinson* (Boston: Roberts Brothers, 1894), vol. 2, p. 237. Dickinson quoted in Shira Wolosky, *Emily Dickinson: A Voice of War* (New Haven: Yale University Press, 1984), p. 44; Emily Dickinson, "I never felt at Home—Below—," #413, in Thomas H. Johnson, *The Complete Poems of Emily Dickinson* (Boston: Little, Brown, 1960); McDannell and Lang, *Heaven,* p. 228; *Daily South Carolinian,* April 24, 1864; Phillip Shaw Paludan, *A People's Contest: The Union and Civil War, 1861–1865* (1988; rpt. Lawrence: University Press of Kansas, 1996), p. 367; *Harper's Weekly,* December 5, 1863, p. 784; poems from *Harper's New Monthly Magazine* 26 (February 1863): 384, and 29 (October 1864): 584.

18. Robert Patterson, *Visions of Heaven for the Life on Earth* (Philadelphia: Presbyterian Board of Publication, 1877); *Harper's Weekly,* December 5, 1863, p. 784; William Branks, *Heaven Our Home: We Have No Saviour But Jesus and No Home But Heaven* (Boston: Roberts Brothers, 1864). The book has twenty-five total chapters and is divided into three parts; part 2 is "Recognition." Rebecca Gratz to Ann Boswell Gratz, September 12, 1861, in David Philipson, ed., *Letters of Rebecca Gratz* (Philadelphia: Jewish Publication Society of America, 1929), p. 427. On heaven and Jews, see Henry Harbaugh, "Heavenly Recognition Among the Jews," *The Heavenly Recognition; or, An Earnest and Scriptural Discussion of the Question, Will We Know Our Friends in Heaven* (Philadelphia: Lindsay & Blackiston, 1865), pp. 85–115.

19. Epes Sargent, *The Proof Palpable of Immortality: Being an Account of the Materialization Phenomena of Modern Spiritualism* (Boston: Colby and Rich, 1875).

20. Robert S. Cox, *Body and Soul: A Sympathetic History of American Spiritualism* (Charlottesville: University of Virginia Press, 2003), p. 169; James Henry Hammond Diary, December 13, 1853, James Henry Hammond Papers, SCL; see Drew Gilpin Faust, *A Sacred Circle: The Dilemma of the Intellectual in the Old South, 1840–1860* (Baltimore: Johns Hopkins University Press, 1977), pp. 66–67. Ann Braude demonstrates the especially close link between spiritualism and feminism in *Radical Spirits: Spiritualism and Women's Rights in Nineteenth-Century America* (Boston: Beacon Press, 1989). On numbers of spiritualists, the *North American Review* estimated at least 2 million in 1855; Harriet Beecher Stowe thought 4 to 5 million in 1869; Emma Hardinge, spiritualist writer, estimated 11 million in 1870. Nina Baym, "Introduction," in Elizabeth Stuart Phelps, *Three Spiritualist Novels* (Urbana: University of Illinois Press, 2000), p. ix.

21. Jean H. Baker, *Mary Todd Lincoln: A Biography* (New York: W. W. Norton, 1987), pp. 218–20, 221; "Lincoln's Attendance at Spiritualist Seances," *Lincoln Lore,*

no. 1499 (January 1963): 1–4; no. 1500 (February 1963): 1–2; John Pierpont, "My Child," online at www.poetry-archive.com/p/pierpont_john.html; Henry Ingersoll Bowditch, *Memorial* (Boston: John Wilson & Son, 1865), p. 49; Bret E. Carroll, *Spiritualism in Antebellum America* (Bloomington: Indiana University Press, 1997), pp. 16–34.

22. Cox, *Body and Soul*, p. 176.

23. Epes Sargent, *Planchette: or, The Despair of Science* (Boston: Roberts Brothers, 1869). "Novel amusement" from broadside "The Boston Planchette," American Antiquarian Society, Worcester, Mass., reproduced in Braude, *Radical Spirits*, fig. 5, after p. 114.

24. R. Laurence Moore, *In Search of White Crows: Spiritualism, Parapsychology, and American Culture* (New York: Oxford University Press, 1977), p. 38; Epes Sargent, *The Scientific Basis of Spiritualism* (Boston: Colby & Rich, 1881), p. 346; John W. Edmonds and George T. Dexter, *Spiritualism* (New York: Partridge & Brittan, 1853), p. 360; Sargent, *Planchette*, p. 279.

25. "The Second Death," *Banner of Light*, October 19, 1861, p. 6; "Message Department," April 26, 1862, p. 6; May 31, 1862, p. 6; July 2, 1864, p. 1.; December 13, 1862, p. 6.

26. *Banner of Light*, April 26, 1862, p. 6.

27. *Banner of Light*, September 19, 1863; July 16, 1864; May 10, 1862; all p. 6.

28. *Banner of Light*, August 29, 1863, p. 6.

29. Ibid. See S. Weir Mitchell's fictional rendering of a spiritualist reunion of an amputee and his limbs, "The Case of George Dedlow," *Atlantic Monthly*, July 1866, online at www.painonline.org/pdf/dedlow.pdf.

30. National Park Service, Civil War Soldiers and Sailors System, Names Index Project, online at www.itd.nps.gov/cwss/info.htm. The data are entered from the General Index Cards of the Compiled Military Service records at the National Archives.

31. *Banner of Light*, May 31, 1862, p. 5; Sweet, *Speaking Dead*, pp. 11, 12, 3.

32. Elizabeth Stuart Phelps, *Chapters from a Life* (Boston: Houghton Mifflin & Co., 1896) pp. 96, 97, 98, 127, 128; Helen Sootin Smith, "Introduction," Phelps, *The Gates Ajar* (1868; rpt. Cambridge, Mass.: Harvard University Press, 1964), p. xxxiv. See Barton Levi St. Armand, "Paradise Deferred: The Image of Heaven in the Work of Emily Dickinson and Elizabeth Stuart Phelps," *American Quarterly* 29 (Spring 1977): 55–78; Ann Douglas, "Heaven Our Home: Consolation Literature in the Northern United States, 1830–1880," *American Quarterly* 26 (December 1974): 496–515; Lisa Long, "The Corporeity of Heaven: Rehabilitating the Civil War Body in *The Gates Ajar*," *American Literature* 69 (December 1997): 781–811; and Carol Farley Kessler, *Elizabeth Stuart Phelps* (Boston: Twayne Publishers, 1982).

33. Elizabeth Stuart Phelps, *The Gates Ajar*, in *Three Spiritualist Novels* pp. 5, 32. See Mark Twain's "burlesque" of *The Gates Ajar*, perhaps the ultimate testimony to its cultural impact, *Extract from Captain Stormfield's Visit to Heaven* (1909; rpt. New York: Oxford University Press, 1996).

34. Phelps, *Gates*, pp. 41, 110, 42.

35. Ibid., p. 50.

36. Ibid., pp. 65, 64.

37. Ibid., pp. 10–11.

38. Catherine Edmondston, *Journal of a Secesh Lady: The Diary of Catherine Ann Devereux Edmondston, 1860–1866,* ed. Beth G. Crabtree and James W. Patton (Raleigh: North Carolina Division of Archives and History, 1979), p. 461; J. Michael Welton, ed., *"My Heart Is So Rebellious": The Caldwell Letters, 1861–1865* (Warrenton, Va.: Fauquier National Bank, 1991), pp. 240, 241; Clara Solomon Diary, entry for June 7, 1861, Louisiana State University; Anne Darden, Diary, entry for July 20, 1861, North Carolina Department of Archives and History. See Drew Gilpin Faust, *Mothers of Invention: Women of the Slaveholding South in the American Civil War* (Chapel Hill: University of North Carolina Press, 1996), pp. 190–95. On both Job and "Though thou slay us," see Peyton Harrison Hoge, *Moses Drury Hoge: Life and Letters* (Richmond, Va.: Presbyterian Committee of Publication, 1899), pp. 235–37.

39. Abraham Lincoln, "Address at Gettysburg, Pennsylvania," November 19, 1863, in *Abraham Lincoln: Speeches and Writings, 1859–1865* (New York: Library of America, 1989), p. 536.

40. Lincoln, "Second Inaugural Address," in *Speeches and Writings,* pp. 686–87.

41. Stephen Elliott, *Ezra's Dilemna [sic]: A Sermon* (Savannah, Ga.: Power Press of George N. Nichols, 1863), p. 17; Stephen Elliott, *Gideon's Water-Lappers: A Sermon* (Macon, Ga.: Burke, Boykin & Co., 1864), p. 20. On providentialism see Mark Noll, *The Civil War as a Theological Crisis* (Chapel Hill: University of North Carolina Press, 2006), pp. 75–94. On religion and nationalism, see Drew Gilpin Faust, *The Creation of Confederate Nationalism: Ideology and Identity in the Civil War South* (Baton Rouge: Louisiana State University Press, 1988), pp. 22–40. With thanks to Katy Park for Latin assistance.

42. Lincoln, "Second Inaugural Address," p. 687.

43. Horace Bushnell, "Our Obligations to the Dead," in *Building Eras in Religion* (New York: Charles Scribner's Sons, 1881), pp. 322, 327.

44. Horace Bushnell, *Reverses Needed: A Discourse Delivered on the Sunday After the Disaster of Bull Run, in the North Church, Hartford* (Hartford, Conn.: L. E. Hunt, 1861); Bushnell, "Obligations," pp. 331, 333, 332, 341, 353. See William A. Clebsch, "Christian Interpretations of the Civil War," *Church History* 30, no. 2 (1961): 212–22.

45. Bushnell, "Obligations," p. 350; Elliott, *Gideon's Water-Lappers,* p. 20; Bushnell, "Obligations," p. 355. See also Horace Bushnell, *The Vicarious Sacrifice, Grounded in Principles of Universal Obligation* (New York: Charles Scribner & Co., 1866).

46. Bushnell, "Obligations," p. 353.

47. Mary Ann Harris Gay, *Life in Dixie During the War* (Atlanta: Constitution Job Office, 1892), p. 195; Henry Timrod, "Ethnogenesis," online at www.poemhunter .com/quotations/famous.asp?people=Henry%20Timrod; also quoted in Malvina Waring, "A Confederate Girl's Diary, March 9, 1865," in Mrs. Thomas Taylor et al., eds., *South Carolina Women in the Confederacy* (Columbia, S.C.: State Co., 1903), vol. 1, p. 280.

48. Presbytery and Ford quoted in Daniel W. Stowell, *Rebuilding Zion: The Religious Reconstruction of the South, 1863–1877* (New York: Oxford University Press, 1998), pp. 26–27; Mary Greenhow Lee Diary, April 15, 1865, WFCHS.

49. John Adger, "Northern and Southern Views of the Province of the Church," *Southern Presbyterian Review* 16 (March 1866): 410, quoted in Noll, *Civil War as a Theological Crisis*, p. 78; Hoge, *Moses Drury Hoge*, pp. 235–37, quoted in Stowell, *Rebuilding Zion*, p. 40.

50. Grace Brown Elmore, *A Heritage of Woe: The Civil War Diary of Grace Brown Elmore, 1861–1868*, ed. Marli F. Weiner (Athens: University of Georgia Press, 1997), pp. 119, 99; Cornelia Peake McDonald, *A Woman's Civil War: A Diary, with Reminiscences of the War, from March 1862*, ed. Minrose C. Gwin (Madison: University of Wisconsin Press, 1992), p. 241.

51. Louis Menand, *The Metaphysical Club* (New York: Farrar, Straus & Giroux, 2001), pp. x, 4. See Oliver Wendell Holmes, *Touched with Fire: Civil War Letters and Diary of Oliver Wendell Holmes, Jr., 1861–1864*, ed. Mark DeWolfe Howe (Cambridge, Mass.: Harvard University Press, 1946). The pathbreaking study of these issues was George M. Fredrickson, *The Inner Civil War: Northern Intellectuals and the Crisis of the Union* (New York: Harper & Row, 1965).

52. Paul Fussell, *The Great War and Modern Memory* (New York: Oxford University Press, 1975), p. 7; "Mother, Come Your Boy Is Dying" [sheet music] (New York: H. DeMarsan, n.d.); "Bless Me, Mother, Ere I Die" (New York: H. DeMarsan, n.d.); "Who Will Care for Mother Now?" (New York: Charles Magnus, n.d.); "Rock Me to Sleep, Mother," in *A Storm in the Land: Music of the 26th North Carolina Regimental Band, C.S.A.* (New York: New World Records, 2002).

53. "Mother Would Comfort Me" (New York: H. DeMarsan, n.d.), Wolf 1472, words and music online at freepages.music.rootsweb.com/~edgmon/cwcomfort.htm; "Mother Would Wallop Me" (New York: H. DeMarsan, n.d.), Wolf 1470; John C. Cross, "Mother on the Brain" (New York: H. DeMarsan, n.d.), Wolf 1473, all from the American Song Sheet Collection, LCP. See southern editions: "Who Will Care for Mother Now?" (Macon and Savannah, Ga.: J. C. Schreiner & Son, 186–); "Rock Me to Sleep, Mother" (Richmond, Va.: C. Nordendorf, 1863); "Mother, Is the Battle Over?" (Columbia, S.C.: B. Duncan, 1863).

54. Twain, *Stormfield's Visit to Heaven*.

55. Bierce quoted in Roy Morris Jr., *Ambrose Bierce: Alone in Bad Company* (New York: Oxford University Press, 1995), p. 182; Bierce quoted in Daniel Aaron, *The Unwritten War: American Writers and the Civil War* (New York: Oxford University Press, 1973), p. 183; Bierce quoted in Morris, *Ambrose Bierce*, p. 137. See Lara Cohen, " 'A Supper of Horrors Too Long Drawn Out': Ambrose Bierce's Literary Terrorism and the Reinstatement of Death," B.A. paper (University of Chicago, 1999), courtesy of Lara Cohen; Cathy N. Davidson, *The Experimental Fictions of Ambrose Bierce: Structuring the Ineffable* (Lincoln: University of Nebraska Press, 1984); Cathy N. Davidson, ed., *Critical Essays on Ambrose Bierce* (Boston: G. K. Hall, 1982).

56. Bierce quoted in Morris, *Ambrose Bierce*, p. 205; Ambrose Bierce, *Phantoms of a*

Blood-Stained Period: The Complete Civil War Writings of Ambrose Bierce, ed. Russell Duncan and David J. Klooster (Amherst: University of Massachusetts Press, 2002); Ambrose Bierce, *The Devil's Dictionary* (New York: Oxford University Press, 1999), p. 161.

57. Ambrose Bierce, "What I Saw of Shiloh," in *Phantoms of a Blood-Stained Period,* p. 103.

58. Ambrose Bierce, "A Tough Tussle," in Ernest Jerome Hopkins, comp., *The Civil War Short Stories of Ambrose Bierce* (Lincoln: University of Nebraska Press, 1970), p. 39.

59. Edmund Wilson, *Patriotic Gore: Studies in the Literature of the American Civil War* (New York: Oxford University Press, 1962), p. 622.

60. Bierce, "Tough Tussle," pp. 39, 41.

61. Ibid., pp. 41, 43, 44.

62. Bierce quoted in Morris, *Ambrose Bierce,* p. 205; Bierce, *Phantoms of a Blood-Stained Period,* p. 21.

63. Ambrose Bierce, "An Occurrence at Owl Creek Bridge," in *Civil War Stories of Bierce,* pp. 45–52; Robert C. Evans, ed., *Ambrose Bierce's "An Occurrence at Owl Creek Bridge"; An Annotated Critical Edition* (West Cornwall, Conn.: Locust Hill Press, 2003).

64. Bierce quoted in Morris, *Ambrose Bierce,* p. 205; Bierce, *Devil's Dictionary,* p. 34.

65. Ambrose Bierce, *The Collected Works of Ambrose Bierce* (New York: Neale Publishing Co., 1911), vol. 8, p. 347.

66. Herman Melville, "The Armies of the Wilderness," in *Battle-Pieces and Aspects of the War: Civil War Poems* (1866; rpt. New York: Da Capo Press, 1995), p. 103; Melville quoted in Lee Rust Brown, "Introduction," ibid., p. viii. See also Robert Penn Warren, "Melville's Poems," *Southern Review* 3 (Autumn 1967): 799–855.

67. Herman Melville, "The March into Virginia," in *Battle-Pieces,* p. 23; Melville, "On the Slain Collegians," ibid., p. 159. See also Stanton Garner, *The Civil War World of Herman Melville* (Lawrence: University Press of Kansas, 1993); Warren, "Melville's Poems," p. 809; Joyce Sparer Adler, *War in Melville's Imagination* (New York: New York University Press, 1981); Andrew Delbanco, *Melville: His World and His Work* (New York: Alfred A. Knopf, 2005).

68. Hawthorne quoted in Lee Rust Brown, "Introduction" to Melville, *Battle-Pieces,* p. iv; Aaron, *Unwritten War,* p. 88.

69. Melville, "Armies of the Wilderness," pp. 101, 102; Melville, "A Utilitarian View of the Monitor's Fight," in *Battle-Pieces,* p. 62.

70. Melville, "Shiloh," in *Battle-Pieces,* 63; "Armies of the Wilderness," p. 103; Melville, "Shiloh," p. 63.

71. Emily Dickinson, "My Triumph lasted till the Drums," #1227, and "They dropped like Flakes—," #409 in Thomas H. Johnson, ed., *The Complete Poems of Emily Dickinson* (Boston: Little, Brown & Co., 1960). See Robert Milder, "The Rhetoric of Melville's Battle-Pieces," *Nineteenth-Century Literature* 44 (September 1989), pp. 173–200; Maurice S. Lee, "Writing Through the War; Melville and Dickinson After the Renaissance," *PMLA* 115 (October 2000): pp. 1124–28.

72. David Higgins, *Portrait of Emily Dickinson, The Poet and Her Prose* (New

Brunswick, N.J.: Rutgers University Press, 1967); Thomas W. Ford, "Emily Dickinson and the Civil War," *University Review—Kansas City* 31 (Spring 1965): 199. For the most systematic exploration of the importance of war to Dickinson, see Shira Wolosky, *Emily Dickinson: A Voice of War* (New Haven: Yale University Press, 1984). Daniel Aaron relegates Dickinson to Supplement 4, a page and a half, in *The Unwritten War* and emphasizes the personal nature of her experience, although at the same time he shows the impact of war imagery on her poetry, pp. 355–56.

73. Emily Dickinson to Thomas Wentworth Higginson, June 8, 1862, and [n.d.] 1863, in Mabel Todd Loomis, ed., *Letters of Emily Dickinson* (Boston: Roberts Brothers, 1894), vol. 2, pp. 304, 310.

74. Emily Dickinson to Fanny Norcross and Loo Norcross, April 1862, *Letters of Dickinson*, vol. 2, p. 243; William A. Stearns, *Adjutant Stearns* (Boston: Massachusetts Sabbath School Society, 1862), p. 106. See also Roger Lundin, *Emily Dickinson and the Art of Belief* (Grand Rapids, Mich.: William B. Eerdmans, 1998), pp. 122–23. The death of another Amherst neighbor at Antietam "in Scarlet Maryland" prompted Dickinson's "When I was small, a Woman died," later the same year, #596 in *Complete Poems of Dickinson*.

75. Emily Dickinson to Thomas Wentworth Higginson, [n.d.] 1863, in *Letters of Dickinson*, vol. 2, p. 309; Emily Dickinson to Fanny Norcross and Loo Norcross, April 1862, ibid., p. 243.

76. Emily Dickinson, "I dwell in Possibility," #657, *Complete Poems of Dickinson*; Emily Dickinson to Thomas Wentworth Higginson, April 26, 1862, in *Letters of Dickinson*, vol. 2, p. 302; "Death is a Dialogue between," #976; "At least—to pray—is left—is left," #502; "We pray—to Heaven—" #489; "I felt my life with both my hands," #351; "Ourselves we do inter with sweet derision," #1144, all in *Complete Poems of Dickinson*.

77. "All but Death, can be Adjusted," #749, in *Complete Poems of Dickinson*.

78. "Suspense—is Hostiler than Death—," #705; "Victory comes late—," #690; "My Portion is Defeat—today—," #639; "It feels a shame to be Alive," #444; "The Battle fought between the Soul," #594, all in *Complete Poems of Dickinson*. See Maria Magdalena Farland, " 'That Tritest/Brightest Truth': Emily Dickinson's Anti-Sentimentality," *Nineteenth-Century Literature* 53 (December 1998): 364–89. Barton Levi St. Armand, *Emily Dickinson and Her Culture: The Soul's Society* (New York: Cambridge University Press, 1984), portrays her as less doubting and more conventional.

79. Helen Vendler, "Melville and the Lyric of History," in Melville, *Battle-Pieces*, pp. 262, 265.

80. "I felt a Cleaving in my Mind," #937, in *Complete Poems of Dickinson*; Wolosky, *Emily Dickinson*, p. xv. See also David T. Porter, *Dickinson: The Modern Idiom* (Cambridge, Mass.: Harvard University Press, 1981), pp. 39, 98, 120. On Amy Lowell's judgment that Dickinson was a uniquely "modern" voice in nineteenth-century American poetry, see S. Foster Damon, *Amy Lowell: A Chronicle* (Boston: Houghton Mifflin, 1935), p. 295. Historian Michael O'Brien has argued that Mary Chesnut's Civil War diary, refashioned in the 1880s but unpublished

during her lifetime, reflects these same modernistic tendencies. A South Carolina aristocrat who survived on wit and irony as she watched her world disintegrate around her, Chesnut has been well known since the appearance of bowdlerized versions of her writings early in the twentieth century. At last in 1981 historian C. Vann Woodward published a carefully edited version of the 1880s manuscript that recognized it as a literary construction—and reconstruction—not a series of daily jottings from the midst of war. Chesnut's effort might be seen to have much in common with those of Bierce, Melville, and Dickinson. Chesnut eschews narrative for voices and fragments, reflecting in her chosen form the substance of her own disbelief—in God, in science, in her society, in herself. O'Brien connects her with Virginia Woolf, suggesting a continuum of doubt and dislocation from an American war to a European conflagration a half century later. Michael O'Brien, "The Flight Down the Middle Walk: Mary Chesnut and the Forms of Observance," in Anne Goodwyn Jones and Susan V. Donaldson, eds., *Haunted Bodies: Gender and Southern Texts* (Charlottesville: University of Virginia Press, 1997), pp. 109–31.

81. Oliver Wendell Holmes, *Occasional Speeches,* comp. Mark DeWolfe Howe (Cambridge, Mass.: Harvard University Press, 1962), p. 82; Reuben Allen Pierson in Thomas W. Cutrer and T. Michael Parrish, eds., *Brothers in Gray: Civil War Letters of the Pierson Family* (Baton Rouge: Louisiana State University Press, 1997), p. 101; James P. Suiter quoted in Earl Hess, *Union Soldier in Battle,* p. 20; Daniel M. Holt, *A Surgeon's Civil War: Letters and Diaries of Daniel M. Holt, M.D.,* ed. James M. Greiner, Janet L. Coryell, and James R. Smither (Kent, Ohio: Kent State University Press, 1994), p. 100; John O. Casler, *Four Years in the Stonewall Brigade* (1906; rpt. Columbia: University of South Carolina Press, 2005), p. 37.

82. Cordelia Harvey, letter from Memphis dated December 6, 1862, published in *Wisconsin Daily State Journal,* December 30, 1862, Cordelia Harvey Papers, WHS, online at www.uwosh.edu/archives/civilwar/women/harvey/harvey6 .htm; Kate Cumming, *Journal of a Confederate Nurse,* ed. Richard Barksdale Harwell (Baton Rouge: Louisiana State University Press, 1959), p. 15. See the almost identical remark by northern nurse Cornelia Hancock in Hancock, *South After Gettysburg,* ed. Henrietta Stratton Jaquette (New York: T. Y. Crowell, 1956), p. 7. On the unspeakability of suffering, see Elaine Scarry, *The Body in Pain* (New York: Oxford University Press, 1985). Paul Fussell writes of the incommunicability of World War I and the failure of language it generated in *The Great War and Modern Memory* (New York: Oxford University Press, 1975), p. 139, as does Jay Winter, *Sites of Memory, Sites of Mourning: The Great War in European Cultural History* (Cambridge: Cambridge University Press, 1995), p. 5. Thomas Leonard writes of the Civil War that "in some ways the most important legacy . . . was silence." Thomas C. Leonard, *Above the Battle: War Making in America from Appomattox to Versailles* (New York: Oxford University Press, 1978), p. 25. See also Allyson Booth, *Postcards from the Trenches: Negotiating the Space Between Modernism and the First World War* (New York: Oxford University Press, 1996), pp. 52, 62.

83. David T. Hedrick and Gordon Barry Davis Jr., eds., *I'm Surrounded by Methodists:*

Diary of John H. W. Stuckenberg, Chaplain of the 145th Pennsylvania Volunteer Infantry (Gettysburg, Pa.: Thomas Publications, 1995), p. 44.

CHAPTER 7. ACCOUNTING

1. Horace Bushnell, "Our Obligations to the Dead, July 26, 1865," *Building Eras in Religion* (New York: Charles Scribner's Sons, 1881), pp. 322, 327, 321, 340. On Bushnell, see Conrad Cherry, "The Structure of Organic Thinking: Horace Bushnell's Approach to Language, Nature and Nation," *Journal of the American Academy of Religion* 40 (March 1972): 3–20, and Daniel Walker Howe, "The Social Science of Horace Bushnell," *Journal of American History* 70 (September 1983): 305–22.

2. James Russell Lowell, "Ode Recited at the Harvard Commemoration, July 21, 1865," in Richard Marius, ed., *The Columbia Book of Civil War Poetry: From Whitman to Walcott* (New York: Columbia University Press, 1994), pp. 372, 380.

3. Clara Barton to Brigadier General D. C. McCallum, April 14, 1865; Barton to Secretary of War Edwin Stanton, draft letter, October 1865, final version dated November 27, 1865, Clara Barton Papers, LC.

4. "To Returned Soldiers and Others" [1865], Clara Barton Papers, LC; Elizabeth B. Pryor, *Clara Barton: Professional Angel* (Philadelphia: University of Pennsylvania Press, 1987), p. 154.

5. On general orders, see Brevet Brigadier General J. J. Dana to Brevet Major General J. L. Donaldson, March 19, 1866, in Whitman, Letters Received, RG 92 E-A-1 397A, and E. B. Whitman, Cemeterial Movement, in Final Report, 1869, RG 92 E646, both in NARA; "Civil War Era National Cemeteries," online at www.va.gov/facmgt/historic/civilwar.asp. See also U.S. War Department, Quartermaster General's Office, *Compilation of Laws, Orders, Opinions, Instructions, etc. in Regard to National Military Cemeteries* (Washington, D.C.: Government Printing Office, 1878); *Roll of Honor: Names of Soldiers Who Died in Defence of the American Union*, 27 nos. (Washington, D.C.: Government Printing Office, 1865–71).

6. Special Order no. 132 in "Report of Captain J. M. Moore," in *Executive Documents Printed by Order of the House of Representatives During the First Session of the Thirty-Ninth Congress, 1865–66* (Washington, D.C.: Government Printing Office, 1866), vol. 3, pp. 264–66; James M. Moore to Quartermaster General Montgomery C. Meigs, July 3, 1865, M619 208Q 1865, Roll 401, NARA. See also Requests received by Colonel James Moore, 1863–66, RG 92 E581, Requests for Information Relating to Missing Soldiers 1863–67, RG 92 E582, and Letters Received by Tommy Baker, Clerk of Office of Burial Records, 1862–67, RG 92 E580, all in NARA.

7. On Andersonville see William Marvel, *Andersonville: The Last Depot* (Chapel Hill: University of North Carolina Press, 1994).

8. Clara Barton, Journal, July 8, July 12, August 5, August 6, and August 17, 1865; Clara Barton to Edmund Stanton, n.d.; all in Clara Barton Papers, LC; Pryor, *Clara Barton*, p. 138.

9. Barton, Journal, August 5–8, and 17, 1865, Clara Barton Papers, LC; see Requests for Information, NARA; Pryor, *Clara Barton*, pp. 138–42; Monro Mac-Closkey, *Hallowed Ground: Our National Cemeteries* (New York: Richards Rosen Press, 1968), p. 32; "Report of Captain J. M. Moore," in *Executive Documents, 1865–66*, vol. 3, pp. 264–66. See also John R. Neff, *Honoring the Civil War Dead: Commemoration and the Problem of Reconciliation* (Lawrence: University Press of Kansas, 2005), and Edward Steere, "Genesis of American Graves Registration, 1861–1870," *Military Affairs* 12 (Autumn 1948): 149–61. See Edmund Whitman Papers, 1830–1876, Schoff Civil War Collection, William L. Clements Library, University of Michigan, Ann Arbor; Class of 1838 Class Book, call #HUD238.714, Harvard University Archives, Cambridge, Mass.; "1838: Whitman, Edmund Burke," Biographical File, call #HUG300, Harvard University Archives, Cambridge, Mass.

10. Earnshaw quoted in Monro MacCloskey, *Hallowed Ground: Our National Cemeteries* (New York: Richard Rosens Press, 1968), p. 34.

11. Meigs quoted in Whitman, "Remarks on National Cemeteries," in W. T. Sherman et al., *The Army Reunion* (Chicago: S. C. Griggs & Co., 1869), p. 227.

12. E. B. Whitman to Thomas Swords, February 13, 1867, in Whitman, Final Report; Circular, January 24, 1866, in E. B. Whitman, Letter Press Book, vol. 1, RG 92 A-1 397A, NARA; Whitman, Final Report.

13. Whitman, Final Report; A. T. Blackmun to E. B. Whitman, n.d. [1865]; John H. Castle to Whitman, January 24, 1866, both in Letters Received, RG 92 A-1 397A, NARA.

14. E. B. Whitman, Report, May 5, 1866, Cemeterial Reports and Lists, RG 92 A-1 397A, NARA; Whitman, Final Report.

15. Whitman to Donaldson, June 26, 1866, in Whitman, Letter Press Book, vol. 1; E. B. Whitman, Daily Journal, vol. 2, RG 92 E-A1-397A, n.p., both in NARA; Whitman, "Remarks on National Cemeteries," p. 229.

16. Lieutenant Thomas Albee to Thomas Van Horne, November 28, 1865; Donaldson to Quartermaster General Montgomery Meigs, December 9, 1865; Barger to E. B. Whitman, February 24, 1866; all in Whitman, Letters Received; [Whitman], Journal of a Trip Through Parts of Kentucky, Tennessee, and Georgia Made to Locate the Scattered Graves of Union Soldiers [1866], vol. 1, p. 93, RG 92 E685, NARA.

17. Whitman, Appendix, Final Report; Whitman, Cemeterial Movement; clipping, April 4, 1866, Letters and Reports Received Relating to Cemeteries, RG 92 E569, NARA.

18. Donaldson to Colonel M. D. Wickersham, April 17, 1866, Whitman, Letters Received; Dana, Remarks of the Quartermaster General, May 26, 1866, Cemetery Reports and Lists RG 92 A-1 397A; all in NARA.

19. See Dan T. Carter, *When the War Was Over: The Failure of Self-Reconstruction in the South, 1865–1867* (Baton Rouge: Louisiana State University Press, 1985); George C. Rable, *But There Was No Peace: The Role of Violence in the Politics of Reconstruction* (Athens: University of Georgia Press, 1984); Eric Foner, *Reconstruction: America's Unfinished Revolution, 1863–1877* (New York: Harper & Row, 1988).

20. Whitman, Final Report; U.S. House of Representatives, Select Committee on the Memphis Riots, *Memphis Riots and Massacres, 1866* (1866; rpt. Miami: Mnemosyne, 1969).

21. Whitman to Donaldson, March 26, 1866, in Whitman, Letter Press Book, vol. 1; Whitman, Cemeterial Reports and Lists; Whitman to Donaldson, March 26, 1866; Whitman to Donaldson, April 18, 1866, Letter Press Book, vol. 1; [Whitman], Journal of a Trip; Whitman to Donaldson, March 26, 1866.

22. Whitman to Donaldson, April 29, 1866, in Whitman, Letter Press Book, vol. 1.

23. Whitman, "Remarks on National Cemeteries," p. 229; Whitman to Donaldson, April 30, 1866, in Whitman, Letter Press Book, vol. 1.

24. Whitman to Donaldson, May 24, 1866, Letter Press Book, vol. 1; Whitman to Brigadier General H. M. Whittlesey, May 15, 1866, Letter Press Book, vol. 1; Whitman to Donaldson, May 24, 1866, Letter Press Book, vol. 1.

25. Dana, Remarks of the Quartermaster General.

26. Whitman to Donaldson, June 26, 1866, Letter Press Book, vol. 1; [Whitman], Journal of a Trip, vol. 2, p. 26.

27. [Whitman], Journal of a Trip, vol. 1, pp. 218, 240; vol. 2, p. 26.

28. Ibid.; vol. 2, p. 26.

29. On Charleston observances, see David Blight, *Race and Reunion: The Civil War in American Memory* (Cambridge, Mass.: Harvard University Press, 2001), pp. 68–71.

30. Whitman to Donaldson, June 19, 1866; Whitman to Donaldson, June 26, 1866; both in Letter Press Book, vol. 1.

31. Whitman to Donaldson, June 26, 1866, Letter Press Book, vol. 1; E. B. Whitman, Speech Draft, n.d., Miscellaneous Records, RG 92 A-1 397A, NARA.

32. Clara Barton to Edwin Stanton, Secretary of War, October 1865, Clara Barton Papers, LC.

33. On gender and contract in this period, see Amy Dru Stanley, *From Bondage to Contract: Wage Labor, Marriage and the Market in the Age of Slave Emancipation* (New York: Cambridge University Press, 1998). See also Drew Gilpin Faust, "'The Dread Void of Uncertainty': Naming the Dead in the American Civil War," *Southern Cultures* 11 (Summer 2005): 7–32. This emerging sense of national obligation represented a development in the history of human rights. See Lynn Hunt, *Inventing Human Rights: A History* (New York: W. W. Norton, 2007).

34. James F. Russling, "National Cemeteries," *Harper's Monthly Magazine* 33 (August 1866): 311, 312, 321.

35. Ibid., p. 322.

36. Wilfred Owen, "Dulce et Decorum Est," online at www.warpoetry.co.uk/owen1 .html.

37. Whitman to Donaldson, October 1, 1866, Letter Press Book, vol. 1; Thomas quoted in Whitman, Final Report.

38. Whitman to Donaldson, September 23, 1866, Letter Press Book, vol. 1; Whitman, Final Report.

39. *Congressional Globe*, 39th Cong., 1st sess., February 15, 1867, p. 1374.

40. Whitman, Final Report; Meigs statement of December 22, 1868, quoted in *Congressional Globe*, 42nd Cong., 2nd sess., May 8, 1872, p. 3220.

41. See www.itd.nps.gov/cwss/poplargrove/poplargrovehist.htm; *New York Times*, July 8, 1866, p. 4.

42. "The National Cemeteries," *Chicago Tribune*, January 23, 1867, p. 2; Steven R. Stotelmyer, *The Bivouacs of the Dead* (Baltimore: Toomey Press, 1992), p. 22.

43. "Report of the Quartermaster General," *Executive Documents Printed by Order of the House of Representatives During the Second Session of the Forty-second Congress* (Washington, D.C.: Government Printing Office, 1872), vol. 2, pp. 135–66; "Report of the Quartermaster General, Secretary of War," *Executive Documents Printed by Order of the House of Representatives During the Third Session of the Forty-first Congress* (Washington, D.C.: Government Printing Office, 1871), vol. 2, p. 210; "Civil War Era National Cemeteries," online at www.va.gov/facmgt/historic/civilwar.asp, total cost from Charles W. Snell and Sharon A. Brown, *Antietam National Battlefield and National Cemetery, Sharpsburg, Maryland: An Administrative History* (Washington, D.C.: U.S. Department of the Interior, National Park Service, 1986), p. 29; Leslie Perry, "The Confederate Dead," clipping from *New York Sun* [1898] in RG 92 585, NARA. See plats of national cemeteries in Whitman, Final Report. Sara Amy Leach, Senior Historian, National Cemetery Administration, Department of Veterans' Affairs, letter to author, October 5, 2004, gives details of African American burials. She notes that segregated burials seem to have been undertaken by custom rather than by explicit regulation. For forms, see "Weekly Report of the Number of Interments," July 28, 1866, Letters and Reports Received Relating to Cemeteries, RG 92 E569, NARA.

44. Whitman, "Remarks on National Cemeteries," p. 225.

45. John Trowbridge, "The Wilderness," *Atlantic Monthly*, 17 (January 1866), 45, 46.

46. "Burial of the Rebel Dead," *New York Times*, January 30, 1868, p. 4; Russell F. Weigley, *Quartermaster General of the Union Army: A Biography of M. C. Meigs* (New York: Columbia University Press, 1959), pp. 308–10.

47. *Examiner* quoted in Mary H. Mitchell, *Hollywood Cemetery: The History of a Southern Shrine* (Richmond: Virginia State Library, 1985), p. 64.

48. "To the Women of the South," in *Daily Richmond Enquirer*, May 31, 1866, clipping in Hollywood Memorial Association Collection, ESBL.

49. Oakwood Ladies Memorial Association, Minutes, April 19, 1866, Oakwood Memorial Association Collection, ESBL.

50. Minute Book, 1867, Hollywood Memorial Association Collection.

51. Henry Timrod, "Ode," in *The Columbia Book of Civil War Poetry*, ed. Richard Marius (New York: Columbia University Press, 1994), p. 418. On Memorial Day, see Blight, *Race and Reunion*, pp. 70–73; online at www.usmemorialday.org/order11.html. See also William Blair, *Cities of the Dead: Contesting the Memory of the Civil War in the South, 1865–1914* (Chapel Hill: University of North Carolina Press, 2004), pp. 44–76.

52. Downing cited in Anne Sarah Rubin, *A Shattered Nation: The Rise and Fall of the Confederacy, 1861–1868* (Chapel Hill: University of North Carolina Press, 2005), p. 234.

53. Ibid., p. 235; Neff, *Honoring the Civil War Dead*, pp. 146–48. On women and politics in the Civil War, see Drew Gilpin Faust, *Mothers of Invention: Women of the Slaveholding South in the American Civil War* (Chapel Hill: University of North Carolina Press, 1996), pp. 207–19.

54. "Virginia—Dedication of the Stonewall Cemetery—Feeling of the Southern People—Miscellaneous Incidents," *New York Times*, October 29, 1866, p. 8. On Ashby, see Confederated Southern Memorial Association, *History of the Confederated Memorial Associations of the South* (New Orleans: Graham Press, 1904), p. 149.

55. Confederated Southern Memorial Association, *History*, p. 92; Rubin, *Shattered Nation*, p. 236. See also Gaines M. Foster, *Ghosts of the Confederacy: Defeat, the Lost Cause, and the Emergence of the New South, 1865–1913* (New York: Oxford University Press, 1987), pp. 36–46.

56. Abram J. Ryan, "Lines Respectfully Inscribed to the Ladies Memorial Association of Fredericksburg, Virginia," December 31, 1866, VHS; Abram J. Ryan, "March of the Deathless Dead," *Poems: Patriotic, Religious* (Baltimore: Baltimore Publishing Co., 1885), p. 39. See Robert K. Krick, *Roster of the Confederate Dead in the Fredericksburg Confederate Cemetery* (Fredericksburg, Va.: published by the author, 1974).

57. Mary J. Dogan to John S. Palmer, July 1, 1869; Dogan to Palmer, June 16, 1870; both in Louis P. Towle, ed., *A World Turned Upside Down: The Palmers of South Santee, 1818–1881* (Columbia: University of South Carolina Press, 1996), pp. 628, 650.

58. Dogan to Palmer, June 16, 1870, February 25, 1871, ibid., p. 686.

59. Gregory A. Coco, *A Strange and Blighted Land: Gettysburg; The Aftermath of a Battle* (Gettysburg, Pa.: Thomas Publications, 1995), p. 136. On Confederate dead at Antietam and the 2,240 bodies reinterred in Washington Cemetery in Hagerstown, see Steven R. Stotelmyer, *The Bivouacs of the Dead: The Story of Those Who Died at Antietam and South Mountain* (Baltimore: Toomey Press, 1992), and Snell and Brown, *Antietam National Battlefield and Cemetery*. Confederate dead also remained in the North at the site of prisoner-of-war camps. See, for example, "Confederate Dead. Cemeteries. Elmira," Confederate Dead Collection, ESBL.

60. Coco, *Strange and Blighted Land*, p. 134.

61. See *Confederate Memorial Day at Charleston, S.C. Re-interment of the Carolina Dead from Gettysburg* (Charleston, S.C.: William C. Maczyck, 1871); Mary H. Mitchell, *Hollywood Cemetery: The History of a Southern Shrine* (1985; rpt. Richmond: Library of Virginia, 1999), pp. 83–92. See also Correspondence Regarding Gettysburg Dead, 1872–1902, and Correspondence and Memoranda Regarding Weaver's Claim, 1871–73, Hollywood Memorial Association Collection, ESBL.

62. Coco, *Strange and Blighted Land*, pp. 143–48; "Ghost of Gettysburg," *Atlanta Journal and Constitution*, November 24, 1996, Dixie Living, p. 3.

63. See David Charles Sloane, *The Last Great Necessity: Cemeteries in American History* (Baltimore: Johns Hopkins University Press, 1991).

CHAPTER 8. NUMBERING

1. Kate Campbell to Mattie McGaw, May 1, 1863, McGaw Family Papers, SCL.

2. Patricia Cline Cohen, *A Calculating People: The Spread of Numeracy in Early America* (Chicago: University of Chicago Press, 1982), p. 205. I. B. Cohen, *The Triumph of Numbers: How Counting Shaped Modern Life* (New York: W. W. Norton, 2005); Alain DeRosières, *The Politics of Large Numbers: A History of Statistical Reasoning* (Cambridge, Mass.: Harvard University Press, 1998).

3. Walt Whitman, *Specimen Days,* in Whitman, *Complete Prose Works* (New York: Appleton, 1910), pp. 114–15.

4. Thomas Wentworth Higginson, *Massachusetts in the Army and Navy During the War of 1861–65* (Boston: Wright & Potter, 1896), vol. 1, pp. viii, ix.

5. William Tecumseh Sherman, *Memoirs of General W. T. Sherman* (New York: Library of America, 1990), p. 607. For a brilliant consideration of Sherman and Civil War casualty figures generally, see James Dawes, "Counting on the Battlefield: Literature and Philosophy After the Civil War," in *The Language of War: Literature and Culture in the U.S. from the Civil War through World War II* (Cambridge, Mass.: Harvard University Press, 2002), quote on p. 29. On McClellan see George B. McClellan, *McClellan's Own Story* (New York: C. L. Webster & Co., 1887), and Stephen W. Sears, *George B. McClellan: The Young Napoleon* (New York: Ticknor & Fields, 1988).

6. On Lee see William F. Fox, *Regimental Losses in the American Civil War, 1861–1865* (Albany, N.Y.: Albany Publishing Company, 1889; rpt. 2002), p. 559. On Lee's manipulation of casualty statistics after Gettysburg, see Shelby Foote, *The Civil War: A Narrative,* Vol. 2: *From Fredericksburg to Meridian* (New York: Random House, 1963), p. 578.

7. William F. Fox, "The Chances of Being Hit in Battle," *Century Illustrated Magazine* 36 (May 1888): 94; Fox, *Regimental Losses,* p. 7.

8. Fox, *Regimental Losses,* p. 57.

9. John William De Forest, *Miss Ravenel's Conversion from Secession to Loyalty* (New York: Harper, 1867), pp. 482–83. See also John W. De Forest, *A Volunteer's Adventures: A Union Captain's Record of the Civil War,* ed. James H. Croushore (New Haven: Yale University Press, 1946), p. 151. On the unreliability of Confederate rolls, see W. H. Taylor to J. E. Hagood, January 13, 1863, Hagood Papers, SCL. On inaccuracies of casualty statistics, see George C. Rable, *Fredericksburg! Fredericksburg!* (Chapel Hill: University of North Carolina Press, 2002), pp. 288–89.

10. J. J. Woodward, *The Medical and Surgical History of the War of the Rebellion,* Part I, Vol. I: *Medical History* (Washington, D.C.: Government Printing Office, 1870), pp. xxx, xxxi; Thomas L. Livermore, *Numbers and Losses in the Civil War in America, 1861–65,* 2nd ed. (Boston: Houghton, Mifflin & Co., 1901), p. 6; "Notes on the Union and Confederate Armies," in Robert Underwood Johnson and Clarence Clough Buel, eds., *Battles and Leaders of the Civil War* (New York: Century, 1889), pp. 767–68. On pensions see Megan McClintock, "Civil War Pensions and the Reconstruction of Union Families," *Journal of American History* 83

(September 1996): 456–80; Theda Skocpol, *Protecting Soldiers and Mothers: The Political Origins of Social Policy in the United States* (Cambridge, Mass.: Harvard University Press, 1992); William H. Glasson, *Federal Military Pensions in the United States* (New York: Oxford University Press, 1918).

11. Mabel E. Deutrich, *Struggle for Supremacy: The Career of General Fred C. Ainsworth* (Washington, D.C.: Public Affairs Press, 1962), pp. 46, 91. The Compiled Military Service Records (CMSR) has become an indispensable tool for Civil War researchers and genealogists. A printed index is now available with a useful introduction by Silas Felton that explains the origins of the CMSR and includes a bibliography of all state rosters. See Janet B. Hewett, ed., *The Roster of Union Soldiers, 1861–1865* (Wilmington, N.C.: Broadfoot, 1997). Robert Krick introduces Janet B. Hewett, ed., *The Roster of Confederate Soldiers, 1861–1865* (Wilmington, N.C.: Broadfoot, 1995), and similarly includes a survey and bibliography of state efforts.

12. Samuel P. Bates, *History of Pennsylvania Volunteers, 1861–1865,* (Harrisburg, Pa.: B. Singerly, 1869–71), vol. 1, pp. iv–v.

13. Higginson, *Massachusetts in the Army and Navy,* vol. 1, p. 568; Silas Felton, "Introduction," in Hewett, ed., *Roster of Union Soldiers,* vol. 1, p. 29.

14. A recent study by James David Hacker identifies other problems in Confederate records, arguing that southern deaths from diarrhea and dysentery have been seriously undercounted and that total numbers of war deaths should be increased from 258,000 to 282,600. Hacker, "The Human Cost of War: White Population in the United States, 1850–1880," Ph.D. diss. (University of Minnesota, 1999), pp. 41–43. Hacker seems to me far too sanguine in his acceptance of figures for both Union and Confederate battle deaths as "reasonably accurate" (p. 15). *Battles and Leaders of the Civil War* concluded in 1889 that "no data exist for a reasonably accurate estimate" of Confederate losses. See "Notes on the Union and Confederate Armies," in Johnson and Buel, eds., *Battles and Leaders of the Civil War,* vol. 4, p. 768). Note too Robert Krick's comment on the "nonchalant Confederate approach to military record keeping," in his introduction to *Roster of Confederate Soldiers,* p. 4.

15. A. S. Salley Jr., comp., *South Carolina Troops in Confederate Service* (Columbia, S.C.: R. L. Bryan Co., 1913), pp. v, vi, vii, viii. The Roll of the Dead prepared by a Confederate widow from Rives's notebooks remained unidentified in the National Archives until 1993. It has now been published as *Roll of the Dead: South Carolina Troops in Confederate State Service* (Columbia: South Carolina Department of Archives and History, 1994).

16. John W. Moore, *Roster of North Carolina Troops in the War Between the States,* Prepared by Order of the Legislature of 1881, 4 vols. (Raleigh, N.C.: Ash & Gatling, 1882), vol. 1, p. v. See, for Tennessee, John Berrien Lindsley, *The Military Annals of Tennessee* (Nashville, Tenn.: J. M. Lindsley & Co., 1886).

17. "Editorial Department," *Southern Historical Society Papers* 1 (January–June 1876): 39; "Confederate Losses During the War—Correspondence Between Dr. Joseph Jones and General Samuel Cooper," *Southern Historical Society Papers* 7 (June 1879): 289.

18. Frederick Phisterer, *Statistical Record of the Armies of the United States* (1883; rpt. New York: Castle, 2002); Fox, *Regimental Losses;* Thomas Livermore, *Numbers and Losses in the Civil War in America* (Boston: Houghton, Mifflin & Co., 1901); Frederick Dyer, *A Compendium of the War of the Rebellion* (1908; rpt. New York: Thomas Yoseloff, 1959). The 1959 reprint has an excellent introduction by Bell Irvin Wiley. See also the review of Dyer in *American Historical Review* 15 (July 1910): 889–91.

19. Fox, *Regimental Losses,* p. 58.

20. Ibid., p. 1; William F. Fox, "The Chances of Being Hit in Battle," *Century Illustrated Magazine* 36 (May 1888): 99.

21. Fox, *Regimental Losses,* pp. 58–59.

22. Ibid., pp. 58, 59, 61.

23. See www.brainyquote.com/quotes/quotes/j/josephstall1137476.html; Fox, *Regimental Losses,* p. 46.

24. Walt Whitman, *Memoranda During the War* (1875; rpt. Bedford, Mass.: Applewood Books, 1993), pp. 74, 73, 74, 75; Walt Whitman, "Reconciliation," in Whitman, *Civil War Poetry and Prose* (New York: Dover, 1995) p. 25; Whitman, "As Toilsome I Wander'd Virginia's Woods," in Whitman, *Civil War Poetry and Prose,* p. 25; Whitman, *Memoranda,* p. 46. It seems possible that Whitman derived his numbers from a letter from Charles W. Folsom, brevet colonel and assistant quartermaster to Brevet Brigadier General A. J. Perry, U.S. Quartermaster, May 27, 1868, that introduced volume 16 of *Roll of Honor: Names of Soldiers Who Died in Defence of the American Union, Interred in the National Cemeteries and Other Burial Places* (Washington, D.C.: Government Printing Office, 1868), p. viii. Folsom's categories and numbers are very similar to Whitman's.

25. For contemporary versions of "All Quiet," see, for example "Editor's Table," *Southern Literary Messenger* 34 (September–October 1862): 589, and "Journal of the War," *DeBow's Review* 2 (July 1866): 68–69.

26. "Only One Killed," *Harper's Weekly,* May 24, 1862, pp. 330–31; Lewis quoted in Robert V. Wells, *Facing the "King of Terrors": Death and Society in an American Community, 1750–1990* (New York: Cambridge University Press, 2000), p. 127.

27. See H. M. Wharton, *War Songs and Poems of the Southern Confederacy* (Philadelphia: John C. Winston, 1904), pp. 153–54, 131–32; "Only," *Harper's Weekly,* January 3, 1863; "One of Many," *Harper's Weekly,* April 16, 1864. "Only a Private Killed" is a refrain from a poem composed by H. L. Gordon and sent to Mrs. E. H. Ogden, November 12, 1861, GLC6559.01.038, Gilder Lehrman Collection, The Gilder Lehrman Institute of American History, NYHS.

28. On Civil War sentimentality, see Alice Fahs, "The Sentimental Soldier," in Fahs, *The Imagined Civil War: Popular Literature of the North and South, 1861–1865* (Chapel Hill: University of North Carolina Press, 2001), pp. 93–119, and Frances M. Clarke, "Sentimental Bonds: Suffering, Sacrifice and Benevolence in the Civil War North," Ph.D. diss. (Johns Hopkins University, 2001). On irony, see Claire Colebrook, *Irony* (New York: Routledge, 2004).

29. Fox, *Regimental Losses,* p. 574.

EPILOGUE

1. Walter Lowenfels, ed. and comp., *Walt Whitman's Civil War* (New York: Alfred A. Knopf, 1960), p. 15; Bierce quoted in Daniel Aaron, *The Unwritten War: American Writers and the Civil War* (New York: Alfred A. Knopf, 1973), p. 183.

2. Bierce quoted in Roy Morris Jr., *Ambrose Bierce: Alone in Bad Company* (New York: Crown, 1996), p. 205; Sidney Lanier to Bayard Taylor, August 7, 1875, in Charles R. Anderson and Aubrey H. Starke, eds., *Letters, 1874–1877, The Centennial Edition of the Works of Sidney Lanier* (Baltimore: Johns Hopkins University Press, 1945), vol. 9, p. 230.

3. Susannah Hampton to Dear Sir, September 14, 1863, Philadelphia Agency, Hospital Directory Correspondence, vol. 2, box 597, U.S. Sanitary Commission Records, NYPL.

4. Melville quoted in Lee Rust Brown, "Introduction," in Herman Melville, *Battle-Pieces and Aspects of the War: Civil War Poems* (1866; rpt. New York: Da Capo Press, 1995), p. viii.

5. Lucy Rebecca Buck, *Sad Earth, Sweet Heaven: The Diary of Lucy Rebecca Buck During the War Between the States* (Birmingham, Ala.: Cornerstone, 1973), p. 50.

6. Frederick Douglass, "The Mission of the War," in *The Life and Writings of Frederick Douglass* (New York: International Publishers, 1950), vol. 3, p. 397.

7. E. B. Whitman, "Remarks on National Cemeteries," in W. T. Sherman et al., *The Army Reunion* (Chicago: S. C. Griggs & Co., 1869), p. 225; Herman Melville, "A Utilitarian View of the Monitor's Fight," in *Battle-Pieces*, p. 62.

8. Walt Whitman, "The Million Dead, Too, Summed Up," *Specimen Days* (1882; rpt. Boston: David Godine, 1971), p. 59.

9. William McKinley, "Speech Before the Legislature in Joint Assembly at the State Capitol, Atlanta, Georgia, December 14, 1898," *Speeches and Addresses of William McKinley from March 1, 1897 to May 30, 1900* (New York: Doubleday & McClure, 1900), p. 159.

10. Douglass quoted in David W. Blight, *Frederick Douglass' Civil War: Keeping Faith in Jubilee* (Baton Rouge: Louisiana State University Press, 1989), p. 238; Ambrose Bierce, "To E. S. Salomon" [1903], in Bierce, *Phantoms of a Blood-Stained Period: The Complete Civil War Writings of Ambrose Bierce*, ed. Russell Duncan and David J. Klooster (Boston: University of Massachusetts Press, 2002), p. 334.

11. Oliver Wendell Holmes, *The Soldier's Faith: An Address Delivered on Memorial Day, May 30, 1895, at a Meeting Called by the Graduating Class of Harvard University* (Boston: Little, Brown, & Co., 1895). Holmes had given an earlier version of this speech in Keene, New Hampshire, on Memorial Day 1884. See harvard regiment.org/memorial.htm.

Acknowledgments

The idea for this book grew out of my earlier work on women of the slaveholding South and crystallized as I recognized that their perceptions of the war were rooted in its terrible harvest of death. I have been engaged in this project for well over a decade, partly because I have undertaken other responsibilities alongside it, but partly because I found the subject so compelling and wanted to do it full justice. If I have in any way succeeded in this purpose, it is because of the many friends, colleagues, and even strangers who have helped. I want first to thank those who read and commented on the whole manuscript, saving me from errors and offering me invaluable perspective on larger conceptual questions: David Blight, Ann Braude, Gary Gallagher, Tony Horwitz, Jennifer Leaning, Stephanie McCurry, James McPherson, Luke Menand, Charles Rosenberg, and Jessica Rosenberg. Others read particular chapters in their areas of expertise, found library materials, guided me to and through manuscript collections, shared treasures encountered in their own research, worked as research assistants, aided in preparation of the manuscript, or contributed in countless other ways. I am deeply indebted to Michael Bernath, Homi Bhabha, Tracy Blanchard, Beth Brady, Gabor Boritt, Tom Coens, Lara Cohen, Gretchen Condran, John Coski, Yonatan Eyal, Henry Fulmer, Jesse Goldstine, James Green, Jenessa Hoffman, Kathryn Johnson, Andrew Kinney, James Kloppenberg, Jeremy Knowles, Lisa Laskin, Paul LeClerc, Millington Lockwood, Chandra Manning, Sandra Markham, Stewart Meyer, Reid Mitchell, Margot Minardi, Lien-Hang Nguyen, Charlie Ornstein, Amy Paradis, Katy Park, Michael Parrish, Charlene Peacock, Trevor Plante, Frances Pollard, George Rable, James Robertson Jr., Neil Rudenstine, Barbara Savage, Elana Harris Schanzer, Kay Shelemay, Theda Skocpol, Susan Stewart,

Allen Stokes, Steven Stowe, Julie Tomback, Helen Vendler, and Ann Wilson. My gratitude to Jane Garrett for patience and faith.

My thanks to Louise Richardson for holding the fort at Radcliffe while I took a sabbatical to write; to Susan Johnson and Anne Brown for running my life; to Janine Bestine and Peggy Chan for running my computers; and to Lars Madsen for taking on so much so well at the last minute. Kennie Lyman did the near impossible in making sure the manuscript was ready to go to press on time. I have been privileged to enjoy the generosity first of the University of Pennsylvania and then of Harvard University in support of my work as a historian, and I have been inspired for the past six years by the intellectual riches of the Radcliffe Institute. I am the grateful beneficiary of the treasures of the many manuscript repositories cited in the notes, and I thank the libraries and museums that have permitted me to use quotations and illustrations. Parts of this book appeared in slightly different form in the *Journal of Southern History,* the *Journal of Military History,* and *Southern Cultures.* In quoting primary materials, I have retained original, often rather creative, spellings without inserting the intrusive *sic.*

Charles Rosenberg and Jessica Rosenberg are great editors and critics. But they know that is the least of it. Thanks to them for believing in this project for so long and for living with my fascination with death.

Cambridge, January 2007

Index

Italicized page numbers indicate illustrations.

Illustration Credits

67 "A Burial Party After the Battle of Antietam." Photograph by Alexander Gardner. Library of Congress. Prints & Photographs Division, Civil War Photographs, LC-DIG-cwpb-01098.

68 "Antietam. Bodies of Confederate Dead Gathered for Burial." Photograph by Alexander Gardner. Library of Congress, Prints & Photographs Division, Civil War Photographs, LC-DIG-cwpb-01094.

70 "Burying the Dead Under a Flag of Truce, Petersburg, 1864." *Frank Leslie's Illustrated Newspaper,* September 3, 1864. Widener Library, Harvard College Library, XPS 527 PF.

72 "Dead Confederate Soldiers Collected for Burial. Spotsylvania, May 1864." Library of Congress, Prints & Photographs Division, Civil War Photographs, LC-USZ62-104044.

74 "A Burial Trench at Gettysburg." Photograph by Timothy H. O'Sullivan. Library of Congress. Prints & Photographs Division, Civil War Photographs, LC-DIG-cwpb-00843.

75 "Rebel Soldiers After Battle 'Peeling' (i.e. Stripping) the Fallen Union Soldiers." *Frank Leslie's Illustrated Newspaper,* February 13, 1864. Widener Library, Harvard College Library, XPS 527 PF.

78 "Burial of Federal Dead. Fredericksburg, 1864." Photograph by Timothy H. O'Sullivan. Library of Congress, Prints & Photographs Division, Civil War Photographs, LC-DIG-cwpb-01840.

81 "A Contrast: Federal Buried, Confederate Unburied, Where They Fell on the Battlefield of Antietam." Caption and photograph by Alexander Gardner. Library of Congress, Prints & Photographs Division, Civil War Photographs, LC-DIG-cwpb-01086.

82 Sketch by Alfred R. Waud. Library of Congress, Prints & Photographs Division, Civil War Drawing Collection, LC-USZ62-15118.

84 *The Burial of Latané,* 1864. Painting by William D. Washington. Courtesy of The Johnson Collection.

86 "Maryland and Pennsylvania Farmers Visiting the Battlefield of Antietam While the National Troops Were Burying the Dead and Carrying Off the Wounded." From a sketch by F. H. Schell. *Frank Leslie's Illustrated Newspaper,* October 18, 1862. Widener Library, Harvard College Library, XPS 527 PF.

93 "Transportation of the Dead!" Gettysburg: H. J. Stahle, 1863. Broadside. The Library Company of Philadelphia.

95 Business card for undertaker Lewis Ernde, Hagerstown, Maryland. Civil War Miscellanies (McA 5786.F), McAllister Collection, The Library Company of Philadelphia.

97 "Embalming Surgeon at Work on Soldier's Body." Library of Congress, Prints & Photographs Division, Civil War Photographs Division, LC-DIG-cwpb-01887.

98 "Dr. Bunnell's Embalming Establishment in the Field (Army of the James)." Library of Congress, Prints & Photographs Division, Civil War Photographs, LC-DIG-cwpb-01886.

105 Detail from "News of the War." *Harper's Weekly,* June 14, 1862. The Library Company of Philadelphia.

108 "The United States Christian Commission Office at 8th and H Streets, Washington, D.C., 1865." Library of Congress, Prints & Photographs Division, Civil War Photographs, LC-DIG-cwpb-04165.

114 "Nurses and Officers of the United States Sanitary Commission at Fredericksburg, Virginia, During the Wilderness Campaign, 1864." Library of Congress, Prints & Photographs Division, Civil War Photographs, LC-DIG-cwpb-01196.

119 Telegram from William Drayton Rutherford to Sallie Fair Rutherford, July 6, 1862. Manuscripts W. D. Rutherford Papers. Courtesy of South Caroliniana Library, University of South Carolina, Columbia.

120 Advertisement for soldiers' identification badges. *Frank Leslie's Illustrated Newspaper*, September 10, 1864. Widener Library, Harvard College Library, XPS 527 PF.

121 "I am Capt O W Holmes, 20th Mass V, Son of Oliver Wendell Holmes, MD, Boston." Note written by Oliver Wendell Holmes Jr. Courtesy of Special Collections Department, Harvard Law School Library, Harvard University.

122 Detail from "News of the War." *Harper's Weekly*, June 14, 1862. The Library Company of Philadelphia.

125 "Ward K at Armory Square Hospital in Washington, D.C." Library of Congress, Prints & Photographs Division, Civil War Photographs, LC-DIG-cwpb-04246.

131 "An Unknown Soldier." *Harper's Weekly*, October 24, 1868. Widener Library, Harvard College Library, P 207.6 F.

132 "Henry Clay Taylor." Henry Clay Taylor Papers WHi-46641. Wisconsin Historical Society, Madison.

133 "Libby Prison, Richmond Virginia, April 1865." Library of Congress, Prints & Photographs Division, Civil War Photographs, LC-DIG-cwpb-02898.

142 "View of the Darlington Court-House and the Sycamore Tree Where Amy Spain, the Negro Slave, Was Hung." *Harper's Weekly*, September 30, 1865. Widener Library, Harvard College Library, P 207.6 F.

147 John Saunders Palmer Jr. with his wife, Alice Ann Gaillard Palmer. From a copy, courtesy of South Caroliniana Library, University of South Carolina, Columbia.

148 Half-mourning dress of Varina Howell Davis. The Museum of the Confederacy, Richmond, Virginia. Photography by Katherine Wetzel.

150 "Women in Mourning, Cemetery in New Orleans." *Frank Leslie's Illustrated Newspaper*, April 25, 1863. Widener Library, Harvard College Library, XPS 527 PF.

151 "View of the 'Burnt District', Richmond, Va." Library of Congress, Prints & Photographs Division, Civil War Photographs, LC-USZC4-4593.

153 "Godey's Fashions for June 1862." *Godey's Lady's Book and Magazine*, June 1862. The Library Company of Philadelphia.

154 "Women in Mourning at Stonewall Jackson's Grave, circa 1866." Courtesy of Virginia Military Institute Archives, Lexington.

158 "President Lincoln's Funeral—Citizens Viewing the Body at the City Hall, New York." *Harper's Weekly*, May 6, 1865. Widener Library, Harvard College Library, P 207.6 F.

168 Henry Ingersoll Bowditch at the time of the Civil War. Courtesy of Harvard University Archives, HUP Bowditch, Henry (1).

195   "The Dying Soldier." Song sheet (New York: Charles Magnus, n.d.), Wolf 5486, American Song Sheet Collection, The Library Company of Philadelphia.

203   "Battle-field of Gaines Mill, Virginia." Library of Congress, Prints & Photographs Division, Civil War Photographs, LC-USZ62-106283.

214   Clara Barton, circa 1865. Photograph by Mathew Brady. Clara Barton National Historic Site/National Park Service.

216   "A Burial Party on the Battle-field of Cold Harbor, Virginia, April 1865." Negative by John Reekie; print and caption by Alexander Gardner. Library of Congress, Prints & Photographs Division, Civil War Photographs, LC-DIG-cwpb-04324.

218   "Miss Clara Barton Raising the National Flag, August 17, 1865," at Andersonville. Sketched by I. C. Schotel. *Harper's Weekly*, October 7, 1865. Widener Library, Harvard College Library, P 207.6 F.

231   "The Soldier's Grave." Lithograph by Currier and Ives. Library of Congress, Prints & Photographs Division, Popular Graphic Art (Historical Print) Collection, LC-USZC2-3015.

242   "Hollywood Cemetery, Richmond, Virginia—Decorating the Graves of the Rebel Soldiers." *Harper's Weekly*, August 17, 1867. Widener Library, Harvard College Library, P 207.6 F.

249   "Confederate Cemetery of Vicksburg." Photo by David Butow, 1997. © David Butow/CORBIS SABA.

263   Walt Whitman. Photograph by Mathew Brady. Library of Congress, Prints & Photographs Division, Brady-Handy Photograph Collection, LC-DIG-cwpbh-00752.

A Note About the Author

Drew Gilpin Faust, a 1968 graduate of Bryn Mawr College, took her M.A. and Ph.D. at the University of Pennsylvania and taught history and American civilization there from 1975, becoming a full professor in 1984 and Annenberg Professor of History in 1989. In 2001 she became Dean of the Radcliffe Institute for Advanced Study at Harvard University, where she also holds the Lincoln Professorship of History. On July 1, 2007, she became the twenty-eighth president of Harvard. She is the author of five previous books, including *Mothers of Invention: Women of the Slaveholding South in the American Civil War* (1996), which won the Francis Parkman Prize of the Society of American Historians and the Avery Craven Prize of the Organization of American Historians. She and her husband live in Cambridge, Massachusetts.

A Note on the Type

This book was set in Caslon, a typeface named after William Caslon (1692–1766). The first of a famous English family of type designers and founders, he started as an apprentice to an engraver of gun-locks and gun barrels in London. In 1716 he opened his own shop, for silver chasing and making bookbinders' stamps. He began type-founding in 1720. A specimen sheet of typefaces, issued in 1734, established Caslon's superiority to all other letter cutters of the time, and soon his types, or types modeled on his style, were being used by most English printers, supplanting the Dutch types that had formerly prevailed. In style, Caslon was a reversion to earlier type styles. Its characteristics are remarkable regularity and symmetry, and beauty in the shape and proportion of the letters; its general effect is clear and open but not weak or delicate. For uniformity, clearness, and readability it has perhaps never been surpassed.

Composed by North Market Street Graphics, Lancaster, Pennsylvania

Printed and bound by Berryville Graphics, Berryville, Virginia

Designed by Anthea Lingeman